Teaching Reading:
Language, Letters & Thought

Teaching Reading

Language, Letters & Thought

Sara Brody, EdD
editor

LARC Publishing
Milford, New Hampshire

Teaching Reading: Language, Letters, and Thought.

For information contact LARC Publishing, P.O. Box 801, Milford, NH 03055, (603) 880-7691.

ISBN 1-886042-12-8

1st edition   2 3 4 5 6 7 8 9 10

Dedicated to caring teachers, parents, principals,
and librarians who lovingly shovel sand
against the tide
to ensure that learners
enjoy the gifts of literacy.

Contents

List of Tables

List of Figures

I. OVERVIEW

Introduction

Reading with understanding empowers us to learn and remember, to record and revise, and to encounter other people's most complex and cherished thoughts. While reading, we draw on our facility with language, identify and interpret printed symbols, and extend our knowledge beyond the confines of our backgrounds. Unique to humans, reading engages us in thinking processes that can develop deep understanding.

Reading is enhanced by good teaching that sensitizes a reader to the nuances of language and the subtleties of print. Effective instructors consider questions concerning when to teach about letters and when to teach about language; when to focus on a single component and when to integrate the whole; when to demonstrate the steps of a process and when to set up unobtrusive environments that let books and readers' curiosity engage spontaneously. These questions arise as we try to engage all learners in the intricate and enriching process of reading.

Given the complexity of reading instruction, what sort of background is offered to teachers of reading? Typically, college preservice programs provide a cursory introduction to reading instruction through one or two courses that review current methodology and materials. Once teachers are in classrooms, they use their ingenuity to learn through experience. Schools and text publishers supplement teachers' resourcefulness with directions in text manuals, an occasional staff development workshop, and articles in teaching journals.

Although the education literature is replete with recommendations concerning how to teach reading, many suggestions seem to conflict with each other. School systems sometimes use these recommendations to shift methods and philosophies of instruction to flow with prevailing attitudes and theories. Often, recommended approaches are instituted broadly without an understanding of students' diverse needs that vary by individual differences such as maturation, experience, and ability.

When teachers use an approach recommended by an article, workshop, or their school system, the responses of their students often indicate that it works for some but not for others. Further, what worked for some children at one time seems to lose its effectiveness, even with these children, when they grow beyond its purpose. At times, this conflict between recommendations and practical experience contributes to feelings of deep dissatisfaction among experienced educators.

Teachers of reading, both specialists and classroom educators, often seek a means of teaching effectively that transcends shifts in trends and materials. They wish to clarify, and express persuasively, their experiential knowledge concerning how and when to teach various components of reading. In essence, educators desire a consistent means of teaching with intentionality, thoughtful planning, and practicality in a way that fosters success and a love of reading.

In response to these issues, this volume was developed to articulate the basic components of reading—what they are, as well as why, when, and how they are taught. The volume attempts to clarify differences in the literature concerning these components and their instruction. The opening chapter presents an overview of reading development, a descriptive model of mature reading, and a discussion of effective teaching practices that encourage vulnerable learners.

Next, language development, a vital precursor to reading, is reviewed through an exploration of its emergence in infants, controversies concerning its etiology, and recommendations for home and preschool activities. In addition, phonemic awareness is explored, along with its role as a bridge between language and reading abilities. Then, several chapters examine the decoding aspect of reading—the learning of letter-sound correspondences, development of fluent reading, and spelling instruction as a path to reading. Within these chapters, the uses of literature to enhance decoding ability are also considered.

The next chapters investigate the comprehension processes of reading—using textbooks and literature to gather information and construct meaning, increasing background knowledge to prepare for reading, teaching word meanings to enhance thought, and extending understanding through writing. In order to assist teachers in determining what reading component(s) require instruction for particular students at particular times, the final chapters examine aspects of formal and informal assessment. These chapters suggest useful and appropriate assessment procedures along with guidelines concerning application of diagnostic findings to relevant and effective instruction.

The chapter authors come to their writing with rich backgrounds in both theory and practice. They have engaged seriously with language and reading research, yet they also possess practical understanding acquired through teaching. In each chapter, an author describes one particular component of reading, along with various views concerning its role in reading; then specific procedures for teaching the component are presented.

When any method or material is suggested, the author describes the underlying principles that render it effective, at a particular maturational time, and for a particular instructional purpose. Often, varied materials are noted that can be used to teach one aspect of reading. In these instances, the similarities, or effective elements that appear across materials, are discussed.

Each chapter provides background that may empower educators to plan and implement instruction with greater success. The writings attempt to support teachers as they draw from alternative materials that achieve the same end, or assemble their own. Some ideas in the volume may confirm what teachers find working in their classrooms; others may suggest variations that can enhance instructional effectiveness. It is hoped that the suggestions encourage teachers as they continue in their efforts to nurture confidence and a deep love of reading among all students.

Chapter 1. Language and Reading: An Overview

Sara Brody, EdD
Rivier College

Language and reading are complex cognitive processes that develop over a long period of time and through extensive practice. Before reading develops, children learn to express their ideas with language. Next, children who receive exposure to written language learn that letters can convey thoughts. With experience and instruction, novices learn how letters represent sounds.

Through practice, readers become fluent decoders and comprehenders of simple written messages, then they move on to the adventure of absorbing unfamiliar ideas and concepts encountered through print. As readers mature, they branch out to explore ever more complex material. Finally, they examine intricate issues through wide reading and use critical thinking to apply their understanding to complex challenges and questions.

Effective instruction enhances readers' ease, enjoyment, and rate of learning. Adept instruction accommodates a reader's developmental level and learning needs. This chapter explores reading from three perspectives. First, we consider the nature of language and reading as they develop in various learners. Next, the cognitive processes that occur during mature reading are examined. And finally, several practical components of exemplary instruction are reviewed.

Developmental View of Reading Maturation

The desired outcome of reading instruction—the ability to read critically, constructively, and with deep understanding of complex issues—is compelling; it may tempt us to focus on teaching the reading process at once, holistically. However, instruction needs to take into account the gradual maturation of human language, cognition, and physiology. In humans, concrete abilities develop early, then serve as a foundation for more complex and abstract skills that unfold later (Fischer, 1980).

A developmental description of reading maturation reflects the way in which reading ability evolves when learners are taught with effective techniques in a nurturing environment. Such a view of reading is supported by a broad array of cognitive, physiological, and educational research. This material has been reviewed in detail, and synthesized comprehensively by Chall (1983a; in press).

Chall's synthesis presents a framework for viewing reading development as a series of stages that begins with a precursor Stage 0, in which language develops, and that culminates in the reading of diverse perspectives to construct personal understanding at Stage 5. Chall's stages offer a useful guideline when making and explaining instructional choices for particular students at particular times. Developmental stages of reading provide conceptual support for effective instructional practices that may not be in vogue at a particular time.

The discussion below draws extensively on Chall's scheme to describe the maturation of reading ability. Her stage delineations are used as descriptors of particular reading levels throughout the chapters of this volume. For a thorough description and analysis of reading stages, readers are referred to *Stages of Reading Development, 2nd edition*, (Chall, in press).

READING STAGES 0 - 5
Stage 0. During their early years, children typically develop great facility with oral language. They learn to communicate using a variety of syntactic structures and a wide range of vocabulary. In addition, children generally recognize thousands

of spoken words by the time they enter first grade. Along with the development of oral language, children who are read to from books, and who tell stories from pictures, learn that print is a special code that somehow preserves and transmits language. When given guidance, these children often begin to recognize a few letters, identify some words on road signs or products, and draw messages with letters or scribbles (Chall, 1983a, p. 14). Chapter 2 in this volume provides a detailed description of language development and supportive activities.

Transition to Stage 1. In languages with alphabetic writing systems, the speech sounds of language correspond to the print system of reading. As children's oral language becomes well established, they can begin to notice the sound patterns of the words in their language. In a step that leads toward becoming readers of an alphabetic system, beginners start to recognize that the words in the sound stream of oral language separate into syllables, and the syllables into initial, medial, and ending sounds (Liberman, 1987).

Phonemic awareness—sensitivity to these sound patterns of oral language—is a crucial understanding that marks the transition from Stage 0 to Stage 1. When phonemic awareness develops, learners can advance in reading. They progress from creating and interacting with speech to actually transforming printed letters into language. Learners demonstrate their phonemic awareness by separating and combining the sounds of spoken words during word play, poetry reading, and other oral language activities (Blachman, 1991; Williams, 1980). Chapter 3 provides a detailed discussion of phonemic awareness and activities that encourage its development.

Stage 1. As phonemic awareness becomes established, novices enter Chall's Stage 1. During this stage, beginners break the barrier of print's secret code. As they extend their knowledge of the relationships between single letters and their sounds, learners begin to recognize letter-sound patterns such as *bug, rug, hug*. As they expand their decoding repertoire, readers increase their opportunities for independent access to the wealth of rich language experiences that are locked in print.

In alphabetic systems, learning the code appears to be a crucial developmental step in reading maturation. When students are similar in physical and cognitive abilities, background knowledge, vocabulary breadth, and exposure to reading materials, it is print-to-sound knowledge that separates those who can read unfamiliar words and sentences independently from those who cannot (Rath, 1990).

Much debate surrounds the teaching of decoding. Research repeatedly demonstrates the effectiveness of teaching letters and their associated sounds directly, an approach commonly referred to as phonics (Adams, 1994; Chall, 1983b). However, some educators contend that children will have a greater love of reading if they discover the code of print on their own through indirect exposure in a less systematic manner (Smith, 1988). Certainly an overemphasis on phonics instruction after the secret of code is mastered would be fruitless. However, learners who have developed phonemic awareness tend to respond with delight and excitement when introduced to the link between sounds and letters, shown how those sounded letters form words, and helped to read those words in sentences and short paragraphs.

Since people learn at different rates, readers vary in the amount of instruction and practice needed to learn the alphabetic code. This variation is prompted by factors such as how often the learner practices, whether a learning disability is present, and the extent of reading exposure available outside the school setting (Stanovich, 1986; 1994). Children with learning disabilities, as well as learners from environments that offer few opportunities for practice, encounter great difficulty if expected to learn the code only from indirect exposure.

Instruction in the sounds of letters and their blending in words is critical for learners. Those who do not receive sufficient supplemental exposure cannot assimilate the code from limited, indirect classroom experiences (Adams, 1994; Chall, 1983b; Perfetti, 1984). Chapter 4 offers a detailed analysis of Stage 1 reading instruction—its historical development, crucial elements, and methods of instruction. In addition, Chapter 6 explores the role of spelling in enhancing decoding ability.

Stage 2. As learners practice reading words, sentences, and then familiar stories, they mature to a subsequent reading stage. Stage 2 is a time of developing fluency and automaticity (unconscious speed and accuracy) in decoding connected text. Stage 2 learners develop advanced decoding skills and acquire fluency during reading and listening to stories that follow common structures to express familiar experiences and emotions (Chall, 1983a).

As they read, beginners develop confidence in their decoding ability. Familiarity with the language and content of simple reading material confirms to beginners that they have read accurately. As learners read words many times in many different sentences, they develop automaticity in sounding words and retrieving meaning in connected text (Chomsky, 1978; Samuels, Schermer, & Reinking, 1992).

Stage 2 is differentiated from Stage 1 since it is not minimal knowledge of letter-sound correspondences that constrains progress. Instead, automaticity and fluency with this knowledge need to develop before a reader can read and comprehend more challenging text independently. Although readers entering Stage 2 can decipher stories, much of their attention is absorbed by sounding out words. Consequently, little attention remains available to comprehend unfamiliar content.

After decoding becomes automatic, through practice with much oral and silent reading, attention becomes free to engage in comprehending unfamiliar text during independent reading (Perfetti, 1984; Stanovich, 1980). Chapter 5 explores the nature of automaticity, its contribution to reading ability, and strategies that enhance fluency and confidence.

Stage 3. As students emerge from Stage 2 with confidence in their ability to decode print and understand the messages of familiar stories, reading takes on a new dimension. As Chall (1983a) aptly states, rather than "learning to read," students now begin to "read to learn." During this stage, learners spend a great deal of time broadening their knowledge of the world around them.

Among Stage 3 readers, language and reading offer a bridge to extend beyond concrete and personally centered messages to an understanding of the larger world. Students typically enter Stage 3 around 4th grade. At the same time, they encounter more difficult texts in the content areas, as well as more sophisticated literature. They begin the process of gathering extensive knowledge by reading specialized text (Chall & Conard, 1991). See Chapter 7 for a discussion of the comprehension aspect of reading.

Stage 3 challenges readers to expand in several ways. These readers need to construct understanding from specialized words and unfamiliar concepts. At the same time, readers need to remember their learnings by incorporating them into a growing collection of background knowledge that will be drawn on in future reading. A great deal of learning in Stage 3 involves the development of a depth and breadth of background knowledge. Students need to enrich their knowledge by internalizing an abundance of word meanings and concepts that reach into a broad array of domains (Brody, 1989). See Chapter 8 concerning background knowledge and Chapter 9 for a discussion of vocabulary development.

During this time, readers also need to extend their language facility to incorporate familiarity with a wider variety of literary genres and expository structures (Liebling, 1989). As instruction focuses on development in a variety of areas shared by reading and language comprehension, writing takes on an important role in clarifying, completing, and generating new understanding. The intertwining of the reading and writing aspects of print encourages agility and thoughtful engagement with the abstract language of reading (Stotsky, 1986). See Chapter 10 regarding the role of writing in development of reading comprehension.

Stage 4. When students have developed the ability to learn unfamiliar information from text and comprehend specialized concepts, they enter Stage 4. Typically, it is in high school or later that learners begin to read, with relative ease, materials that present abstract concepts and issues from multiple points of view (Chall, 1983a). As they continue to read widely, students seem to develop automaticity in their ability to gather meaning from unfamiliar text—a skill that required careful attention during Stage 3.

Learners begin to read selectively from vast collections of source material by concentrating only on the parts that are relevant to their studies. As their automaticity in "learning the new" from unfamiliar texts develops, readers appear to assimilate new concepts and multiple meanings with fluent ease. During the wide reading of this stage, they gather material voraciously from diverse sources and multiple points of view to develop their stock of background knowledge (Chall, 1983a). Chapters 7 - 10 briefly discuss the extension of strategies beyond Stage 3 instruction and their application to the complex reading materials that assist in the development of Stage 4 reading ability.

Stage 5. Once readers achieve automaticity in gathering and assimilating knowledge from unfamiliar material, readers may advance to Stage 5, the ultimate stage of reading ability. Generally at the college level, Stage 5 readers create new, complex knowledge by synthesizing the material they are reading with the knowledge and beliefs they have acquired over time (Chall, 1983a).

Readers at Stage 5 make use of what is learned from reading but extend their understanding beyond any of their earlier conceptions or viewpoints. This new understanding exceeds what is expressed by its constituent parts. Many of the activities recommended in Chapters 7 - 10 for Stage 3 and 4 reading lay the groundwork for later development of Stage 5 reading.

Variation. Variation occurs in the rate at which learners acquire reading ability. How quickly reading matures at any particular stage is influenced by the way in which reading is taught as well as by a number of additional factors. The amount of time spent practicing, through reading at school and at home, affects how quickly reading matures.

Some children come to school from homes that provide extensive exposure to books along with practice in identifying letters and their sounds through activities such as games with magnetic letters, writing little notes, playing "school" with older siblings, conversing about letters with parents during bedtime reading, and observations of signs during car trips. When these children enter school, some of them need little or no instruction in letters and their sounds.

Since early home instruction in letters and sounds, books and listening, is invisible to teachers, some children appear to learn how to read in school simply by sharing books and ideas. Many other children begin 1st grade with limited knowledge of letters and little exposure to stories and literary language. These children can become very able readers, but only if school provides appropriate instruction at critical stages (Chall & Snow, 1988).

The extent to which earlier stages are mastered before a later one is introduced also influences development. For example, the extent that a reader masters decoding fluency during Stage 2 influences how much attention can be allocated to the comprehension of unfamiliar text during Stage 3. In addition, the extent that a learner develops rich vocabulary and background knowledge during Stage 3 determines how effectively background knowledge can support the reading of texts that present varied points of view during Stage 4 (Wilson & Anderson, 1986).

Variation in learners' cognitive abilities also influences rate of reading maturation. Students who experience learning disabilities often require additional time to develop competency in the beginning reading stages (Lerner, 1993). Even physical factors influence the rate of progress through developmental stages, and a check of eyesight and hearing is wise when reading is not progressing as expected. Further, emotional factors such as unresolved family issues, or fear of failure, influence reading growth.

When using a stage framework, there is a danger of viewing reading maturation too precisely. It is crucial to recognize that readers vary in developmental rate and also experience vacillations in ability. During any one time, some developing readers may need instruction in certain areas at one stage and in other areas at a higher or lower stage. For example, readers who possess rich oral vocabularies in a particular content area as well as many sight words may be able to gather new meaning from content text despite limited decoding skills.

Such students could be considered Stage 3 readers since they use content texts to learn new information in a familiar field. Yet they are also Stage 1 readers since instruction in letter-sound correspondences is needed before they can read texts concerning content from a less common field or texts with fewer sight words to support guessing from context.

A reader's place within the stages varies depending on the abilities the learner has developed, the difficulty of the text under study, and the reader's familiarity with the text's subject matter (Applebee, Langer, & Mullis, 1987). Even within one piece of writing, a mature reader sometimes gathers complex information carefully, sounds out unfamiliar words slowly, and synthesizes all that is read with previous knowledge to form a new understanding of a complicated issue.

Application of the stages to assessment and instruction. A developmental view of reading can refine assessment and instructional planning by providing a description of progressive abilities that a learner needs to acquire in order to become a mature reader. Debates concerning whether students need to learn decoding strategies or complex vocabulary meanings are clarified by considering which of these skills are underdeveloped and blocking further reading progress for a specific individual at a specific point in development.

Knowledge of developmental reading stages helps educators focus on what is needed by learners who possess particular abilities rather than on the sometimes less helpful issue of what should be taught during a particular grade in school. An appreciation of developmental levels can reduce the errors that accompany blanket prescriptives that assume all learners of a certain age or grade possess the same abilities and proceed at the same rate.

A stage view of reading maturation also enlightens debates concerning whether readers ought to learn through direct or indirect instruction (Chall, 1983a). When students are learning new skills, for which they have little knowledge or experience, direct teaching of the rudiments provides information needed to make progress (Gagne & Driscoll, 1988). However, as students learn the fundamental workings of new skills and need to develop fluency, indirect instruction through an abundance of independent reading makes sense.

Instruction shifts between direct and indirect within a single lesson as well as over a period of time. For example, students may be taught directly the pronunciation and meanings of several unfamiliar vocabulary words, then develop automatic decoding and understanding through independent reading of texts in which the words appear multiple times. Chapters 11 and 12 discuss formal and informal means of assessing reading ability and planning relevant instruction.

Summary. Essentially, a developmental view of reading suggests various stages during which students learn particular aspects of reading ability. During certain stages readers need to acquire competencies for which they have little knowledge or background. In other stages, readers need to extend their automaticity with an already learned skill. Teachers can use a developmental view of reading to determine the nature of their students' learning needs. At times this will suggest that students need to be taught the foundations of certain competencies with direct instruction. Other stages will suggest a need for opportunities to practice in a more unstructured, leisurely environment with motivating assignments and materials that encourage extensive reading.

A Model of Mature Reading

My graduate students in reading and educational disabilities have urged me to begin this section with a note encouraging readers to move on to the practical teaching strategies that begin on page 24 if the content of this reading model becomes too dry. My students agree that the model provides useful background, but they caution that readers should skip this model section if it seems too abstract (rather than setting aside the entire book!) since this section is not representative of the rest of the text. Their advice is included here with my encouragement that it be heeded.[1]

If additional explanation is desired, the reader could refer to the glossary or return to this section later. I include this section since a theoretical description of a reader's thought processes may be useful when planning lessons or explaining an instructional choice to an administrator or school committee.

Unlike a stage view, which explains reading at various levels of development, a theoretical model of the reading process describes the cognitive activity (mental

---

[1] I am indebted to my Rivier College graduate students whose discussion of manuscript drafts contributed immeasurably to the writing of this book.

processing) that appears to occur in adults during mature reading. Theoretical models are postulated by researchers after careful observations of readers who participate in intricate perception tasks. These models express researchers' best guesses concerning the nature of cognitive reading processes since technology does not yet let us watch in detail the various components of reading as they function within the brain. Although theoretical models are only hypothetical guesses, they offer a useful means of understanding the nature of reading.

The discussion below provides a composite sketch of the cognitive processes that appear in commonly cited reading models. In particular, this outline draws heavily on the work of LaBerge & Samuels (1974), Rummelhart & Ortony (1977), Kinsch & van Dijk (1978), Stanovich (1980), Lesgold & Perfetti (1981), Just & Carpenter (1981; 1987), Perfetti & Curtis (1986), and Adams (1994).[2]

THE PROCESS OF MATURE READING IN ALPHABETIC SYSTEMS

Reading involves the understanding of thought conveyed by print. To understand written messages, readers draw meaning from text in one of two ways. When approaching text that is written in an alphabetic system, readers often decode letters to their corresponding sounds, and then use those sounds to recognize the word and its meaning. In contrast, readers respond to text written in a logographic (picture) system, such as Chinese, by memorizing the look of a printed word as a "picture," and then connecting it with its meaning.

Even in an alphabetic writing system, beginners sometimes read without attending to the sounds of letters. However, total reliance on the perceiving of words as logographs (pictures), without making use of letters to represent specific sounds, requires the memorization of each word.

An alphabetic system, such as English, lets readers use letters as symbols of sounds. Rather than memorizing thousands of words, readers in an alphabetic writing system can learn letter-sound correspondences and thereby use the decoding

---

[2]If a reader is interested in a more detailed understanding of the historical development of theoretical reading models, background appears in the synthesis by Samuels & Kamil (1984). For a sense of the type of tasks that establish the role of decoding, see the work of Perfetti (1984), Stanovich, Cunningham, & Feeman (1984) or, Lesch & Pollatsek (1993). And for insight into meaning processes and their interaction with decoding, refer to the models proposed by Just & Carpenter (1981; 1987), Perfetti & Curtis (1986), or Adams (1990).

approach. Decoding is an efficient means of comprehending unfamiliar written messages since it does not require readers to memorize each word to be read.

During decoding, readers translate letters to speech sounds, and process those sounds as language. This occurs through the use of neural signals that are sensitive to the sound structures of language. **Neural signals** are messages that travel among brain cells. The language-sensitive neural signals connect letters with their sounds, group the sounds into word patterns, and match the word patterns with meaning. Researchers refer to three types of neural signals used in this process—graphic (visual) codes, phonological (sound) codes, and lexical (meaning) codes. (Please see Figure 1.a, following page.)

Graphic codes are neural signals that represent letters. They represent information that is gathered *visually* from the page. Graphic codes are triggered when we see letters. They are activated in a part of the brain that processes visual stimuli. They connect with another part of the brain that processes sound stimuli; here, visual codes trigger phonological (sound) codes.

Phonological codes, triggered in the sound processing area of the brain, are neural signals that represent the *sounds* of a language. Phonological codes are triggered by graphic (visual) codes during reading, or by oral language when someone speaks to us. When phonological codes are triggered, they connect with a third part of the brain, an area that processes meaning. Here, phonological codes trigger **lexical codes**. Lexical codes are sometimes referred to as semantic codes since they represent *meanings*.

A comprehension mechanism sorts and arranges these lexical codes to construct understanding. Information from the comprehension mechanism is fed back to the sound and visual centers to confirm or correct decoding accuracy. When a confirmation is received, work on a small group of letters is complete and the eye proceeds to the next group of letters on a printed page.

In a mature reader, the process from seeing letters to confirming their meaning takes an average of 0.239 second per word during the reading of a college science text. The actual time varies based on the length and familiarity of a word as well as its location in a sentence and paragraph (Just & Carpenter, 1981; Lesch & Pollatsek, 1993).

Schema development and unique individual understanding. Each reader possesses a large collection of assorted knowledge even before beginning to read a

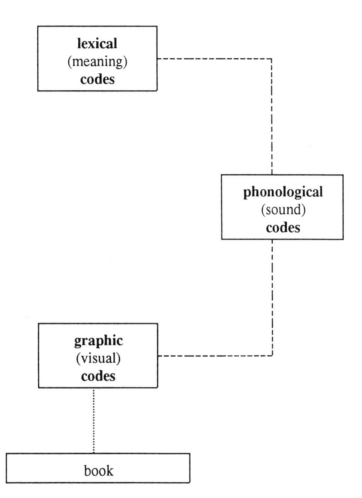

Figure 1.a. Decoding by graphic-phonological-lexical connection.
When a reader's eyes perceive letters, graphic codes are triggered
in a part of the brain that processes **visual** stimuli. These graphic
codes trigger phonological codes in an area of the brain that
processes **sound** stimuli. These phonological codes then trigger
lexical codes that represent **meanings**.

piece of text. This knowledge rests in the reader's lexicon (mental dictionary). The lexicon is a collection of word meanings, concepts, beliefs, text structures, and narrative plots that the reader continues to develop over a lifetime of internalizing experiences perceived through the five senses. To be accessible during reading, these meanings need to be associated with lexical (meaning) codes. Storage as lexical codes seems to allow each bit of knowledge in the lexicon to be expressible and accessible through language. This seems to facilitate processing among lexical, phonological, and graphic codes.

During reading, lexical codes are selected from the lexicon to match the visual and sound codes triggered by print. A comprehension mechanism processes lexical codes in the sequence in which they are selected. As a reader progresses through a text, meanings represented by lexical codes are arranged and integrated in a process that constructs a meaningful understanding of the text—a text schema.

As a text is read, adjustments and repairs are made to the developing schema. These adjustments are made to accommodate unanticipated information as it is triggered in the lexicon by the print or by related thinking during reading. After a piece of text has been read, the reader's personal schema of the text is complete. This mental representation of the text as a whole, the text schema, is a reader's understanding of what a writer set out to convey when placing letters on paper in a specific order.

During reading, the accuracy, clarity, and completeness of a schema is influenced by the availability and repleteness of meanings stored in a reader's lexicon. In addition, schema construction is influenced by a reader's immediate emotional state and feelings concerning stored understandings. These determine how much weight is given to various concepts as they are drawn from the lexicon. Thus, a schema develops from the interaction of a text and the personal store of a reader's lexicon and is influenced by differences in readers' backgrounds. Consequently, when several people read a particular selection of text, each reader develops a personal schema or individualized understanding of the text.

Similar construction of understanding occurs during oral communication. When people communicate with speech, each listener forms a schema of the spoken message. This conversation schema represents an understanding of a conversation as a whole. Given this theoretical model of comprehension, it is not surprising that two people often disagree about what was said or read after participating in one conversation or reading one set of directions.

The role of phonemes in reading. As discussed above, phonological (sound) codes are triggered either by the sounds of letters that we read or by the sounds of language that we hear. The individual sounds that make up phonological codes are called phonemes. Phonemes are the smallest units representing the sounds of spoken language. Human understanding of spoken language relies on our unique sensitivity to phonemes. To understand *spoken* language, we hear the stream of spoken sound separated into specific small groups of phonemes.

Phonemes represent sounds in spoken language just as letters represent units of print in written language. Just as the letter *t* is the letter *t* whether it is printed by a typewriter, written by me, or printed by you, the phoneme /t/ is the phoneme /t/ whether its sound is said by you, your neighbor, or me.

In English, one letter often corresponds to one phoneme as with /t/ or /d/. But sometimes it takes several letters grouped together to spell one phoneme as in /th/ or /sh/. Further, some phonemes are spelled several different ways. For example, the single letter *f* corresponds to the phoneme /f/, but the pair of letters *ph* also corresponds to the phoneme /f/.

During reading, it appears that **individual letters** trigger graphic (visual) codes that in turn trigger an individual phoneme. *Or,* **small groups of letters** trigger graphic (visual) codes that in turn trigger small groups of phonemes. Either single phonemes or small groups of phonemes form phonological (sound) codes. For example, *t* will trigger /t/ or *tion* will trigger /sh/u/n/.

In any language, certain phonemes cluster in common sound patterns that form phonological codes typical of that language. For example, in English, a phonological code is typically formed by the phoneme group /d/i/s/, but not by the phoneme group /v/l/k/. /D/i/s/ but not /v/l/k/ typically forms a phonological code since /d/i/s/ is a common sound pattern in English but /v/l/k/ is not. Further, the common sound pattern of /d/i/s/ connects readily with a meaning in the lexicon while /v/l/k/ does not. Phonological codes are formed readily by specific groups of phonemes when the phoneme groups represent common sound patterns and meaningful lexical codes in a given language.

Direct graphic - lexical access. During beginning reading, the connection of graphic codes to corresponding phonological codes is usually facilitated by "hearing" the sounds of phonemes inside the head. The "hearing" of the phonemes seems to assist in grouping phonemes properly to form familiar phonological codes.

In contrast, during mature reading we seem to read without "hearing" words in our heads. Instead, mature readers *visually* perceive letters in groupings that are phonologically regular. Thus, graphic codes represent letters in clusters that follow phonologically regular patterns. This seems to allow graphic codes to connect directly with corresponding lexical codes. (See Figure 1.b, following page.) That is, instead of matching letters to their sounds and then the sounds to their meaning, mature readers match groups of letters to their lexical codes after perceiving the letters in phonologically regular clusters.

Evidence concerning a graphic - lexical connection through visual sensitivity to phonological patterns is supported by the nature of high fluency reading among readers who were profoundly deaf from birth. Liberman (1987) describes the process of graphic - lexical connection as a function of visually perceiving phonological codes:

> But there are some congenitally, profoundly deaf individuals who can read well, even up to the college level. What about them? Recently, Vicki Hanson and her associates at Haskins asked that question in a series of experiments (Hanson 1982; Hanson and Fowler, 1987). What they found was that the successful deaf readers were not limited to reading English as if it were a logographic [picture system of]...words learned by rote memory. Instead, despite profound hearing loss since birth, they were able to use abstract phonological information both in reading and in short term memory, much as the successful hearing reader does. In reading, for example, they demonstrated phonological sensitivity by responding differentially to rhyming and nonrhyming pairs of words (save/wave vs. have/cave) and by being able to identify the real word equivalents of nonwords ("flame" for *flaim*; "tall" for *taul*). (p. 5).

Even among deaf learners, in an alphabetic reading system, it appears that a direct graphic - lexical connection depends on deep knowledge of the phonological structure of language. These findings indicate the power of common phonological groupings and their integral role in communicating among graphic, phonological, and lexical codes during the cognitive processing of written and oral language.

The power of phonological patterns is further illustrated by their consistent use during the interaction of decoding and understanding. As illustrated in Figure 1.b, even when direct graphic - lexical connections occur, post-lexical reconnections to corresponding phonological codes, or graphic codes representing phonological units, appear to check that correct lexical codes were accessed (Stanovich, Cunningham, & Feeman, 1984; Lesch & Pollatsek, 1993). It would seem that these

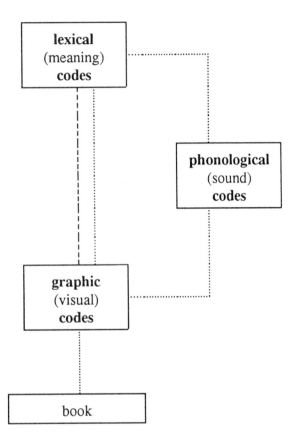

Figure 1.b. Decoding by direct graphic-lexical connection.
Mature readers seem to perceive groups of letters in visual clusters
that represent common phonological patterns. These visual clusters
seem to be used to form a direct graphic-lexical connection, as
represented by the dashed line.

After visual and meaning codes connect, there is a check back to
phonological codes and/or visual codes to assure that correct lexical
codes were triggered.   (The dotted lines represent post-lexical
reconnections to corresponding phonological codes and/or to graphic
codes representing phonological units.)

verification reconnections may also help in remembering what was read by confirming content through additional processing.

An example summarizing the reading process. In essence, during reading a decoding mechanism picks up print from the page when the eyes rest on a letter or small group of letters. This information is momentarily held in the brain as a graphic (visual) code. The graphic code in turn triggers a corresponding phonological (sound) code. Then the phonological code triggers a lexical code—a meaning selected from the reader's lexicon to correspond with the phonological code that triggered it.

During mature reading, the connection to lexical codes may occur directly from graphic codes formed by perceiving letters in phonologically regular clusters. As graphic codes connect either directly with lexical codes, or through phonological to lexical codes, these lexical (meaning) codes are arranged and rearranged to create a sensible understanding of the text. As it is developing, this understanding is continually checked for consistency with the written word.

For example, if the eyes rest on the letters, *in the morning*, the eyes and brain work together to transform the printed letters into graphic (visual) codes that represent the letters in the reader's brain. These graphic codes connect with phonological (sound) codes. To help make this connection occur, a reader sometimes "hears in the head" the sound of /in/the/morn/ing/. The phonological codes for /in/the/morn/ing/ rapidly connect with the reader's mental dictionary (lexicon) and select corresponding lexical (meaning) codes.

The meanings are selected from the lexicon in the exact order that the words are read, then they are rearranged for maximum coherence as additional letter groups are read. For example, the lexicon first receives /in/ and prepares to use either the meaning [inside] or [during]. Then the brain processes /the/ and leans toward [inside] for /in/ since /the/ suggests that some kind of object will follow. Next the lexicon receives /morn/ and starts to lean toward [during] for /in/.

The next bit of information /ing/ completes the meaning and [during] is selected instead of [inside]. If the reader had accidentally decoded the example phrase as *in the morned*, when the lexicon received /ed/, a meaning would not be found for /morned/. A message would be sent back through phonological and graphic codes to recheck the letters on the page to see if they might be *ing*.

THEORETICAL MODELS AND INSTRUCTION

Models of mature reading suggest that reading instruction needs to fill several roles. One function of instruction is to assist students in developing automaticity, unconscious speed and accuracy, in the neural "athletics" of connecting print to graphic (visual) codes, graphic codes to phonological (sound) codes, and phonological codes to lexical (meaning) codes. Another function of instruction is to enlarge a reader's pool of meanings, along with their corresponding array of lexical codes, in preparation for constructing a schema of an unfamiliar text.

Automaticity. During precursor Stage 0, children generally develop automaticity in connecting the phonological codes of spoken words with their corresponding lexical (meaning) codes. The challenge facing novice readers is to make letter-to-sound connections as automatic as sound-to-meaning connections.

Deep memory of graphic (visual) codes and their connections to phonological (sound) codes develops through practice. Until a wide range of graphic codes, and their connections to phonological codes, are well embedded in memory, beginning readers focus much of their conscious attention on the decoding of individual letters, syllables, and words. As a consequence, beginning readers often experience a *bottleneck* effect when trying to pay attention to both decoding and comprehension of a text (Perfetti, 1984).

Even mature readers sometimes practice decoding in order to develop automaticity with particular words. For example, readers of this chapter who were unfamiliar with the terms *graphic*, *phonological*, and *lexical*, focused attention on the decoding of these words. It may have taken a second or third reading before the graphic, phonological, and lexical codes for these terms embedded solidly in memory. Once the codes were set in memory, readers no longer needed to sound the words nor check on each word's meaning. Finally, readers could focus attention on how these concepts fit together to express ideas about the process of reading comprehension.

Expanding the lexicon. When students enter Stage 3, they need to expand their lexicons. One effective approach is through instruction that directly connects linguistic expressions with all sorts of information, experiences, feelings, perceptions, beliefs, and text structures. This occurs during vocabulary instruction, discussion of readings, related writing projects, as well as in other contexts. As readers expand their lexicons, they more easily sequence, check, adjust, and repair their schemata of unfamiliar texts.

Components of Effective Instruction

Sensitive instruction increases the rate at which students progress in reading and enhances their facility with a repertoire of reading competencies. Whether students are learning the sound of the letter *t*, the meaning of the word *dyspedagogia*[3], or a strategy for synthesizing convoluted schemata, they are aided by skillful instruction. Such instruction nurtures students through their fear of failure while avoiding practices that foster apathy.

Well timed support, accompanied by sufficient modeling, encourages students to navigate purposefully through the learning of specialized concepts and unfamiliar processes. Effective instruction includes opportunities for students to express their knowledge in written or oral language. The discussion that follows considers several salient instructional characteristics that enrich learning.

SCAFFOLDING

Scaffolding is a means of developing agility with a complex skill or process while focusing on only one or several of its components at a time. During scaffolded instruction, teachers supply supports that bridge gaps in their students' knowledge, experience, or dexterity. Aided by these supports, students can practice one essential component that contributes to a broader, more complex ability or understanding. At any stage of reading, properly executed scaffolds create learning experiences that ensure success (Case, 1980; Fisher, 1980).

An illustration. The use of scaffolding is illustrated by the process of learning to ride a two-wheeled bicycle with training wheels. Properly adjusted training wheels barely hover above the ground when a rider is balanced. The moment balance is lost, or until balance is gained, the rider can trust the training wheels to offer reliable protection against a painful spill. Even while riding in balance, the novice feels secure that the training wheels are ready to provide support should the sense of balance or the skill of balancing be jarred by uneven pavement.

In addition, when a novice is learning to ride, the feel or sound of training wheels momentarily touching the ground provides a cue to shift weight and regain balance. During responsive teaching, scaffolding, such as training wheels, is provided for precisely as long as and to the extent that it is needed. As with training

---

[3]*dyspedagogia* - Weak academic performance resulting from poor teaching.

wheels, learners recognize their need for support yet are glad to accomplish the independence of functioning beyond the scaffolds.

Scaffolds in full contexts. Scaffolds sometimes support a process in its full context by taking care of related activities. For example, students may be learning a strategy for finding details that contribute to main ideas in a science text. While searching for details, unfamiliar vocabulary words may surface. A teacher could scaffold the process by directly stating the meaning of the unfamiliar words.

Such scaffolding would encourage students to proceed with finding details, without interruption. The scaffold would spare students the frustration inherent in a forced shift away from the fragile work of schema construction to the process of defining words. Such a shift would remove attention from the process under study and threaten to dismantle tentative understanding.

At another time, students may be learning to develop meanings of unfamiliar words in text through use of context or a computerized meaning search. In this instance, a teacher would scaffold by stating a brief schema summary each time the developing schema was forgotten during definition activity. Students would experience success with the definition strategy since the word would fit meaningfully into the freshly summarized text. Such scaffolding would enable students to concentrate on the practice of one component while engaging in a broader process.

Scaffolds in constrained contexts. At other times, scaffolds narrow an activity's context to decrease the number of processes vying for attention. For example, novices learning the alphabetic principle may be overwhelmed if asked to read a bit of text concerning *mice*. A teacher can provide the scaffold of a constrained context by teaching, in isolation, the letter-sounds of *mice* and how they blend into *mice*.

When students are learning the letter *m* and its corresponding sound in isolation, the meaning of a text is not present to provide a contextual cue. When the symbol is presented, a teacher would scaffold the learning of *m* by forming her lips for the sound. When necessary, the teacher would begin to make the sound as well. As students begin to sound the phoneme, the teacher fades the prompt. To acknowledge growth and encourage further development, teachers need to reduce scaffolds gradually and shift toward fuller contexts as students' needs for practice with single components decrease.

Teachers need to determine when practice within a broader context encourages learners by providing intrinsic cues and when a larger context creates overwhelming confusion. When a broad ability involves many unfamiliar components, temporary practice with one or several of the central components, in isolation, reduces distractions and develops confidence. In this instance, the teacher's scaffold provides a replacement context, external reminders or cues that trigger the skill under study.

Teach in segments. At any stage of reading, fluid scaffolding enables a teacher to assist hesitant students by segmenting an instructional component into easily achieved parts. Small segments demand only minimal effort and minor risk while producing noticeable success. Success achieved during nonthreatening exertion motivates students to risk a little more exposure and invest a little more effort. When further investment leads to continued success, students commit to the process of learning, and become actively involved.

For example, a teacher may segment the instructional component of telling the plot of a story into smaller steps by asking the following questions one at a time. "Tell what happened first." "What happened next?" "Then what happened?" "And how did it finally end?" The teacher asks only one of these questions at a time and gives verbal clues or points to clues in the book to remind a student of the answer. By confirming a student's response to the one small question before asking the next small question, the teacher ensures success at a task that would have seemed formidable if presented at once as, "What was the plot of the story?"

At times, a teacher will accidentally provide an activity that is too challenging, with too little scaffolding. If this is acknowledged immediately as a teaching error, and treated as an indicator to break instruction into smaller segments with added scaffolds, students' commitment to learning will remain intact. The smaller, achievable objective initiates a successful experience that overrides a momentary sense of failure.

Immediate adjustments in segment size and degree of scaffolding bolster students' courage to remain committed to the process of learning (Brody, 1987). For example, if a teacher asks a student to tell the plot of a story and the student is not ready, the teacher could say, "Let me try to ask my question a better way." Next, while pointing to the relevant section of text, the teacher would ask, "What happened here in the story?"

Model. Across reading stages, teachers can convey a concept or process through modeling—demonstrating each segment of a process or concept while describing it. An oral explanation alone may be difficult to understand, particularly when a complex process or intricate concept is explained. Conversely, a graph, picture, or demonstration, without oral or written explanation, may convey a feeling for the concept, but leave students with no language to retrieve or describe necessary details of the concept for later use. For maximum effectiveness, lessons need to employ both linguistic explanation and visual demonstration.

Model and apply. After viewing a model while hearing its explanation, students need to engage with the matter themselves in order to understand it fully. To scaffold for immediate success during these engagements, teachers need to explain and model not only the concept, but how to apply it as well. This explanation and demonstration should include a context similar to the one assigned to the student. For example, if the student is assigned to engage with an unfamiliar vocabulary word by using it in a meaningful sentence, a teacher would explain its meaning and demonstrate its use in a sentence. This would model how to use the word when speaking or writing.

When beginning to engage with a concept, students may need the scaffold of a highly specific suggestion for application. For example, a student may hesitate to use the word *hectic* in a sentence. A teacher could scaffold the application by suggesting that students tell sentences about a time of day when things are hectic at home. This would assist the student in retrieving an appropriate situation from which to develop a sentence. In another instance, if students are to share a detail found in a paragraph, a teacher can model the application process by pointing out one detail, then asking a student for another. As a scaffold, the teacher may direct the student to a specific sentence in which to locate another detail.

Apply in varied contexts. Learning is enriched by many opportunities to engage successfully with a concept in a variety of contexts. Such opportunities motivate students to practice further so long as sufficient modeling and scaffolding assure success. As automaticity develops through practice, the concept can be used in wider and more varied contexts with less support; then attention can turn to less-practiced components.

As automaticity increases, engagement with a concept in varied contexts offers openings to explore nuances that were not communicated during initial instruction. When nuances surface during students' efforts to use the concept in a specialized application, adjustments and details become meaningful.

Teach the exceptions. Exceptions and complicated details are best taught during practice when varied contexts and decreased scaffolds reveal them. In this way, exceptions are introduced when students are ready to absorb them as specialized cases of a general concept or process. Occasionally, students will raise exceptions early in the learning process. It is generally wise to state that they are specialized cases and focus on a variety of examples that support the common generalization.

For example, in words with double vowels, the first vowel is often long and the second vowel silent as in *boat* or *lean*. When learning this rule, a student may question it since it does not hold for a *piece* of *bread*. In this instance, it is important to acknowledge the difference, but equally important to focus quickly on the many words that follow the rule (such as *bead, soak, neat, rail*) to indicate that it is worth learning and using.

It is necessary to acknowledge a specialized case when it is raised early by a student. This assures the student that the concept was understood even though it contains a contradiction. Study of a general concept, before introducing or exploring exceptions in depth, embeds the central concept or process as the main schema. This assures that exceptions are not assumed to be the general case.

ANTIDOTES TO FEAR OF FAILURE

Some learners exhibit deep hesitation when approaching reading. Students who have tried and failed need particular support and encouragement if they are to develop reading ability and confidence. Models and scaffolds aid thought and memory to assure an abundance of immediate success. They also offer emotional support and encouragement—assuring that success is achievable and that mistakes along the way are acceptable.

Confirm and assure. When students fear failure, their fright lends an added drain to their attentional resources. Since attention is limited, as much of it as possible needs to be free to engage with text during reading. Fearful students will not be able to focus all the attention needed on reading if they feel compelled to continually monitor whether they are carrying out a process correctly.

Even with scaffolding, success needs to be confirmed with immediate feedback. Immediate, continual, low-key confirmations from a teacher decrease self-conscious worry. Sensitive confirmation encourages hesitant students to focus all their attention on reading rather than reserving some of their attention for self-checking.

Continual confirmatory feedback needs to be very brief and cause minimal disruption to the flow of reading and instruction. For example, when students are beginning to read connected text, they should not need to look up from the print to check for a confirming smile or nod. The confirmation should be communicated by a teacher with a soft *um-hum* or *yeah* that unobtrusively indicates success without drawing attention from the text. When a student errs, a soft restating of the last word read correctly, or pointing to the spot that needs repair, interrupts the flow minimally.

Quietly hearing of their continual success encourages learners to involve themselves a little more in the learning process. As students develop automaticity with introductory components, these begin to serve as self-applied scaffolds during later learning. Consistent and accurate graphic - phonological - lexical connections serve as internal scaffolds that manifest themselves as confidence. These automatized scaffolds assure that text is read accurately. With successful practice, students slowly replace verbal confirmations from a teacher with internal recognition that what they hear and understand through their reading makes sense.

Provide missing background. Learners vary in the extent of their background at each stage of learning. Some develop sufficient mastery and background at one level to generalize the central components to a next level for themselves. Others, who lack background and security, need scaffolds and models that teach the intricate details of an unfamiliar component before they can attempt to try it independently. Teachers can reduce anxiety by providing models and scaffolds instead of expecting fearful learners to guess. Instead of assuming that hesitant students are timid, teachers need to recognize that these learners lack the background that enables their peers to seem more daring and confident.

Students with learning disabilities, and learners who come from homes where little reading has occurred, need clear procedures to follow as they encounter unfamiliar reading processes. When teachers provide these supports, students with limited background and experience progress well.   Their progress develops background and confidence, and encourages the daring required for later levels of reading to mature.

Model vulnerability. As teachers, we encourage learners to take a variety of risks: to explain what they read, to pronounce unknown words, to use a spelling dictionary, to forge into the unknown and learn from mistakes. We state that no one knows everything, that it is fine to need to learn, acceptable not to know an answer.

Many mature adults avoid these self-exposing activities assiduously, and hesitant learners fear them immensely.

Modeling these challenging activities, which often are accompanied by deep feelings of vulnerability, intensifies the effectiveness of good teaching. When teachers publicly look up the spelling of a word, say they need to look for information that they do not know, or pause during oral reading to sound through a long word, they model that it really is all right to be a learner and to use the strategies that are under study.

Expect success. When teachers believe that their students will learn, students have a higher success rate (Rosenthal & Jacobson, 1968). Teachers communicate their expectation that students will learn by offering material in manageable segments with supportive scaffolds and models. They freely re-teach portions of the material in smaller segments when necessary. They also test students on what has been taught, rather than on abstruse applications. Such assessments communicate clearly that expectations are met and develop students' confidence that they will encounter success as they continue to learn.

In contrast, "setting high expectations" is sometimes invoked as an explanation for giving students assignments that are too large, too complicated, and unaccompanied by sufficient support. While done in the name of expecting success, this nearly guarantees failure for students who can learn the material, but not without a teacher who takes the time to teach prerequisite background and to present the assignment in manageable steps.

The expectation of success can be communicated through the simple verbal nuance of asking students *to do* a task rather than asking *whether* they *can* do it. For example, teachers can communicate positive expectations by asking students, "Read this sentence," rather than asking, "Do you think you can read this sentence for me?" We tend to use "will you" or "can you" questions to seem less demanding or threatening. One effect is to communicate an unsureness in students' abilities. By directly asking students to do things that we have taught them or things that we think they can do, and by consistently accompanying such requests with sufficient scaffolds for students to experience success, we communicate that we anticipate success.

Conclusion

Reading is a complex and intricate process involving print and language. To enhance reading progress, instruction needs to take into account variations in maturational level, learning abilities, text difficulty, extent of mastery, and extensiveness of background knowledge. These can be viewed against an understanding of developmental stages of reading, cognitive processes of mature reading, and guidelines of effective instruction. In the chapters that follow, each component of reading sketched in this overview will be examined in depth. Discussion will include recommendations that engender confidence and security in growing readers.

32

References

Adams, M.J. (1990; 1994). *Beginning to read: Thinking and learning about print*. Cambridge, MA: MIT Press.

Applebee, A.N., Langer, J.A., & Mullis, I.V. (1987). *The nation's report card: Learning to be literate in America*. Princeton, NJ: Educational Testing Service.

Blachman, B.A. (1991). Getting ready to read: Learning how print maps to speech. In J.F. Kavanagh (Ed.), *The language continuum: From infancy to literacy*. Parkton, MD: York Press.

Brody, S. (1987). *Study skills: Teaching and learning strategies for mainstream and specialized classrooms*. Milford, NH: LARC Publishing.

Brody, S. (1989). Elements of effective reading instruction in grades 4 and 5: Lessons from recent research. Unpublished qualifying paper. Harvard Graduate School of Education.

Case, R. (1980). The underlying mechanism of intellectual development. In *Cognition, development, and instruction*. NY: Academic Press.

Chall, J.S. (1983a). *Stages of reading development*. NY: McGraw-Hill.

Chall, J.S. (1983b). *Learning to reading: The great debate (2nd ed.)*. NY: McGraw Hill.

Chall, J.S. (in press). *Stages of reading development (2nd ed.)*.

Chall, J.S., & Conard, S.S. (1991). *Should textbooks challenge students?* NY: Teachers College Press.

Chall, J.S., & Snow, C. (1988). School influences on the reading development of low-income children. *Education Letter*. Published by the Harvard Graduate School of Education in association with Harvard University Press, 4(1), January.

Chomsky, C. (1978). When you still can't read in third grade: After decoding what? In S.J. Samuels & A.E. Farstrup (Eds.), *What research has to say about reading instruction (2nd ed.)*. Newark, DE: IRA.

Fisher, K.W. (1980). A theory of cognitive development: The control and construction of hierarchies of skills. *Psychological Review*, 87(6), 115-169.

Gagne, R.M., & Driscoll, M.P. (1988). *Essentials of learning for instruction (2nd ed.)*. Englewood Cliffs, NJ: Prentice Hall.

Hanson, V.L. (1982). Short-term recall by deaf signers of American Sign Language: Implications of encoding strategy for order recall. *Journal of Experimental Psychology: Learning, Memory, and Cognition*, 8(6), 572-583.

Hanson, V.L., & Fowler, C.A. (1987) Phonological coding in word reading: Evidence from hearing and deaf readers. *Memory & Cognition*, 15(3), 199-207.

Just, M.A., & Carpenter, P.A. (1981). Cognitive processes in reading: Models based on readers' eye fixations. In A.M. Lesgold & C.A. Perfetti (Eds.) *Interactive processes in reading*. Hillsdale, NJ: Erlbaum, 177-213.

Just, M.A., & Carpenter, P.A. (1987). *The psychology of reading and language comprehension*. Boston, MA: Allyn and Bacon, Inc.

Kinsch, W., & vanDijk, T. (1978). Toward a model of text comprehension and production. *Psychological Review*, 85, 363-394.

LaBerge, D., & Samuels, S.J. (1974). Toward a theory of automatic information processing in reading. *Cognitive Psychology*, 6, 293-323.

Lerner, J. (1993). *Teaching children with learning disabilities*. Boston: Houghton Mifflin.

Lesch, M.F., & Pollatsek, A. (1993). Automatic access of semantic information by phonological codes in visual word recognition. *Journal of Experimental Psychology: Learning Memory and Cognition*, 19(2), 285-294.

Lesgold, A.M., & Perfetti, C.A. (Eds.) (1981). *Interactive processes in reading*. Hillsdale, NJ: Erlbaum.

Liberman, I. (1987). Language and literacy: The obligation of the schools of education. In *Intimacy with language: A forgotten basic in teacher education. Conference proceedings*. Baltimore, MD: The Orton Dyslexia Society.

Liebling, C.R. (1989). Inside view and character plans in an original story and its basal adaptation. *Theory into Practice*, 28(2).

Perfetti, C.A. (1984). Reading acquisition and beyond: Decoding includes cognition. *American Journal of Education*, Nov. 93, 40-60.

Perfetti, C.A., & Curtis, M.E. (1986). Reading. In R.F. Dillon & R.J. Sternberg (Eds.), *Cognition and instruction*. NY: Academic Press.

Rath, L. (1990). Phonemic awareness: Its role in reading development. Unpublished qualifying paper, Harvard Graduate School of Education.

Rosenthal, R., & Jacobson, L. (1968). *Pygmalion in the classroom: Teacher expectation and pupils' intellectual development*. New York: Holt, Rinehart and Winston, Inc.

Rummelhart, D.E., & Ortony, A. (1977). The representation of knowledge in memory. In R.C. Anderson, R.J. Spiro, & W.E. Montague (Eds.) *Schooling and the acquisition of knowledge*. Hillsdale, NJ: Erlbaum.

Samuels, S.J., & Kamil, M.L. (1984). Models of the reading process. In P.D. Pearson, (Ed.), *Handbook of Reading Research*. New York: Longman.

Samuels, S.J., Schermer, D.R., & Reinking, D. (1992). Reading fluency: Techniques for making decoding automatic. In S.J. Samuels & A.E. Farstrup (Eds.), *What research has to say about reading instruction (2nd ed.)*. Newark, DE: IRA.

Smith, F. (1988). *Understanding reading: A psycholinguistic analysis of reading and learning to read (4th ed.)*. Hillsdale, NJ: Erlbaum.

Stanovich, K.E. (1980). Toward an interactive-compensatory model of individual differences in the development of reading fluency. *Reading Research Quarterly*, 16, 32-71.

Stanovich, K.E. (1986). Matthew effects in reading: Some consequences of individual differences in the acquisition of literacy. *Reading Research Quarterly*, 21(4), 360-406.

Stanovich, K.E. (1994). Romance and reality. *The Reading Teacher*, 47(4), 280-291.

Stanovich, K.E., Cunningham, A.E., & Feeman, D.J. (1984). Intelligence, cognitive skills, and early reading progress. *Reading Research Quarterly*, 19(3), 278-303.

Stotsky, S. (1986). Asking questions about ideas: A critical component in critical thinking. *The Leaflet*, Fall, 39-47.

34

Williams, J.P. (1980). Teaching decoding with an emphasis on phoneme analysis and phoneme blending. *Journal of Educational Psychology*, 72, 1 - 15.

Wilson, P.T., & Anderson, R.C. (1986). What they don't know will hurt them: The role of prior knowledge in comprehension. In J. Orasanu (Ed.) *Reading comprehension: From research to practice*. Hillsdale, NJ: Lawrence Erlbaum Associates.

II. LANGUAGE

Chapter 2. Language: Structure and Acquisition

Melissa Farrall, PhD
Rivier College

Long ago, in a distant time and place, unknown beings opened their mouths, and through a precisely articulated sequence of sounds, exchanged thoughts. What triggered those first words we will never know. We will also never know whether the significance of that moment was appreciated in any way. Did the two people look at each other knowingly? Was there relief or joy or pride? The advent of language, however inauspicious and modest its beginnings, distinguished the history of the human species by allowing men and women to convey needs, thoughts, and desires to one another, as well as from one generation to the next.

The debate over those first words, and whatever precipitated them, has raged for more than two thousand years. Since that time, philosophers, philologists, psychologists, and a host of others have all engaged in the study of language in an attempt to describe the system by which articulated sounds are used to convey information and carry on the affairs of their society (Francis, 1958). In addition, the study of language involves yet another dimension. Language is seen by some to be a manifestation of the inner workings of the brain. The abstract principles that govern the structure of language may be the product of a unique biological design. Whether language is biological, social, or some combination thereof, the study of language teaches much about humans, how we think and how we learn. We may ultimately even satisfy our curiosity about why it is that we speak and animals do not.

This chapter is about language—its structure and the stages in which it is acquired. We will review the interrelationships and patterns that make up the intricate structures of language, and examine the process by which humans use language to communicate. Part One of the chapter will review the terminology of language study, analyze the developmental stages of language acquisition, and offer strategies to aid in its evolution. Part Two examines several prominent theories concerned with the nature of cognition and language acquisition.

PART ONE

TERMINOLOGY

Before proceeding with the discussion, we will review the jargon commonly employed by linguistic enthusiasts. **Language** is the communication of thoughts and feelings by means of a formalized system of abstract symbols and rule-governed structures. Such systems may include signs, gestures, speech-sounds, and letters of the alphabet. It is important to note that, with the exception of a small category of words known as onomatopoeias (*buzz, moo*), the relationship between a symbol and its meaning is arbitrary. For example, a table is not called a *table* because its sound has a "tablelike" quality, and it is unlikely that we will ever determine a causal relationship between words and the objects or abstractions that they represent.

Because language is essentially a human creation, all languages share certain common properties. Whether we speak French, Swahili, or Urdu, we have an unlimited vehicle for communication. Any language provides a means to refer to the past, the present, and the future. In addition, all languages include vehicles that assist us in creating new vocabulary, and comprehending infinite sets of well-formed sentences. All of this is made possible by the application of humans' immeasurable cognitive resources to a finite set of discrete sounds or gestures that are then linked together in accordance with the rules of grammar.

Speech is defined as the oral expression of language. It is a complex physical process involving the precise interaction of three main functions of the human vocal apparatus. These functions include: the production of air from the lungs; the constriction of airflow in the larynx; and the modification of airflow by the anatomical structures of the vocal tract (For those wishing to learn about the production of speech, please see Hulit & Howard's [1993] *Born to Talk*).

Linguistics is the science of language and it encompasses a broad range of specialties and interests. **Historical linguists** study the history of written languages in order to document the ways in which they change. **Comparative linguists** classify language into various groups and families in order to posit an explanation for both the diversity and universality of human speech. **Psycholinguists** examine the relationship between language and cognitive processes. Recently, this field has focused considerable attention on the biological and neurological aspects of language by scrutinizing emergent language in the child. Finally, **structural linguists** focus on the study of the system, or the structural components, of language. Winograd (1983) compared structural linguistics to chemistry. In his view, the goal of linguistics, as for chemistry, is to define a set of primitive elements and their rules for combination. In this way, we are able to understand how to generate more complex structures of language.

Structure of language. The structure of human language traditionally is divided into four main branches: phonology, morphology, syntax, and semantics. **Phonology** is the study of the patterns and distribution of speech sounds. Within phonology there are two areas of concentration, **phonetics** and **phonemics**. The distinction between phonetics and phonemics causes endless confusion, which I attempt to clarify below.

Phonetics is the study of speech sounds, called **phones**, and their production, transmission, and reception. Although we speak of speech sounds as discrete bits of acoustic data, this is not really the case. Speech is continuous, and the precise articulation of individual sounds is limited by our physical design and our ability to manipulate our speech organs from one position to another. To most of us, a *t* is just a *t*. To a phonetician, the precise pronunciation of a *t* is dependent upon its phonetic environment. The spoken word, *titillate*, may contain three different *t* phones. The transcription, [t' I t ̚ leit], shows that the first [t'] is aspirated, the second [t ̚] is unreleased, and the third [t] is unaspirated. The specific phones produced vary with each individual and are influenced by local accents.

In contrast, **phonemics** is the study of **phonemes**. Phonemes are **consistent** representations, in our brains, of the major sounds of speech. For example, in our brains, the phoneme /t/ represents every *t* in *titillate*. Our ability to translate the phones we hear to phonemes that represent them is most apparent when we hear someone speak with an accent. In our minds, we recognize what the speaker is saying despite encountering a set of phones that vary from those we are accustomed to hearing. For example, the phoneme /a/ represents both the phone *a* in *what* pronounced by someone from Britain and the phone *a* in *what* pronounced by someone from Michigan. The fact that we understand each other, even when, on an acoustic level, pronunciation differs considerably, is a testament to the substantial capacity of the brain and its ability to translate phones to phonemes.

As we advance to more complex structures of language, we find that phonemes are organized into meaningful groups called morphemes. **Morphology** is the study of words and word building. **Morphemes**, the smallest units of meaning in a word, are categorized into two classes: free morphemes and bound morphemes. A free morpheme can stand on its own as, for example, the word *house*. Bound morphemes cannot stand alone but must be attached to another morpheme. By adding the morpheme -*s* onto a noun, we signify the plural. If we add the bound morpheme *un* to a verb we can turn the world upside down by undoing whatever has already been done.

Syntax involves the rules for the formation of grammatical sentences. Although as native speakers we may not understand the difference between a noun and a verb, we do know how to generate well-formed sentences. Non-native speakers often apply their own rules of syntax when learning to speak foreign languages. The sentence, "Throw me down the stairs my hat," is an example of how speakers may apply rules of syntax from another language to English.

Finally, **semantics** concerns meaning. Knowledge of semantics allows us to make decisions such as whether to use the adverb *badly* or *awfully*. "It is awfully good" is correct. "It is badly good" is not. Over the years there has been much discussion as to whether meaning should be considered part of language structure. Since meaning is part of the knowledge that a speaker utilizes to communicate verbally, it seems crucial to include meaning as part of the structure of human language.

Communication and the Speech Chain

Whether we choose to communicate through speech, writing, or sign, communication is a fragile process requiring the speaker and the listener to perform a series of complex operations in order to come to a common understanding. Denes & Pinson (1973, pp. 1-6) call this process the **speech chain** and they break it down into a series of six steps that are summarized below:

1. The speaker has an idea, a feeling, or a conscious need, and a desire to express it.

2. Within the speaker's mind, the concept is put into language.

3. The language that represents the concept initiates neurological activity that conveys the proper neural impulses from the brain to the organs of speech in order to produce the actual message.

4. The message is a series of pressure patterns in the air called **sound waves**. Sound waves cause air particles to move and collide into one another, creating compression between some particles and spaces between others.

5. The movement of the air particles in sound waves causes a series of vibrations in the listener's eardrums. The ear functions to transform these vibrations into neural impulses that travel along the acoustic nerve to the brain.

6. Finally, these neural impulses are mapped into progressively more abstract representations in the listener's consciousness and they are stored into memory as ideas, feelings, or desires. The speech chain, however, does not end here. In order for comprehension to occur, the listener must actively compare the new information to what is already believed to be true. This is achieved by plugging the new data into the established network of schemata and by noting how they differ or conform. Critical thinking occurs when we, on the basis of our analysis, decide to alter or expand our existing network of thought in order to reflect the larger perspective.

Life would be much simpler if the messages that speakers sent were the messages received. Unfortunately, the nature of the communicative process is such that problems can occur at many points along the way. The speaker may have deficits in cognitive processing or poor articulation. The room may be noisy and distracting. The listener may be hearing impaired, lack focused attention, or have difficulty with cognitive functioning.

Even assuming that all these functions are performed fluently and without disruption, the communicative effort may still be in vain. Comprehension may not occur if the speaker and the listener do not share a common background knowledge to support their communication. The expression, "They don't speak the same language," is used frequently when two individuals are not able to communicate their points of view. The language to which this expression refers is not the oral language, but the language in the head. Perhaps the expression should be rephrased to read, "They don't have the same background knowledge."

To further appreciate the complexities of the communicative process, we must understand that oral language is only part of the message. When human beings speak, we also provide additional information in the form of nonverbal cues such as gestures, facial expression, eye contact, tone of voice, emotion, and even significant pauses. Each of these cues provides a context for the interpretation of language. With them, we are able to distinguish a truthful, "I didn't do it," from its less than honorable counterpart. Being able to discern the communicative intent behind an utterance is as important as the language in and of itself. The study of **pragmatics** is the analysis of language in terms of the situational context, including the knowledge and beliefs of the speaker, as well as the relation between the speaker and the listener.

Stages of Speech and Language Development

Many parents feel that an eternity passes before their children articulate their first recognizable words. During this time of waiting, tremendous achievement and cognitive growth occur as all the speech and language related mechanisms are finely tuned to work so precisely that we often forget just how complex the process is. The following briefly describes the most significant features of the stages of language development that lead to and follow children's first utterances (see Table 2.1, following page). For those wishing to delve further into the subject, a more thorough examination can be found in Sharon James's *Normal Language Acquisition* (1990).

Although the stages are presented here with references to specific age spans, it is important to note that these are guidelines and not absolutes. To a certain degree, variation in language acquisition is normal. Some children may enter the one-word stage at twelve months of age and others at fourteen months. We accept these variations as part of the diversity of nature.

There are, however, children whose development, for some reason or other, departs significantly from the norm. These children can be helped, and when there is a question, it is prudent to have a child evaluated by a speech and language pathologist. Federal law mandates that the local school districts provide services for the identification of such children, at no cost to the parent, from birth. Remedial

Table 2.1. Summary of the Stages of Language Development.

Stages of Language Development

Prebirth Stage
Sensory stimulation promotes neurological development.

Infancy: Setting the Stage for Speech
Prefer human voices and smiling faces. Non-verbal dialogue and turn-taking.

Birth	Vegetative sounds
2 months	Locke's "Goo Stage"
5 months	Marginal babbling
6 months	Babbling
9 - 18 mos	Non-reduplicated babbling, phonetically consistent forms

The One-Word Holophrastic Stage (12 months)
The use of one word to express a thought or concern. Single syllable or doubling of single syllable words such as *wawa*. Over/underextend meaning.

Pragmatics:	Satisfy needs and wants. Control behavior of others.
	Interact with others. Express feelings or attitudes.
	Rudiments of turn-taking.

The Two-Word Telegraphic Stage (Between 18 and 24 Months)
Two-word utterances characterized by elimination of unstressed syllables, deletion of final consonants, and substitution of sounds made in front of mouth (/b/, /p/, /d/, /t/, /m/, /n/, /w/). No prepositions, auxiliary words, or conjunctions. No morphological markers for number, person, or tense. No pronouns. Negation signaled by *no* or *not* in initial position.

Pragmatics:	Language of requests. Provide information.
	Comment, remember, question, and predict.

Preschool Years to Fluency (Ages Two to Five)
Language explosion. Morphemes, pronouns, auxiliary verbs, function words, and phrases appear. Negation develops in stages. Overextension of grammar. Fluency.

Pragmatics:	Question formation. Interrogatives, *why, who,* and *how* appear.
	Sustain turn-taking for one or two turns. Fewer interruptions.
	Mechanics of conversational timing. Semantic softeners.
	Conversational repair to suit the needs of the listener.

The School-Aged Child
Effective use of language. Passives with action verbs. Full use of the passive does not occur until adolescence. Principal of minimum distance. Metalinguistic ability.

Pragmatics:	Maintain conversation for several turns.
	Sustained conversational repair. Artful hints.

services are available beginning with the age of three, when warranted. Assistance in determining whether a child needs remediation can be received by contacting one's elementary school principal.

PREBIRTH STAGE

According to the research conducted by John Locke (1993), an infant in the womb is able to experience and process a wide variety of sensory stimuli that are thought to promote neurological development in the brain. Recent research has determined that beginning at about twenty-six weeks, the fetus is able to respond to the stimulus of the mother's voice, as well as other ex utero voices and sounds, amidst the noise of turbulent blood flow. Of these stimuli, maternal vocalizations are said to be the most apparent, possibly explaining why newborns not only prefer their mother's voice, but also the sounds of their mother's native tongue. It has been suggested, by Locke, that the fetus learns its first lessons about language when the mother reacts to being kicked.

INFANCY: SETTING THE STAGE FOR SPEECH

As stated above, newborns come into the world with a strong preference for the maternal voice and a distinct predilection for the sounds of their native tongue. According to Locke (1993), from the earliest moments of life in the outside world, infants actively seek out stimulation that they find pleasurable. This stimulation includes melodious humans voices and smiling faces. In particular, the infant's gaze is drawn to the eyes, for their expression reveals much about the nature of our communication.

Locke suggests that early mother-infant interactions are linguistically significant. Through the process of nurturance, infants become closely attuned to all the cues, verbal and nonverbal, that a mother emits concerning her emotional state. The primary reason for this is survival. Mother is the infancy equivalent of meals on wheels, and one must be able to flag down the driver for a delivery.

The attachment between parent and child also provides opportunities to develop many language-related processes, such as turn-taking. Infants, in their quest for nourishment and stimulation, actively solicit attention in the form of a friendly face or a familiar voice through eye contact and manual gestures. They are even able to identify whether a mother is in a nurturing mood and modulate their behavior accordingly. In a similar fashion, mothers are continually evaluating and responding to an infant's signals to gather information about the child's physical and emotional well being.

Through a sequence of prompting, attending, and reassessment, infants participate in a nonverbal dialogue with their parents, and this forms a base for language acquisition and later social expertise. This phenomenon, called turn taking, performs two main functions critical to language instruction. It allows the infant to attend to and reproduce parental speech, and it allows the parent to monitor the quality of the utterance and provide feedback.

Assuming that an infant learns to take turns and specifically attend to verbal input, further speech and language development hinges on the ability to process auditory information. This is by no means a simple process, and difficulty can occur in any one of several areas, all of which are critically important to the development of language and reading skills. In short, speech perception, i.e. the ability to discriminate, sequence, and store speech sounds, provides the mechanisms by which the brain processes linguistic data. For a more detailed discussion of the ability to process auditory information, please see Chapter 3 on phonemic awareness.

Speech production in the infant. With their first cries, infants announce their arrival into the world. Their initial sounds—cries, burps, sneezes, and coughs—are reflexive or what is often called **vegetative.** The term, vegetative, refers to what has traditionally been recognized as the passive condition of the child. As time passes, infant crying becomes less frequent and more specialized. Mothers learn to recognize distinct cries of hunger, pain, and anger.

By the age of about two months, infants begin to coo vowel-like sounds in response to pleasurable attention. Locke refers to this period as the "Goo Stage." By the end of the first five months of life, these vowel-like utterances are enriched with consonant-like sounds, as well as squeals, growls, and bilabial trills, more commonly known as "raspberries." According to Stark (1979), this versatile vocal repertoire is called **marginal babbling.** It is a transitional behavior that precedes the development of true babbling.

At about the age of six months, the infant begins to **babble.** Cries and gurgles are gradually augmented with a large repertoire of repeated consonant-vowel syllables, beginning most commonly with the sounds that are produced in the front of the mouth (/b/, /p/, /t/, /d/, /m/, and /n/). Locke (1983) notes that no matter what the native language, all children babble the same set of sounds and they all share a passion for auditory stimulation. Locke suggests that these babbled sounds are determined by phonetic, i.e. anatomical, physiological, and aerodynamic, factors. In support of this argument, he notes that the set of sounds produced during the babbling stage does not differ among those with retardation, neonatal brain damage, or congenital deafness. Locke (1993) notes, however, that the onset of babbling is delayed in those with severe hearing impairments.

Gradually, between nine and eighteen months of age, this repertoire expands and children's articulations become more dependent upon linguistic input. It is at this point that deaf children's vocal output begins to stall, while hearing children initiate an activity referred to as **non-reduplicated babbling** (Stark, 1980). Children who engage in non-reduplicated babbling often give the impression, through intonational patterns, stress, rhythm, and phrasing, that they are expressing themselves with adult language. All of the cues are present that we, as adults, interpret to signify communicative intent. Contrary to expectation, however, there are no meaningful words.

In addition to non-reduplicated babbling, children at this age engage in a parrot-like imitation of sounds called **echolalia** in which they imitate speech without understanding. Non-reduplicated babbling and echolalia are signs that infants from an early age are apt observers who are able to witness, remember, and apply knowledge with artistry. They are also indications that children are exploring, enjoying, and fine tuning functions of motor control and sensory feedback while, on a neurological level, the left hemisphere of the brain is being primed to process speech data.

In order for children to advance from babbling to speech, they must develop an understanding of the function of language. This realization generally occurs at about one year of age, but from nine to ten months of age, children begin to use **phonetically consistent forms.** Phonetically consistent forms occur when children use identical patterns of sound in order to reference a particular object or situation. Von Raffler-Engler (1973) described her son's use of /i/ to signify objects he wanted and /u/ for his sign of disapproval. Although we cannot call these utterances language, the use of a phonetically consistent form is a critical step toward using language to accomplish specific goals.

THE ONE-WORD (HOLOPHRASTIC) STAGE
Sometime around the first birthday, child and parent enter a new mode of communication that is based upon language. Language at the one-word stage is used to call attention to objects that capture the interest of the child through motion, noise, and their potential for manual play. To those other than family members, these words may be completely unintelligible. To parents, these words are a source of great pride.

The one-word stage of language development is distinguished by the child's use of recognizable words to refer to familiar people, animals, and objects in the home, as well as simple actions or states (Bloom, 1973). Attempts to classify this vocabulary according to adult standards of grammatical function have determined that words at this stage consist mostly of nouns and verbs. Function words, such as auxiliary verbs, articles, and prepositions, are used rarely (Nelson, 1973).

Classifications of first words. When children speak, we often forget that their first words are not products of adult minds. From a child's perspective, a "doggie" might be any furry animal that walks on four legs. This might include a cow, a camel, or the tomcat next door. On the other hand, the word "doggie" could be restricted to none other than the family pet. Although our considerable linguistic knowledge allows us to draw many conclusions about language, adult grammar is not child grammar. Attempts to classify children's first words into nouns, verbs, and other formal categories of grammar may reveal less about the child's use of language than about our own desire to impose *our* structure in order to see the world in our own reflection. In studying the child's acquisition of language, we must, therefore, exercise caution not to let our adult perspectives detract from appreciating the structure of the child's mind.

What then can be said about children's language at the one-word stage? Children's first recognizable attempts at language are said to be **holophrastic**. This means that children use one word to express a thought or a concern that, at a later stage, will be expressed in a phrase or complete sentence. A child who says the word, "ball," may actually be saying, "Give me the ball," or "Look at the ball," or "That is a pretty ball." We have no way of knowing what nonverbal and perhaps verbal thoughts may be serving as the motivation for the utterance.

There has been much speculation as to how children learn the meanings of words as they are generally understood by adults. Vygotsky (1934/1986) proposed that children develop meaning through the internalization of experience. With each new opportunity, word meanings acquire greater depth to reflect a more mature view of the world. This process may be illustrated as children, with their primitive grasp of meaning, typically **overextend** and **underextend** their words. Overextension occurs when children apply a single word to anything with a similar form or characteristic. "Wawa" might be used to signify water, juice, milk, or a lake. On the other hand, underextension occurs when children restrict the more general meaning of a word to a specific narrow reference. In this case, "doggie" may be used only with respect to the family pet or, the word "mama" jealously guarded for use with one's own.

Vygotsky's groundbreaking work on the relationship of thought, language, and experience was expanded upon by Clark in his research concerning children's acquisition of semantics. According to his **semantic feature hypothesis** (1973), words do not represent an object or action in its entirety but rather a cluster of many bits of information called **semantic features**. Although different words may have features in common, each word, in theory, represents a unique semantic set. When children learn the meaning of a new word, they focus on one or two of the object's physical semantic features, such as shape, size, movement, texture, or taste, to serve as the basis for understanding. A child, for example, may initially perceive a grandparent to be someone old and wrinkled. Only later, after the child has acquired a broader sampling of semantic features, does a child understand a grandparent by virtue of the blood relation. It is through experience that children broaden their perspective to encompass more of the pertinent semantic features and come to use words as understood by adults.

Pragmatics in the one-word stage. In order to present a complete picture of the one-word stage of language development, we must consider not only the grammatical and semantic aspects of language, but also the **pragmatics.** Pragmatics is the analysis of language in terms of situational context. It takes into consideration the communicative intent of the speaker, as well as the relationship between speaker and listener.

When children learn language, their ability to interact with others acquires new depth and potential. It becomes possible for children to overtly articulate their wishes, needs, and intentions. If only, however, communication were as simple as that! Language always occurs in a context. We, as listeners and speakers, have a prior history of conversations and events that create within us a base of knowledge, expectations, and prejudices. Effective communication depends not only on our ability to generate well formed sentences, but also on our ability to read the many extralinguistic cues, such as facial expression, gesture, and emotion, **and** compare new information to an already established data base of what we believe to be true.

When Halliday (1975) researched the development of pragmatics in his son, Nigel, he found that Nigel's communicative repertoire increased with the advent of the one-word stage. In the stage prior to language, Nigel was able to perform four functions of communicative intent including: satisfying needs and wants, controlling the behavior of others, interacting with others, and expressing feelings or attitude. With language, Nigel was also able to investigate and explore his environment, imagine and pretend, and inform others of his thoughts and experiences.

Other researchers (Greenfield & Smith, 1976) note that children at this stage not only begin to adjust their messages according to their assumptions about the listener's prior knowledge, but that they are also grappling with the rudiments of conversational turn taking (Bloom, Rocissano, & Hood, 1976). From birth, the child has been alternately prompting, reacting, and reassessing his caretakers through nonverbal means. It is the challenge of the one year old to integrate language into this communicative effort and initiate the long road to social ease and proficiency. Children may have the ability to express thoughts, but they may not understand how to use that ability to convey their desires efficiently and with consideration. These are skills that continue to develop well into adulthood.

THE TWO-WORD TELEGRAPHIC STAGE
Language during the two-word stage, which often begins between the ages of eighteen and twenty-four months, is often referred to as "**telegraphic.**" During this stage, children typically put two words together in a style reminiscent of the compact language of the old Western Union telegrams. Utterances such as *cookie gone, no go,* and *mommy up,* are all indicative of two-word stage expression. There are no function words such as prepositions, auxiliary verbs, and conjunctions, and there are no morphological markers for person, number, or tense. Pronouns are forgone for the more specific *mommy* and *truck,* and negation is expressed by negative words, such as *no* or *not,* placed at the beginning of the utterance. Telegraphic speech is an important milestone in the development of language, for it signals the child's preliminary grasp of sentence structure or **syntax**.

Grammar in the two-word stage. Although the logic sometimes escapes adults, children appear to use basic rules of syntax when putting two or more words together. There has been much discussion about the nature of these rules. There is some acceptance of Roger Brown's (1973) proposed grammar based on **semantic-relations**. By examining the two-word utterances produced by English, Swedish, Finnish, Samoan, and Spanish children, Brown found that children's utterances could be classified according to their semantic relations as demonstrated in the following examples:

Mommy eat	agent + action
Hit kitty	action + object
My cookie	possessor + object
Dirty car	attribute + object
Daddy car	agent + location

Brown suggests that this analysis is in accord with children's early cognitive development and their acute interest in objects and actions. Even though this may be the case, it is important to remember that the analysis is based upon adult logic. What children at this age actually understand about parts of speech and their different functions has not yet been ascertained.

Pragmatics in the two-word stage. From the perspective of pragmatics, the above examples show that children in the two-word stage are able to perform a variety of communicative acts. They can describe objects and actions, identify locations, and indicate who is performing a given act on what. According to Halliday (1975), these acts now form the basis for three new communicative functions.

The **pragmatic** function, often called the "language of request," allows children to interact with and act upon their environment. In this case, language becomes the vehicle for fulfilling needs and regulating the behavior of others. The **mathetic** function is related to learning or discovery. Children use language to satisfy their curiosity about the world. To this end, they comment, remember, question, and predict. Finally, the **informative** function, which is the last function to emerge, occurs when children use language to provide information. These pragmatic skills, together with an understanding of the basic rules of conversation such as turn-taking, allow children to enter and enjoy the world of the verbal arts.

Comprehension in the two-word stage. The final consideration of the skills that make up the communicative process is comprehension. I have written to some degree about children's early understanding of meaning—their tendency to overextend or underextend by viewing the world through a lens focused on one or two distinct physical features—and the difficulty adults have in perceiving what children actually understand. Their comprehension depends not only on linguistic data, but also on a multitude of nonverbal and contextual clues that accompany verbal information. Children's comprehension is significantly greater than their ability to produce language, yet they often appear to understand much more than, in reality, they do. This perception is often enhanced by children's ability to learn new vocabulary (James, 1990). How often do children learn adult expletives after being exposed to only one unfortunate slip of the tongue!

PRESCHOOL YEARS TO FLUENCY

Generally after the second birthday, children's verbal activity assumes a new intensity that makes some parents wonder why they ever waited so anxiously for that very first word. Children's language explodes into a rich variety of grammatical and conceptual relations. Morphemes, pronouns, auxiliary verbs, function words, and even phrases appear. Children learn how to negate sentences (an apparent favorite), bombard caretakers with questions, and demand action. Sentences become more adult-like and, by the fifth year of life, children converse freely and skillfully. Although it is certainly possible to write extensively about the many milestones of linguistic achievement that occur during the preschool years, the discussion below is limited to some of the more pertinent highlights. (For more detail, see James, 1990).

Grammar in the preschooler. The period from twenty-seven to thirty months is generally distinguished by a process that Brown (1973) refers to as the **"modulation of meaning."** Meaning is modulated, or clarified, when morphemes are introduced into simple sentences in order to make the meaning more precise. For example, when the morpheme *-ed* is added to a verb, the speaker is able to reference and express thoughts or incidents that occurred in the past. When the morpheme *-s* is added to a noun, the speaker indicates a quantity of more than one. Similarly, prepositions such as *in* or *on* leave no doubt that ice cream was left *in* the freezer and not *on* it.

As children begin to utilize grammatical morphemes in their speech, they often **overextend** or **overgeneralize** their use without consideration for the many nuances of the English language. We often hear sentences such as, "I eated the cake," or, "There were many mooses." In adult language, these errors are interpreted to be signs of poor grammar, but with young children, these errors are evidence of progress in mastering the many rules of language and their application with some regularity.

During the preschool years, children learn how to substitute pronouns for nouns. Pronoun use is by no means a simple task; its complexities often plague individuals well into adulthood. Note, for example, the incorrect sentence, "They saw him and I," in which the subjective *I* is commonly substituted for the objective *me*. This incorrect usage occurs so often that many assume it to be correct by virtue of having heard it said by friends and personalities in the media.

For adults and children, correct pronoun use requires the ability to make judgments about gender and number, and determine whether they are subjects, objects, or modifiers. Three year olds typically have difficulty with these assessments, as in the example, "His name is Mommy." By the time that children are ready to enter school, however, with the exception of the above inaccurate *him and I,* pronoun use is regular and, for the most part, correct.

Between the ages of two and five, we see the advent of structured language. In order to generate more complex utterances, children must be able to form sophisticated grammatical constructions. The development of these grammatical constructions can be understood best by examining how children acquire the ability to negate and form questions. Negations first appear in one-word utterances such as *allgone* or *no*.

In 1966, Klima and Bellugi determined that negation in multiword utterances develops in three phases. In the first phase, *no* is put at the beginning of the utterance as in the examples, "No sleep," or, "No go bed." In the second stage, *no* is moved to the internal position preceding the verb, "Lucas no take bath." It is at this point that the negative forms *can't* and *don't* appear. These forms are somewhat misleading to adults for the child has no sense that these forms are indeed contractions. They are, in fact, **negative preverbs** that are used interchangeably with *no* and *not*. It is interesting to note that auxiliary verbs, such as *can, do, does,* or *did,* do not appear until later. Finally, according to Klima and Bellugi, it is only in the final stage that the negative particle assumes its proper form as in the sentence, "Daddy is not happy."

A similar process is found in the development of questions. Normally adults form yes-no questions by moving the auxiliary verb to the front of the sentence as in the example, "Was he happy?" In the event, however, that the sentence has no auxiliary verb, then the appropriate form of *do* must be supplied, "Does the kitty bite?" Two-year-old children have not yet acquired auxiliary verbs, and they are not privy to the axioms of movement necessitated by the formation of interrogatives according to adult standards. Yes-no questions, therefore, are marked by rising intonation at the end of the utterance.

In addition to yes-no questions, children's early use of the interrogative forms includes the question words, *what* and *where,* reflecting, perhaps, their acute interest in naming and location. Gradually, by thirty-one to thirty-four months, children learn to create questions by adding the auxiliary verbs and inverting word order according to the adult rules of syntax and grammar. Additional interrogatives, *why, who,* and *how* also appear.

Pragmatics in the preschooler. By the time children have reached the age of two and a half, they are capable of sustaining a topic of conversation for one or two turns, and they are actively working on strategies in order to prolong and improve the effectiveness of their interactions with others. One of the most significant signs of this effort is that children talk much, much more—requesting, describing, repeating, and responding.   Although this speech is sometimes incomprehensible, the originality is often startling.

Children during this stage are beginning to master some of the more subtle features of conversation.   They are able to participate in two- and three-party conversations with fewer and fewer interruptions.   Often younger children misinterpret syntactic junctures or pauses as an indication that they may take the floor (Ervin-Tripp, 1979). As their social awareness becomes more finely tuned, they are not only able to perceive the difference between a syntactic juncture and a pause signaling the end of the speaker's turn, but they are better able to maintain the conversational rhythm by shortening their response time to match that of adults. Having mastered the mechanics of conversational timing, the child can then focus more on the quality of the communication itself.

Sometime between the ages of one and two, children recognize that their language is not always understood, and that they now have sufficient vocabulary and pronunciation skills to fix breakdowns in communication (Gallager, 1977). **Conversational repair** is the art of responding to a listener's requests for clarification by revising, and attempting to clarify, the original utterance.   Initially these attempts at repair may actually cause more confusion than the original misunderstanding.   As children's active vocabulary increases, however, they have more tools with which to accomplish the job, and they become more adept at adjusting their speech to suit the needs of the listener.

Responding to the listener's need for clarification is the first indication that a child is grasping the concept of style and its importance in communication. Eventually, a child comes to understand the importance of the word, "please," and the etiquette of the indirect request.   In middle-class, American culture, it is considered more correct to phrase requests with delicacy and a certain degree of uncertainty in order to convey the proper respect and avoid the appearance of assertion and threat.

The subtleties of etiquette require syntactic forms known as **semantic softeners** (Becker, 1984). These indirect forms include hints, pauses reflecting apparent or feigned uncertainty, and modal forms of verbs such as *could, would,* or *might.* Four-year-old children who have mastered these forms will still say, "Gimme that toy," but more and more frequently they can be heard to exhibit the proper social deference when requesting assistance from those who are older, larger, or in positions of authority.

THE SCHOOL-AGED CHILD

By the time that children enter school, they can use language effectively to express their wants, needs, and desires, discuss events in the past, present, or future, carry on conversations for several turns, and consider the impact of their speech on the listener. This does not mean, however, that their acquisition of language has come to an end. School-aged children are continually refining their use of syntax, semantics, and pragmatics to incorporate more complex forms of expression and comprehension.

The passive voice and the school-aged child. The development of the passive voice in children is perhaps one of the more difficult challenges of language acquisition. Young children seem to have an understanding of passive sentences long before they can produce them. This may be related to contextual cues rather than to understanding the construction itself. By the age of five, most children are able to understand some forms of passives that are constructed with action verbs, such as, "Nolan was punched by Lucas." Passives with nonaction verbs, "Nolan was loved by Lucas," prove to be more of a challenge. In either case, those passives actually produced by five-year-olds tend to be of the shortened form, "Nolan was punched."[1]

Unfortunately for preschoolers, the action-nonaction issue is not the only complexity that stands in the way of early progress with passive constructions. There is also the question of reversible and nonreversible passive sentences. A passive sentence is considered to be reversible if either of the two nouns can function as the agent. If the sentence, "The dog was chased by the cat," is reversed, the sentence will still make sense.

---

[1]Having mastered many of the regular features and rules of language, school-aged children are free to focus on the more subtle aspects of syntax that allow them to understand and produce increasingly complex sentences. Carol Chomsky (1969), investigated the **principle of minimal distance (PMD)** which states that, as a rule, the noun that most directly precedes the verb will be the subject of the sentence. This rule allows us to interpret sentences that might otherwise be unclear. Consider the example, "Mommy told Nolan to clean his room." According to the PMD, the noun (Nolan) immediately preceding the infinitive verb (to clean) acts as the subject of the infinitive, and there should be no doubt in anyone's mind that it is Nolan who is to clean his room. There are, however, exceptions to this rule. In the example, "Mommy promised Nolan to clean his room," the PMD does not apply. It is the mother who has assumed that responsibility. Verbs such as *ask, tell,* and *promise* comprise a small group of verbs that violate the PMD, and are learned as exceptions only when the more generally applicable rules are in place.

In the example, "The tomato was eaten by the boy," the reversal would not hold true unless, of course, we were retelling bad science fiction from the 1960s. Horgan (1978) found that reversibility plays an important role in children's ability to comprehend and produce passive constructions. Children under the age of four produce more reversible than nonreversible passive sentences. Due to the difficulty in ascertaining meaning in passive constructions, the production of full passive sentences does not occur for many children until they reach the age of adolescence.

Pragmatics and the school-aged child. Children of school age make considerable progress in their ability to maintain a conversation for several turns and repair conversational breakdowns. Preschoolers often attempt to clarify confusing messages through repetition and revision of the original utterance. This facility, however, is generally limited to one or two attempts. Once they are of school age, children are able to focus their attention and respond to a sequence of at least three requests for clarification by providing additional information (Brinton, Fujiki, Loeb, & Winkler, 1986). As this skill becomes more keen, school-aged children are able to actively assess and determine the original point of misunderstanding and address that point directly.

During this period, school-aged children also expand their facility to prompt responses through artfully crafted hints. By the age of eight, requests are carefully phrased in order to acknowledge the possible inconvenience to the listener and, thereby, curry the necessary favor (Ervin-Tripp & Gordon, 1986). At this time, children not only resort to careful phrasing, but also attempt to manipulate adults through subtle hints. The statement, "My tummy is hungry," is an example of a not-so-veiled request for food that is intended to make the listener think that she thought of the snack idea all by herself.

Between the ages of five and eight, the focus on communicative style is enriched by a growing appreciation for the medium itself. The term, **metalinguistic ability**, applies to the conscious awareness of the phonological, semantic, syntactic, and pragmatic aspects of language. It is this awareness that allows us to determine a well-formed sentence, enjoy a good riddle, and appreciate literature as art.

SUMMARY

Children come into the world actively seeking stimulation and the adoring gaze of their mothers' eyes. They are alert and perceptive, and socially aware. By focusing their attention on nonverbal cues, they learn much about the mechanics that govern conversational interactions. During the first year of life, children, driven by a love for auditory stimulation and assisted by their mothers, labor to coordinate the many specific mechanisms of motor control and sensory feedback. Bit by bit, they learn to babble. Their speech gradually acquires all the trappings of language—the rhythm and phrasing, the intonation and emotion, and finally, the pronunciation itself. By the time of their first birthdays, they will have achieved a cognitive milestone that is unique to the human species. Children understand that specific sequences of sounds can be used to designate meaning. From then on, language is not simply a means for amusement, it becomes a means for communication.

Children's first attempts at language are limited to single words that reflect their interest in the immediate environment. By the age of eighteen months, they will succeed in putting two words together. Almost overnight, this primitive telegraphic speech explodes with a rapidly expanding vocabulary, grammar, and syntax. As children acquire linguistic knowledge, they focus on how to make their communicative efforts more effective by modifying their styles of expression to suit the needs of their listeners.

The dawning awareness of the capacity of language to satisfy specific wants and desires accompanies yet another cognitive milestone in the life of human beings. At some time between the ages of five and eight, children become able to focus not only on the message, but on the medium itself. The many nuances of pronunciation and expression that children work so single-mindedly to learn and use in speaking fluently are now called upon to embellish and enrich the communicative process.

Strategies for Promoting Language Development

How do parents and preschool educators teach language or at least promote its development? Chomsky's followers would argue that language cannot be taught at all. Recent research by cognitive and language theorists, however, suggests quite the opposite (see pages 92-95 this chapter). The work of these cognitive and language theorists, as well as studies conducted by researchers and educators, is reflected in the strategies offered below.

STRATEGIES FOR ALL CHILDREN
Inclusive conversations. Regardless of age, children must be provided with opportunities for conversational interactions that promote their active participation. Children must be made to feel that their presence is welcome and that their words are worthy of attention. Parents need to follow their child's lead and expand their conversational repertoire to comment with enthusiasm on everything from spilled milk to the pile of wash waiting to be done. Any person, place, or thing that captures

children's eyes is fair subject for conversation. The subject matter is less important than warm, fuzzy conversational exchanges.

Eye contact. Parents and caretakers should be careful to maintain positive eye contact, and show with their body language that they are attending to every word. It may help to get down on the floor when speaking with young children. By entering their immediate field of vision in a non-threatening manner, we may reduce distraction and allow children to focus, not only on our words, but on nonverbal facial cues.

Extension. In general, whether children are at the babbling stage or engaged in refining language usage, linguistic development can best be promoted through activities that expand upon children's present level of linguistic achievement (see **zone of proximal development** in Part II of this chapter, pages 70-71). Adults can scaffold children's speech by using repetition, modeling, and prompts to extend the content and the complexity of utterances. Children who are at the one- and two-word stages, for example, are encouraged to develop more expressive and grammatically correct language, *if* parents expand upon their children's original utterances and model the use of descriptive adjectives and adverbs. Five-year-olds, who have mastered the basics of declarative sentences, may be encouraged to tackle basic etiquette and modal forms of verbs as illustrated below:

Child: Mommy, I want pickles.
Parent: (eating toast) What *would* you like?
Child: Pickles.
Parent: You *would like* some pickles?
Child: Yes.
Parent: Say, "I would like some pickles, please."
Child: I would like some pickles, please.
Parent: (Offers the child pickles) I would like some pickles, too. Please.

Requests for clarification. Let children know when they are not understood. It allows them to confirm their ability to read doubt or confusion signaled by nonverbal aspects of communication, and it offers them an opportunity for conversational repair. Selectively and gently offer responses such as, "I do not understand what you are saying," or, "Try again." When accompanied by appropriate scaffolding, such a request shows children that we care about their concerns. The results will be clearer pronunciation, larger vocabularies, improved syntax, and perhaps higher self-esteem.

Acknowledge meaning. Children, like adults, enjoy feeling successful. Children who are constantly rebuked for errors in pronunciation and grammar are reluctant to take risks to express themselves, thereby inhibiting language development. Correcting mistakes in language can be done without implying weakness or fault. For example, in response to the utterance, "I goed to the store," the corrected verb can be modeled with an intonation that acknowledges the meaning of the utterance and not the improper form. With the acknowledgment, "You went to the store!" the child feels interest and enthusiasm, while hearing the correct usage.

Storytime. Read to children at every opportunity—in bed, in the bath tub, while waiting for the doctor—in order to expose them to new vocabulary, syntactic forms, and sequences of events. Storytime can be fun as parents read slowly and with exaggerated expression. I find that storytime not only provides children with oodles of good language, but that it can also serve as a graceful transition between the activities of the day and the quiet of the night. Children delight in hearing the same stories again and again, as it provides them with practice in receptive language, as well as the comfort that comes from knowing what is going to happen. Retelling and discussing the plot of a story offer wonderful opportunities to activate new vocabulary not typically used in the household.

Create communication opportunities. Speech and communication practice are stimulated by creating opportunities for children to choose, refuse, accept, request, and engage in repetitive turn-taking sequences and routines (Siegel-Causey & Wetherby, 1993). During daily activities, take time to ask children which of two options is preferred such as which shirt to wear or what toy to select. In addition, offer activities or objects that can be refused or accepted without creating a difficulty. Encourage children to request by placing cues for a tempting activity or object within sight but out of reach. Follow repetitive sequences when eating meals, playing games, cleaning, or dressing, and accompany these sequences with repetitive sequences of words. For example, "Pass the butter," at dinner is a common sequence along with "Good-bye; have a nice time," at parting.

Evaluate interactions. Videotaping conversations with young children provides a means not only to capture precious moments on tape, but also to assess the effectiveness of adult-child interactions. The lens of the camera allows parents and educators to observe both verbal and nonverbal communication with uncompromised clarity. Questions that should be asked include: Is the adult providing opportunities to extend the child's use of language? Are there opportunities to choose, refuse, accept, request, and engage in repetitive turn-taking sequences and routines? Is the adult providing the child with models, prompts, and opportunities for practice? Is the child being corrected in a gentle, caring manner? Finally, what nonverbal signals are being sent? Many young children are skilled interpreters of nonverbal communication. If words say "yes," and the body says "no," children are faced with understandable confusion and a problem of trust.

STRATEGIES FOR INFANTS

Respond and acknowledge. Higher expectations improve performance. Adults can assume that infants are ready, from the day of their birth, to actively socialize and learn about the world. We can be sensitive to children's moods and to their ability to make eye contact. Talk to them using exaggerated facial expressions, enunciation, and intonation, offer direct and tender eye contact, and employ a simplified vocabulary and syntax. Let infants know, through the use of questions, commands, and appropriate pauses, that their comments are anxiously awaited. Acknowledge any and all sounds, such as coos, babbles, smiles, and whimpers, as valuable contributions to the conversation.

Word play. Exploit infants' natural love of speech-sounds by repeating syllables in a rhythmic fashion ("Tum dee, tum dee," has always been a personal favorite). Help them enjoy rhythm through the kinesthetics of clapping and bouncing games. Word play and nursery rhymes promote phonological awareness and provide opportunities for practice in listening and comprehension. For a more detailed discussion, see Chapter 3.

Consistent responses to repeated sounds. Listen carefully for early utterances and intonational patterns that are used consistently. The utterance, "bah," may be an early attempt at the request, "Bottle, please." Success is a great motivator. Help infants make that leap into the world of verbal communication by responding to certain sounds or gestures with consistent efforts to meet their apparent need, whether for food, hugs, or comforting words.

Singing. Infants' love of music can help them learn simple words and phrases. Songs modified to have just one word, such as "The Mommy Song," "The Car Song," and "The Kitty Song," allow children under the age of two to participate in music and enjoy the pleasure that it brings, as well as to increase their vocabulary with intensive practice.

Ritual actions and phrases. Model rituals of etiquette, such as greetings, good-byes, and introductions in which speakers commonly engage. Include infants in these rituals to make them feel as though they are part of the social fabric of home and community.

STRATEGIES FOR PRESCHOOLERS

Answer questions. Language proficiency requires practice. It is a credit to our design that we learn language as preschoolers, for there is no other stage of life in which we would have the physical stamina to pursue language in the manner required by mother nature. Preschoolers require a tremendous amount of attention as they delight in their new communicative ability and explore the world verbally. This period can be very trying for parents who are bombarded unceasingly with questions and observations. However, it takes no more energy on the part of the parent to answer their questions and then redirect their interest to less demanding pursuits than it does to tell children to be quiet.

Shared stories. Make story telling an interactive experience. The activity, "Story Soup," allows everyone to add something to the pot and contribute to the fun. Children are asked to pick various story elements, such as character, setting, and conflict. Parents and caretakers are charged with calling upon all their imaginative talents in order to weave these elements into a fairly believable plot. Although suggestions may stretch creative limits, adults enjoy challenges, and children love to hear their ideas incorporated into a tale that may become a family favorite.

Personalize stories. Make up and tell stories in which children play the roles of the heroes and protagonists, and use their creativity to resolve problems. In addition to developing familiarity with plot structure and the roles that characters play, these stories enable children to visualize themselves as heroes who have much to offer the world. Storytime can offer a forum for working out family dilemmas, such as children who will not pick up toys, or who are afraid of the dark.

STRATEGIES FOR SCHOOL-AGED CHILDREN

Preschoolers and children of school age with speech and language difficulties may require direct instruction and opportunities for practice beyond what typical conversations normally offer. Some educators, in an attempt to recreate a normal conversational environment, inadvertently lessen the amount of practice that children actually receive. Classroom language instruction should be designed to maximize speech as much as possible per instructional period without sacrificing either the pragmatic aspects of language or entertainment value of such lessons.

Children with speech and language disabilities may benefit from techniques commonly used in foreign language instruction. These involve songs, memorized dialogues, dictation, choral responses, and repetitive practice of clearly routinized activities such as greeting, shopping, or eating in a restaurant.

Word play.   Jokes and riddles are an ideal opportunity to promote metalinguistic awareness in five- and six-year-old children. Many five-year-olds reach the stage of language awareness in which they want to understand the humor behind the joke and not just laugh along with the crowd. To many in the five-year-old crowd, the humor in the following joke is not readily apparent unless they understand that the word "ball" can have two meanings:

Question: Why would Cinderella not make a good football player?
Response: Because she ran away from the ball.

By directly teaching that words can have more than one meaning, and by explaining what in particular makes a joke funny, we help children come to appreciate a whole new world of play with language.

Awareness of style. According to Rath (1987), older siblings often become interested in the speech of their younger brothers and sisters. They may engage in their own form of child-directed speech by experimenting with their words. While it is not necessary, or fruitful, to treat older children to an in-depth analysis of their siblings' language, it is an opportunity to convey the idea that people speak in different styles. This basic understanding of style is the first step to appreciating artistic forms of language.

Role play. As five- and six-year-olds expand their contact with the world, they may come home with inappropriate forms of language. At these times, parents and educators need to remember that such vocabulary, however distressing, is evidence of children's remarkable ability to acquire language and perceive meaning. There is, after all, no doubt that five- and six-year-old children understand the emotional impact of such words.

The pragmatics of language require much time, effort, and direct explanation. Five- and six-year-olds, as they continually refine their language efforts, are ready to work on their social skills and focus on the niceties of social interaction. Role playing to model the etiquette of language usage capitalizes on children's love of theater, and allows them to practice their newly acquired social expertise.

LANGUAGE FACILITATION IN THE CLASSROOM

Language usage in the classroom is much more formal than the language used at home. It requires that students be able understand the individual communication style of the teacher, to recall and sequence ideas in a logical fashion, and express themselves succinctly. Without these particular skills, success in class activities or on the playground is unlikely. In addition, facility with language provides a rich background that enhances the process of learning to read.

A thorough assessment of children experiencing speech and/or language difficulties in school should include an assessment of the teacher's language usage in the classroom. Tape-recorded or videotaped sessions allow teachers and specialists to examine the whole communicative process between speaker and listener. Hallahan and Kauffman suggest that "learning how to be clear, relevant, and informative, and how to hold listeners' attention are not only problems for students with language disorders, but also problems for their teachers" (1993, p. 273). They point out that the teacher's role is not merely to instruct about language, but also to model its use. If their students are to succeed, teachers need to express themselves clearly, provide proper feedback to students, and ask questions that are within the linguistic and cognitive abilities of children.

PART I CONCLUSION

Familiarity with the stages of language acquisition allow parents and educators to keep a watchful eye on children's progress and promote its advancement. Critical components of effective language teaching in the home or in school encourage children to take risks and reach for their potential. This is accomplished through the modeling and scaffolding of language usage in social and academic environments, and by providing opportunities for practice and feedback coupled with high expectations, affection, and respect. Such activities further language development and foster language facility, and, in turn enhance learners' progress as they make the transition to learning to read.

PART TWO

Humans have always been intrigued by words and language. Apart from their obvious utility, words have been accorded the power to move boulders from cave entrances, reveal secrets of the soul, explain the meaning of life, and turn princes into frogs. Considering their many, many applications, it is no wonder that the nature of language has been fiercely contested by an endless list of poets, theologians, philosophers, philologists, psychologists, biologists, neurologists and, yes, even grammarians.

At one time or another, various disciplines have staked their claims to the progenitorship of language, resulting in a spectrum of theories that is often referred to collectively as the nature versus nurture debate. Theorists who engage in this debate present a variety of arguments ranging from pure nature—we are born biologically wired with language through our genetic nature—to pure nurture—language is learned through a painstaking process of stimulus and response nurtured by environment.

Since language, reading, and cognition are so deeply intertwined, a thorough examination of reading instruction begs for at least a brief review of several prominent theories concerning the nature of cognition and language. This part of the chapter sketches these theories and notes their influence on instructional methods during the past two centuries. Readers who prefer to focus on the more practical aspects of instruction are urged to skip this discussion and proceed to Chapter 3.

This discussion begins with a brief overview of philosophers—Déscartes, Locke, and Rousseau—whose early efforts created a philosophical climate that made the study of cognition and language possible. Next, the relationship of cognition and language is examined through the antithetical views of Vygotsky and Piaget, psychologists who provide the theoretical bases for the diverse instructional methods used in the East and the West. Then, their contributions to current thinking concerning the role of biology and the environment are explored further through a review of late 20th century research in cognitive psychology from Fisher, Case, and Gardner (see Table 2.2, following page).

We then step back four decades into the volatile history of the nature-nurture controversy to consider, in a more detailed discussion, the figures who galvanized the fields of linguistics and cognition in the mid twentieth century. The work of Skinner, the leading proponent of the nurture or behaviorist school of cognitive development, is presented in contrast to Chomsky and Lennenberg, whose research made language an area of focus in its own right.

Finally, we return to the 1990s, where linguists join the cognitive psychologists in letting nature and nurture enjoin as linguistic theory expands to encompass new understandings in the areas of infant cognition and neuropsychology. Here the research of Catherine Snow and John Locke, 20th century social interactionists, suggests how nature and nurture work together to enable humans to communicate their needs, wants, and desires in order to survive.

The Philosophy of Language

RENÉ DÉSCARTES (1596-1650)

How does language develop? Until the time of the Renaissance, European philosophers related the question back to God for they considered language as mysterious and divine as the creator that it reflected. Then, in the mid-seventeenth century, René Déscartes proposed that the soul was independent from the body and that the mind was independent from the brain. By dividing humans into two realms, the corporal and the spiritual, Déscartes ended the prohibition on the study of the human body, and the field of biology was established.

During the course of the debate as to what features of humans were to be assigned to the corporal realm, considerable testimony was heard about the biological properties of language. Déscartes recognized that language was an attribute specifically linked to the human species, and should, therefore, be studied as a corporal phenomenon. His fellow philosophers, however, did not agree. It was decided that language should remain in the hands of God; and it was not until the mid-twentieth century that the study of language came into its own.

Table 2.2. Nature vs. Nurture: Imprecise Framing by Theory and Era.

Nature (Genetics)	Interaction (Genetics & Environment)	Nurture (Environment)
	Philosophers	
	Déscartes (mid-17th century)	
		Locke (late 17th century)
Rousseau (mid-18th century)		
	Psychologists	
Piaget (20th century)		Vygotsky (20th century)
Chomsky (1957 onward)		Skinner (mid-20th century)
	Cognitive Psychologists (late 20th century) Fischer Case Gardner	
	Cognitive Linguists (late 20th century) Locke Snow	

Even though Déscartes' efforts to promote the study of language as a biological phenomenon failed, his recognition of the broader issue, the mind/body dichotomy, laid the philosophical foundations for modern psychology, linguistics, and neuropsychology. During the seventeenth and the eighteenth centuries, the study of philosophy divided into two schools of thought that are recognized today as the forbearers of the nature versus nurture controversy.

JOHN LOCKE (1632-1704)

In 1690, English philosopher John Locke (1632-1704) proposed that children were not miniature adults with innate capabilities and preformed characters, but that they were essentially empty organisms (Crain, 1992). In his description of young children, Locke coined the term "*tabula rasa*" (blank slate) as he explained that all knowledge was the result of sensory experience. Although Locke personally ascribed the origin of language to divine intervention, his **environmental views** on learning laid the foundation for the school of **empiricism** and for those who believe that language is a product of **nurture**.

JEAN JACQUES ROUSSEAU (1712-1778)

In contrast, Jean Jacques Rousseau is considered father to the **innatists**. Although he agreed with Locke that children differ significantly from adults (Crain, 1992), Rousseau argued that children are not blank slates but that they possess innate qualities that would develop and flower into healthy individuals if left to **nature**. According to Rousseau, children grow into adulthood according to an inner biological timetable that unfolds in a predetermined sequence of unique characteristics. Rousseau's metaphor for this biological process was "nature," and it has become the rallying cry for present day **innatists** in their quest to prove the **genetic** regulation of language.

In the following discussion of language acquisition, theories of cognitive and language development have been selected that present an overview of the different positions in the nature versus nurture controversy. As students of language acquisition, we should not feel the need to pledge our allegiance to a particular position at the expense of the insight of another. The authorities represented here have all made significant contributions to our understanding of language acquisition, and they each, in their considerable wisdom, have succeeded in clarifying important aspects of a complex and often astonishing process.

Human Development and Language:
Vygotsky and Piaget

LEV SEMYONIVICH VYGOTSKY (1896-1934)

In 1917, Bolshevik forces in Russia anticipated a new utopian society and renounced their cultural and intellectual heritage as bourgeois. Those that survived the ensuing civil war, with its famine, epidemics, and cruelly utilitarian focus, were faced with the arduous task of developing a new proletarian workers' culture. Many members of the Russian intelligentsia could not make the adjustment. They no longer had any place in a movement that declared creativity, humanitarianism, and aesthetics to be products of bourgeois decadence. There was to be no expression outside the confines of Marxist ideology and Stalin's fanaticism.

Lev Vygotsky, psychologist at the Moscow Institute of Psychology in the 1920s, was one of the few scholars who was able to produce innovative and high quality research within the dictates of Marx and Lenin. During this time of upheaval, devastation, and Five-Year Plans, Vygotsky was determined to create a psychology of thought and language that would help to build a new socialist society. To this end, he devised a theory of language development that acknowledged both the intrinsic development of cognition proposed by Piaget and the influence of the socio-historical environment on thought as stressed by Marx.

At the time Vygotsky began his research, the study of the intellect was being contested by two schools of philosophers. Adherents of John Locke's concept of empiricism sought to relate basic elements of thought to the realm of the physical being, originating in environmentally produced sensations. The disciples of the philosopher Immanuel Kant, on the other hand, believed that ideas belonged to the sphere of the human mind which could not be dissected into discrete observable elements. A crisis was brewing among the philosophers: Was thought a phenomenon of the body or of the soul?

Bridging senses and thought. Vygotsky felt that both disciplines failed to grasp the essence of the problem. One focused on biological processes, the other on abstract thought. Neither explained the relationship between the higher functions of thought and elementary sensory and reflex processes. Vygotsky, therefore, sought to establish a study of the mind that would bridge the schism between sense and thought, and satisfy the empiricist craving for sensory verification without alienating those who considered thought to be a mental phenomenon that could only be investigated intuitively. The soul was soon to become the property of modern psychology.

Until his death in 1934, Vygotsky worked to free psychology from its empiricist limitations and to create a theory of development that would explain how socio-historical influences change the human capacity for language and thought. Utilizing Engel's writing on tool use, Vygotsky proposed that human beings develop "psychological tools" or *signs* that enable them to facilitate higher level thought processes (1930/1978). Vygotsky's *primary sign systems* included writing, numbering, and speech. Of these, speech was considered to be the most important.

Speech as a tool. Speech distinguished humans from the animal kingdom by enabling them to discuss the past and the future, to transmit information from generation to generation, and to communicate needs and desires. It is important to note, however, that for Vygotsky, speech was not just the verbal manifestation of thought. Instead speech was a tool, in and of itself, that gave humans the capacity to think critically and solve problems. Speech, he proposed, interacted with thought and enhanced it in ways that were not yet appreciated.

In *Thought and Language*, published posthumously in 1934, Vygotsky developed a theory concerning the close correspondence of thought and speech. According to Vygotsky, children's speech is social from its very first utterance, a view that would come as no surprise to any doting parent. As children develop, speech becomes multipurpose. In addition to the original communicative or social function, speech begins to act as an internal mechanism that modifies existing structures to facilitate higher level mental operations.

Speech becomes the medium that allows the cognitive structures of children to interact with, and be altered by, the socio-historical environment. In Vygotsky's scheme of development, early egocentric speech is not a purposeless form of monologue that reflects children's self-absorbed condition. Instead it is part of the process by which children work to internalize social forms of behavior and initiate internal dialogue and thought.

According to Vygotsky, development of thought unfolds in three stages:

1. Children experience speech and develop an understanding of the relationship between an object and its label while interacting with others.

2. At about the age of three, children begin to comment on objects and processes to themselves; they also refer to objects not in the immediate perceptual field. As children become involved in challenging tasks and nonautomatic processes, they articulate their problem-solving in order to

guide their own activities. Gradually, this self guiding speech becomes more telegraphic and less grammatical, and it occurs less frequently.

3. By the age of eight, this overt problem-solving speech becomes less obvious as it is internalized in the form of linguistic thought.

Interaction of speech and thought. Vygotsky elaborated that speech and thought develop and function together to foster higher level cognitive skills. He acknowledged a preintellectual stage in speech and a prelinguistic stage in thought during which speech and thought develop independently and from distinct biological roots. By about the age of two, thought and speech have merged together in an interrelationship based upon meaning. In this relationship, thought acquires a verbal form and speech becomes intellectual, or meaningful. We see evidence of this emerging cognitive state as infants leave babbling to enter the one-word stage and utter their first meaningful words. From this age on, thought and speech intermingle, influencing and enhancing each other's growth.

Words replace gestures. In Vygotsky's scheme of development, children's initial attempts at language are nothing more than verbal gestures, or extensions of the child's system of nonverbal communication. Gradually, through the process of operating with these word-gestures, children undergo a series of tiny "molecular" changes in their cognitive structures to form the word's inner symbolic meaning. Initially, word meaning may be limited to one of the many specific physical properties that make an object complete. A *ball* is a *ball* because of its ball-like nature. As thought becomes enriched through language, meaning evolves from the fundamental understanding of words as attributes to the mature perception of words as symbols.

According to Vygotsky, the moment heralding children's awareness of the symbolic function of language and the onset of verbal thought has been vastly exaggerated. Stern (cited in Vygotsky, 1934/1986), for example, maintains that this moment occurs like an epiphany conferring upon children the ability to make far-reaching generalizations about the nature of language and enabling them to use language symbolically. Vygotsky sees this moment differently. Such knowledge does not materialize out of thin air and it is not present in the genetic code. In fact, Vygotsky believes that generalizations about the symbolic nature of language are well beyond the two-year-old's overall intellectual capacity.

Concepts are refined. The process of "molecular change" that governs the development of meaning also regulates the formation of concepts. In a child's mind, the initial symbolic meaning of a word is a primitive generalization. Through experience this generalization is tuned, by small degrees, to more accurately portray a comprehensive view of the reality it is intended to designate. This process eventually leads to the formation of a clearly delineated concept; the concept, in turn, becomes an intellectual tool for further analysis and problem-solving.

According to Vygotsky, concept formation is affected by varying internal and external conditions. In this respect, he differs from Piaget, who proposed that children learn entirely through their own spontaneous mental efforts. In Vygotsky's opinion, concept formation is not only dependent upon the spontaneous mental efforts of the child, but to a greater degree upon the influence of the socio-historical environment. If thought is determined by language, i.e. by the linguistic tools of a child's particular socio-historical environment, then higher level cognitive functions can be promoted through instruction in language and guided opportunities to explore the nature of the world all around.

Zone of proximal development and scaffolding. Vygotsky's views on the role of instruction in cognitive development are best understood through two notions: *zone of proximal development* and *scaffolding*. The *zone of proximal development* is the difference between an actual developmental level, as determined by a child's ability to work independently, and the level at which problems can be solved with assistance from more capable peers and adults (1934/1986). It is, in effect, a measure of a child's potential for learning when placed in a supportive instructional atmosphere. (This method of assessment differs substantially from Piaget's technique, which required that children be observed independently in their problem-solving efforts.)

Scaffolding refers to the instructional process by which a child is provided with cues in order to ensure successful confrontations and mastery of more challenging tasks. By utilizing the zone of proximal development, together with the technique of scaffolding, instruction becomes a vital component that stretches proficiency.

In Vygotsky's view, education that is adapted to the current level of proficiency maintains the status quo. By failing to utilize the higher range of the zone of proximal development, educators do not fully develop the potential for learning. According to Vygotsky, instruction that aims at a child's present level of proficiency provides opportunities for practice, while tasks within the upper range of the zone of proximal development encourage children to tackle and master even higher levels of skill with support. Both of these types of activities are necessary in order for children to learn, develop confidence, and progress.

Scaffolding with child-directed speech. An example of how we utilize the zone of proximal development and scaffolding occurs very naturally between parents and children. According to research conducted by Catherine Snow (1986), adults engage in a unique form of communication with infants and small children. Snow calls this "child-directed speech." During child-directed speech, adults reduce extraneous information and simplify their language in order to enter a child's zone of proximal development for language. The simplified vocabulary, grammar, and syntax let a child focus on the content of the utterance without being overwhelmed by irrelevant data. With adult scaffolding, children use words or syntactic structures that could not have been uttered independently.

During child-directed speech, scaffolding occurs as parents provide cues in the form of exaggerated intonation, enunciation, and facial expression in order to focus attention on the important information. As parents try to solicit speech from children, they often try to exploit the child's upper range of the zone of proximal development. In the following conversation with a two-year-old, note how the parent is using repetition, modeling, and prompts, to enable the child to articulate the word "red" and to use it in a two-word utterance.

Parent:	What's that?
Child:	An apple
Parent:	What kind of apple?
Child:	An apple
Parent:	Is it a red apple?
Child:	Yes
Parent:	Do you like red apples?
Child:	Yes, good
Parent:	Can I have some red apple?
Child:	Child offers the apple.
Parent:	Mmm. Red apples are good.
	What kind of apples do we like?
Child:	Red apple.
Parent:	Mmmmm.

Afterword. During his short lifetime, implications of Vygotsky's work were considered not only for classroom and home instruction but also for the larger political agenda. Vygotsky's theories on the development of language and thought tantalized those who were already entranced by the prospect of molding future generations of Soviet citizens. Eventually, his work was decreed to be too "mental," and after two years in print, his research was banned from publication by the Central Committee of the Communist Party. Officially, it was not published again until the thaw of 1956 under Nikita Khrushchev. Consequently, although he was born in the same year as Piaget, his work was not generally available until Piaget's contrasting views were well established.

JEAN PIAGET (1896-1980)

Jean Piaget's constructivist theory of cognitive development has been the monumental yardstick according to which all other theories of development are evaluated and compared. All psychologists know precisely where they stand with respect to Piaget's views and every teacher implements to some degree his notions of developmental education. Piaget was the first Western psychologist to focus on the qualitative differences between adult and child thought, and to propose a stage theory elucidating the process by which children grow to take their place with adults.

Piaget's stage theory presents a developmental approach to cognitive maturation that suggests children progress through a series of distinct stages in an invariant sequence. Although each stage is attributed to a specific age level, Piaget did not consider the age boundaries to be inviolate nor that children would enter or exit a given stage on cue because we have turned another page on the calendar. He accepts that most children develop according to a pace of their own and that each child's individual path is part of the diversity that we enjoy in human nature.

Even though Piaget's stage theory has been interpreted as innatist by some, Piaget rejected the possibility that development was subject to the forces of biological maturation (Ginsburg & Opper, 1988). In his view, stages of development do not result from the regulation of genetic matter, but rather from children's need to self stimulate and interact with the world. This self stimulation begins in infancy with the internal organization of chaotic sensorimotor activity and the gradual development of increasingly complex modes of thought and action. Through a meticulous process of growth and adaptation, children emerge from their original state of limited self awareness to consider multiple perspectives, use language abstractly, and interact with the environment.

Assimilation and accommodation. The confusion over Piaget's innatist leanings results from his comparison of the processes of cognitive growth and adaptation to biological tendencies found in all organisms. By rooting his theory of cognitive development in these biological processes, Piaget hoped to establish a precedent in nature for his vision of the child as an organism that grows by altering cognitive structures through assimilation and accommodation. According to Piaget, **assimilation** is the process by which new information is incorporated into existing cognitive structures as the result of experience. He compares it to the process of eating or digestion.

In contrast, **accommodation** occurs when existing cognitive structures need to be altered to encompass a new understanding. This is similar to adding a new wing to a house when another child is born. These two processes allow children to adjust and organize their thinking in order to gain an understanding of the world. They are part of an active construction process, in which children, like biological organisms, seek to build increasingly complex and differentiated modes of thought.

It is Piaget's opinion, therefore, that learning is the result of children's spontaneous efforts to reorganize their cognitive structures. He suggests that it cannot be hurried or rushed, and that no amount of direct instruction will alter or accelerate children along the path to adulthood. Piaget's influence in the field of education lies primarily in the concept of indirect instruction. According to Piaget, children do not learn through the direct transmission of information from teacher to pupil, but rather by exploration in an environment that offers opportunities to problem solve at a level compatible with interest and ability.

Role of language. Unlike Vygotsky, Piaget does not accord language any special status with respect to other cognitive abilities. It is simply one of many autonomous behaviors that follows from a child's efforts to participate in the world. It is not, as others have proposed, a mechanism for cognitive development. He proposes that language occurs when children interact with their environment utilizing their knowledge in order to generate higher levels of mental operations through experience. Although Piaget has admitted in discussions of higher stages (formal operations) that language may be necessary for some forms of reasoning, language is, in his scheme of development, a reflection of the inner cognitive state and not a mechanism of change.

Piaget has classified the cognitive development of children into four distinct stages through which all children advance as they mature. These stages are briefly described as below:

Sensorimotor stage (birth - 2 years). Piaget characterizes the period from birth to two years of age as a prelanguage stage in which children have no understanding of objects existing apart from themselves (1936/1974). They organize sensory input in order to generate simple reflex reactions and they begin to develop physical action schemes to deal with their environment. Caretakers often facilitate this stage by providing infants with a colorful dashboard of knobs, buttons, dials, and bells, known as a busybox. Such a toy provides infants with an opportunity to develop fundamental understandings of deliberate physical actions, and cause and effect.

According to Piaget, children's thought prior to two years of age is nonverbal. He suggests that, even though the child may begin to articulate individual words, the concept of meaning and the idea that words signify objects has not yet stabilized. Although children in this age group are capable of speech, Piaget is reluctant to categorize these utterances as evidence of language. In his view, language has a communicative function that is beyond the cognitive capacity of the sensorimotor stage.

Preoperational stage (years 2 - 6). In Piaget's scheme of development, the preoperational stage from age two to age six is distinguished by two phenomena: the realization that words are symbols, and the acquisition of language (1936/1974). One cognitive milestone of this stage is the development of object permanence. **Object permanence** allows children to separate from their environment and understand that objects exist independently in their own right. An object that is out of the perceptual field does not cease to exist. As children learn to distinguish themselves from external actions and objects, they develop a sense of subject, verb, and object.

Preoperational speech allows children to increase their sphere of activity to include the past and the present, and to invoke objects that are not within perceptual range. Children begin to grasp the relationship between word and referent. In the beginning, however, words are not arbitrary symbols but are understood as physical attributes along with color, shape, and texture. A dog, for example, is a dog because of its "dogness." Gradually, children come to understand that words are arbitrary, that they are symbolic, and that people and things may be called by different names.

According to Piaget, preoperational speech lacks communicative intent because children are cognitively unable to consider a point of view apart from their own. He attributes this to the basic egocentric nature of the child (1923/1974). Although the word "egocentric" is often used in a pejorative sense, Piaget was not suggesting in any way that children's abilities are inferior to those of adults. He was simply trying to convey the overall character of children's cognitive functioning and limited awareness of their environment.

Egocentric speech. The function of egocentric language has stimulated a great deal of controversy since many psychologists disagree about the role of early speech. In Piaget's opinion, egocentric speech serves no function. It is an external manifestation of internal thought. He describes three subclasses of egocentric speech: repetition, monologue, and collective monologue. He suggests that repetitions are motivated by children's need for self-stimulation and their love of hearing themselves talk. Monologues externalize inner thoughts as though children were thinking aloud. Collective monologues are fashioned when two children speak in turns without acknowledging the other's contribution to the conversation. Gradually, egocentric language wanes, as children discover that language can be used to communicate with others. Egocentric speech atrophies and socialized language appears.

According to Piaget, preoperational thought is transductive—a term borrowed from the field of biology to signify the shifting of thought from one particular to another (1946/1962). Children lack the ability to associate objects into classes and so they deal in particulars. Consider the statement, "If my daddy hasn't come home yet, then it can't be dinnertime." To adults this association may seem unsystematic and illogical. To a child, however, this kind of thinking results from an inability to extract essential from nonessential and make generalizations. In this particular case, the child does not yet understand that dinnertime is a general time period during which many events occur and that it occurs independently of a parent's arrival home.

Concrete operations stage (years 7 - adolescence). At about the age of seven, children enter the stage of concrete operations (1964/1968). They can think logically and systematically when referring to tangible objects that can be physically manipulated. Children in this stage are able to classify objects based upon physical characteristics and they begin to order objects according to size and weight.

One of Piaget's most significant contributions to our understanding of this age is the **principle of conservation** in which children come to realize that water is conserved when poured from one size glass into another. In an earlier stage, children would focus only on one dimension of the glass, the larger height or width. This tunnel vision would obscure the fact that the quantity of liquid had not changed as the liquid was poured from one glass to another.

As children develop and acquire the ability to perform mental operations, they can reverse the experiment in their minds to see that no liquid has been added or taken away, and that the lesser width may, in effect, cancel out the larger height. Finally, children may say that the whole operation can be inverted by pouring the water back into its original container. The three arguments, that of identity, compensation, and inversion, require the use of mental operations that are reversible and the ability to consider multiple dimensions at one time.

During this period, egocentric language becomes less and less frequent as children become active participants in a world of objects, people, and actions that have properties and points of view of their own. The development of concrete operations is reflected in children's use of language as they perform linguistic transformations from the active to the passive voice and from declarative to interrogatory sentences.

Formal operations stage (adolescence - adulthood). The stage of formal operations, which characterizes the period from adolescence into adulthood, is distinguished by the capacity to think abstractly and hypothetically (1964/1968). Older children can hypothesize, perform experiments, analyze, and execute abstract reasoning. Adolescents develop a method of analysis that systematically reviews all possible solutions and their implications. According to Piaget, adolescents experience another period of egocentrism as they become intrigued with their intellectual capabilities and visions of creating utopian societies. It is only upon assuming the responsibilities of adulthood and confronting the realities of the socialized world that they learn the limits of their own thoughts.

In summary, Piaget believes that language is only one of many behaviors that result as children develop higher level cognitive skills. His approach to learning is similar to that of Rousseau and the European educator, Montessori. He suggests that children will learn spontaneously in an environment that is appropriate to their cognitive level. This learning is the result of a constructivist process that is governed neither by external stimulus nor biological predisposition; and, it cannot be hurried through attempts at direct teaching.

Cognitive Psychology and Language:
Fischer, Case, and Gardner

Although Piaget's work has been instrumental in furthering our understanding of the specific nature of children's thought, his theory of cognitive development has troubled scholars on both ends of the nature-nurture continuum. Behaviorists and innatists challenged the basic notion of an internal constructivist process as the primary mechanism of cognitive development. Behaviorists felt slighted by the diminutive role that Piaget attributed to the environment. They felt that Piaget's approach was too cerebral, and that he focused on a realm inaccessible to scientific inquiry and empiricist methodology. Innatists, on the other hand, were concerned that Piaget's theory lacked a proper biological foundation. They asked, "What is self-stimulation and how specifically does cognitive development occur?" Research conducted by cognitive psychologists of the late 20th century attempts to clarify these issues.

KURT W. FISCHER

Kurt Fischer (1980) attempts to bridge the nature-nurture controversy by positing a theory of cognitive development that is the result of interaction between the organism and the environment. According to Fischer, children mature into adulthood by virtue of experiences that gradually transform collections of skills from infantile sensory-motor actions into the representational abstract thought processes of the adult mind.

Skill theory. Fischer's approach differs from Piaget's in that he defines development in terms of skill levels and tiers, and not stages. Piaget's stages are discrete modes of thought that occur in an invariant sequence. For example, the formal operations stage is qualitatively different from the sensory motor stage. In contrast, progress through skill levels, as proposed by Fischer, is continuous and gradual. Each level is built upon increasingly complex skills, incorporating skills from preceding levels. These levels may be grouped into tiers, similar to Piaget's stages, that specify skills of different types: sensory-motor, representational, and abstract. According to Fischer, cognitive development occurs as humans move through skill levels by virtue of their particular experience in individual domains.

Individual variation. Unlike Piaget, Fischer also notes that the paths of cognitive development will vary from individual to individual (1980). Some will follow paths within particular skill domains, such as basket weaving and reading. Others may not learn how to basket weave at all. In addition, Fischer's rules for transformation from one level to another allow for different paths within the same domain, some being more efficient than others. Ultimately, the environmental and individual factors that contribute to cognitive development ensure tremendous variety in human interests and capabilities.

Skill theory offers an explanation concerning why people develop strengths and weaknesses. Human beings act upon their environment in ways that respond to specific circumstances, or stimuli. As a consequence, human behavior is controlled both by the biology of the organism and by the specific nature of the environmental stimulus it encounters. According to Fischer (1980), the quality of the stimulus has as much to contribute to the development of skills as does the predisposition of the individual. For example, children who daily observe clay pots of varied shapes and sizes being produced from clay lumps of one size have been reported to learn the principle of conservation earlier than Piaget's stages would predict.

Because of the qualitative differences in the substance of an individual's experiences, cognitive development will be uneven. Fischer calls this **décalage**, a term originally coined by Piaget to acknowledge discrepancies in abilities within specific stages. According to skill theory, only the skills that are afforded the most opportunity for practice and application in a supportive environment will develop and attain optimal levels of performance.

Optimal levels. The concept of optimal levels of performance is one of the central hypotheses of skill theory. The optimal level is the upper level of achievable performance in a particular domain. It is not a global description of a child's abilities, but rather a description of performance of an individual skill under ideal conditions. Such conditions include: tasks that are familiar and highly practiced, a supportive atmosphere, and children who are healthy and motivated. Without a high degree of environmental support, people ordinarily perform at their **functional level.** (The optimal/functional distinction is equivalent to the upper and lower boundaries of Vygotsky's zone of proximal development.) According to Fischer (1987), in order to independently bridge the gap between these two levels of performance, children must, with exposure and practice, internalize strategies that produce optimal performance without support.

ROBBIE CASE

Case (1980) examines the mechanisms of how children internalize strategies at a more microscopic level. His theory of intellectual development is compatible with Fischer's Skill Theory. Case focuses specifically on how children revise their strategies to deal with challenges of increasing complexity. He proposes the following:

1. Each major stage as described by Piaget is divided into a series of substages. As children mature, they advance through the substages by developing increasingly complex strategies for problem-solving.

2. In order for particular strategies to develop, children must be exposed to relevant opportunities for practice and application.

3. The ability to incorporate more complex routines into basic strategies depends not only upon experience, but also upon the child's ability to manipulate and coordinate information in memory. Case refers to the

maximum number of items with which a child can work at any one time as **working memory.**

4. He suggested that working memory capacity does not change substantially after the age of two. Instead, as children develop automaticity in their strategies, there are gradual ongoing changes in the allocation of working memory. Since strategies that are automatized require less working memory, practice increases the amount of working memory available to learn new strategies. This available memory is referred to as **functional memory**.

5. As sufficient functional memory is freed by the mastery of particular skills, functional memory resources become available to focus on higher order operations of the next stage.

According to Case (1980), as children develop, they continually engage in a process in which they automatize lower level skills, make functional memory available, and focus on automatizing increasingly complex skills.

Skill theory and the concept of working memory provide a means to assist educators in evaluating the specific mechanisms that produce changes in the quality or the character of the educational experience. These theories suggest that the child and the environment must work together in order to facilitate cognitive development.

If décalage is the norm, and not the exception, then educators must be prepared to accommodate a wide variety of skills and approaches in an environment that encourages active and comfortable participation with the support of direct teaching, demonstration, modeling, repetition, and independent practice. Children who are actively supported and involved in learning can more quickly internalize given strategies in order to progress to more complex challenges and increase their levels of performance.

HOWARD GARDNER

The concepts of skill theory and décalage add considerable weight to Gardner's theory of **multiple intelligences** (1983; 1993). Gardner defines an intelligence as the ability to solve problems in a way that is of value to a particular culture or community. Based on his research with brain-damaged patients, gifted individuals, and normal children and adults, as well as those of different cultures, Gardner suggests that there is significant evidence postulating the existence of relatively discrete human intelligences that are often unrecognized and unappreciated in traditional educational environments.

Seven intelligences. Without demeaning the more conventional linguistic and logical-mathematical intelligences, Gardner submits that musical, bodily-kinesthetic, spatial, interpersonal, and intrapersonal skills also warrant consideration in the classroom. Instruction that takes into account these intelligences could prepare individuals more fully for the varied challenges that life has to offer, and let society profit from a more diverse pool of developed talent.

Gardner (1993) describes seven intelligences that he has identified on the basis of his research into the nature of the mind. He selected these intelligences by using strict criteria that include: potential isolation by brain damage, the existence of individuals with exceptional ability, the identification of a specific information-processing mechanism, and potential representation in a symbolic system.

In Gardner's view, the first two—linguistic intelligence and logical mathematical intelligence—have been elevated in Western society to a position that obfuscates all other modes of thought. This view is shared by Robert Ornstein (1986) who refers to this limited view of intellect as "the Western intellectual tradition," otherwise known as TWIT. According to Gardner (1993), Piaget mistook his study of logical-mathematical intelligence to be the study of all intelligence, the error of which is confirmed by a straight "A" student who has insufficient intellectual resources to succeed in the real world.

Gardner (1993) proposes that the other intelligences—spatial, musical, bodily-kinesthetic, inter- and intra-personal—deserve equal consideration, and he describes them in this way. Spatial intelligence is the ability to form a mental model of the three-dimensional world and operate within it. Sculptors, architects, and chess players all display evidence of spatial intelligence. Musical intelligence is exemplified by Mozart's ability to generate patterns and harmonies that have captivated listeners for centuries. Bodily-kinesthetic intelligence is evidenced by dancers, athletes, and surgeons who are able to use their bodies to solve physical problems. Interpersonal intelligence is the ability to understand other people, a talent critical to public figures who are dependent upon our good will. Intrapersonal intelligence is the capacity to understand oneself and apply that understanding to achieve one's goals in life.

Gardner proposes that multiple intelligences are the fruits of our biogenetic design coupled with the values encouraged by our culture or environment. According to Gardner, the functioning of specific neurological structures in the brain vary genetically, and these differences appear as variations in cognitive functioning. Certain talents or weaknesses, therefore, may be the result of inherited tendencies to form marked neural connections related to specific abilities, such as linguistic, spatial, or bodily-kinesthetic functioning. Because of this biogenetic predisposition, Gardner suggests that individuals can be "*at promise* for the flowering of a certain talent*,*" in the same way that they can be at risk for disease (1983, p. 35).

Support from Gazzaniga. The neuropsychologist, Michael Gazzaniga (1993), drawing on research in the field of immunology, suggests that the brain has stored within it a vast compendium of potential knowledge that is hardwired into the brain's neural networks. According to the theory of **selectionism**, stimulation alters the way specific cells communicate with each other, creating preferred pathways of neural circuits. The process of selection signals these circuits, turning potential forms of knowledge into an accessible resource. These findings lend support to Gardner's theory.

Fostering talent. If human beings are genetically predisposed to develop certain abilities, how then is this potential turned into talent? According to Gardner, cultural values play a considerable role in fostering specific intellectual capabilities. Inherent in cultural identity is the tendency to promote those particular intelligences that are of value to a culture. What may be nurtured as a talent in Tibet may atrophy from neglect or lack of appreciation in Illinois. Gardner suggests that academic environments have evolved in such a way as to reward verbal and logical mathematical talents, while discouraging those skills that fall outside of the traditional scholarly arena.

Gardner's theory of multiple intelligences is a plea to educators to recognize and cultivate the richness and diversity that the human mind has to offer. By acknowledging our innate promise for a variety of intelligences, and by understanding the timely effect of stimulation on cognitive growth, educators can utilize our natural inclinations and abilities to better facilitate the educational process and help us, as a species, enjoy our potential.

Behavior or Brain Structure:
Skinner and Chomsky

The theories of Fischer, Case, and Gardner are the result of centuries of fiercely contested debate over the nature of cognitive development. Their work would have been impossible without the insight and genius of two of their predecessors, Skinner and Chomsky, who each, in his own way, galvanized the fields of cognition and linguistics, and inspired a multitude of young scholars to take up the call to explore the mind and its vehicles for expression.

In order to appreciate more fully the genesis of cognitive psychology and the roles that nature and nurture play in language development, this review steps back to the mid-20th century to consider the contributions of these leading proponents of the Behaviorist and the Innatist schools of thought. Following the discussion of Skinner and Chomsky, the chapter concludes by returning to the close of the 20th century to examine the work of Locke and Snow, and the current theory of Social Interactionism.

B.F. SKINNER AND THE BEHAVIORIST SCHOOL (1905-1990)

In the mid-20th century, B.F. Skinner was the major proponent of empiricist thought. He, in the tradition of Locke, called for science to be based strictly on principles of observation that could be applied and quantified. Skinner rejected the work of developmentalists, such as Piaget, on the grounds that their theories were dependent on immeasurable mental processes that were beyond the proper boundaries of science. In Skinner's view, environment alone shapes behavior, and although gradual changes in behavior may have the appearance of developmental stages, these internal stages are unimportant with respect to environmental considerations. This focus on the environment to the exclusion of internal cognitive processes is called **behaviorism**.

In 1948, B.F. Skinner published *Walden Two*, a fictional account of an utopian community founded on the precepts of behavioral engineering. Although Skinner wrote the book as a creative exercise exploring the potential of a society in which individual growth was fostered through environmental and social considerations, the public reacted with distaste and suspicion. Many mistakenly interpreted Skinner's utopian vision to be a world in which people would function as robots in response to invasive external stimuli. Descriptions of Skinner's utopia were often embellished with references to dehumanization and loss of individuality. These erroneous impressions, together with highly sensationalized portrayals of Skinner's home life, caught the public's imagination and implanted in many a distrust of technologically designed societies.

However, Skinner was not advocating an end to freedom and dignity. Instead, he found the inner person was equivalent to an impenetrable black box that was fraught with intangible mental states. To him, the inner person was of no scientific interest since thoughts and feelings could not be observed or measured. In his view, the black box of human mental states had no place in the tradition of empiricist thought, which sought to anchor science to sensory experience. Instead, Skinner examined human nature by observing its external manifestations in behavior.

Theory of behavioral psychology. Skinner considered behavior a question of stimulus and response, and focused his research on examining the question of how environment controls behavior. His theory of psychology rests upon three main premises:

1. Animal and human organisms actively emit behaviors of various kinds.

2. When a behavior is emitted, it has consequences that may either increase or decrease the likelihood that the behavior will occur again.

3. The consequences are a product of the organism's physical and social environment.

Conditioning. Although Skinner's research is often equated with that of Pavlov, his focus was quite different. Pavlov worked largely within the area of reflex type responses, called **respondents**, in which initially neutral stimuli become conditioned to elicit specific acts of behavior such as the ringing of a bell and salivation. Skinner's interest was primarily in behaviors that affect the physical and social environment. Such behaviors, called **operants,** act on the environment to produce consequences, and, in turn, are affected by these consequences. These behaviors include any of the activities in which humans engage: speech, reading, studying, playing games. **Operant conditioning** is the process by which these behaviors are changed.

Reinforcement contingencies. In his study of respondents and operants, Skinner examined the three "contingencies of reinforcement." The contingencies of reinforcement are the circumstances under which behavior occurs, the behavior itself, and the consequences that the behavior produces.

The effects of reinforcement mold behavior along certain lines. A **positive reinforcement** increases the frequency of a particular behavior by adding something pleasurable to the environment to increase the likelihood that the behavior will occur again. Positive reinforcers that are related to our biological functioning such as food, sleep, and water, are called **primary reinforcers. Conditioned reinforcers** are originally neutral stimuli that gain power to change behavior by virtue of their association with one or more primary reinforcers. Examples of conditioned reinforcers include smiles, attention, and praise.

Negative reinforcement strengthens a behavior by the removal of unpleasant or aversive stimuli. An example of negative reinforcement is a mother who is conditioned by her children to give them cookies to quiet their crying. A **punishment** decreases or extinguishes behaviors. This term often causes confusion, for punishment does not imply that the individual who is performing the behavior is actually made to feel bad. Punishment refers only to the fact that the behavior itself is lessened. A child's crying, for example, could be punished by rewarding him with candy. Skinner did not advocate punishment (as it is more typically understood) because of its potential for abuse and unwarranted side effects, he acknowledged that it is probably the most commonly used form of behavior control.

Language as behavior. According to Skinner, language is one of many behaviors that result from operant conditioning. In his view, language is not a tool for expressing ideas, feelings, and desires, but rather a behavior that is shaped by the community of the speaker (1957). As children begin to babble, they imitate the models provided by their caretakers. Articulations that approximate adult speech are recognized and reinforced, others are extinguished. Gradually, early attempts at speech are shaped to the pronunciation and grammatical standards of the adult community. The utterance, "dada," for example, is slowly shaped into the generally accepted pronunciation of the word "daddy" through selective reinforcement of more precise articulations.

According to Skinner, children gradually learn to sequence words into phrases and sentences, and participate in conversations through a procedure known as **chaining** (1957). As behaviors are shaped bit by bit, they are also linked into successions of discrete acts. For example, a child, upon the stimulus of parting from friends, may say, "good-bye." The "good-bye" is reinforced by the good wishes of those leaving. In return, the child utters, "Have a nice day!" which is, in turn, reinforced, perhaps by laughter or a smile. After several farewells, in which each act of this behavior is reinforced, the child may, upon the next departure, respond with a chain of utterances all precipitated by the one event, "Good-bye. Have a nice day!"

Skinner's *Verbal behavior,* published in 1957, sought to examine all the conditions under which speech is acquired. What models of speech has the child heard? What was the nature of the environment? What reinforcers or punishments were experienced as the child uttered similar responses?

Language and thought. Even though Skinner held that the practices of a verbal community determine how people speak, he also acknowledged that verbal behavior can be emitted without environmental support. Speakers may, in effect, become listeners and reinforce their own behavior through the process of thinking. According to Skinner (1967), thinking consists of humans' reactions to and revisions of their own verbal behavior. Thinking, however, holds no place in science for it cannot be made public and it cannot be measured. It is important to understand that in Skinner's theory, thought and feelings do not cause behavior. This suggests that if we follow through on a desire, it is because that particular behavior has been reinforced and not because humans are self-motivating.

The question of free will poses the most difficulty for many of Skinner's readers. According to Chomsky (1967), Skinner's work seems to impose limitations on the way in which behavior is to be studied by viewing the speaker as little more than an empty black box that contributes minimally to the process of language acquisition. By disavowing the nature in which an organism inputs and organizes information, Skinner seems to be leaving out the most critical aspect of what causes humans to act. Skinner's focus on experience suggests that humans should not be able to produce and understand an infinite variety of sentences that they have never before experienced. Yet it seems that there is some fundamental process, independent of environmental feedback that contributes to language development.

Summary. Although Skinner's theory of verbal behavior seems to omit crucial aspects of human cognition, we should not be too quick to abandon all of his work as we examine the other end of the nature versus nurture spectrum. Whether or not we accept Skinner's categorizations of verbal behavior, there is undoubtedly much that we learn through reinforcement, which we apply to a variety of behaviors including speech. Although Skinner experienced a fall from grace with the advent of Chomsky and the innatists, Skinner is recognized with great acclaim for his research in the behavioral approach to teaching and for providing educators with the concept of programmed instruction.

NOAM CHOMSKY

In the early 1950s, science and technology were enjoying an unprecedented popularity. It was widely accepted that the future held the promise of better living through technological advances, and Americans were poised to reap the material benefits. Empiricism, the idea that all knowledge is based on sensory experience, was hailed as the foundation of progress, and intellectual communities were vigorously positioning themselves to ride the empiricist wave to new heights of wisdom and glory.

In accord with Skinner's theory, structural linguists of the time undertook to bring their work into the realm of empirical science (Newmeyer, 1980). Their goal was to develop a grammar, which by virtue of its integrity and strict adherence to scientific methodology, would explain how it was possible for humans to speak and understand each other. This was to be achieved through a painstaking process of defining all the elements of language according to their fundamental building blocks. In this way, each element would be verifiable through experience and experiment.

Speech was recorded, segmented into phonemes that were combined and classified as morphs, and once again as morphemes. By beginning with phonemes, the basic building blocks of language, and developing an inviolate hierarchy of grammatical levels, linguists intended to define the process by which children learn language. Unfortunately, structuralist methodology was at odds with the medium. Not all linguistic phenomena could be observed, and the attempts to apply empiricist logic to language often resulted in conclusions that clashed with common sense.

The theory of innateness - nature prevails. In 1957 Noam Chomsky, a young instructor at MIT, published a work that shook the foundation of the empiricist world view. Chomsky's *Syntactic Structures* proposed a grammar that structural linguists could **not** verify through experience and experiment. It was instead a multidisciplinary "theory of language" that was based, not on observation, but on intuition.

Although it was not explicitly stated, Chomsky rejected the basic tenets of empiricism and, instead, took a posture that had its roots in the rationalism of Rousseau. According to Chomsky, children were not born as blank slates *(tabulae rasae)* to be formed by their environment. Children came into the world already possessing an innate knowledge of grammar and a unique facility for language acquisition. Without this innate knowledge, Chomsky reasoned, surely the task of acquiring language would be insurmountable.

In his argument, Chomsky points to the environmental realities that shape children's linguistic knowledge. Children do not learn through meticulous observation and selective reinforcement. Many children learn language without the slow and careful shaping performed by indulgent caretakers. In addition, Chomsky posits that children are able to understand and produce sentences that are beyond their own experience. Chomsky cites the example of the command, "Your money or your life!" Strictly speaking, according to Chomsky's interpretation of Skinner's theory, we should not be able to understand that utterance unless, of course, we have a past experience of being killed (1967).

This point of view was more overtly expressed in 1959 when Chomsky reviewed B.F. Skinner's *Verbal Behavior*, in which the behaviorist defended his "babble-luck" theory of language acquisition. As discussed above, Skinner posited that children learn language strictly through input from the environment. In his view, language develops as children babble random sequences of phonemes. Adults encourage and reinforce correct sequences. The others are extinguished. Chomsky could not accept Skinner's view of language acquisition as a labor-intensive mechanical process. In his review of *Verbal Behavior*, Chomsky states

> "The actual observed ability of a speaker to distinguish sentences from nonsentences, detect ambiguities, etc., apparently forces us to the conclusion that this grammar is of an extremely complex and abstract character, and that the young child has succeeded in carrying out what from the formal point of view, at least, seems to be a remarkable type of theory construction" (1959, p. 57).

Chomsky's words sent shock waves through the intellectual community. In the eyes of many structuralists, these words were no less than heresy. Numerous attacks appeared in print. More and more linguists, however, became intoxicated with a new appreciation for the mystery of language and the magnitude of the task facing the young child. In an era dominated by science and logic, Chomsky asked linguists to make a leap of faith. He suggested that children were not learning language from their mothers. Instead, children were acquiring language because of their biology.

The human species, Chomsky proposed, is endowed with a unique capacity for language; and this capacity determines the form and the range of human mental activity (1980). In support of his theory, Chomsky put forth three major observations.

1. Only humans are able to speak and understand language.
2. All languages have fundamental features in common.
3. Language is developmental.

Both opponents and supporters of Chomsky embarked on a quest to determine through research whether the capacity for language was indeed unique to humans. The uniqueness criterion was fundamental to Chomsky's argument concerning a genetic basis for language, and the question was posed as to whether other species were capable of using a communication system similar to that of humans.

Early chimp studies. In the late 1960s a project was conducted by Alan and Beatrice Gardner testing the ability of a one-year-old female chimpanzee named Washoe to learn language (1969). Certain practical difficulties were inherent in an undertaking of this type. The first difficulty concerned what language Washoe should learn. A previous attempt at teaching language to a chimp named Vicki raised serious doubts about a chimp's ability to master spoken language. After five years of being raised as a human child, Vicki's spoken vocabulary consisted of a paltry four words. It appeared that the chimp's vocal apparatus was simply insufficient to handle the phonetic diversity required by oral speech. For this reason, it was decided to teach Washoe American Sign Language.

According to the Gardners, instruction in American Sign Language offered an opportunity to compare Washoe's ability to acquire language with that of human children. There was an expectation that Washoe's learning would follow a similar developmental sequence, beginning with babbling and eventually producing infinite combinations of words into sentences of unrestricted length. Like humans, young chimps engage in spontaneous gestural play, play that was equated to verbal babbling.

In Washoe's case, there was great hope that the gestural babbling would, as it does in humans, lead to the functional use of signs and an ability to generate two-sign utterances. Washoe eventually mastered approximately one hundred sixty signs, and was able to use them in two-sign combinations (1975). There remained, however, significant doubt as to whether Washoe was producing spontaneous combinations of signs or whether her efforts were due to her undeniable talent for mimicry and her ability to get what she wanted.

Nim Chimpsky. In the mid 1970s, psychologist Herbert Terrace (1979) initiated a study at Columbia University which was designed to explore further the chimp's facility for language. Over a period of four years, a chimpanzee named Nim Chimpsky was taught how to express approximately one hundred twenty-five signs that he appeared to combine effectively in two- and three-sign combinations.

Terrace began to experience uncertainty about his protégé's ability to use language when he noticed two curiosities about the chimp's speech. First, Nim's use of three-sign combinations failed to provide any new information over the preceding two-sign combinations. The content of "play me Nim" was largely redundant to the earlier form, "play me." (1979, pp. 210-211). In addition, researchers neglected to examine the role of Nim's instructors. What was at first attributed to Nim's originality and spontaneity now appeared to be an apt imitation of Nim's role models.

The question now remains as to whether Nim was meeting the basic requirements of human language—the ability to produce and understand an infinite set of sentences.

Human language unique.   Clearly, there are considerable difficulties inherent in the comparison of chimp speech to that of humans.   Although the possibility of communicating with another species is very intriguing, the reality may be that chimps lack the same capacity to use language and that the behavioral manifestations of these capacities are different.   According to Ed Walker, "Birds, bees, bats and people fly, but to infer correspondences between these species just because they all engage in 'flying' would be to confuse quite different acts which all have the same nature," (1978, p. 204).   He argues that this is a classic simulation problem in which the solutions that produce the same answer to a problem may not be at all related.

Chimp acquisition of human language appears to differ substantially from the process by which humans learn to express themselves.   Humans develop language spontaneously; they produce infinite sets of sentences; and they are capable of expression beyond their immediate needs.   If we understand language in the sense that humans use it, then we have to admit that chimps do not share in the human capacity for expression.

Language universals.   Chomsky argued that language experience is essentially the same for all.   Wherever people exist, regardless of culture or race, humans learn to speak by organizing words into grammatical sentence forms. Humans, regardless of their experience or native tongue, have the capacity to generate questions, commands, and negations.   They are able to use rules that let them reference the past, present, and future.   In Chomsky's view, it is these universal features of grammar that attest to the innateness of language in humans.

According to Chomsky, it is universal grammar that allows children to invoke complex rules of language unconsciously, even rules that are beyond the conscious understanding of most adults.   By drawing on a universal grammar, children are able to focus on and master the particular constructs, or idiosyncrasies, of their native tongue.   While unconsciously using universal rules, a child can transform a thought from its neurochemical origins into a grammatical string of words, with an efficiency that IBM could envy.

Certain fundamental constraints are inherent in a universal grammar.   An example of one such constraint is that all transformational rules must be **structure-dependent** (1975).   In order to understand what is meant by **structure-dependence** and the role it plays in language, consider the following examples of how a question is formed from a declarative sentence:

    (1)   The boy is in the room.
                Is the boy in the room?

    (2)   The book is on the table
                Is the book on the table?

If we were to write a rule governing the transformation of a declarative sentence into a question, we might propose that the sentence is read from left to right until we reach the first verbal element which we then move to the front of the sentence. If this rule is correct, example (3) would be transformed as follows:

    (3)   The boy who is ill is in the room.
                Is the boy who ill is in the room?

According to Chomsky, we understand that the above question is ungrammatical, or ill-formed, because it violates one of the basic constraints of how the human mind organizes bits of information. The universal grammar tells us that before we operate on a string of words, we must analyze the structure of the phrases and always keep the noun phrase intact (1975, pp. 30-32).

Chomsky's transformational grammar. Chomsky's transformational grammar is based on the premise that as human beings translate a thought into a grammatical utterance, they operate on two discernible levels: the **surface structure** and the **deep structure** (1957). The deep structure may be interpreted as the kernel of meaning that exists on a neurological level prior to its formulation in language. The surface structure is the sentence that is produced and articulated, once the individual phrases have been processed by the rules and/or transformations for that particular language. It is important to note that each language has its own rules and transformations. Consider the following sentences:

         John read the book.
         The book was read by John.

Although on the surface these sentences may appear to be different, their deep structure is the same. The transformation used to change the active voice into the passive is called the passive transformation. Speakers of English perform this transformation fluently without effort even though they might not be able to explain the rules governing the change.

Biological basis of language.   Nature temporarily won over nurture. Linguists no longer asked "How is language designed?" or "How can language be taught?" but rather "How does language mirror our neurological and biological design?" In fact, many of Chomsky's followers argued that language was not learned at all, but that it blossomed spontaneously as a function of biological maturation. They ask how else children could acquire the complexities of language at a time when they are not capable of intricate intellectual achievements in other domains.

Chomsky and his followers pointed to the fact that language acquisition occurs in predictable steps during specific maturational stages of development and that this capacity wanes after the onset of puberty. For these reasons, it was thought that the capacity for language must on some level be linked to biological development.

Chomsky suggested that we think of this innate capacity as the product of a linguistic organ of the mind subject to all the physical laws of biological growth. This linguistic organ was given the acronym of **LRCS** standing for **"language-responsible cognitive structure."** It provided a means to initiate the study of the biological basis for language that Eric H. Lennenberg proposed would prove that "reason, discovery and intelligence are as irrelevant for an explanation of the existence of language as for the existence of bird songs or the dance of bees" (1967, p. 1).

According to Lennenberg, the LRCS is a structural network of neurons. Although it may vary somewhat from individual to individual, as do physical organs in general, the primary function of this network is the regulation of the onset and development of language through biological and neurological processes.   In Lennenberg's scheme, the LRCS regulates a child's ability to learn its mother's tongue and fosters development during the period from birth to puberty. Lennenberg refers to this time as the **"critical period."** Although he acknowledges that it is possible to acquire a second language in adulthood, Lennenberg notes that this is only achieved through a conscious and labor-intensive effort, and then usually with an accent.

Even though second-language acquisition in adulthood is not as easily accomplished as it is in childhood, there remains no doubt that it can be done. In fact, college programs, as a rule, require the successful study of a second language. It is important to understand that language learning often occurs well beyond the critical period. Sometimes nature's way requires help, and it is the province of the educator to assist and enable children to make the most of the talents with which they were born.

Social Interactionism

The social interactionist view of language acquisition is often touted as a compromise position that allows both the nature and the nurture contenders to coexist within the stormy psycholinguistic community. It is much more, however, than a compromise position. Whereas the nature school seeks to justify their approach by focusing on the commonalties of language, social interactionists concentrate their efforts on the interaction between parent and child. Social interactionists examine how parent and child participate together, and equally, in communicative and social activities that gradually develop the linguistic, cognitive, neural, motor, perceptual, social, and affective capacities for spoken language.

Social interactionists suggest that language acquisition arises from the intense bond between parent and child. Although proponents of this theory acknowledge the role of genetic predisposition, it is, in their minds, only one contributing factor. They seek to explain the development of language by investigating the nature of the parent-child relationship from two main perspectives: the parents' role in language facilitation through child-directed speech and the child's cognitive and linguistic abilities beginning with the time prior to birth.

Parental role in child-directed speech. Child-directed speech, otherwise known as "motherese," occurs when parents, caretakers, and older children interact with infants and toddlers (Snow, 1986). Some may do this with more ease and artistic flair than others, but it appears that those with language engage in a special form of communication with young children. This form of communication is specifically designed to capture and sustain attention, and promote comprehension.

When directing speech to children, adults often, by their own standards, lose all sense of decorum. They speak with high-pitched voices and exaggerated intonation, facial expressions, and gestures. Using short, simple sentences, adults contrive conversations based on whatever appears to be of immediate interest of the child. Possible ambiguities are clarified as parents drop the pronoun "I" from their speech in order to model more immediately useful (and rewarding) vocabulary such as "mama" and "papa."

In general, child-directed speech is characterized by simplified vocabulary, abundant repetitions, and numerous invitations to participate in conversation prompted by questions and commands. From the first day of life, there is an assumption on the part of most parents that children are aware and active participants in the social milieu. Unconsciously acting on their assumption, these parents provide their children with natural models and endless occasions to practice.

Shaping child-directed speech. As children acquire language, parents and caretakers adjust their expectations of children's ability to communicate. During each stage of language acquisition, parents are always one step ahead of their children, prompting, encouraging, and otherwise increasing the range of the zone of proximal development. Initially, infant smiles, burps, and other sounds are reinforced just as though children were speaking their minds.

With time, however, parents become more selective in their reinforcement. Children who babble sequences of speech sounds vaguely identifiable as "mama" or "papa" experience effusive approval of their command of expression. Less recognizable utterances are now ignored. As children advance to the stage of telegraphic speech, they are encouraged to expand upon their utterances and include adjectives and adverbs. Trucks are no longer just trucks, they are now blue, or big, or noisy.

Parents do not set out to teach their children language. Language occurs as a result of the intense desire on the part of the caretakers and the child to bond and communicate. Even though many caretakers may not be specialists in linguistic transformations, all human beings have significant experience in the area of communication that they gladly and capably pass on to their children.

Innate abilities. One of the arguments in support of the innateness of language is that linguistic rules and their numerous exceptions simply could not be mastered without some innate sense of the acceptable forms of language. Although linguistic knowledge seems in some ways be innate, we are left with a multitude of unanswered questions concerning the biogenetic mechanisms and their interaction with both the physical and mental organs of speech. We might ask, "What is the intrinsic nature of the child? What prompts children to pay attention to language and exercise their language-related abilities? Can these processes be influenced by caretakers?" These questions go beyond Piaget's theory of egocentrism to formulate a description of what it is really like to be a child.

As part of this effort, more and more research is focusing on the sundry speech- and language-related mechanisms that are gradually tuned and integrated into verbal and non-verbal communication. As researchers delve into these areas with greater exactitude, they are examining the nature of infant experience prior to birth. Although research has traditionally begun at birth (largely due to convenience), infant experience actually begins earlier, in the womb.

Prenatal learning occurs, according to John Locke of Harvard Medical School, in a "sensational" place. Here "auditory, thermal, tactile, and other sources of sensory stimulation, as well as opportunities for movement, occur at a developmental period when much of the infant's processing machinery is already turned on" (1993, p. 23). Locke even goes so far as to suggest that certain critical decisions are made with respect to the child's nature and development prior to the child's entrance into the world. It is this acknowledgment of prenatal experience and learning that is forcing psycholinguists to reconsider capacities that were previously assigned to the relatively obscure realm of genetic predisposition or were assumed to be acquired after birth.

According to Locke, an infant seeks out and actively prompts the particular kinds of stimulation that it enjoys and that foster the development of the brain. Compared to all other stimuli, the human face, particularly that of the mother, compels the child to attend to facial movements, expression, and voice. This attentiveness initiates the child into the social community. Locke believes that as social beings, infants use strategies for language acquisition that are commonly attributed to nonnative speakers attempting to socialize with those who are fluent (1993). He describes these strategies as the infantile equivalents of:

- Participating in group activities and pretending to know what is going on.

- Choosing words carefully to give the impression that one can speak the language.

- Counting on friends for assistance.

Infants also utilize certain cognitive strategies. They actively solicit attention by using their available talents effectively. Eye contact, smiling, laughing, kicking, and speech sounds, all serve to attract notice and provide a much-desired opportunity for social intercourse. Verbal and nonverbal cues are all taken into consideration along with an implicit assumption that a conversation is relevant to its immediate surroundings. Infants seek patterns of what is already known, and they focus on the larger event allowing the details to fill in later. Finally, children learn new means of expression and they practice them actively.

Conclusion

Much research in the areas of language and cognition, and their development in children, has contributed to clarification of our understanding of the stages of language development and the nature of effective interactions to support that development. The work of philosophers, linguists, and cognitive psychologists has enhanced the range of perspectives from which we can view the nature of the language process itself.

In the opinion of the social interactionists, language is formed as the result of a closely interwoven relationship between parent and child in which each plays an active role. The child is motivated by the desire to bond and seeks the stimulation of verbal and nonverbal social interaction. The parent, as a nurturer, provides that stimulation in a form that the child is able to digest by directing speech and nonverbal cues to the communicative level of the child. In this respect, Locke's social-interactionist conceptions are in agreement with Vygotsky's views, since both conceive of learning as the product of a unique association between the generations. Vygotsky refers to a genetic predisposition for social relations; and these are enacted as the parent scaffolds the child in the zone of proximal development (1934/1986).

Social interactionists credit the innate desires to nurture, bond, and communicate with the development and the integration of linguistic, cognitive, motor, social, and affective functions. In Vygotsky's view, children experience the world through language. The social interactionists have broadened his perspective to demonstrate how children actively savor their environment through all of their senses.

References

Akmajian, A. and Demers, R. (1984). *Linguistics*. Cambridge, MA: MIT Press.

Becker, J. (1984). Implications of ethology for the study of pragmatic development. In S. Kuczaj, II (Ed.), *Discourse development: Progress in cognitive development research*. New York: Springer-Verlag.

Bloom, L. (1970). *Language development: Form and function of emerging grammars*. Cambridge, MA: MIT Press.

Bloom, L. (1973). *One word at a time: The use of single-word utterances before syntax*. The Hague: Mouton.

Bloom, L., Rocissano, L., & Hood, L. (1976). Adult-child discourse: Developmental interaction between information processing and linguistic interaction. *Cognitive Psychology*, 8, 521-552.

Braine, M. (1963). The ontology of English phrase structure: The first phrase. *Language*. 39, 1-13.

Brinton, B., Fujiki, M., Loeb, D., & Winkler, E. (1986). Development of conversational repair strategies in response to requests for clarification. *Journal of Speech and Hearing Research, 29*, 75-81.

Brown, R. (1973). *A first language: The early stages*. Cambridge, MA: Harvard University Press.

Case, R. (1980). The underlying mechanism of intellectual development. In *Cognition, development, and instruction*. New York: Academic Press.

Chomsky, C. (1969). *The acquisition of syntax in children from 5 to 10*. Cambridge, MA: MIT Press.

Chomsky, N. (1957). *Syntactic structures*. The Hague: Mounton.

Chomsky, N. (1959). Review of B.F. Skinner, *Verbal behavior*. *Language, 35*, 26-57.

Chomsky, N. (1965). *Aspects of the theory of syntax*. Cambridge, MA: MIT Press.

Chomsky, N. (1967). Review of Skinner's verbal behavior. In L.A. Jakobovits & M.S. Miron, (Eds.), *Readings in the psychology of language* (pp. 142-171). Englewood Cliffs: Prentice Hall.

Chomsky, N. (1968). *Language and mind*. New York: Harcourt, Brace & World.

Chomsky, N. (1975). *Reflections on language*. San Diego, CA: Pantheon.

Chomsky, N. (1980). *Rules and Representations*. New York: Columbia University Press.

Chomsky, N. and Walker, E. (1978) The linguistic and psycholinguistic background. In E. Walker, (Ed.), *Explorations in the biology of language* (pp.15-26). Montgomery, VT: Bradford Books.

Clark, E. (1973). What's in a word? On the child's acquisition of semantics in his first language. In T. Moore (Ed.), *Cognitive development and the acquisition of language*. New York: Academic Press.

Crain, W. (1992). *Theories of development: Concepts and applications*. Englewood Cliffs, NJ: Prentice Hall.

Damasio, A. and Damasio, H. (1992). Brain and language. *Scientific American, 267* (3), 88-111.

Deese, J. (1970). *Psycholinguistics*. Boston: Allyn & Bacon, Inc.

Denes, P. and Pinson, E. (1973). *The speech chain*. New York: Doubleday.

Ervin-Tripp, S. (1979). Children's verbal turn-taking. In E. Ochs & B. Schieffelin (Eds.), *Developmental pragmatics*. New York: Academic Press.

Ervin-Tripp, S. & Gordon, D. (1986). The development of requests. In R. Schiefelbusch (Ed.), *Language competence: Assessment and intervention*. San Diego, CA: College-Hill Press.

Fischer, K.W. (1980). A theory of cognitive development: The control and construction of hierarchies of skills. *Psychological Review, 87*(6), 477- 531.

Fischer, K.W. (1987). *Cognitive development in real children: Levels and variations*. Paper presented at the Conference on Teaching Thinking and At-risk Students, November, Philadelphia, PA.

Francis, W.N. (1958). *The structure of English*. New York: The Ronald Press Company.

Gallager, T. (1977). Revision behaviors in the speech of normal children developing language. *Journal of Speech and Hearing Research, 20*, 303-318.

Gardner, H. (1983). *Frames of mind*. New York: Basic Books.

Gardner, H. (1993). *Multiple intelligences: The theory in practice*. New York:Basic Books.

Gardner, A., & Gardner, B. (1969). Teaching sign language to a chimpanzee, *Science, 165*, 664-672.

Gardner, A., Gardner, B. (1975). Evidence for sentence constituents in early utterances of child and chimpanzee, *Journal of Experimental Psychology, 104*, 244-267.

Gazzaniga, M. S. (1993). *Nature's mind: The biological roots of thinking, emotions, sexuality, language, and intelligence*. New York: Basic Books.

Ginsburg, H. and Opper, S. (1988). *Piaget's theory of intellectual development (3rd ed.)*. Englewood Cliffs, NJ: Prentice Hall.

Greenfield, P. & Smith, J. (1976). *The structure of communication in early language development*. New York: Academic Press.

Hallahan, D.P., & Kauffman, J.M. (1993). *Exceptional children: Introduction to special education*. Boston: Allyn and Bacon.

Halliday, M. (1975). *Learning how to mean: Explorations in the development of language*. New York: Edward Arnold.

Hockett, C. (1968). *The state of the art*. Paris: Mouton.

Horgan, D. (1978). The development of the full passive. *Journal of Child Language, 5*, 65-80.

Hulit, L. and Howard, M. (1993). *Born to talk: An introduction to speech and language development*. New York: Macmillan Publishing Company.

James, S. (1990). *Normal language acquisition*. Austin, TX: Pro-Ed.

Klima E. & Bellugi, U. (1966). Syntactic regularities in the speech of children. In J. Lyons & R. Wales (Eds.), *Psycholinguistic Papers*. Edinburgh: Edinburgh University Press.

Lennenberg, E. (1967). *Biological foundations of language*. New York: Wiley.

Locke, J.L. (1983). *Phonological acquisition and change*. New York: Academic Press.

98

Locke, J.L. (1993). *The child's path to spoken language*. Cambridge:Harvard University Press.

Nelson, K. (1973). Structure and strategy in learning to talk. *Monographs of the Society for Research in Child Development, 38.*

Newmeyer, F.J. (1980). *Linguistic theory in America: The first quarter-century of transformational grammar*. New York: Academic Press.

Ornstein, R. (1986). *Multimind: A new way of looking at human behavior*. New York: Anchor Books.

Piaget, J. (1962). *Play, dreams and imitation in childhood*. (C. Gattegno and F.M. Hodgson, Trans.). New York: W.W. Norton & Co. (Original work published 1946.)

Piaget, J. (1968). *Six psychological studies*. (A. Tenzer and D. Elkind, Trans.). New York: Vintage Books. (Original work published 1964.)

Piaget, J. (1973). *The child and reality*. (A. Rosen, Trans.). New York: Grossman Publishers. (Original work published 1972.)

Piaget, J. (1974). *The language and thought of the child*. (M. Gabain, Trans.). New York: Meridian. (Original work published 1923.)

Piaget, J. (1974). *The origins of intelligence in children*. (M. Cook, Trans.). New York: International Universities Press. (Original work published 1936.)

Rath, L. (1987). *Child language and education*. Unpublished manuscript.

Siegel-Causey, E., & Wetherby, A. (1993). Nonsymbolic communication. In M.E. Snell (Ed.), *Instruction of students with severe disabilities 4th ed*. New York: Merrill.

Skinner, B.F. (1957). *Verbal behavior*. Englewood Cliffs, NJ: Prentice Hall.

Skinner, B.F. (1967). Thinking. In L.A. Jakobovits & M.S. Mirron (Eds.), *Readings in the psychology of language* (pp.128-141). Englewood Cliffs, NJ: Prentice Hall.

Skinner, B.F. (1948). *Walden Two*. New York: Macmillan.

Slobin, D.I. (1979). *Psycholinguistics (2nd ed.)*. Glenville, IL: Scott, Foresman and Company.

Snow, C. (1986). Conversations with children. In P. Fletcher & M. Garman (Eds.), *Language acquisition: Studies in first language development*. Cambridge: Cambridge University Press.

Stark, R. (1979). Prespeech segmental feature development. In P. Fletcher & M. Garman (Eds.), *Language Acquisition*. New York: Cambridge University Press.

Stark, R. (1980). Stages of speech development in the first years of life. In G.H. Yeni-Komshian, J.F. Kavanagh, and C.A. Ferguson (Eds.), *Child phonology: Vol. 1. Production*. New York: Academic Press.

Terrace, H.S. (1979). *Nim*. New York: Alfred A. Knopf.

von Raffler-Engel, W. (1973). The development from sound to phoneme in child language. In C. Ferguson & D. Slobin (Eds.), *Studies of child language development*. New York: Holt, Rinehart & Winston.

Vygotsky, L.S. (1978). *Mind in society*. In M. Cole, V. John-Steiner, S. Scribner, & E. Souberman, (Eds.) Cambridge, MA: Harvard University Press. (Work written in 1930.)

Vygotsky, L.S. (1986). *Thought and language* (A. Kosulin, Trans.). Cambridge, MA: MIT Press. (Original work published 1934.)

Walker, E. (1978). Current studies of animal communication as paradigms for the biology of language. In E. Walker (Ed.), *Explorations in the biology of language* (pp.203-218). Montgomery, VT: Bradford Books.

Winograd, T. (1983). *Language as a cognitive process: Vol. 1. Syntax.* Reading, MA: Addison-Wesley Publishing Company.

Chapter 3. Phonemic Awareness: Segmenting and Blending the Sounds of Language

Linda K. Rath, EdD
Harvard University

Phonemic awareness is said to be the *sine qua non* of reading acquisition for an alphabetic language and a major source of individual variation in reading and spelling performance for students of all ages (Liberman & Shankweiler, 1979; Stanovich, 1986). Findings related to phonemic awareness suggest practical ways to predict reading achievement, promote reading success, and prevent reading failure. This chapter provides an overview of these findings and presents a set of suggestions for implementing them in the classroom and clinic.

The term "phonemic awareness" was adopted recently by linguists and cognitive psychologists in an effort to explain one of the many complex processes involved in literacy acquisition. **Phonemic awareness** is an understanding that spoken words can be decomposed structurally into sound units, called phonemes. This awareness allows one to analyze a spoken word into phoneme segments and to blend or manipulate the segments to form a new word. Phonemic awareness plays a key role in literacy acquisition. When learners realize that speech is composed of discrete sound units, they can then begin to learn how to associate speech sounds with the letters they see in print.

Although the term **phonemic awareness** is new, the concept is not. In decades past, numerous educators examined these issues under other names. Describing similar findings, earlier researchers called the underlying processes **auditory perception, blending,** or **analysis** (Chall, et al. 1963; Monroe, 1932; Rosner, 1974; Vernon, 1957), and even **ear-training** or **reading readiness** (Dolch & Bloomster, 1937; Gates & Bond, 1937).

The 1980s heard the optimistic claims of many researchers who agreed that in **phonemic awareness** they had isolated a key to reading acquisition. Research findings on the subject were hailed as "the single most powerful advance in the science and pedagogy of reading this century" (Adams et al., 1991, p. 392). Meanwhile, national assessments over the same decade reflected declining scores on tests of reading achievement. National Assessment of Educational Progress (NAEP) data indicated a leveling off in scores among 9-year-olds from 1980-1984, a steep decline between 1984 and 1986, especially among the lowest achievers, and further slippage in subsequent years (Mullis & Jenkins, 1990; NAEP, 1985). It is now common to find increasing numbers of public school students in primary grades labeled "learning disabled" because they have encountered problems with reading acquisition.

As often occurs, there has been a mismatch between progress in theory and progress in practice, between the research on reading development and the reality of reading education. The purpose of this chapter is to highlight recent discoveries and old truths about phonemic awareness and its potential role in the prevention of reading failure. We examine this component of reading ability in an effort to synthesize and present important evidence that can be used to inform and improve instructional practice.

What Is Phonemic Awareness?

Phonemic awareness refers to an individual's knowledge that spoken words are composed of discrete sound units. Changing one of these phoneme units will create a new and different word. For example, in the words "bit" and "pit" only the initial phonemes are different, /b/ and /p/, and this leads to two different words. Phonemes vary considerably based on the context in which they occur, and they are "coarticulated" with other sounds in words—overlapping so as to be hard to distinguish as individual units. This abstract and elusive quality of phonemes makes them difficult for young children to grasp (Liberman & Shankweiler, 1979; Read, 1978).

While five-year-olds may not be aware of specific phonemic distinctions, their implicit phonemic understanding enables them to comprehend spoken language. In fact, most humans are adept at **implicit** phonemic processing—perceiving the difference between *pin* and *pen*, or *wet* and *went*, especially in the context of a meaningful utterance. However, as individuals, we are strikingly diverse in our ability to segment, analyze, and synthesize these sounds consciously, in order to perform deliberate phoneme manipulations (Rozin & Gleitman, 1977).

Speaking and listening seem to be performed with relative consistency from person to person and are thought to be biologically determined; as humans we are born with this capacity to communicate by speaking and listening (Mattingly, 1972). In contrast, other linguistic activities or skills are thought to be secondary, and not necessarily natural for humans. Reading, writing, or even speaking Pig Latin, are such secondary linguistic behaviors. They rely on one's awareness of and ability to **process** language, controlling and manipulating it as a medium. In this more abstract behavior, individual variation can be far ranging.

Variation in language awareness. To demonstrate phonemic awareness in particular, one must pay attention to the sounds of words rather than to their meanings. This requires a shift in attention from an automatic focus on the message to a more deliberate, analytic focus on the words as objects in and of themselves (Lundberg, 1978). These and similar concerns for the forms of language are called *meta*linguistic behaviors. Tasks that are used to assess phonemic awareness are often called *meta*phonology tasks. They require that the sound units of words be recognized, identified, segmented, blended, manipulated, and the like.

Language awareness might be thought of as a broad continuum that has very skillful metalinguistic performers at one end and poor performers at the other. The most metalinguistically adept individuals demonstrate extraordinary keenness for language forms and the subtle possibilities of sound and sense. For example, author Natalie Babbitt writes:

> The alphabet is still a miracle to me—how those twenty-six funny shapes can group themselves in endlessly different ways to make words with endlessly different meanings. I still play alphabet games with myself, games like trying to think of five words that are exactly the same except for the vowels, like bAg, bEg, bIg, bOg and bUg. Just by changing the vowels, you can utterly change the meaning (1986, p. 43).

While this exquisite delight in our written language system may be common among poets and linguists, it is not something that the typical reader or speaker of English ordinarily celebrates.

In order to become competent at reading and writing English, a learner must possess enough awareness to be able to note how phonemic elements are represented in our alphabetic writing system. Those who experience reading disability are often unable to make this connection and generally tend to be at the low end of the language awareness continuum. Along with a reading disability, they are likely to have difficulty with other complex language processing skills.

Researchers studying disabled readers have found that they often misunderstand spoken sentences containing embedded clauses, are unaware of morphological connections between words, and have a hard time detecting ambiguity and analyzing syntactic structure (Bialystok & Mitterer, 1987; Crain, 1989; Johnson, 1986; Menyuk & Flood, 1981). In a recent study of reading disabled young adults, one subject's insight summed up their experience: "I know I talk it alright, but I just don't know language." (Blalock, 1982, p. 608).

ACQUIRING KNOWLEDGE OF SOUNDS AND SYMBOLS

A learner with an awareness of the phonemic structure of spoken language has gained an underlying ability crucial to the acquisition of literacy. Once a learner develops phonemic awareness, the correspondences between phonemes and graphemes (letter symbols) in written English can be mastered. Phonemic awareness is the insight upon which spelling knowledge depends. Learners must then discover how the forty-two phonemes of English are represented by the twenty-six letters of the alphabet.

Acquiring a general knowledge of sound/symbol correspondence is a special challenge in English because of the complexities of the English spelling system (*orthography*). Ours is a "morpho-phonemic" system, one that sacrifices the simplicity of one-to-one sound-symbol relationships in order to reflect meaning-based connections (Chomsky, 1970). For example, in the words "nation" and its derivative "national," the letter "a" is preserved even though it represents a different sound. In the word "sign," a silent "g" remains as a trace to make the connection to "signature" more apparent.

If our spelling system had perfect one-to-one correspondence, the word pairs "nation" and "national" or "sign" and "signature" would look very different from one another. Our alphabet symbols are able to map phonemes, one by one, while at the same time preserving morphemes (units of **meaning**, like "sign"). Flexible and sophisticated enough to include words from many languages, the English spelling system, alas, is not user-friendly for beginning readers and writers.

PHONEMIC PROCESSING SKILL

In addition to phonemic awareness and knowledge of English spellings, a learner's **phonemic processing skill** is a factor in reading and spelling performance. One must possess the ability to perform segmental speech acts, to hold the segments in short-term memory, and to blend sounds to form words (or blend words to form larger units of meaning). For example, imagine a first grader who encounters the following sentence while reading independently: *Suddenly, it started to rain.*

Many young readers will substitute the more familiar *Sunday* for *suddenly*. Their understanding of the sentence, then, may be somewhat different from what the author intended. Learners who are more successful can segment "sud-den-ly" into chunks, try out different sounds while maintaining the letter sequence, reblend the word, and crosscheck to make sure that it makes sense in context. This is an extremely complicated process, requiring several precise and controlled steps. It is an impossible task to accomplish for a young learner without phonemic awareness and/or with a language-processing disorder.

PHONEMIC AWARENESS AND LEARNING 'PHONICS'

Phonics instruction for beginning readers aims to present the correspondences between letters and the speech sounds they commonly represent. With its emphasis on *decoding* the symbols of written language, phonics as a method of instruction was once thought to be successful only when children had achieved a certain "mental age" or "readiness" for reading (Dolch & Bloomster, 1937). But earlier researchers also noted that children who easily learned to read noticed the separate sounds in spoken words (Durrell & Murphy, 1953). For decades, perhaps even centuries, educators have recommended activities that focus on rhyme, alliteration, and within-word sound patterns to provide the "ear-training" necessary as a foundation for instruction in the principles of phonics.

Now, it is widely acknowledged that **phonemic awareness**, rather than mental age, is the pre-requisite that enables instruction in phonics to be effective. Moreover, phonemic awareness and phonics instruction seem to interact. Direct instruction in spelling and decoding of printed letters (phonics instruction) serves to foster phonemic awareness. Thus, the phonic method may be a vehicle for teaching phonemic awareness, which, in turn, enables the acquisition of reading skill.

Whereas experts in prior decades spoke more globally of the optimum mental age and "readiness" for reading, more-recent studies explore the specific understandings and misunderstandings of children and the cognitive demands of each particular task. For example, many researchers have found that preschool children are frequently confused about what is meant by "word" or "sound." When asked, "Which word is longer, 'snake' or 'butterfly'?" preschool children commonly say "snake," because they all know that snakes are long and skinny. When asked, "What is the first sound in 'cat'?" they are likely to say "MEOW!" For these children, conventional phonics instruction is sure to be confusing at first. As they gain more experience with language **forms** in books and environmental print, as they learn to rhyme, match words and sounds, note letters, etc., such children stand a better chance of understanding how language is represented by the features of print.

In general, the emphasis of current research represents a continued movement away from a global notion of "readiness" (Chall & Stahl, 1981). Investigators of literacy acquisition are offering more specific delineations of the numerous interactive processes needed for learning to read and of the various abilities and understandings required for the execution of each process.

How Phonemic Awareness Relates to Reading and Spelling Achievement

Dozens of studies have been conducted in recent years to "operationalize" the concept of phonemic awareness and to explore its importance as a predictor of subsequent reading achievement, an enabler of literacy progress, and a marker of reading disability. The following section presents a brief summary of the research on phonemic awareness as a predictor and an enabler. A discussion of phonemic awareness as a marker of reading disability will be presented later in the chapter.

PHONEMIC AWARENESS AS A PREDICTOR

Researchers have found that children in kindergarten display a broad range of individual variation when asked to perform tasks that require attention to words as objects containing sounds. In some of these tasks, kindergartners match and produce rhyming words or words that begin with the same sound. In another task they blend together familiar words that are made from segments slowly spoken by the examiner (e.g. /f/.../æ/.../t/ = fat). More difficult tasks ask kindergartners to count sound segments as they speak words slowly, or to isolate each sound as they pronounce a word. The strength of a child's performance is likely to predict later achievement on measures such as standardized reading and spelling tests (Stanovich, Cunningham, & Cramer, 1984).

In one extensive study, for example, researchers administered a phoneme segmentation task to 534 children at the beginning of kindergarten. Twenty months later, at the end of first grade, the same students took a reading achievement test battery. It turned out that their rankings on the summed achievement tests closely mirrored the rankings they had achieved on the phoneme segmentation task (Share, Jorm, Maclean, & Matthews, 1984).

A simpler task to administer, a spelling test that encourages and analyzes "invented spelling," can be given at the end of kindergarten or the beginning of grade one. When this type of task is used to estimate phonemic awareness, correlations with later reading achievement scores are moderate to strong (Mann, Tobin, & Wilson, 1984; Morris & Perney, 1984; Zifcak, 1981).

This strong relationship between phonemic awareness and reading achievement is found so consistently that educators commonly agree that phonemic awareness is the best predictor we know of reading achievement in the primary grades. It surpasses other factors such as IQ, general language proficiency, socioeconomic background, and even knowledge of alphabet letters (Adams, 1990; Griffith & Olson, 1992).

Clearly, kindergartners with a high level of phonemic awareness will have a head start in first grade. This superior preparedness enables them to out-perform agemates on all aspects of reading, from spelling, to word reading, to reading comprehension. Of course, comprehension of contextual materials in the lower grades is rarely a conceptual challenge; if the words can be decoded, the simple stories with familiar vocabulary can be understood (Chall, 1983).

When such a strong correlation is found between variables in education, the next question is often: "Is this a **causal** connection?" In other words, does phonemic awareness **cause** growth in literacy, or does it, perhaps, represent some other underlying factor, such as exposure to print or experience with books? To answer this question, researchers have conducted numerous experimental studies in which some groups of children receive special phonemic awareness training and are compared to untrained "control groups" who come from similar backgrounds with similar educational profiles.

PHONEMIC AWARENESS AS AN ENABLER

In these experimental studies, a variety of interventions that foster phonemic awareness were found to enhance student achievement on subsequent phonemic awareness tasks and on reading and spelling achievement tests. Children who receive specific training consistently and significantly out-perform their control-group peers. Interventions have proven to be successful with kindergartners in whole-class instruction, before they are even introduced to formal reading instruction (Lundberg, Frost, & Petersen, 1988; Rosner, 1974).

Other successful interventions have included phonemic awareness as an important component in early reading instruction, linking phonemic awareness to letter knowledge and the analysis of spoken words to printed word analysis. Using concrete objects, like blocks or moveable letters, researchers have helped children, individually and in small groups, by demonstrating the match between within-word sounds and the letters we use to represent them (Blachman, 1987; Bradley & Bryant, 1985; Ehri & Wilce, 1987; Elkonin, 1973; Wallach & Wallach, 1979; Williams, 1979).

A few interventions have been conducted with older students, underachievers or Special Education students. In these studies, as well, activities that required phoneme segmentation and blending improved student performance on subsequent phonemic awareness tasks and on follow-up tests of word and passage reading (Torneus, 1984; Vellutino & Scanlon, 1987; Williams, 1980).

Because of this strong evidence from experimental studies, researchers are confident that there is a **causal** connection between variables. Phonemic awareness **enables** progress in literacy development, at least in terms of promoting skills such as decoding and encoding with accuracy. Without intervention, children who lack phonemic awareness at the beginning of first grade are likely to fall behind their peers in reading and spelling achievement.

This was the case for a group of ten first graders who were studied by Fox and Routh (1983). At the end of grade one, these students performed poorly on a phoneme segmentation task. Their average word-reading achievement scores fell two years behind the average scores of their classmates. The same students were tested again at age ten. At this point, they could perform well on the phoneme-segmentation task, but they had **all** repeated a grade in school, and their reading and spelling test scores were still falling below the class average. Predictably, without some type of intervention, lack of phonemic awareness becomes a reading disability. This is what has become known as "Matthew Effects" in reading: the poor keep getting poorer while the rich are getting richer (Stanovich, 1986).

What about those students who are "rich" in phonemic awareness when they come to school? What might be the source of this awareness? What type of developmental course does it follow?

Stages and Sequence in Phonemic Awareness Development

Normally, many children demonstrate implicit or tacit phonemic awareness in the preschool years. They engage in play with rhyming and nonsense words (sometimes endlessly and to the exasperation of their parents). By age five they can usually recognize rhyming words and tell when words begin with the same sound (Chomsky, 1979).

Explicit language awareness comes later, usually by age six or seven, and often by virtue of formal instruction. It is the focused, guided attention to the details of written language, which gives rise to a more analytic, systematic awareness of language forms, that is crucial for the development of competence as a reader and writer.

Several studies published in educational journals during the 1980s suggest a sequence of development that leads to an increasing refinement of phonemic awareness (Lewkowicz, 1980; Stanovich, Cunningham, & Cramer, 1984; Yopp, 1988). Taken together, these studies provide a fairly consistent picture of developing skill, which confirms earlier studies by Chall et al. (1963), Bruce (1964), and Rosner & Simon (1971). The sequence appears to be unvarying, systematic, and perhaps developmentally determined. Below, I have synthesized this research into a description of the sequence in which phonemic awareness is likely to develop for a typical, English-speaking child.

By age five, many children demonstrate:

1. ...awareness of the word as a discrete unit.

2. ...awareness of the syllable as a discrete unit. For example, they can segment multi-syllable words into syllables and tap or count the syllables. They can delete a syllable, giving an appropriate response when asked to "say cowboy without the cow."

Somewhat later, as kindergartners, many children are able to perform:

3. ...rhyme identification, particularly if they are given examples to judge.

4. ...initial consonant matching. They can identify words with the same beginning consonant and may be able to produce initial consonant matches. These partial segmentation tasks are an early form of explicit phonemic awareness. It is at this point in development that some children begin to produce invented spelling, if their knowledge of letter names is strong.

5. ...partial phoneme segmentation. Having mastered steps 1-4, a child is next able to segment a spoken syllable into two parts (C-V; V-C; or C-VC). This skill of splitting a syllable into an **onset** and **rime** is described at length by Adams (1990).

...phoneme synthesis (blending) can often be achieved at this stage, particularly with two spoken segments to be blended into one (V-C more easily than C-V).

By age six, many children are able to perform:

6. ...final sound matching and segmenting of simple spoken words (CV-C).

...blending together of two more complex segments (first CV-C, then C-VC or CC-VC).

Somewhat later, many children have learned to perform:

7. ...blending of three spoken phoneme segments (C-V-C or CC-V-C). While this task is difficult for kindergartners and for many first graders, it can be learned. Helfgott (1976) found that blending (C-V-C) was generally simpler than segmenting for her kindergarten sample, and Yopp's data (1988) confirm this order.

...complete phoneme segmentation: saying, tapping, counting, and marking phonemes. At this stage, children can be encouraged to use invented spelling to represent phoneme segments. This depends on knowledge of letter names and their sounds, which adds additional demands to the task.

By age 8, many children can perform:

8. ...advanced phoneme segmentation. However, peeling apart consonant clusters into individual phonemes continues to be difficult for some subjects through the elementary years and even into adulthood (Rath, 1994).

9. ...phoneme manipulation tasks. These comprise Yopp's "compound" category, for they require segmentation plus deletion, reversal, or substitution, and then re-blending of a word. Most kindergarten children and many first graders are unable to perform these compound phonemic awareness tasks, which prove to be more appropriate measures for older students. Rosner & Simon's *Auditory Analysis Test* (1971) is organized according to their predictions of rank order of difficulty in deleting spoken sounds—syllables and phonemes. From kindergarten to grade six, individuals progress quite systematically through the test levels, deleting initial consonants, final consonants, then medial consonants (e.g. "Say 'man' without the /m/"; "say 'steak' without the /k/"; "say 'desk' without the /s/.").

Although the **sequence** of development appears to be unvarying, the **rate** of development varies widely and depends upon many interacting factors related to nature (constitution/neurophysiology/heredity) and nurture (environment/ instruction/experience).

With regard to "nurture," it appears that phonemic awareness only develops under certain conditions. Unlike verbal communication, it does not simply "emerge" in all individuals at a specific point in development, regardless of culture and experience. For example, illiterate adults who have not learned to read the alphabetic language that they speak also do not demonstrate phonemic awareness (Morais et al., 1979). Expert readers in a non-alphabetic language, such as Chinese, also tend to perform poorly on phonemic awareness tasks (Read et al., 1986). From this evidence, we can gather that phonemic awareness development depends on successful experiences with the alphabetic features of a written language.

Even among able students learning to use an alphabetic writing system, the phonemic properties of the language often need to be demonstrated explicitly and concretely. Insight into the phonemic structure of English rarely occurs without some formal or informal instruction that highlights within-word sounds (Byrne, 1984; Gough & Hillinger, 1980).

However, some preschoolers seem to be remarkably sensitive to language sounds and adept at tasks that require phonemic awareness. Others are just as insensitive and oblivious. The source of this individual variation has been a topic of interest to researchers in the 1980s, particularly because it has **not** proven to be correlated as strongly with "mental age" as had been previously supposed. While standard IQ measures generally account for a small portion of the variation in performance, other factors play an even stronger role.

NORMAL VARIATION

Several recent correlational studies have explored the factors that might explain variation in phonemic awareness. Some investigators hypothesize that a child must be able to engage in concrete operational thought as a correlate of phonemic awareness, since a focus on form, rather than meaning, is required. They find that there is a moderate, but statistically significant, relationship among a child's performance on a battery of Piagetian conservation tasks, a phoneme-tapping task, and a syntactic awareness task (Tunmer et al., 1988).

Another study of first graders also documents a significant relationship between phonemic awareness and comprehension of complex spoken sentences (Mann et al., 1987). Researchers in England have found that the mother's education and a child's knowledge of common nursery rhymes account for considerable variation in the phonemic awareness of preschoolers (Maclean et al., 1987).

A vast body of ethnographic research has been building steadily through the decade as well, presenting "naturalistic" examples of how literacy-related activities foster reading acquisition. Researchers have tried to describe how and why children begin, before receiving formal instruction in school, to learn to read. (See, for example, Durkin, 1966; Mason, 1980.) The term "emergent literacy" is used to describe those literacy-related behaviors that are the explorations of novices into the domain of written language. (See Anderson et al., 1985; Teale, 1986.)

Some studies describe family and cultural environments that foster or inhibit early literacy (Heath, 1986; Taylor, 1983). Specific, scaffolded interactions between child and adult are reported in great detail (Bissex, 1980; Snow 1983). In many of these descriptions, a storybook is used as an opportunity to teach a child about the conventions of literacy, including sign-symbol relations (Snow & Ninio, 1986). The story does not merely get read, but adult and child collaborate to build the knowledge of code and convention that will lead to independent reading. The "big books" included in a "Whole Language" approach are meant to replicate this literacy experience, giving children a chance to interact with good books and adults who know how to present them interactively (Holdaway, 1979).

In addition to frequent storybook reading events, writing and spelling activities are prominent in the lives of emergent readers. Ferreiro (1986) documented the discoveries of two precocious preschoolers as they explored the letter-sounds in their own names and the names of family members. Others have shown how systematically inventive spellers make progress from early stages of scribbling to increasingly phonetic spelling as their phonemic awareness becomes more sophisticated (Bissex, 1980; Chomsky, 1979; Clay, 1975; Read, 1971).

While some stress that it is the desire to communicate that drives inventive spellers, that making meaning is critical (Sulzby, 1986; Wells, 1986), others note that inventive spellers are often unconcerned with audience and product; it is the **process** of representing sounds with letters that engages their attention (Read, 1978). Families that foster preschool inventive spellers have a number of things in common: storybook reading is frequent, adults spend time reading and writing for their own purposes, alphabet learning has been valued and advanced through playful as well as rote behavior, and environmental tolerance for spelling errors is high (Read, 1971).

While invented spellings may serve as one window into the development of phonemic awareness (Mann et al., 1987), this behavior does not always lead to an easy entry into reading. Bissex (1980) documents her son's frustrations in learning how to **de**code conventional spellings. Having learned how to map sounds onto plausible symbols, he had to accommodate his logical system to the more complex and less predictable patterns of English orthography.

Schickedanz (1990) records her son's journey through the creative literacy playground of his kindergarten year and into the obstacle course of first grade. She provides the scaffolding he needs to scale these obstacles, leaving the reader to wonder why such assistance is not provided by the teacher. These case studies of individual learners show how many tricky little steps there are in the literacy-acquisition process. They describe confusions and difficulties encountered by even the brightest and most phonemically aware. More than demonstrating how "natural" it is to learn to read, these studies reveal that children need a great deal of guidance along the way from responsive, perceptive, well informed adults.

Our English spelling system is complex, and, unfortunately, many high-frequency words are not spelled as they sound. Even the simplest storybooks for young children contain words that contradict the patterns and principles that children need to learn at the early stages. For this reason, some researchers argue that **writing** (phonetic encoding) is the simpler, more accessible skill for young children and can serve as useful preparation for a guided entry into reading. Many years ago, Montessori (1912) was convinced by her observations of preschoolers that spelling/sounding activities should precede reading efforts, as a self-generative and active way for children to use their knowledge and curiosity. Her argument has been taken up more recently by Bissex (1980), Chomsky (1971), Frith (1986), and Read (1981).

SUMMARY

Much work has been done to explain the development of phonemic awareness, its correlates, and the conditions that promote its growth. Exposure to nursery rhymes during storytime, and focused attention to print on signs in the environment, appear to be important experiences for stimulating phonemic awareness. Scaffolded interaction between adult and child, through sharing an interest in letters, signs, words, messages, and stories, is central in early literacy development. Clearly, interest has grown in the writing-and-reading connection and in the constructive process of mapping sounds with letters to develop an awareness that will enable reading in the early stages.

While there has been some consensus in the field, arguments and debates continue. On the one hand, many argue that literacy is a natural, developing process that emerges gradually in environments that emphasize and celebrate the communicative purposes of print. On the other hand, some researchers persistently ask about those children who do **not** acquire the conventions of literacy in a print-rich, book-loving, story-writing environment. The following section surveys the studies that examine children with severe reading and spelling difficulties and highlights the role of phonemic awareness in their problematic literacy development.

Phonemic Awareness and Reading Disabilities

An abundance of recent research has examined the symptoms, causes, and correlates of extreme individual variation in literacy acquisition. In general, a theory of dyslexia as a language-based disorder has gained wide-spread acceptance. In particular, a lack of phonemic awareness has emerged as one of a number of reliable markers of developmental dyslexia. To explain the characteristics of developmental dyslexia, the following definition is often used:

> A disorder manifested by difficulties with learning to read despite conventional instruction, adequate intelligence, and socioeconomic

opportunity. It is dependent upon fundamental cognitive disabilities, which are frequently constitutional in origin (Critchley, 1970, p. 11).

The constitutional origin of dyslexia is currently thought to be traceable to disorders in language processing mechanisms (Vellutino, 1978). One (or several) of these mechanisms affect the development of linguistic awareness in general and phonemic awareness in particular. In addition to this, or, perhaps, as a cause or consequence, a deficit in short-term memory for verbal information contributes to a slow rate in storing the precisely sequenced sound segments of spoken words (Byrne & Shea, 1979; Katz, 1986; Mann, 1984; Vellutino & Scanlon, 1987).

The lively discussions of different subtypes of dyslexia that appeared in journals of the '70s are rarely seen in journals today. Formerly, individuals with severe spelling problems, who mangle letter order (e.g., "nature" = "nartue"), were thought to have specific visual-perceptual disorders, and were called "diseidetic." These spelling difficulties are now thought to be "artifacts of deficiencies in verbal processing or of selective attention" (Chall & Stahl, 1981, p. 1546).

NEUROLOGICAL ASPECTS

Neuroscientists have tried to locate the cause(s) of developmental dyslexia by examining brain cell structure (autopsy studies), EEGs, and computer images of the working brain as it responds to different tasks. They have found that some dyslexics have an atypical brain structure, with a hemispheric symmetry that is not found in most brains (Galaburda, 1985). It may be that delays in neuronal migration during fetal life result in unusual patterns of neural circuitry that make particular language-processing tasks difficult for dyslexics (Geschwind, 1986). Some dyslexics have been found to project unusual left parietal waveforms in CAT scans (Hynd & Semrud-Clikeman, 1989). The neurological anomalies that may be sources of reading dysfunction, and their effects on reading, are discussed in further detail below.

Phonemic sequencing disorder. The difficulty dyslexics have with segmenting and analyzing speech sounds is currently hypothesized to be part of a broader dysfunction in executing sequential motor programs in general. Dyslexics often display what are called "soft signs" of neuropathology: their finger-tapping responses are awkward, eye-movement patterns are agitated, and nonsense syllable repetitions are halting and inaccurate. These individuals often have difficulty with other fine motor tasks such as handwriting, dancing, or piano playing. In fact, the same nervous system pathways that subserve sequenced motor behavior are those that subserve speech production (Wolff, 1989). Evidence suggests that a single mechanism, such as precise timing, is the common denominator for both fine-motor performance and for sequential speech acts (Ojemann cited in Gibson, 1988).

A motor organization/timing theory is one promising explanation for the severity of the problem some individuals have with processing and producing speech sounds sequentially. Adult poor readers consistently have difficulty when asked to remember and repeat numbers, letters, or words (Read & Ruyter 1985). It seems to be the **production** of sounds in sequence rather than **discrimination** that is difficult for many with a reading disorder (Catts, 1986). Since the fine-motor pathway for speech is located in the peri-Sylvian language region of the left hemisphere (Rudel, 1988), it may be that the Galaburda/Geschwind focus on structural anomalies located on the left side of the brain is the apt locus of causality for this particular syndrome.

Selective attention dysfunction. Another theory implicates "control processing," also called "executive function," as the mechanism that is at fault in dyslexic subjects (Bialystok & Mitterer, 1987). Dyslexics have difficulty "changing horses in midstream" (Denckla, 1983), as in shifting attention from meaning to form, or from bottom-up to top-down processing. An interaction between information processing strategies is a crucial part of fluent reading (Lesgold & Perfetti, 1982).

Dyslexics appear to be more single-minded than normal readers and less able to switch focus to integrate processes at the appropriate time, or to exhibit an organized, planful approach. Denckla (1983) notes dyslexics' inability to "pull back" from language meanings and focus on language forms. She questions a "missing link" in their efforts to learn to read—a lack of awareness about the phonemic structure of words.

Other neurologists have observed signs in dyslexics of "a lack of appropriate cortical arousal that may signal problems in the capacity for selective focused attention" (Kirk, 1989, p. 24). Denckla (1983) also noted an "underactivation of frontal contribution" in the brains of dyslexics that might be responsible for a dyslexic's "disorganization and mis-allocation of cerebral resources" (p. 40).

Clearly, the issues of phonemic processing and awareness have emerged as central in the profile of dyslexia, if not its cause. A recent medical journal definitively refers to dyslexia as a "specific aptitude deficit, leading to underachievement in reading by children of otherwise normal intelligence" (Rosenberger, 1992). The aptitude that appears to be lacking in dyslexics is that aptitude for *meta*linguistics, for analyzing sounds or words in sequence.

Again, the cause of such a deficit may be a disorder in the motor system for speech, which causes difficulties in sequential processing of linguistic elements. Alternatively (or in addition), it may be that a disorder in the pre-frontal cortex causes a selective-attention problem that impedes fluent switching between meaning and form. This might delay the dawn of phonemic awareness for some affected subjects. Perhaps further research will clarify these two factors and explain the ways in which they are differentiated and interrelated.

DEFICIT OR DELAY?

Progress has been made in resolving the question of dyslexia's status as a deficit or a developmental delay. The majority of the evidence points toward an existing deficit that holds back performance and knowledge acquisition.

Evidence for deficit among dyslexics. Dyslexics are significantly less adept than their "reading-age mates" (younger, normal readers who are matched on achievement test scores) on a number of oral tasks: in segmenting and manipulating speech sounds, particularly in segmenting consonant blends (Morais, et al., 1984) and Pig-Latin production (Olson et al., 1989); in repeating nonsense words (Snowling, et al., 1986); and in producing rhymes (Bryant & Bradley, 1985; Read & Ruyter, 1985). One study concludes that dyslexic subjects have a "unique phonological coding deficit" that is "highly heritable" but also somewhat responsive to intensive, phonics-based training (Olson et al., 1989).

Snowling et al. suggest that dyslexics have a systemic difficulty in establishing "a new articulatory-motor programme" (p. 80), and that this causes their poor performance on nonword repetition tasks. They further argue:

> If they find the repetition of nonwords difficult, then new word learning will be compromised. It follows that dyslexics may take longer to establish lexical representations for words which they encounter auditorily than age-matched normal readers (1986, p. 515).

In other words, a systemic difficulty/deficit within an individual's naming/speech production system interferes with literacy development. This dysfunction limits their ability to build word knowledge, so that many dyslexics are slower to expand their meaning vocabulary as well as their recognition of infrequent words in print. They need considerably more time and practice than most in learning new words.

In addition, dyslexics seem to be slower in terms of learning and applying the alphabetic principle. Many do not seem to realize that the letters in words encode the speech sounds in precise order. Researchers have found that dyslexics are less able to induce and/or use rules and patterns for solving verbal tasks, especially those involving reading and spelling (DiBenedetto, Richardson, & Korchnower, 1983; Manis, et al., 1987; Morrison, 1984; Snowling, 1981).

Once again, this could be a consequence of a selective attention dysfunction. Alternatively, it may be that because of the difficulties experienced with phoneme analysis and production, dyslexics are impeded in their ability to store accurate phonemic representations in memory (Byrne & Shea, 1979). In order to compensate for this deficiency, some may adopt a meaning-based reading strategy, which is initially less difficult. Perhaps they try to store words holistically, as isolated pictures to be remembered.

This strategy of reading words as logographic wholes may further hold back spelling and reading development, as it may distract the student from seeing the more productive phonetic connections among words. While able readers may be recognizing patterns and learning the principles to apply in spelling or reading independently, disabled readers may be memorizing individual words, a practice that becomes unmanageable once many words have been introduced.

Evidence for delay in non-dyslexics. Some researchers object to the deficit theory and offer evidence in favor of a developmental lag theory. They present findings from subjects who are more broadly drawn from the school, and not the more severely affected clinical population. These students are often referred to as "garden variety" poor readers, for their difficulties may be neither constitutional, nor neurological, in origin. Their low achievement in reading may be more related to instruction, motivation, or experience (e.g. lack of exposure to books at home, health problems that have led to school absences, emotional issues that interfere with academic growth). For these students, performance on tasks of speech segmentation, digit span, rhyme production, etc., is only slightly, and not significantly, worse than the performance of younger, normal readers, matched for reading age (Beech & Harding, 1984; Backman et al., 1984; Siegel & Ryan, 1988; Treiman 1984).

Evidence influenced by research design. The question of deficit versus developmental lag is answered differently depending on the nature of the research studies used to examine the issue. Using a strict definition of "dyslexia" and considering studies based on the performance of children who are of average intelligence or above consistently leads to a conclusion for a deficit. Using a more liberal definition of dyslexia that includes "garden variety" poor readers leads to a conclusion for delay in development as an underlying condition (Olson et al., 1989; Shaywitz et al., 1992). The answer varies with: the number of readers studied;

whether severe dyslexics or "garden variety" poor readers were examined; and whether readers with rich or limited educational experiences were studied.

In many instances, authors comment on the "generally impoverished phonemic-processing skills" (Beech & Harding, 1984, p. 359) of all poor readers and their weak knowledge of phonological information (Bruck, 1988). However, this symptom does not always suggest dyslexia. In some cases this could result from lack of instruction or from instruction that has not been effective. Very little instructional background information is included in these comparative studies, and so the reader is left to wonder whether the poor performance indicates a neurological anomaly, a lack of effective instruction, or a combination of the two.

Historical evidence for deficit among dyslexics. Over fifty years ago, neurologist Samuel Torrey Orton published his findings with regard to reading disability (1937). Although his theory of causation—lack of established cerebral dominance—has not been substantiated (Chall, 1967), he was very close to today's mark in connecting reading problems with a developmental language disorder. He was aware of the cluster of subskills that generally mark the dyslexic population, noting "...a difficulty in repicturing or rebuilding in the order of presentation, sequences of letters, of sounds or units of movement" (p. 145).

> It is this process of synthesizing the word as a spoken unit from its component sounds that often makes much more difficulty for the strephosymbolic child than do the static reversals and letter confusions (p. 162).

He argued that the only way for students with this speech/motor deficit to achieve reading skill is to engage in intensive, systematic practice with letters and sounds.

Similarly, Marion Monroe's experience with poor readers more than sixty years ago (1932) convinced her that the links connecting motor organization, language, and reading are strong. She found that, for children with reading deficits, an emphasis on overt motor responses (particularly in articulation) could serve as an aid in sound discrimination and maintaining attentional focus.

M.D. Vernon accurately anticipated today's focus on phonemic awareness as a factor in the nature and origin of "backwardness in reading" (1957). Having reviewed the reading research conducted from 1920 to 1958, she recognized that:

> The word was so deeply embedded in the sentence, and so impregnated with its meaning, that it could hardly be thought of in isolation....Thus the child

> has to learn that: (a) each word and its sound pattern are separate entities, with their peculiar, invariable, and universal characteristics; (b) each word's sound pattern can be analyzed into a succession of sounds, with a characteristic and invariable sequence; (c) these unitary sounds can be generalized, in the sense that they occur, in approximately the same form, but in different sequences in different words; (d) the sounds correspond to different letter shapes, visually perceived; but (e) unfortunately in the English language the relationship between sounds and visual percepts vary considerably from word to word (p. 39).

She wrote that reading disability involves the "mechanisms by which linguistic tasks are carried out, rather than the understanding and use of words as such" (p. 191). She also noted the link to "slow speech development" and "motor incoordination" (p. 190) and suspected that these signs are congenital and related to cortical function or dysfunction.

SUMMARY OF DISABILITY RESEARCH

Researchers have arrived at some agreement on the subject of developmental dyslexia. It is generally thought to be a language-related disorder that is connected to verbal processing difficulties, which may be traced to neuro-motor disorders. Alternatively, or in addition, a selective attention dysfunction may result in metalinguistic disability.

Some researchers hypothesize that extreme individual variation in reading and language performance results from hereditary or pre-natal factors that cause neurological anomalies. Affected individuals are not merely developmentally delayed but constitutionally different, just as each of us is unique and yet similar to others. Some educators do not subscribe to the theories presented above, objecting to the medical or deficit model of reading difficulty. However, evidence continues to build in support of the theories that were once put forth by Orton and Vernon.

Fostering Phonemic Awareness: Teaching Strategies

The research literature on phonemic awareness contains a host of suggestions for parents of young children as well as for teachers. Not surprisingly, many of the ideas are specific examples of the type of instruction recommended and implemented by Vernon in the 1950s. She favored varied and engaging reading methods, with an emphasis on rhymes and word games, spelling, story-writing, and opportunities to practice phonetic analysis and blending.

In this section I will describe specific games and activities that focus attention on language elements, particularly word and sound units. For the most part, I will confine my recommendations to activities that have been tested by educational research. The first group includes listening-speaking-movement games, with no reference to print or letters. The second group emphasizes sound-to-print mapping (encoding). The third group emphasizes print-to-sound mapping (decoding). These games and activities may be viewed as preventive measures and used with young children, on an individual or whole-class basis, to call attention to details that are often overlooked. Finally, I will mention briefly several intensive and systematic instructional programs that we know can be effective for students with persistent phonemic processing disabilities.

LISTENING-SPEAKING-MOVEMENT GAMES

The following games/activities provide a place to begin focusing attention on the elements of spoken language: sentences, words, syllables, and sounds. A playful approach is recommended, one that encourages creativity and curiosity. In attempting these activities and games, remember to appreciate and examine children's errors and misconceptions, for they are the best guide to the next step in instruction.

A preschool program. Lundberg (1987) describes the preschool training program he developed and implemented with fellow researchers in Sweden. Daily "sessions" included the whole group (15-20 children), and the program was on-going for six months. The slow but steady nature of the program was purposeful, to give those with limited metalinguistic talent a chance to catch on and perform with the others. The sequence was as follows:

...*weeks 1 and 2*: listening games, nursery rhymes, and action songs (e.g., games like "Bear Hunt," "Duck, Duck, Goose"; songs like "If You're Happy and You Know It," "My Hat it Has Three Corners," "Chester").

...*week 3*: sentences and words are introduced as concepts...games that focus on segmenting spoken sentences into word units (e.g., clap or march to each word in "Humpty Dumpty sat on a wall...")...games comparing word length (e.g., "Whose name is longer, Sam or Melissa?").

...*month 2*: syllables are introduced...children clap hands to the syllables (introduced as "beats" in their names) then to other multisyllable words in the classroom...marching, walking, dancing with syllabic intonation...plastic markers used to represent syllables...rhyming games, sorting words that rhyme (pictures or objects).

...*month 3*: phonemes are introduced, but only those in initial position...*vowels* and *continuant consonants* are the ones to focus on at this stage, because they can be exaggerated without distortion. (E.g. in "S...am" or "M...ary" or "A...dam," it is easy to elongate the initial phoneme without distorting it. In "T...om" the initial sound is a *stop consonant*, which cannot be elongated without distorting it by adding a vowel.) When including stop consonants, use a repetition technique: "T-t-t-t-om," or "P-p-p-p-amela," and apply to games of matching words that contain the same initial phoneme or to sorting objects or pictures that begin with the same sound.

...*month 5*: phonemes within words are introduced, beginning with words with two sounds (e.g. "m...e", "ea...t") and progressing slowly to more complex words....guessing games where teacher says word in segments and students blend the word together.

It is essential that teachers focus on *sounds* without considering or introducing any information on letters at this stage. (This can be confusing, as many of us have difficulty segmenting words by phoneme. For example, "face" is "/f/.../e/.../s/"; "arm" is '/a/.../r/.../m/'; and "floor" is "/f/.../l/.../o/.../r/.")

While this type of session is preferred by many teachers who like the structure of a set time for such activities, other teachers may favor a more integrated approach, where the same kinds of activities are performed in the context of other pursuits. It is important to remember that phonemic awareness requires attention to sounds *in the speech stream*, so these games can and should be played along with songs, stories, nursery rhymes—in short, whenever an opportunity for language play arises.

Songs and rhymes. Yopp (1992) presents a host of songs and rhymes that have been developed to highlight phonemes in *spoken* language and have been field-tested in preschool and kindergarten classrooms. She categorizes the recommended activities into the following groups: sound-matching activities, sound-isolation activities, blending activities, sound-addition or -substitution activities, and segmentation activities. One example, in the sound-substitution category, takes the

"Fe-Fi-Fiddly-i-o" chorus of "I've Been Workin' of the Railroad" and creates new versions: Ze-zi-Ziddly-i-o, Me-Mi-Middly-i-o, etc. A sound-segmenting game can be sung to the tune of "Twinkle, Twinkle, Little Star:"

> Listen, listen to my word.
> Then tell me all the sounds you heard: *mice*
> /m/ is one sound
> /i/ is two
> /s/ is last in *mice*, it's true.

Yopp urges teachers to maintain an informal and fanciful tone in these games and to encourage social interaction, for this is what inspires language play.

For kindergarten children, nursery **rhymes** should be an important part of the curriculum. Children should recite them, act them out, sing them, clap to them, rap to them. Revising the rhymes can be fun:

> There was an old woman who lived in a ...tent.
> She had so many children she never knew where they ...went.

Words in sentences and nursery rhymes can be counted by moving tokens, taking baby steps, passing or bouncing balls. A good rhyming game called "Head or Feet" asks children to point to the body part that rhymes with each word spoken: bed...seat...sled...heat, etc. Other words might rhyme with *hand* or *knee,* or *nose* or *ear* (Cunningham, 1990a).

Of course, many books besides nursery rhymes play with speech sounds. Several examples are *Green Eggs and Ham* (Seuss, 1960)*, Don't Forget the Bacon!* (Hutchins, 1976), *Sheep in a Jeep* (Shaw, 1986), *Who Said Red?* (Serfozo, 1988). Alphabet books, particularly those like *Animalia* (Base, 1986) that present multiple words beginning with the same sound (e.g., "Lazy lions lounging in the local library"), can be extremely useful as listening exercises. A more complete list of books that play with language sounds can be found in Griffith & Olson (1992).

Name games. Name games can be played at line-up times, e.g., "If your name has /s/ (the sound, not the letter) in it, you can get in line." (Cindy should line up along with Jason and even Max!) "If your name has /v/ in it...," etc. When helpers are needed their names can be announced in segmented form (S-a-m and K-i-t) and blended together by the class. Name games can be a good way to sort into random groups, e.g. "Those with one-beat names stand here"; "those with two-beat names stand here," etc.

Word games. For older students, language play can continue on a more sophisticated level. Word games like "*A* My Name is *A*lice," knock-knock jokes, tongue-twisters, and secret codes all encourage children to monitor and manipulate language, building sensitivity and skill as they do. The mastery of Pig Latin or "Op-Talk" can be a rewarding challenge for elementary school linguists. Such metalinguistic activity seems to train children for other linguistic challenges, giving them an advantage over less playful language-users (Cazden, 1974).

ACTIVITIES THAT EMPHASIZE SOUND-TO-PRINT MAPPING

Modeling. The most obvious and productive way to emphasize sound-to-print mapping is to demonstrate just how print becomes the representation of sounds spoken in sequence. Whenever written communication is required during the day, when words are written on the board, when messages are sent home to parents, a teacher can make the process very explicit. She can say the sounds in sequence (slowly pronouncing each *phoneme,* not naming the letters) as she writes the correct letters that map each sound.

Modeling and demonstrating the process is a very important technique. Articulating questions about ambiguous or unusual spellings encourages children to attend to these oddities as well. Although the steps in the process may be automatic to us, we need to show these individual steps to young learners. They need to see how we write letters one at a time, representing the sounds we speak in careful sequence. This should also make young children more inclined to begin their own attempts at writing their ideas for signs, messages, and stories.

Reading Recovery composition process. A scaffolding technique for assisting children with all the steps in the composition process is used consistently in Reading Recovery sessions with individual first graders (Pinnell, Fried, & Estice, 1990). Children think of a sentence, story, or message they want to record and say the whole thing to the teacher. The child writes the story while the teacher helps as needed, along the way. Children are encouraged to do as much as they can—to use as much knowledge as they have, and the teacher collaborates by filling in any missing information.

With unfamiliar words, the Reading Recovery child is helped to hear and mark the component sounds, using a token and sound-box technique suggested by Elkonin (1973). Invented/phonetic spellings are valued, but teachers show children the conventional spellings and explain how the two are similar and different. In this way the child gets reinforced for predicting the phonemic-phonetic match, but the conventional spellings are the ones that get recorded and practiced. When a story has been completed, the teacher usually makes a neat, conventionally spelled version and cuts it into small pieces for the child to reassemble. This reinforces the learning and turns the sound-to-print activity into a thoroughly related print-to-sound activity. Teachers can cut the story into segments of different sizes—phrases, words, phonemes—depending on the ability of the child or the teaching emphasis for that session. This technique and its effectiveness in experimental research is also described by Jansky (1981).

The intensive techniques that are used in Reading Recovery aim to provide "something extra" for first graders who have developed misconceptions about the reading-writing process and are at risk for failure. In my opinion, Reading Recovery techniques hold potential benefit for all children who are trying to practice their reading strategies and improve their spelling skills. Sensitive, responsive teachers can and should provide direct instruction to all, adapting duration and activities, as needed, to avoid excessive drill as readers master phonemic awareness.

Other less-structured ways to encourage invented/phonetic spelling are common in the literature (e.g., Clay, 1975; 1987; Hansen, Newkirk, & Graves, 1985). Ideas for bridging the gap to conventional spelling are presented very thoughtfully in Cunningham (1990a, pp. 93-105) and Gentry & Gillet (1993).

ACTIVITIES THAT EMPHASIZE PRINT-TO-SOUND MAPPING

As noted in an earlier section, researchers have found that the development of phonemic awareness is enhanced when children see how the sounds we speak relate directly to letters and letter clusters. In interventions to foster phonemic awareness, researchers have shown that using moveable letters in careful manipulations has helped young children and older special education students gain a more concrete understanding of an abstract system (Blachman, 1987; Cunningham, 1991; Ehri & Wilce, 1987; Williams 1980).

Another way to make the sounds within words *visible* to children is attempted with *Words in Color* charts (Gattegno, 1968). Each of the forty-two phonemes of English is assigned a color, and these colors indicate the sounds one hears in a word. For example, "eight" and "ate" are shown with the same colors; the colors in "kiss" match the colors in the middle syllable of "orchestra." The use of color allows for a kind of one-to-one correspondence that is otherwise lacking in English, giving extra guidance to children in their efforts to map sounds onto print.

This is not the place to go into great detail concerning the many programs that assist learners in discovering and mastering print-to-sound correspondence, since the process of learning to decode is covered in detail in Chapter 4. I will mention just one specific, well-documented program and note the components that numerous others share.

In the model first-grade reading program developed by Blachman (1987), children learn to identify sounds represented by letters on small cards. Then they blend them to form words, reversing and substituting sounds as they go: 'nap,' 'pan,' 'pin,' etc. The children write these words and read them back. They find and read them in little paperbacks that serve as "transitional" readers, books with vocabulary that is controlled so as to be decodable for beginners (e.g., *A Pig Can Jig,* Rasmussen & Goldberg, 1976; *Six Kids*, Modern Curriculum Press, 1978). These activities are just one component of an overall reading program that also includes literature, some basals, and creative writing.

In general, comprehensive programs for teaching reading in first grade seem to yield greater gains, on average, when they contain a systematic phonics component (Adams, 1990; Chall, 1967; 1983). The more successful programs are those that introduce individual sound elements (letters and the sounds they usually represent) to be blended into words and sentences. Chall called this "synthetic" phonics and recommended it as less confusing than "analytic" phonics.

Another important component for beginning readers is that they have access to short, simple books written with consistency in letter-sound correspondence. These books reward children who are struggling to practice letter-sound mapping; they enable success. Like invented/phonetic spelling, they serve a purpose for a short time, to help children understand one particular strategy used in reading and writing. The research on materials of this kind shows that first graders who use these books develop stronger skills and more independence at word analysis and spelling than those who have used only texts written to introduce high frequency "sight" words (Beck & Block, 1979; Juel & Roper-Schneider, 1985; Slavin et al., 1990).

If the above strategies are implemented by well informed, attentive teachers, we might substantially improve the quality of instruction offered to beginning readers. It has been estimated that 80% of kindergartners with limited awareness of phonemes go on to become "reading disabled" (Fox & Routh, 1983). In this we have a fairly accurate marker to which efforts at prevention can be directed. For some, however, the disability may persist. Many of the awareness games described above would be inappropriate for older readers, who would need instruction in phonemic awareness but with content that is sensitive to their maturity. In particular, their instruction could include working with repetitive poetry that expresses mature themes and with activities directly tied to printed letters and words.

INSTRUCTIONAL PROGRAMS FOR READERS WITH DISABILITIES

Research indicates that effective instructional techniques are those that help older dyslexics attend to sounds by presenting an organized, step-by-step system for processing written language. Clark (1988) presents a thorough discussion of these different programs and a review of the research base that supports their effectiveness. Her basic recommendation underscores the need for explicit phonics instruction for most dyslexic students.

Many code-emphasis reading programs are available, and those that emphasize individual phonemic elements and the blending of these into words provide the focus that dyslexics seem constitutionally inclined to overlook. For example, the *Auditory Discrimination in Depth* program, designed by Charles and Patricia Lindamood (described in Clark, 1988), trains teachers to tackle the phonemic awareness "aptitude deficit" by providing clear and persistent instruction in speech analysis. Such programs demand a great deal of teacher direction and focused time on task. They are highly structured and time consuming. There simply is no quick fix.

Programs to bypass the disability and rely on other strengths have been unconvincing for those with the "specific aptitude deficit" that results in dyslexia. Without the ability to focus on phonemes in sequence, a student predictably will have great difficulty with spelling, accurate oral reading, and decoding new words. Devices such as tape recorders, talking computers, and spell checkers will help students to compensate for this disability so as to function in a literate world. However, students without equal access to this technology, or students who want to become more self-reliant, will need to gain phonemic awareness and to be shown how to use it in learning to encode and decode written language.

Considering that dyslexia may be the linguistic reflection of a motor-organization difficulty, it makes sense to break the reading process down into a series of skills and to teach these skills step-by-step, from simple to more complex. Once a step is "over-learned" it can become automatic, and a new step can be attempted. This is the strategy of the Orton-Gillingham approach, where decoding is taught letter-by-letter, sound-by-sound, with multi-sensory practice. Proponents of this method—teachers, students, and their grateful parents—are convinced of its benefits.

The method works best when used consistently, on a daily basis. One-to-one tutorial support is usually recommended, and phonetically regular texts are used so that students can practice applying the rules and generalizations learned to decodable words in context. Over the decades, the *Let's Read* series (Bloomfield, Barnhart, & Barnhart, 1965) also has been used for this purpose.

There are many variations on the Orton-Gillingham prototype: *Alphabetic Phonics, Project Read, Total Reading, Won Way, Wilson Reading System*, and even IBM's *Writing to Read* program, to name but a few in current use. Full descriptions of these programs can be found in Clark (1988) or at Educators Publishing Service in Cambridge, MA. With all of the above programs, learners are not permitted to bypass their phonemic processing difficulties. They must master phonemic processing, over time, and with a great deal of practice.

Considering that dyslexia may signal a failure in selective-attention mechanisms, the focused, systematic approach seems sensible. However, there may be a problem in integrating the various component processes involved in reading. Perhaps a focus on the smallest elements of language alone is not sufficient to help students make meaningful connections based on context and general knowledge.

In other words, the Orton-Gillingham type of approach, if used exclusively, may overly reinforce the single-mindedness that characterizes students with this type of disability. For these students, the additional use of a program such as Reading Recovery shows promise, since the student is constantly reminded to use cross-checking strategies while reading in such programs. Students are urged to predict, to guess, and to confirm or disconfirm by alternately checking print features and considering underlying meaning.

If used in addition to the bottom-up path that Orton-Gillingham recommends, a program such as Reading Recovery may help readers learn how bottom-up and top-down processes must work interactively and continually when we read books and write stories. Note that the behaviors practiced in Reading Recovery sessions are always done in the context of a meaningful literacy task. Also, note that Reading Recovery was designed as a preventive, not a remedial, program. Older readers are not eligible for this program at the present time. Future research will be needed to document the progress of "Recovered" students and, perhaps, to determine how to implement a program with similar goals for an older population.

Assessment of Phonemic Awareness

Many different tests have been used in research exploring phonemic awareness. Often, the researchers design and administer experimental tasks that have not been validated with a broad population. However, the three tests listed below are frequently used as comparison measures and have been found to be reliable. Although they provide norm-referenced information, suggesting age- or grade-level expectations, unfortunately, the norms are both dated and limited. Therefore, these tests are best used for the qualitative data they provide. (For additional information concerning phonemic awareness assessment see Chapter 11, p. 347.)

1. The Sound Blending subtest of the *Illinois Test of Psycholinguistic Abilities* (Kirk, McCarthy & Kirk, 1968)

2. Rosner's *Test of Auditory Analysis Skills* (in Rosner, 1979)

3. *Roswell-Chall Auditory Blending Test* (Chall, Roswell, & Blumenthal, 1963)

Less-formal measures are also used for assessing phonemic awareness in the context of writing/spelling tasks. The Diagnostic Survey used with first graders in Reading Recovery includes a sentence dictation task that is analyzed for phonemic accuracy (Clay, 1979). Another researcher recommends using nursery rhymes to assess kindergartners' phonemic awareness as it develops over time (Hall, 1985). If these rhymes have been committed to memory, it is easier for children to focus on sounds one at a time, and re-reading what they have written becomes a snap. In January, one kindergarten class produced the following range in their renditions of "Jack and Jill"

child #1:   +L+ < V↑_OO > TT+...

child #2:   J N J N OP O L...

child #3:   JAK N JL YAT UP THE HEL....

It is easy to use this information to gauge the status of each child's phonemic awareness development. A well-informed and sensitive teacher can then use her knowledge of sound-symbol relations and the stages of spelling development to determine where to aim instruction that meets each child's needs. Child #3, for example, is using "Y" to represent the /w/ sound. This is common among young children, since the name of the letter "Y" begins with the /w/ sound, whereas the name of the letter "W" begins with the /d/ sound. There is sound logic behind this error. A few re-readings of *Mrs. Wishy-washy* (Cowley, 1980), along with some reminders from the teacher, and this confusion is likely to be corrected.

A highly predictive spelling list to be used at the beginning of first grade is suggested by Morris & Perney (1984), and two separate "Spelling Features Lists" for grades K-2 and grades 3 and up are included in Gillet & Temple (1990, p. 192). A quick check to assess decoding ability can be implemented via "The Names Test" (Cunningham, 1990b), which comprises 25 unusual but phonetic first and last names to be decoded (e.g. "Vance Middleton"). Grade-level means, and suggestions for qualitative interpretation are included.

A more comprehensive battery of tests is recommended for older students whose difficulties with reading may **not** stem from a phonemic awareness deficit. At the Harvard Reading Laboratory we found that many of our students were accurate at decoding and spelling but still scored below grade level expectations on tests of vocabulary and comprehension. For these students, of course, the activities described above would not be necessary.

A broad scale assessment of the separate (but interacting) components of reading ability to establish how different strengths and weaknesses might affect a student's performance is certainly recommended. This can be accomplished with a battery of written and oral tests, or with a composite measure such as the *Diagnostic Assessment of Reading* included in the *DARTTS* assessment kit recently developed by Roswell & Chall (1991). Designed to be administered to a student in 20-30 minutes, the assessment instrument has been validated with children in grades 1-12 and includes *Trial Teaching Strategies* to guide the teaching process.

The Phonemic Awareness of Reading Teachers

A word of caution to teachers, especially to those of you who may be new to the teaching of reading: You probably ought not assume that, just because you are an expert reader, your own level of phonemic awareness is high. Many excellent reading teachers have difficulty performing the tasks used to assess this factor (Rath, 1994). When asked to count the phonemes in the word *question*, for example, only 19% of the 117 reading teachers sampled were accurate in their count. *Test yourself:* How many individual sounds do you hear when you say the word *question* out loud?

Many teachers indicate that *question* has 4 sounds: *qu e s tion*, presumably because they are thinking about patterns learned and taught in phonics.

In the Orton-Gillingham approach, these combinations of letters that reliably represent sound patterns are called "phonograms."

However, when counting phonemes, **each speech sound that requires a different mouth position is counted alone.** Therefore, to pronounce *question*, we form our mouths in 7 different positions: */k/ /w/ /e/ /s/ /ch/ /ə/ /n/*, in order to articulate seven discrete phonemes. The dictionary is a reliable guide in these matters; its phonetic spellings with diacritical markings accurately map the sequence of sounds in all cases. Young inventive spellers, so focused on sounds and so innocent with regard to English spelling patterns, come close to these dictionary representations in their own attempts to spell words like *question*.

For those interested in further testing or improving their own phonemic awareness, a short quiz has been included in the appendix of this chapter. For those who would like to clarify questions about phonics, phonetics, and the phonemic structure of language, Durkin (1981) is helpful.

Summary and Conclusion

Phonemic awareness plays a critical role in literacy development. Educators and researchers have recognized for decades that a young child who focuses on the sound units in spoken words is likely to learn to read with ease and early success. Recently, investigators have engaged in a flurry of research to explore the reasons for and implications of this notion. They have continued to document the key role of phonemic awareness as a gateway to literacy acquisition; without this awareness, children have difficulty learning to read and spell English accurately. The important findings from this research can be used to inform the practice of professionals in classrooms and clinics, as they suggest a variety of strategies for assessing phonemic awareness, fostering it, and connecting it with reading and spelling instruction.

In learning more about the subject of phonemic awareness, teachers may become more attentive, themselves, to the phonemic structure of English. Such a focus has the potential to broaden teachers' knowledge of spelling—its underlying patterns and principles as well as its many challenges. Teachers with knowledge and confidence in this area will have a better chance of ensuring that students gain the understanding that is crucial for successful literacy development.

APPENDIX

A Phonemic Awareness Quiz for Reading Teachers
(Answers appear at end of quiz.)

In order to make the task of focusing on phonemes simpler for students, teachers should begin by selecting examples of words that contain all *continuant* sounds. These are easier to say at a slow speed, lingering on each sound. For example, all the phonemes in **fan** are *continuants*. Try saying this word very slowly, pronouncing each separate sound for a second or two: /f/.../æ/.../n/.

Now try saying **top** in the same exaggerated way. Do you see how hard it is to hold the sounds in **top**? That is because the two consonants in **top** are *stop* sounds. They <u>stop</u> the stream of air in the oral cavity when we say them. In English, the letters that usually represent *stops* are: **p, t, d, b, k, g,** and sometimes **ng**. It is more difficult to hear each phoneme in words that contain *stops*.

I. Continuants and Stops
Look at the words in each numbered set below. Say them aloud <u>very</u> slowly. Decide which word contains *stops*, and cross it out.

1. fish, dish, wish
2. zoom, moon, root
3. live, love, give
4. slow, crow, throw
5. trees, freeze, sneeze
6. clear, here, there
7. books, lines, waves
8. twin, swim, flies
9. mother, father, sister
10. enough, tough, through

Teachers may want to present words in this slowed-down way and ask children to blend them together and say them fast. Another exercise asks children to produce slow pronunciations, noting or marking each discrete phoneme. It is handy to have a pack of cards with illustrations that represent words to be analyzed.

Try to think of at least **10** all-*continuant* words that are easily illustrated. Examples: **nose,** but not **lips; shoe,** but not **sock; mouse,** but not **cat.**

II. Word Reversals
Say one of the following words out loud. Then *reverse the order of the sounds*, and say the new English word that results. Write the new word with its conventional English spelling. (Hint: It helps to close your eyes as you say each of the numbered words, trying to pay attention to the *phonemes*. Don't worry about existing *letters* or resulting spelling changes. Just reverse the *sounds, not* the letters.)

1. pin _____
2. tub _____
3. sick _____
4. time _____
5. judge _____
6. cuts _____
7. face _____
8. easy _____
9. teach _____
10. talk _____
11. ice _____
12. checks _____
13. votes _____
14. chance _____
15. enough _____

III. Phoneme Counting

Count the number of phonemes you hear in each of the words below. It may help if you circle the letter or letter cluster that represents each sound. (Remember, each time you change the position of your mouth—including lips and tongue—you are forming a new phoneme.)

number:

	number:		number:	
_____ 1. sun	_____ 5. laughed	_____ 9. station
_____ 2. grass	_____ 6. quickly	_____ 10. everything
_____ 3. deeply	_____ 7. started	_____ 11. Christmas
_____ 4. thought	_____ 8. people	_____ 12. psychology

IV. Phoneme Discrimination

Read the first word (in boldface) in each line, and note the sound that is represented by the underlined letter or letter cluster. Then select the word or words on the line that contain **the same sound.** Circle the word or words you have selected.

1. **paper**	a. village	b. survey	c. contain	d. sleigh
2. **rose**	a. dazzle	b. anxiety	c. azure	d. tissue
3. **push**	a. overlook	b. jump	c. should	d. soup
4. **return**	a. smashed	b. two	c. listen	d. castle
5. **salad**	a. physician	b. usual	c. reception	d. has
6. **this**	a. both	b. their	c. thunder	d. mother
7. **factor**	a. similar	b. restore	c. never	d. create
8. **Stephen**	a. of	b. soften	c. phrase	d. several
9. **nurse**	a. prefer	b. percent	c. journey	d. cure
10. **thin**	a. there	b. gather	c. sympathy	d. thousand

Answers:

I. Continuants and Stops. These words contain stops: 1. dish, 2. root, 3. give, 4. crow, 5. trees, 6. clear, 7. books, 8. twin, 9. sister, 10. tough.

II. Word Reversals. 1. nip, 2. but, 3. kiss, 4. might, 5. judge, 6. stuck, 7. safe, 8. easy, 9. cheat, 10. caught, 11. sigh, 12. sketch, 13. stove, 14. snatch, 15. funny.

III. Phoneme Counting. 1. 3 (s-u-n), 2. 4 (g-r-a-ss), 3. 5 (d-ee-p-l-y), 4. 3 (th-ough-t), 5. 4 (l-au-gh-ed), 6. 6 (k-w-i-ck-l-y), 7. 7 (s-t-a-r-t-e-d), 8. 5 (p-eo-p-ə-l), 9. 6 (s-t-a-t-io-n), 10. 7 (e-ve-r-y-th-i-ng), 11. 7 (Ch-r-i-st-m-a-s), 12. 8 (ps-y-ch-o-l-o-g-y).

IV. Phoneme Discrimination. 1. b,c,d; 2. a,b; 3. a,c; 4. a,b; 5. c; 6. b, d; 7. a,c; 8. a,d; 9.a,c; 10. c,d.

Author's note: The above exercise is *meant* to be challenging, so please don't be discouraged if your accuracy rate is low. I am used to encountering experienced, competent teachers who answer only 50% of the above quiz correctly. We all have room for improvement in areas of knowledge and expertise. If you are confused about any of the above examples, you are encouraged to consult dictionaries and linguistic texts for reference (e.g., Fromkin, V., & Rodman, R. [1988]. *An Introduction to Language, Fourth Edition.* Orlando, FL: Holt, Rinehart, and Winston). Or, contact me with questions *via* this publisher.

References

Adams, M.J. (1990). *Beginning to read: Thinking and learning about print.* Cambridge, MA: The MIT Press.

Adams, M.J., et al. (1991). Beginning to read: A critique of literacy professionals and a response by Marilyn Jager Adams. *The Reading Teacher, 44*, 370-395.

Alegria, J., Pignot, E., & Morais, J. (1982). Phonetic analysis of speech and memory codes in beginning readers. *Memory and Cognition, 10*, 451-456.

Anderson, R. C., Hiebert, E.H., Scott, J.A., & Wilkinson, A.G. (1985). *Becoming a nation of readers.* Washington, DC: National Academy of Education.

Babbitt, N. (1986). My love affair with the alphabet. In Reading is Fundamental, *Once upon a time....* NY: G.P. Putnam's Sons, 42- 45.

Backman, J., Bruck, M., Hebert, M., & Seidenberg, M.S. (1984). Acquisition and use of spelling-sound correspondences in reading. *Journal of Experimental Child Psychology, 38*, 114-133.

Base, G. (1986). *Animalia.* NY: Abrams.

Beck, I.L., & Block, K.K. (1979). An analysis of two beginning reading programs: Some facts and some opinions. In L.B. Resnick & P.A. Weaver (Eds.), *Theory and practice of early reading (Vol.1)*, Hillsdale, NJ: Erlbaum, 279-318.

Beech, J.R., & Harding, L.M. (1984) Phonemic processing and the poor reader from a developmental lag viewpoint. *Reading Research Quarterly, 19*, 357-366.

Bialystok, E., & Mitterer, J. (1987). Metalinguistic differences among three kinds of readers. *Journal of Educational Psychology, 79*, 147-153.

Bissex, G. (1980). *GNYS AT WORK.* Cambridge, MA.: Harvard University Press.

Blachman, B.A. (1987). An alternative classroom reading program for learning disabled and other low-achieving children. In R. Bowler (Ed.), *Intimacy with language: A forgotten basic in teacher education.* Baltimore, MD: Orton Dyslexia Society, 49-55.

Blalock, J.W. (1982). Persistent auditory language deficits in adults with learning disabilities. *Journal of Learning Disabilities, 15*, 604-609.

Bloomfield, L., Barnhart, C.L., & Barnhart R.K. et al (1965). *Let's Read.* Cambridge, MA: Educators Publishing Service.

Bradley, L., & Bryant, P. (1985). *Rhyme and reason in reading and spelling.* Ann Arbor: University of Michigan Press.

Bruce, D. J. (1964). The analysis of word sounds by young children. *British Journal of Educational Psychology, 34*, 158-170.

Bruck, M. (1988). The word recognition and spelling of dyslexic children. *Reading Research Quarterly, 23*, 51-69.

Bryant, P., & Bradley, L. (1985). *Children's reading problems: Psychology and education.* Oxford, UK: Basil Blackwell Inc.

Byrne, B. (1984). On teaching articulatory phonetics via an orthography. *Memory and Cognition, 12*, 181-189.

Byrne, B., & Shea, P., (1979). Semantic and phonetic memory codes in beginning readers. *Memory and Cognition, 7,* 333-338.

Catts, H.W. (1986). Speech production/ phonological deficits in reading disordered children. *Journal of Learning Disabilities, 19,* 504-508.

Cazden, C. (1974). Play with language and metalinguistics: One dimension of language awareness experience. *The Urban Review, 7,* 28-39.

Chall, J. S. (1967). *Learning to read: The great debate.* NY: McGraw Hill.

Chall, J. S. (1983). *Stages of reading development.* NY: McGraw-Hill.

Chall, J. S., Roswell, F. G., & Blumenthal, S. H. (1963). Auditory blending ability: A factor in success in beginning reading. *The Reading Teacher, 17,* 113-118.

Chall, J.S., & Stahl, S.A. (1981). Reading. In H. Mitzel (Ed.), *Encyclopedia of educational research (5th edition).* NY: The Free Press, Macmillan, 1535-1559.

Chomsky, C. (1970). Reading, writing, and phonology. *Harvard Educational Review, 40,* 287-309.

Chomsky, C. (1971). Write first, read later. *Childhood Education,* March, 296-299.

Chomsky, C. (1979). Approaching reading through invented spelling. In L.B. Resnick & P.A. Weaver (Eds.), *Theory and practice of early reading (Vol. 2).* Hillsdale, NJ: Erlbaum, 43-65.

Clark, D.B. (1988). *Dyslexia: Theory and practice of remedial instruction.* Parkton, MD: York Press.

Clay, M. (1975). *What did I write? Beginning writing behavior.* Portsmouth, NH: Heinemann.

Clay, M. (1979). *The early detection of reading difficulties.* Portsmouth, NH: Heinemann.

Clay, M. (1987). *Writing begins at home.* Portsmouth, NH: Heinemann.

Cowley, J. (1980). *Mrs. Wishy-washy.* Bothell, WA: The Wright Group.

Crain, S. (1989). Why poor readers misunderstand spoken sentences. In D. Shankweiler & I.Y. Liberman (Eds.), *Phonology and reading disability,* 133-165. Ann Arbor: Univ. of Michigan Press.

Critchley, M. (1970). *The dyslexic child.* Springfield, IL: Charles C. Thomas.

Cunningham, P.M. (1990a). *Phonics they use.* NY: Harper Collins.

Cunningham, P.M. (1990b). The names test: A quick assessment of decoding ability. *The Reading Teacher, 44,* 124-129.

Cunningham, P. M. (1991). Research directions: Multimethod, multilevel literacy instruction in first grade. *Language Arts, 68,* 578-584.

Denckla, M.B. (1983). Learning for language and language for learning. In U. Kirk (Ed.), *Neuropsychology of language, reading and spelling,* 33-43. NY: Academic Press.

DiBenedetto, B., Richardson, E., & Kochnower, J. (1983). Vowel generalization in normal and learning disabled readers. *Journal of Educational Psychology, 75,* 576-582.

Dolch, E.W., & Bloomster, M. (1937). Phonic readiness. *Elementary School Journal, 38,* 201-205.

Durkin, D. (1966). *Children who read early.* NY: Teachers College Press.

Durkin, D. (1981). *Strategies for identifying words (2nd ed.).* Boston, MA: Allyn & Bacon.

Durrell, D.D., & Murphy, H.A. (1953). The auditory discrimination factor in reading readiness and reading disability. *Education, 73,* 556-560.

Ehri, L.C., & Wilce, L.S. (1987). Does learning to spell help beginners learn to read words? *Reading Research Quarterly, 22,* 47-65.

Elkonin, D.B. (1973). USSR. In J. Downing (Ed.), *Comparative reading.* NY: Macmillan.

Ferreiro, E. (1986). The interplay between information and assimilation in beginning literacy. In W.H. Teale & E. Sulzby (Eds.), *Emergent literacy.* NJ: Ablex.

Fox, B., & Routh, D.K., (1983). Reading disability, phonemic analysis, and dysphonetic spelling: A follow-up study. *Journal of Clinical Child Psychology, 12,* 28-32.

Frith, U. (1986). A developmental framework for developmental dyslexia. *Annals of Dyslexia, 36,* 69-81.

Galaburda, A. (1985). Developmental dyslexia: A review of biological interactions. *Annals of Dyslexia, 35.*

Gates, A.I., & Bond, G.L. (1937). The necessary mental age for beginning reading. *Elementary School Journal, 37,* 495-508.

Gattegno, C. (1968). *Words in Color.* NY: Educational Solutions, Inc.

Gentry, J.R. & Gillet, J.W. (1993). *Teaching kids to spell.* Portsmouth, NH: Heinemann.

Geschwind, N. (1986). Dyslexia, cerebral dominance, autoimmunity and sex hormones. In G.T. Pavlidis, & D.F.Fisher (Eds.), *Dyslexia: Its neuropsychology and treatment.* Chichester, UK: John Wiley & Sons, Ltd.

Gibson, C. (1988). The impact of early developmental history on cerebral asymmetries: Implications for reading ability in deaf children. In D. Molfese & S. Segalowitz, (Eds.), *Brain lateralization in children: Developmental implications.* NY: The Guilford Press.

Gillet, J.W., & Temple, C. (1990). *Understanding reading problems: Assessment and instruction (3rd ed.).* Glenview, IL: Scott Foresman.

Gough, P.B., & Hillinger, M.L. (1980). Learning to read: An unnatural act. *Bulletin of the Orton Society, 30,* 179-96.

Griffith, P.L., & Olson, M.W. (1992). Phonemic awareness helps beginning readers break the code. *The Reading Teacher, 45,* 516-523.

Hall, S.E.M. (1985). OAD MAHR GOS and writing with young children. *Language Arts, 62,* 262-265.

Hansen, J., Newkirk, T., & Graves, D. (1985). *Breaking ground.* Portsmouth, NH: Heinemann.

Heath, S.B. (1986). Separating "things of the imagination" from life: Learning to read and write. In W.H. Teale & E. Sulzby (Eds.), *Emergent literacy.* Norwood, NJ: Ablex Publishing.

Helfgott, J. (1976). Phonemic segmentation and blending skills of kindergarten children: Implications for beginning reading acquisition. *Contemporary Educational Psychology, 1,* 157-169.

Holdaway, D. (1979). *The foundations of literacy.* Sydney, Australia: Ashton Scholastic.

Hutchins, P. (1976). *Don't forget the bacon!* NY: Morrow.

Hynd, G.W., & Semrud-Clikeman, M. (1989). Dyslexia and neurodevelopmental pathology: Relationships to cognition, intelligence, and reading skill acquisition. *Journal of Learning Disabilities, 22.*

Jansky, J. (1981). The clinician in the classroom: A first-grade intervention study. *Bulletin of the Orton Society, 31.*

Johnson, D. (1986). Remediation for dyslexic adults. In G.T. Pavlidis & D.F. Fisher (Eds.), *Dyslexia: Its neuropsychology and treatment.* Chichester, UK: John Wiley & Sons, Ltd.

Juel, C., & Roper-Schneider, D. (1985). The influence of basal readers on first grade reading. *Reading Research Quarterly, 20,* 134-152.

Katz, R.B. (1986) Phonological deficiencies in children with reading disability: Evidence from an object naming test. *Cognition, 22,* 225-157.

Kirk, S.A., McCarthy, J.J., & Kirk, W.D. (1986). *Illinois Test of Psycholinguistic Abilities.* Urbana, IL: University of Illinois.

Kirk, U. (1989). Neurological aspects of learning difficulty. In F.G. Roswell & G. Natchez, *Reading disability: A human approach to evaluation and treatment of reading and writing difficulties.* NY: Basic Books, 17-40.

Lesgold, A.M., & Perfetti, C. (1982). *Interactive processes in reading.* Hillsdale, NJ: Erlbaum.

Lewkowicz, N. K. (1980). Phonemic awareness training: What to teach and how to teach it. *Journal of Educational Psychology, 72,* 686-700.

Liberman, I.Y., & Shankweiler, D. (1979). Speech, the alphabet and learning to read. In L.B. Resnick & P. Weaver (Eds.), *Theory and practice of early reading (Vol. 2).* Hillsdale, NJ: Erlbaum, 109-134.

Lundberg, I. (1978). Aspects of linguistic awareness related to reading. In A. Sinclair, R.J. Jarvella, & W.J.M. Levelt, (Eds.), *The child's conception of language.* NY: Springer-Verlag, 83-96.

Lundberg, I. (1987). Phonological awareness facilitates reading and spelling acquisition. In R. Bowler, (Ed.), *Intimacy with language: A forgotten basic in teacher education.* Baltimore, MD: The Orton Dyslexia Society, 56-63.

Lundberg, I., Frost, J., & Petersen, O. P. (1988). Effects of an extensive program for stimulating phonological awareness in preschool children. *Reading Research Quarterly, 23,* 263-284.

Maclean, M., Bryant, P., & Bradley, L. (1987) Rhymes, nursery rhymes, and reading in early childhood. *Merrill-Palmer Quarterly, 33,* 255-282.

Manis, F., Savage, P., Morrison, F., Horn, G., Howell, M., Szeszulski, P., & Holt, L. (1987). Paired associate learning in reading-disabled children: Evidence for a rule-learning deficiency. *Journal of Experimental Child Psychology, 43,* 25-43.

Mann, V. A. (1984). Longitudinal prediction and prevention of early reading difficulty. *Annals of Dyslexia, 34,* 117-136.

Mann, V.A., Tobin, P., & Wilson, R. (1987). Measuring phonological awareness through the invented spellings of kindergarten children. *Merrill-Palmer Quarterly, 33,* 365-391.

Mason, J.M. (1980). When DO children begin to read: An exploration of four-year-old children's letter and word reading competencies. *Reading Research Quarterly, 15,* 203-227.

138

Mattingly, I.G. (1972). Reading, the linguistic process, and linguistic awareness. In J.F. Kavanagh & I.G. Mattingly (Eds.), *Language by ear and by eye*. Cambridge, MA: MIT Press.

Menyuk, P., & Flood, J. (1981). Linguistic competence, reading, writing problems, and remediation. *Bulletin of the Orton Society, 31*, 13-28.

Modern Curriculum Press (1978). *Six kids*. Phonics Practice Readers. Cleveland, Ohio

Monroe, M. (1932). *Children who cannot read*. Chicago: University of Chicago Press.

Montessori, M. (1912). *The Montessori method (1964 ed.)*. NY: Schocken Books, Inc.

Morais, J., Cary, L., Alegria, J., & Bertelson, P. (1979). Does awareness of speech as a sequence of phones arise spontaneously? *Cognition, 7*, 323-331.

Morais, J., Cluytens, M., Alegria, J., & Content, A. (1984). Segmentation abilities of dyslexics and normal readers. *Perceptual and Motor Skills, 58*, 221-222.

Morris, D., & Perney, J. (1984). Developmental spelling as a predictor of first-grade reading achievement. *The Elementary School Journal, 84*, 442-457.

Morrison, F.J. (1984). Word decoding and rule-learning in normal and disabled readers. *Remedial and Special Education, 5*, 20-27.

Mullis, I.V.S., & Jenkins, L.B. (1990). *The reading report card, 1971-88: Trends from the nation's report card*. Princeton, NJ: Educational Testing Service and National Assessment of Educational Progress.

NAEP (1985). *The reading report card: Progress toward excellence in our schools*. NJ: NAEP & ETS.

Olson, R., Wise, B., Conners, F., Rack, J., & Fulker, D. (1989) Specific deficits in component reading and language skills: Genetic and environmental influences. *Journal of Learning Disabilities, 22*, 339-348.

Orton, S.T. (1937). *Reading, writing, and speech problems in children*. NY: Norton & Co., Inc.

Pinnell, G.S., Fried, M.D., & Estice, R.M. (1990). Reading Recovery: Learning how to make a difference. *The Reading Teacher*, January, 282-295.

Rasmussen, D., & Goldberg, L. (1976). *A pig can jig*. Basic Reading Series. Chicago, IL: SRA.

Rath, L.K. (1994). The phonemic awareness of reading teachers: Examining aspects of knowledge. Unpublished doctoral dissertation. Cambridge, MA: Harvard University Graduate School of Education.

Read, C. (1971). Preschool children's knowledge of English phonology. *Harvard Educational Review, 41*, 1-34.

Read, C. (1978). Children's awareness of language, with emphasis on sound systems. In A. Sinclair, R.J. Jarvella & W.J.M. Levelt, (Eds.), *The child's conception of language*. NY: Springer-Verlag, 65-82.

Read, C. (1981). Writing is not the inverse of reading for young children. In C.H. Fredericksen & J.F. Dominic (Eds.), *Writing (Vol.2)*. Hillsdale, NJ: Erlbaum.

Read, C., & Ruyter, L. (1985). Reading and spelling in adults of low literacy. *Remedial and Special Education, 6*, 43-52.

Read, C., Yun-Fei, A., Hong-Yin, Nie, Ban-Qing, D. (1986). The ability to manipulate speech sounds depends on knowing alphabetic writing. *Cognition, 26*, 31-44.

Rosenberger, P.B. (1992). Dyslexia—is it a disease? *New England Journal of Medicine*, Jan.

Rosner, J. (1974). Auditory analysis training with pre-readers. *The Reading Teacher, 27*, 379-381.

Rosner, J. (1979). *Helping children overcome learning difficulties (2nd ed.)*. NY: Walker.

Rosner, J., & Simon, D.P. (1971). The auditory analysis test: An initial report. *Journal of Learning Disabilities, 4*, 384-392.

Roswell, F., & Chall, J.S. (1991). *Diagnostic Assessment of Reading with Trial Teaching Strategies*. Chicago, IL: Riverside Press.

Rozin, P., & Gleitman, L.R. (1977). The structure and acquisition of the alphabetic principle. In A.S. Reber & D.L. Scarborough (Eds.), *Toward a psychology of reading*. Hillsdale, NJ: Erlbaum.

Rudel, R. (1988). *Assessment of developmental learning disorders: A neuropsychological approach*. NY: Basic Books.

Schickedanz, J. (1990). *Adam's righting revolutions*. Portsmouth, NH: Heinemann.

Seuss, Dr. (1960). *Green eggs and ham*. NY: Random House.

Serfozo, M.K. (1988). *Who said red?* NY: Macmillan.

Share, D.J., Jorm, A.F., Maclean., R., & Mathews, R. (1984). Sources of individual differences in reading achievement. *Journal of Educational Psychology, 76*, 466-477.

Shaw, N. (1986). *Sheep in a jeep*. Boston, MA: Houghton Mifflin.

Shaywitz, S.E., Escobar, M.D., Shaywitz, B.A., Fletcher, J.M., & Makuch, R.. (1992). Evidence that dyslexia may represent the lower tail of a normal distribution of reading ability. In *The New England Journal of Medicine, 326*, 145-50.

Siegel, L.S., & Ryan, E.B. (1988). Development of grammatical sensitivity, phonological, and short-term memory skills in normally achieving and learning disabled children. *Developmental Psychology, 24*, 28-37.

Slavin, R., Madden, N.A., Kaarweit, N.L., Livermon, B.J., & Dolan, L. (1990). Success for all: First-year outcomes of a comprehensive plan for reforming urban education. *American Education Research Journal, 27*, 255-278.

Snow, C.E. (1983). Language and literacy: Relationships during the preschool years. *Harvard Educational Review, 53*, 165-189.

Snow, C.E, & Ninio, A. (1986). The contracts of literacy: What children learn from learning to read books. In W.H.Teale & E.Sulzby (Eds.), *Emergent literacy*. Norwood, NJ: Ablex Publishing Co.

Snowling, M. (1981). Phonemic deficits in developmental dyslexia. *Psychological Research, 43*, 219-234.

Snowling, M., Goulandris, N., Bowlby, M., & Howell, P. (1986). Segmentation and speech perception in relation to reading skill: A developmental analysis. *Journal of Experimental Child Psychology, 41*, 489-507.

Stanovich, K.E. (1986). Matthew effects in reading: Some consequences of individual differences in the acquisition of literacy. *Reading Research Quarterly, 21*, 360-407.

Stanovich, K.E., Cunningham, A.E., & Cramer, B.B. (1984). Assessing phonological awareness in kindergarten: Issues of task comparability. *Journal of Experimental Child Psychology, 38*, 175-190.

Sulzby, E. (1986). Writing and reading: Signs of oral and written language organization in the young child. In W.H. Teale & E. Sulzby (Eds.), *Emergent literacy*. Norwood, NJ: Ablex Publishing Co.

Taylor, D. (1983). *Family literacy*. Portsmouth, NH: Heinemann.

Teale, W.H. (1986). Home background and young children's literacy development. In W.H.Teale & E.Sulzby (Eds.), *Emergent literacy*. Norwood, NJ: Ablex Publishing Co.

Torneus, M. (1984). Phonological awareness and reading: A chicken and egg problem? *Journal of Educational Psychology, 76*, 1346-1358.

Treiman, R. (1984). Individual differences among children in reading and spelling styles. *Journal of Experimental Child Psychology, 37*, 463-477.

Tunmer, W.E., Herriman, M.L., & Nesdale, A.R. (1988). Metalinguistic abilities and beginning reading. *Reading Research Quarterly, 23*, 135-158.

Vellutino, F.R. (1978). Toward an understanding of dyslexia: Psychological factors in specific reading disability. In A.L. Benton & D. Pearl (Eds.), *Dyslexia*. NY: Oxford University Press, 63-111.

Vellutino, F.R., & Scanlon, D. (1987). Phonological coding, phonological awareness, and reading ability: Evidence from a longitudinal and experimental study. *Merrill-Palmer Quarterly, 33*, 321-363.

Vernon, M.D. (1957). *Backwardness in reading: A study of its nature and origin*. NY: Cambridge University Press.

Wallach, M. A., & Wallach, L. (1979). Helping disadvantaged children learn to read by teaching them phoneme identification skills. In L.B. Resnick & P. Weaver (Eds.), *Theory and practice of early reading, (Vol. 3)*. Hillsdale, NJ: Erlbaum.

Wells, G. (1986). *The meaning makers: Children learning language and using language to learn*. Portsmouth, NH: Heinemann.

Williams, J. P. (1979). The ABDs of reading: A program for the learning disabled. In L.B. Resnick & P. Weaver (Eds.), *Theory and practice of early reading, (Vol. 3)*. Hillsdale, NJ: Erlbaum.

Williams, J.P. (1980). Teaching decoding with an emphasis on phoneme analysis and phoneme blending. *Journal of Educational Psychology, 172*, 1-15.

Wolff, P. (1989). Presentation at Harvard Graduate School of Education.

Yopp, H. K. (1988). The validity and reliability of phonemic awareness tests. *Reading Research Quarterly, 23*, 159-177.

Yopp, H. K (1992). Developing phonemic awareness in young children. *The Reading Teacher, 45*, 696-703.

Zifcak, M. (1981). Phonological awareness and reading acquisition. *Contemporary Educational Psychology, 6*, 117-126.

III. LETTERS

Chapter 4. Beginning Reading: Learning Print-to-sound Correspondence

Cheryl Rappaport Liebling, PhD
Rivier College

In 1985, the Commission on Reading issued a report, *Becoming a Nation of Readers*, that called for a view of reading "as part of a child's general language development and not as a discrete skill isolated from listening, speaking, and writing" (Anderson et al., 1985, p. 20). The Commission described reading as part of the language arts; and it suggested that the overriding purpose of instruction is to help students become capable in communicating and understanding meaning through spoken and written language. In addition, the Commission spoke loudly and clearly about the need for beginning readers to become fluent and automatic decoders of words if they are to gain access to meaning and effective communication: "The issue is no longer, as it was several decades ago, whether children should be taught phonics. The issues now are specific ones of just how it should be done" (Anderson et al., 1985, p. 36).

Since recent findings concerning beginning reading remain consistent with the recommendations of the Commission on Reading, this chapter discusses how to teach beginners to read by emphasizing the code and the integration of reading with the language arts. Learning the code in beginning reading requires direct, systematic, explicit instruction regarding the relationship of print to sound as well as encouragement to practice newly developing reading strategies with connected text. Progress in beginning reading is enhanced by opportunities for learners to listen, and follow along, while fluent readers share children's literature, along with ample occasions to use both written and spoken language.

This chapter begins with a summary of historical trends concerning how beginning reading is taught. This is followed by a description of Stage 1 reading (Chall, 1983a) that identifies various aspects of word recognition, along with strategies that help students "break the code." The final section discusses implementation of a Stage 1 beginning reading program by presenting several classroom assessment strategies, a framework for providing instruction within primary-grade classrooms, and several promising intensive intervention programs.

History of Beginning Reading Instruction in the United States[1]

Colonial period through the early 19th century. From colonial times well into the 19th century, the predominant approach to beginning reading was the ABC method. It emphasized the identification of letters by name along with recognition of simple letter-sound relationships. Children learned the names of letters and recited these in sequence in order to memorize words appearing in religious texts. In essence, most children learned to read by spelling aloud written words.

Throughout the colonial period and until the mid-19th century, the primary purpose of reading was to study the *Bible*. A commonly used teaching material was the *New England Primer*, a book that used religious text as the content for instruction. The *Primer* emphasized memorization and recitation as children learned to spell and decode words of one-to-five syllables. Later, children practiced reading words within short verses and religious texts. Many students also used hornbooks, hand-held boards that fit in a child's palm. On each board was written the alphabet, two-letter combinations of a vowel and a consonant, and *The Lord's Prayer*.

Between the Revolutionary and Civil Wars, the reading of patriotic documents became another purpose for reading. Through reading, a sense of pride in the American democratic system of government could be instilled. At this time, Noah

---

[1]This discussion is drawn from Adams (1990), Chall (1983b), Heilman (1993), and Smith (1986). The reader is urged to consult these texts for more detailed information concerning the history of beginning reading instruction.

Webster developed *The Elementary Spelling Book*. Webster continued to emphasize reading by spelling; his book included spelling rules, lists of words and syllables to memorize and recite, and fables, moralistic stories, and poetry. Stress marks were added to words, within stories and poetry, to encourage correct pronunciation, regardless of regional dialect.

Mid-19th century. During the mid-19th century, instruction in the **sounds** associated with printed letters gradually came to replace the earlier **alphabet spelling** (Smith, 1986). Using the sound approach, children associated a letter with its most typical sound by means of a key word; for example *B is for ball*. After learning the symbol-sound relationship, children practiced reading one-syllable words containing the phonics generalization.

The *McGuffey Eclectic Readers*, published from 1840 through the turn of the century, provided children with instruction in both the spelling of words and the association of letters with sounds in sequence. The *McGuffey Readers* represented the first attempt to control the complexity of vocabulary and grammar by limiting the number of different words and types of sentence structures within a selection of text. An effort was made to consider the developmental capabilities of students and to provide appropriate reading materials.

During this time, American schools were beginning to place students in separate grades, and the *McGuffey Readers* offered texts for each grade level. Although the *McGuffey Readers* were the most popular instructional texts of the day, they were only one of several series in use. *Bumstead's Reader*, also published at that time, recommended use of a sight method for instruction.

By the mid-1800s, educators were considering alternative teaching approaches for reading instruction. Horace Mann was especially vocal in this debate. He had visited European schools and was inspired by the ideas of Pestalozzi, a Prussian who advocated consideration of the child when designing instruction. As an alternative to the memorization of the alphabet, Pestalozzi proposed that letter sounds be learned, a few at a time, as needed to read a word, rather than in alphabetical order. Mann promoted Pestalozzi's approach, and hence the importance of the relationship of print to meaning. Although it is sometimes thought that Mann wished to abolish phonics instruction, the passage below (in which Mann describes a lesson given in the Pestalozzian manner) suggests quite the opposite. Instead, it indicates that Mann supported the teaching of letter sounds, and their blending into words, but rejected the teaching of letters by name in alphabetical order. Mann writes:

The teacher first drew a house upon the blackboard....By the side of...it, he wrote the word *house*....With a long pointing rod...he ran over the form of the letters,—the children, with their slates before them and their pencils in their hands, looking at the pointing rod and tracing the forms of the letters in the air....

The next process was to copy the word *house*, both in script and in print, on their slates. Then followed the formation of the sounds of the letter of which the word was composed, and the spelling of the word. Here the *names* of the letters were not given as with us, but only their powers, or the sounds which those letters have in combination. The letter *h* was first selected and set up in the reading frame, and the children, instead of articulating our alphabetic *h* (aitch), merely gave a hard breathing,—such a sound as the letter really has in the word *house*....

In every such school, also, there are printed sheets or cards containing the letters, diphthongs, and whole words. The children are taught to sound a diphthong, and then asked in what words that sound occurs (Mann, 1842 in Smith, 1965, pp. 77-78).

Late 19th/early 20th century. Toward the late 19th century, educators decided that the future of the country depended, in part, upon the intellectual abilities of the American people. This realization was coupled with a more enlightened view of childhood as distinctly different from adulthood. The purposes of reading expanded to include acquisition of information, and engagement in a pleasurable activity. As a consequence, many children were introduced to a variety of reading materials including: moralistic verses and stories such as *Mother Goose* and *Aesop's Fables*; adventure stories such as *Robinson Crusoe*; fairy tales such as *Cinderella*; poetry; and, turn-of-the-century contemporary fiction such as *Rebecca of Sunnybrook Farm, The Five Little Peppers, Little Women, and Huckleberry Finn* (Norton, 1991).

As interest in education and literature grew during the early 20th century, so too grew the call to emphasize meaning from the start. The reading textbooks of the late 19th and early 20th centuries such as *Stepping Stones to Literature, The Arnold Primer*, and *The Rational Method in Reading*, emphasized the reading of whole, connected text by whole word identification (Smith, 1986). By the late 1920s, many educators encouraged students to read silently, nearly from the start.

Mid-20th century. By the 1930s, American reading instruction came to rely on basal programs that introduced a set of sight words before sound-symbol relationships were explored. From this time into the 1960s, the "look-say" method received greater emphasis than phonics. Controlled vocabulary and syntactic simplicity characterized the basal stories.   Phonics and spelling-sound pattern exercises were offered as supplementary material, while visual configuration and context appeared to be the primary methods for word recognition.

The public reaction of this period nonetheless continued to express concern for the use of phonics as a word recognition strategy during beginning reading. This concern reached its peak in 1955 when many parents in the United States agreed with Rudolph Flesch (1955) that an emphasis on sight word recognition, rather than phonics, was preventing many children from becoming fluent readers and, therefore, from achieving the American dream. Parental interest in Flesch's polemic stirred educators and government leaders alike.

During the 1960s, considerable government resources were allocated to research the relative merits of various beginning reading programs. A number of supplementary phonics programs appeared. Among these were linguistic readers such as *Let's Read* (Bloomfield & Barnhart, 1965). These materials were used to teach word families through practice with rhyming word-lists and sentences with rhyming patterns. Another program, *Words in Color* (Gattegno, 1968), used color to help students establish the correspondences between print and sound.

Chall's (1967; 1983b) synthesis of the research on beginning reading instruction found that phonics instruction, along with many opportunities to read, was preferable to a sight approach in helping children become independent readers. Twenty years after Chall's initial study, her findings were reaffirmed by Adams (1990). Using more sophisticated statistical and research design methods than were available earlier, Adams continued to find that "approaches in which systematic code instruction is included along with meaningful connected reading result in superior reading achievement overall" (Adams, 1990, p. 12).

Late 20th century. Despite the proliferation of supporting research and instructional materials for teaching phonics and word families, by the late 1970s, many educators were still undecided as to the "best" method for instruction. While programs varied in emphasis, the basals of this era tended to include the following: workbooks for the teaching of phonics and spelling-sound patterns; simple stories with controlled vocabulary and syntax; and detailed scripts for the teacher including directions as to how to introduce a story, questions for comprehension discussion, and postreading activities.

While these basals were seen as comprehensive by many educators, others questioned their literary value, the scripting for teachers, the insufficient connection between word recognition exercises and stories, and the limited integration of reading and language arts.

Furthermore, educators began to reexamine their notions of reading. Conceptions of reading now characterized the reading process as "constructive" since readers create meaning by integrating text information with knowledge gained from prior experience. The "Whole Language" movement arose in the late 1980s to draw on the use of literature instead of basals in an attempt to focus reading instruction more fully on the meaning of text and the "constructive" quality of the reading process. This effort reflected a shift in the ongoing debate concerning whether to place more emphasis on decoding or on meaning in beginning reading programs.

As the 20th century draws to a close, educators are trying to teach both decoding and meaning, at appropriate times, rather than viewing them as mutually exclusive (Spiegel, 1992). Such an approach is supported by theoretical models of reading that postulate the simultaneous processing of letter, sound, meaning, and contextual information during skilled reading.[2]

Stage 1: Beginning Reading - Learning the Code

During beginning reading, learners need to focus on print, a notion that runs counter to the paramount purpose of reading—understanding the meaning of text (Chall, 1983a). Although the central purposes of reading are comprehension and communication, the recognition of words is a necessary step toward comprehension. Since "over 94% of the different words children read occur fewer than ten times in every million words of text" (Adams, 1990, p. 34), it is crucial that learners become automatic decoders of words as quickly as possible so that their attention in reading can focus upon meaning. Mastery of decoding skills by beginning readers will eventually aid in critical thinking during reading and writing.

Beginning readers generally are learning to decode words that are already in their spoken vocabularies, words for which meaning is immediately associated, once accurate decoding occurs. As Chall (1983b) notes, most beginning readers understand 4,000 or more spoken words, yet are learning to read approximately 600 words during Stage 1. Consequently, while being "glued to print" appears to be a less mature approach to reading than reading for comprehension, Chall (1983b)

---

[2]For further information on conceptualizations of skilled reading, See Chapter 1 of this volume and Adams, M.J. (1990; 1994).

makes the convincing argument that attentiveness to the actual words written by the author, rather than their meaning, is an essential phase in the development of fluent reading.

As discussed in Chapter 3 of this text, the most consistent predictor of beginning reading success is phonemic awareness, a skill that reflects the learner's ability to identify, segment, and blend individual sounds within spoken words. Coupled with the identification of letters by name, phonemic awareness paves the way for the mapping of print to sound during Stage 1 of the reading process.

In addition, children's experiences with language and print prior to learning to read can facilitate early success in reading. Among the characteristics frequently attributed to children who learn to read with ease are: considerable background knowledge gained from wide-ranging experiences, familiarity with written language through listening to books read aloud, drawing and attempting to write for communicative purposes, and pretending to read by telling stories of simple texts (Adams, 1990, 1994; Chall, 1983b). Furthermore, young children who learn to read easily generally attend to environmental print and communicate ideas and emotions with effective use of vocabulary and grammar.

Stage 1 reading can be viewed as a "window of opportunity." On the outside are Stage 0 emergent-literacy experiences that help learners begin to appreciate the communicative power of language within highly contextualized environments. On the inside lies the world of written language by which ideas and emotions are shared through print. Stage 1 of reading development is the window that links spoken and written language. Beginning readers "climb" through the window as they learn to decode print. The decoding of print enables readers to comprehend the meaning of written language.

As learners begin to read, they must acquire the range of word recognition strategies that skilled readers call upon when they encounter unfamiliar words. Direct, explicit instruction in these strategies helps beginning readers attend to print and to the relationship of print to sound. As the same time, an effective instructional program also emphasizes the links between spoken and written language.

Such a program includes direct decoding instruction, application of decoding to the reading of connected text, and integration of reading and language arts activities through discussion, writing, and practice in reading simple, engaging stories. In addition, during the school day, beginning readers need to hear more sophisticated texts read aloud by fluent readers in order to become familiar with more complex language patterns, words, and concepts. In combination, these activities constitute a rich instructional program.

INSTRUCTIONAL STRATEGIES

The outcome that signals mastery of Stage 1 reading is the ability to decode and comprehend simple stories independently. Students attain this proficiency by achieving the word recognition goals described below. Such mastery enables readers to shift their attention to comprehension. Most often, these goals are achieved in the primary grades; however, older students and adults who experience difficulties in learning to read need to achieve these goals in order to become fluent readers who concentrate on text meaning.

Goal #1: Use letter-sound correspondences and an understanding of the alphabetic principle when blending sounds to read and write one-syllable words, especially those characterized by the CVC pattern.

Goal #2: Decode by analogy when reading and writing words that are part of rhyming word families. This process enables learners to transfer letter-sound pattern information to words of similar patterns.

Goal #3: Recognize high frequency, irregularly-spelled words by sight as logographic wholes. These words are learned through memorization, participation in language experience, reading aloud, and discussion and writing activities.

Goal #4: Draw on context to confirm word recognition within meaningful sentences.

In combination, mastery of these four goals represents a powerful constellation of strategies for becoming a skilled reader of connected text. The following discussion describes instructional strategies that help learners achieve these goals and illustrates them with sample teaching lessons.

Goal #1 instruction: Use of letter-sound correspondences.

> Phonics is more likely to be useful when children hear the
> sounds associated with most letters both in isolation and in
> words, and when they are taught to blend together the
> sounds of letters to identify words...
> (Anderson et al., 1985, p. 118)

In a recent study, Ehri & Robbins (1992) conclude that beginning readers need to understand the relationship of letters to sounds, to divide words into subunits, and to blend parts of known words with parts of unfamiliar words before they will succeed in decoding by analogy. Their work further confirms that it is necessary to begin Stage 1 instruction by teaching letter-sound correspondence and blending.

This initial step involves the teaching of the correspondences of graphemes (printed letters) to phonemes (sounds). Some students already have some familiarity with these correspondences, but others require considerable practice in discriminating the visual shapes of letters, identifying the names of letters, and associating particular sounds with letters. The amount of time spent on instruction should be adjusted to students' levels of understanding. The following broad scope and sequence for teaching letter-sound correspondences is often recommended:

- Introduce several consonants. These are introduced before vowels since consonants are more frequently found in the initial position in words. However, all consonants need not be taught before introducing some vowels. As suggested in Chapter 3, it is helpful to begin by introducing consonants that are characterized as **continuant sounds** such as **f, m, n, s,** and **w.** These sounds can be pronounced at a slow speed without excessive distortion. Consonants characterized as **stops** such as **p, t, d, b, k,** and **g** can then be introduced.

- As students begin to learn consonants, they use initial letter-sound correspondences along with context to identify words. They also use some final letter-sound correspondences to identify words. At this point, learners need to become familiar with the terminology *consonant* and *vowel*.

- Next, introduce the short vowels **a, e, i, o, u,** and the vowel digraph **ea** as in **ea**ch. Also teach consonant digraphs **ch, sh, th,** in which two consonants combine to form one sound, and consonant blends, **pl, st, tr,** in which the two consonant sounds can be discerned. (The short vowels and consonant digraphs are introduced before the long vowels in order to reveal the code of CVC words.)

- Then, introduce the consonant digraphs **wh** and **ck,** the consonant blends **br, cr, dr, fr, gr, pr, bl, cl, fl, ld, nd, sc, tw,** silent consonants **kn, wr,** long vowels **a, e, i, o, u, y,** key generalizations such as the **silent e rule,** and vowel diphthongs such as **ow, oi,** and **oy.**

- In addition, introduce the soft sounds for **c** and **g,** the consonant digraph **ph,** consonant blends **sk, sl, sm, sw str, squ, thr,** silent consonants **gn** and **mb,** vowel digraphs **oa, ay,** and **ai, ei** as in **eight** and **receive, ey** as in **honey, oo, ow, ue,** and the vowel diphthong **ou.** Introduce r-controlled vowels: **ar, er, ir, or, ur, ear,** and **our.** Learners also need to tackle final consonant blends such as **ng** and **nt.**

Following is a lesson plan that describes the teaching of a vowel letter-sound correspondence in which a short vowel appears in the medial position of the CVC (consonant-vowel-consonant) pattern. An explicit instructional approach, sometimes termed *synthetic phonics*, is favored so as to avoid confusion during instruction. The example can be followed to teach a range of letter-sound correspondences. A similar lesson plan would be followed to teach an initial consonant. (For an example of a plan that introduces an initial consonant, turn to page 169.)

Sample Lesson Plan for Teaching Vowel Letter-Sound Correspondence with Blending.

Instructional Goal: To teach a decoding strategy that enables students to associate the short *a* with **Aa** as in *tan* and to blend sounds to form one-syllable words of the CVC pattern.

1. Introduce short vowel sounds after students have learned to recognize several consonant letter-sound relationships in the initial and final positions of words. Tell students that they will learn what is called the "short" sound of **a**, and that it corresponds to the letter **Aa.** Short /a/ can be pronounced in isolation prior to pronouncing it within a CVC word.

2. Begin by presenting, on a piece of oaktag, a short poem that contains words with the short /a/ sound. Read the selection aloud after asking students to listen for words that have the short /a/ sound, as in the word **at** or **hat.** Pronounce the short /a/ in isolation then move to saying the sound within words. While reading the text aloud, pause to underline the **Aa** in the words having the short /a/ sound within one-syllable words of the CVC or VC pattern. In the following text from *One Fish, Two Fish, Red Fish, Blue Fish* (Seuss, 1960), students read about different kinds of fish:

> Some are sad.
> And some are glad.
> And some are very very bad.
> Why are they sad and glad and bad?
> I do not know.
> Go ask your dad.

3. Explicitly demonstrate the blending of a CVC word such as *dad*, **for which the students have already learned the consonant sounds. While blending** /d/-/a/-/d/, point to the word in the text. Next, ask students to practice blending the sounds as you point to each sound in left to right progression. Ask students to write the letters of the word on an index card as they are sounded. Ask students to point to, sound, blend, and read the word on the index card.

4. Now ask students to help you "echo" reread the text. This time, pause to sound and blend those words that contain the short /a/ sound and consonants that have been learned.

5. After the rereading, write on the chalkboard words containing /a/ for students to enter into a wordbank (of index cards) or a reading/writing notebook. Be sure to use words for which students have already learned the consonants. These may include: **sad, fan, pan**, and **man**. As each word is written on the board, make a special effort to point to the letters and blend the sounds from left to right. Students should read each word after the teacher.

   Following the reading of the word, write it in a simple sentence on the board. (Use CVC words that also are formed with /a/ to write the sentence.) Students can write the sentence on the back of their index cards while the teacher dictates the sentence slowly. Encourage students to use their letter-sound knowledge to spell words accurately. After a set of words is written on the board and in notebooks or on index cards, ask students to take turns reading their words and sentences. This might be done in pairs.

6. Provide additional practice through matching games, practice exercises, reading of sentences or stories composed of these words, and flashcards. Practice exercises may ask a student to: spell a word containing the short /a/ such as _a_ when associated with a picture of a hat; pronounce a word represented by a picture and decide whether the word includes a short /a/; identify and color all words in a drawing that contain the short /a/; or select the correct word from several choices in order to complete a sentence in a meaningful manner.

   Using their set of wordbank cards or their reading/writing notebooks, students can practice reading the words in sentences. Students can also use their wordbank cards to practice reading the words while engaging with peers in games such as BINGO, Fish, or Concentration. Students should be encouraged to refer to their notebooks or index cards during language experience and writing activities.

While teaching a particular letter-sound correspondence, teachers can draw on many simple texts that utilize predictable patterns, rhyming, and particular phonics generalizations. When working on the short vowel sounds, for example, teachers can turn to the following books for compatible text: *Green Eggs and Ham* (Geisel, 1960), *Hop on Pop* (Geisel, 1991b), *Wings on Things* (Brown, 1982), or *The Cat in the Hat* (Seuss, 1957). Alphabet books such as *On Market Street* (Lobel, 1981), or *Brian Wildsmith's ABC* (Wildsmith, 1962), offer simple texts that emphasize individual letters, words in which the letters appear, and illustrations to contextualize the words.

Many authors, such as Marjorie Flack, Jack Kent, Verna Ardema, Molly Bang, Judy Blume, Betsy Byars, Pat Hutchins, and Stan and Jan Berenstain write books that emphasize predictable patterns, rhyme, and phonics generalizations (Norton, 1991; Routman, 1988). Trachtenburg (1990) provides a useful list of stories for beginning readers according to the phonics generalizations that are emphasized in the text. In addition, Modern Curriculum Press and Educators' Publishing Service publish a large variety of stories that emphasize specific phonics generalizations.

Many teachers question whether it is necessary for children to state phonics generalizations that guide pronunciation. Some feel that it is not so important for students to state rules as to apply them through practice in reading and constructing the correspondence. However, it is occasionally beneficial to describe a rule that particularly helps readers and writers decide on the correct pronunciation or spelling of a word. For example, teachers often point out that the vowel within a CVC pattern is generally "short" or that the letters **Cc** and **Gg** generally take "soft" sounds when coming before an *e, i,* or *y.* (See Chapter 6 for other perspectives.)

Summary of goal #1 instruction. Knowing letter-sound correspondences provides learners with a very useful strategy for unraveling unfamiliar words independently in order to read connected text.[3] Exemplary phonics instruction has been characterized as (a) systematic, (b) grounded in a student's phonemic awareness, (c) clear and explicit, (d) integrated into a comprehensive beginning reading and language arts program, (e) focused on reading real words in isolation and in context

---

[3]For more detailed suggestions for the teaching of phonics, see Barr & Johnson (1991), Burns, Roe, & Ross (1992), Heilman (1993), and Miller (1993).

rather than memorizing rules, and (f) oriented toward helping students become independent in word recognition (Stahl, 1992).

Goal #2 instruction: Decoding by analogy. Once students have developed an understanding of the alphabetic principle, they are ready to learn to decode by analogy (Gaskins et al., 1991; Goswami & Mead, 1992). When readers decode by analogy, they blend the **onset** sound of a word with the larger unit of **rime**, typically composed of a vowel and a final consonant or consonant blend.

For example, in reading the word *hat*, a student learns to blend the onset /**h**/ sound with the rime /**at**/ to form **hat**. Once students have learned letter-sound correspondences, this may be an easier process and may result in less distortion of sounds than blending individual segments as in /**h**/-/**a**/-/**t**/. The following instructional scope and sequence is recommended when teaching students to decode by analogy.

- First, introduce, one-at-a-time, common word families based on rimes such as **-at, -an, -ap, -it, -ip, -in, -eg, -et, -ot, -og, -ug**. For any one rime, teach students to substitute initial consonants to create familiar words. Also, list unknown words that follow the pattern, and ask students to decode the unknown words by analogy.

- Introduce the primary word families throughout Stage 1. Practice blending onset sounds with each rime in reading and writing words. Always follow with opportunities to read these words in sentences to promote decoding in context. Wylie & Durrell (cited in Adams, 1990, p. 85) identify thirty-seven phonograms, or word families, from which at least five hundred primary-grade words can be generated: **-al, -all, -ain, -ake, -ale, -ame, -an, -ank, -ap, -ash, -at, -ate, -aw, -ay, -eat, -ell, -est, -ice, -ick, -ide, -ill, -in, -ine, -ing, -ip, -ir, -ock, -oke, -op, -ore, -uck, -ug, -ump, -unk**.

- During instruction, introduce students to the major one-syllable patterns: **CVC** (as in *hat)*, **CVCe** (as in *cake)*, and **CVVC** (as in *boat)*.

- In addition, use poetry and predictable stories to help students decode by analogy. By the conclusion of the beginning reading program, students should decode words that are characterized by the major letter-sound patterns and apply that ability to the reading of simple text.

Sample Lesson Plan for Teaching Decoding by Analogy.

Instructional Goal: To teach a decoding by analogy strategy that enables students to blend the onset sound of a word with the rime in familiar and unfamiliar words within rhyming families.

1. Select a rhyming family such as the **-all** family for instruction. Use the consonant substitution technique to teach students to decode by analogy. Begin instruction by telling the students that they will be reading words in the **-all** family. Write **-all** on the board, pronounce it, and ask the students to read it.

2. Read aloud a poem, or story segment, that emphasizes the word family you will be teaching. Write the text on a large piece of oaktag. Ask students to listen as you read the text aloud, pointing to the words in the **-all** family. Ask students to read along with you as you repeat the text. Read slowly to help students practice blending the onset and rime of each word in the family, as in the following example taken from *Hop on Pop* (Geisel, 1991b):

ALL
TALL
We are **all tall.**

ALL
SMALL
We are **all small.**

ALL
BALL
We **all** play **ball.**

BALL
WALL
Up on a **wall.**

ALL
FALL
Fall off the wall.

3. Underneath **-all** on the board, write **tall**. Pronounce **-all** and **tall**, and ask students to repeat after you. Erase the *t* to yield **-all**, and ask students to watch as you substitute *b* for *t* to yield **ball**. Pronounce **ball**, and ask

students to repeat after you. Students should then generate new words by substituting the *onset* letter/sound: **call, hall, fall.**

As words are generated, make a chart by writing them on the board. You may also want to introduce some unfamiliar rhyming words, such as **gall** and **pall**, to see whether students can decode by analogy even when the words are uncommon. This provides an opportunity to expand your students' vocabulary. Work with students to create short oral sentences that include several of the rhyming words.

4. Ask students to list some target words from the poem and the board exercise in their reading/writing notebooks. Then ask them to copy several sentences from the target poem or story into their notebooks.

5. Now reread the segment, and ask students to underline each word in the **-all** family as the class reads in unison. Students can make word-family index cards and add **-all** family words to their wordbanks. They can also read the charts and sentences from their notebooks to peers and family.

6. As students learn rhyme families, they can spell words of a particular family during dictation of simple sentences. Practice in spelling words that are part of predictable families reinforces the patterns that students are reading. These dictations can be included in word-family notebooks.

7. For those students who require additional support, practice exercises and lists of rhyming words reinforce an understanding of the patterns. In these exercises, students read simple sentences and select rhyming words to complete riddles; circle words that rhyme within stories; connect words to pictures; or select a word that best completes a sentence (Gregorich & Henkel, no date). Using flashcards, a student may be asked to select words from cards that are part of particular word families. The teacher might draw a ladder on the board with **-at** as the bottom rung. Students search the flashcards for words that are part of this family. On each successive rung of the ladder, another word is added: **mat, pat, cat,** etc. (*Golden Step Ahead*, 1989).

Reading by analogy is an important part of an integrated reading and language arts program. Once students become attentive to the rhyming patterns of words in poems and simple stories, they often show an increased interest in reciting and writing poetry as well as participating in choral reading and dramatizations. These activities reinforce the students' knowledge of word families while extending their enjoyment and familiarity with language.

By the conclusion of the beginning reading period, typically by the end of grade 2, most students are very attentive to rhyming patterns; they also recognize words automatically by generating analogous relationships among words in families. This strategy, in combination with a solid understanding of phonics, facilitates the rapid identification of words that is a prerequisite to fluent reading with understanding.

Goal #3 instruction: Rapid recognition of sight words. The primary purpose of sight word recognition is to promote rapid entry to the reading of connected text. Teachers often provide sight word instruction to help students recognize common "glue" words (such as *the, is, are*), as well as content words (such as *beautiful, airplane, pretty*), that appear frequently in beginning reading texts.

Many sight words contain letter-sound correspondences that are not taught until late in the letter-sound instructional sequence. Some of the words contain inconsistent letter-sound correspondences and may always be recognized primarily by visual configurations. Sight words are memorized as logographic wholes through repeated exposures during the reading of stories, short sentences, and flashcards. The following scope of instruction will help beginning readers develop sight word recognition.

- Teach students to recognize function words, such as **the, their, they, to, do, does, get, have,** and **your**, that carry little meaning, but act as the "glue" that binds content words together in sentences. Many of these words contain consistent letter-sound patterns (such as **it**), but some do not (such as **have**). Whether they are consistent or inconsistent, "glue" words should be overlearned and recognized automatically so that beginning readers can read simple texts.

  Common function words include: **a, about, again, all, am, an, and, are, as, at, away, be, but, could, did, do, down, from, for, had, has, have, he, her, here, him, how, I, in, is, it, just, may, me, must, my, near, no, not, oh, of, on, one, she, so, some, soon, that, the, them, then, there, they, this, to, too, two, up, us, want, was, we, were, what, when, where, who, will, with, yes, you,** and **your**.

- In addition, teach students to recognize common content words that are irregular in the correspondence of letters and sounds. Among these words are: **beautiful,**

child, father, language, library, mischief, mother, neighbor, special, and **woman.** In all, some two hundred and twenty-five words that beginning readers frequently encounter can be considered irregular in their letter/sound correspondence (Heilman, 1993). These words need to be taught because they appear so often in texts for beginning readers.

Among common content words are the following: **airplane, apple, baby, back, ball, birthday, black, blue, boy, boat, came, can, come, cookies, cow, cowboy, daddy, dinner, eat, farm, father, girl, good, good-by, happy, house, find, green, known, laugh, little, look, mother, morning, night, party, pie, play, pretty, put, said, saw, show, something, splash, surprise, toy, walk, white,** and **yellow.** Many teachers refer to graded sight-word lists such as the Dale-Chall (1948) list to verify that students have had exposure to words that appear commonly in their reading.

■ Encourage students to read and reread beginning children's literature to promote their skill in sight word recognition.

To learn sight words, students generally write particular words on index cards and generate sentences in which the words appear. For example, *the* is a common sight word. A teacher might take this word from the reading of a simple sentence or text segment, write it on the board, and pronounce it. Students might repeat the pronunciation, trace the letters in the air, close their eyes and spell the word, and enter the word in their word banks or notebooks.

Through practice in reading sight words, either in isolation or within a simple sentence, students are expected to memorize pronunciation and to identify words quickly on the basis of visual configuration. This process can be facilitated if students are encouraged to use phonics for decoding regular letter-sound correspondences such as the *i* in *is*. To identify *is*, students can use their knowledge of phonics to decode the short *i* while the teacher can point out that the *s* represents the sound /z/.

Sometimes teachers select simple text and preteach unfamiliar words as sight words to give students the sense of reading a story long before large numbers of patterns and generalizations can be decoded. When used as a supplement to decoding instruction, and viewed as an initial extension of the stages of emergent reading described by Sulzby (1985), reading primarily by sight with the help of a motivating picture and connection to familiar content may have some benefit among students who can memorize with ease.

For example, in the "Little Book" *Painting* (Cowley, 1990), which is part of the StoryBox series, a student would memorize a set of fourteen words prior to reading the story. These words include: **Toby, painted, the, floor, and, wall, cupboard, table, chair, cat, then, Mom, came,** and, **in.** Many of these words will be decoded through phonics eventually, or by analogy or structural analysis. However, the motivation to read independently can be boosted by success in reading simple texts early, particularly among students who memorize easily.

Additional techniques for sight-word development include: the use of flashcards and word lists to establish a core reading vocabulary; the use of Big Books in which students follow along as the teacher reads aloud and points to individual words; language experience stories; and the use of highly predictable story lines. Many teachers involve students in sight word recognition practice through games such as Concentration, Go Fish, or BINGO.

Summary of goal #3 instruction. While sight words contribute to initial entry to connected text, reliance on sight-word recognition as the primary word-recognition strategy for Stage 1 is an inefficient means for accurate and automatic decoding of text. As studies of fluent readers have shown, unanalyzed sight words are only a small part of all of the words that mature readers recognize automatically. The far greater number of words are identified by means of decoding letter-sound correspondences.

Goal #4 instruction: Using context. With practice, readers learn to couple an understanding of decoding with their background knowledge of vocabulary, syntax, and content to confirm the accuracy of word identification. When combining these strategies, readers generally exhibit a high level of word recognition. Although it is generally inadvisable to encourage readers to guess word identification solely from contextual information, it is important that students use their knowledge of sentence and paragraph context to verify the accuracy of their decoding. In addition, beginners need to rely somewhat on context for word recognition until a full range of decoding generalizations are learned. An instructional scope for teaching students how to use context during decoding is described below.

■ Teach students to use context to provide confirming clues during beginning decoding of letter-sound correspondences. Beginning readers can learn this strategy through exercises in which specific phonics generalizations are highlighted in conjunction with word clues that focus on meaning. For instance, Heilman (1993) offers many examples of exercises in which a learner might be asked to write a word that fits a decoding generalization and a context clue as in the following examples:

g_t_   Clue: opening in a fence (gate)
r_s_   Clue: pretty flower (rose)
pea__   Clue: fruit (peach)
mo__   Clue: insect (moth).

■ In addition, teach students to use repeating sentence and story patterns to predict word identification and to confirm the appropriateness of an identified word within text. Through the choral reading of "Big Books" with predictable sentence and story patterns and the rereading of familiar stories, beginning readers learn to anticipate repeated words.

■ Encourage advanced beginning readers to self-correct their decoding when their comprehension indicates that they mispronounced a word in context. When a mispronunciation affects meaning, encourage the reader to attempt self-correction. If the error does not affect meaning, let the student continue reading. After the section of reading is concluded, ask the student to pronounce misread words.

Sometimes students are not aware of misreading a word that is important to the understanding of text. In such cases, the students may be reading text that is too difficult and a recommendation to read simpler text may be in order.

SUMMARY OF INSTRUCTIONAL STRATEGIES

A combined strategy of phonics, decoding by analogy, use of sight words, and drawing on context to confirm decoding accuracy helps beginning readers master the outcome of decoding and comprehending simple stories. It is crucial that teachers assure that each student learns the four recognition strategies drawn on by skilled readers. Instruction should provide extra practice for those who need it and the opportunity to move to advanced reading activities for those who have mastered decoding.

Implementation of Stage 1 Reading Programs

When beginning readers are successful in word recognition, they are well on the way to becoming independent readers and writers. Word recognition strategies can be taught in integrated reading and language arts classrooms that provide a variety of oral and written activities. Several factors that contribute to effective implementation of Stage 1 reading programs are taken up below. This section begins by presenting several types of assessments that can facilitate flexible planning. Next, a sample structure for a beginning reading classroom is provided; and finally, a few intensive programs designed to enhance Stage 1 reading are considered.

ASSESSMENT OF STUDENTS' LEARNING

The assessment of students' learning can take many forms. Observation of classroom performance, informal inventories of students' reading strengths and needs, and formal evaluations are all valuable means of measuring reading progress. Many teachers assess their students at the beginning and end of each year to determine growth. In addition, some teachers establish a regular schedule of assessment, such as an eight-week cycle, to encourage instructional modifications to meet the changing needs of growing students.

Observation of classroom performance. Assessment through observation of classroom performance is often indistinguishable from instructional activities. It could include work that the student is completing as part of a reading and language arts program as well as the opportunity to read more challenging text. Observation during instruction enables teachers to determine whether a student would benefit from adjustments in classroom practices. When progress is insufficient, educators reflect on their findings to adjust instruction and reteach concepts in different ways.

Assessments of classroom performance could include one or more of the following activities: the reading of an unfamiliar story to a group of peers or younger children; participation in a discussion about a book that several students have read; communicating ideas and emotions through writing or drawing about a book that has been read; or, a dramatic retelling of a story that has been read.

Teachers are expanding the range of activities used for informal assessment. Through the use of portfolios, observation or "kid-watching," conferences, and audio and videotapes, teachers gather information from a variety of perspectives to gain an understanding of each student's progress.

Informal inventories. In addition to teacher-designed assessment, published informal and criterion-referenced inventories can be helpful tools in identifying students' strengths and needs.[4] Teachers may make simple assessments of storybook reading using Barr, Sadow, & Blachowicz's (1990) print awareness assessment or

---

[4]For further information on informal assessment, see Roskos & Walker (1994).

Sulzby's emergent reading of familiar storybooks classifications (1985). Alternatively, Clay (1993a) offers a diagnostic survey that includes letter identification, print concepts, and reading isolated words.

To gauge reading abilities, many teachers ask students to read a familiar book of their own choosing, along with a more difficult book selected by the teacher. The teacher conducts an analysis of errors and discusses the story with the child to determine comprehension of the text and the extent that oral reading inaccuracies interfere with understanding (Clay, 1993a; Goodman, Watson, & Burke, 1987). Other teachers use published informal reading inventories to gather similar information (Bader & Wiesendanger, 1994; Burns & Roe, 1993; Leslie & Caldwell, 1990; Woods & Moe, 1989).

Formal assessment measures. An assessment instrument such as the *Diagnostic Assessment of Reading with Trial Teaching Strategies* (Roswell & Chall, 1991) draws together the information gathered while teaching with more formal assessment. It provides useful information on strengths and needs along with an opportunity to attempt a variety of instructional interventions while evaluating their effectiveness. For those students who appear to require intensive intervention, formal diagnostic testing is advisable. (See Chapters 11 and 12 of this volume.)

STRUCTURING THE BEGINNING READING CLASSROOM

Teachers in the early grades face a daunting task since their students are quite diverse in their language and literacy knowledge. This diversity in abilities requires substantial flexibility and reflection. Teachers need to provide direct instruction in decoding to students who are learning Stage 1 reading strategies, while providing advanced instruction to students who have mastered Stage 1 reading goals.

Characteristic of the beginning reading classroom is an atmosphere that "invites" learners to engage in spoken and written communication (Routman, 1991). This invitation is grounded in daily, engaging reading and writing experiences. Many teachers allocate at least a daily two-hour block to a reading-language arts program. This block is divided into half-hour segments during which students first participate in a whole group reading, listening, and discussion activity, then move to three other types of activities: guided reading and writing, shared reading and writing, and independent work with words.

Whole group segment. Teachers often begin the reading-language arts block by reading a story to the whole group. Typically, the teacher sits in front of the group of students gathered in the reading corner of the room. While reading aloud, the teacher involves learners in the reading by encouraging them to participate in the story and to respond to the story's content. At the same time, the teacher models effective decoding strategies by using techniques described earlier in this chapter.

For this activity, books are often chosen that use a letter-sound correspondence or word family that is under study. Teachers often use books with repetitive story parts, rhythm, and rhyme as well as songs. As students practice reading stories that contain a high percentage of the patterns that are under study, they can draw analogies between words that they have encountered and unfamiliar words that are consistent with previously learned patterns.

Appropriate stories, poems, and songs for group reading can be written on large sheets of chart paper or may be available as "Big Books." The use of large print facilitates group or "echo" reading in which learners repeat words and phrases as the teacher reads aloud. Beginning readers often need to read aloud since oral reading gives them an opportunity to connect print to speech. They also benefit from practicing word-recognition strategies while reading simple texts containing common words and phonetically regular words.

Guided segment. The heart of the daily instructional program is guided reading and writing—a 30 minute block during which the teacher works with a small group of students. During guided reading, teachers provide direct instruction in word-recognition strategies using lesson plans such as the examples described earlier (p. 152, 156). Within each guided session, students learn and practice print-to-sound and sound-to-print word recognition and writing strategies.

In addition to direct reading and writing instruction in the four decoding skills and strategies described earlier, students read orally and discuss the reading as soon as they can recognize most of the words in a given selection. For those students who come to school already decoding text fluently, instruction is planned to increase their opportunities to read for meaning along with opportunities to improve their use of letter-sound correspondences in writing.

Some teachers are finding that all aspects of instruction can occur with mixed-ability grouping (Cunningham et al., 1991). However, many others continue to advocate homogeneous groups for the guided reading instruction half-hour block during Stage 1 because of the diversity of their students' needs:

While I believe strongly that small groups should be heterogeneous and grouped according to interests and not abilities, for me the exception is first grade, especially early in the school year (Routman, 1991, p. 39).

Teachers are encouraged to utilize flexible regrouping rather than static homogeneous groupings when ability grouping is instituted. Such regrouping lets teachers assess developing skills and regroup according to needs.

Shared segment. During the shared reading and writing segment, pairs of students work collaboratively in reading books and creating stories. At times, teachers find it useful to pair students of different abilities to provide help and encouragement during the shared reading of books. Other times, it is helpful to pair students of similar ability while they practice a skill to mastery, or enjoy shared reading of material they have mastered. Students practice reading aloud to one another, reread stories practiced earlier, and discuss or write about books they have read. They may also collaborate on practice exercises assigned by the teacher.

Beginning readers engage in paired reading and discussion by using books written with familiar language, predictable patterns, rhymes, and repetitive content words. In addition to tackling books on their own, these readers can discuss stories, reread stories, and engage in shared or guided reading with fluent readers.

Among the host of appropriate books and series for young beginning readers are the "I Can Read" Books such as *Little Bear* (Minarik, 1957), *A Bargain for Frances* (Hoban, 1970), *The Smallest Cow in the World* (Paterson, 1991), and *Frog and Toad* (Lobel, 1970). The "Puffin Easy-to-Read" books include titles such as *Tales of Oliver Pig* (Leeuwen, 1979), and the "Ready-to-Read" books include titles such as *Wiley and the Hairy Man* (Bang, 1976).

Independent segment. The final block of the program is devoted to independent work. For 30 minutes each day, students read self-selected books, write or draw in journals about their reading, complete practice exercises, or use computer software that provides additional practice. This is also a time for groups of students to engage in book talks or post-reading sharing activities. For students who can benefit from additional guided direct instruction, the independent block can be used instead to provide additional direct teaching such as the intensive approaches described later in this chapter.

During the independent segment, students sometimes engage in independent writing activities that can have a powerful effect on reading by reinforcing the association of symbols with sounds in word recognition. Beginning readers sometimes make an early entry into independent writing by the use of invented spelling. While there is a clear advantage to motivating students by de-emphasizing spelling and editing skills during the "idea generation" phase of writing, teachers should help students produce "final" copy that is grammatically correct and properly spelled. By taking the time to help learners proofread and edit text, teachers encourage beginning readers and writers to become attentive to correct spellings and sentence structure, which reinforces Stage 1 development.

Finally, it is of great importance that beginning readers develop a love of reading and come to see reading as an important activity for free-time and pleasure. Encouraging children to read for pleasure as well as to gather information is an important psychological component of the beginning reading phase of literacy.

INTENSIVE READING-LANGUAGE ARTS INTERVENTIONS

Many educators agree that early and intensive intervention is crucial to preventing later school failure. In addition to sparing children from years of school failure, such programs foster reading development and decrease the need for subsequent special education and remedial services (Slavin et al., 1993). A variety of instructional interventions have demonstrated success or shown promise in preventing reading failure. Several of these, described below, include: *Project READ* (Calfee & Wadleigh, 1992; Enfield, 1987; Hopfenberg & Levin, 1993), *Success for All* (Slavin et al., 1992; Wasik & Slavin, 1993), and Reading Recovery (Clay, 1993b; Deford et al., 1991; Pinnell et al., 1994).

Project Read. *Project READ* (Enfield, 1987) is an intensive reading-and-writing approach that uses direct instruction to teach four strands: decoding-spelling, concept-vocabulary development, composition, and story reading. *Project READ* is considered a systematic and multisensory program that can be part of the daily classroom experience for all students. However, some schools use the program only for students who are behind most of their peers in reading ability. The program is generally used in grades one through three, although its materials go through grade nine. Many schools are using the program, and some cite impressive statistics concerning its effectiveness.

The decoding-spelling strand of *Project READ* is based upon the Orton-Gillingham-Stillman approach to the teaching of letter-sound correspondences (Enfield, 1987). During Strand 1 of the reading program, students learn to decode one syllable words. As decoding abilities progress, this strand also teaches syllabication, recognition of affixes and roots, and the use of context and the dictionary to aid in word recognition. Strand 2 emphasizes vocabulary and comprehension as well as composition. Strand 3 focuses on writing, as students learn to form letters, spell, and create grammatical sentences.

Students read both linguistically controlled stories and texts with uncontrolled vocabulary. Semantic maps, story graphs, and analysis of story structure are used to help students develop comprehension and create stories. Finally, the program links instruction to assessment through observation of performance and portfolios.

In a typical phonics lesson, the teacher begins by reviewing sounds that were taught in earlier lessons. To emphasize reading, the teacher uses flash letter-cards as the students pronounce corresponding sounds. To emphasize spelling, the teacher pronounces a sound, and students select the matching letter card. New sounds are introduced in a similar manner. In addition, students trace a letter as the sound is pronounced. Kinesthetic approaches include the use of a sand tray, raised letters, and tapping on a table. Students trace letters in the air, on a table, on raised-letter cards that show directionality, or on the board with chalk.

Practice in decoding words occurs as students blend sounds to read short words or syllables. Encoding (spelling) practice reinforces reading as students pronounce each sound while writing its corresponding letter. Oral reading follows as students point, to track each letter, while the sounds are blended. Students read phonetically regular words independently to reinforce correspondences that have been introduced, as in the following examples. The first example provides practice with **Pp-/p/, Hh-/h/, Jj-/j/**, and the second provides practice with **"Magic E"** and **Ii-/i/**).

Tan

Tan fan,
Tan pan,
Tan ham,
Tan jam.
Tan!
(Greene & Enfield, 1986, p. 11)

A Bike Trip

Mike had his red and white bike.
Mike was on a five mile trip.
Mike sat to rest.
His dog, Spike, was at his side.

"I like to bike," said Mike.
"Next time I will take a nine mile trip!"
                    (Greene & Enfield, 1986, p. 131)

Students are also encouraged to read any texts that interest them. Termed "stretch reading," this is an opportunity to read uncontrolled vocabulary. Teachers are urged to help with difficult text by pronouncing any words that students are unable to decode independently. Decoding and spelling are linked throughout the program, with emphasis on correct spelling as a means of learning the sequence of sounds in words. In addition, students are expected to use correct capitalization and punctuation. For example, the teacher reads a sentence aloud. Students write the sentences on paper. They correct their own work by underlining errors as the teacher spells aloud and writes the sentence on the board. Correct spellings, capitalization, and punctuation are written above errors.

Project READ has been endorsed by the Accelerated Schools project (Hopfenberg & Levin, 1993). This school reform and restructuring initiative indicates that *Project READ's* instructional approaches are beneficial in helping at-risk students achieve academic success.

Success For All. *Success For All* (Allington, 1992; Karweit, 1993; Madden et al., 1991; Slavin et al., 1991, Wasik & Slavin, 1993) involves a comprehensive restructuring of the educational services provided to children in preschool through grade 5. The goal of *Success for All* is to accelerate the progress of at-risk students. *Success for All* was developed to ensure that students in participating Chapter 1 schools develop adequate reading ability and receive the instruction needed for academic success. *Success For All* is implemented in many urban schools. It has documented success in drastically reducing retention and special education placements.

Beginning in grade 1, students are flexibly grouped cross-age and cross-grade for 90 minutes per day. This adaptation of the "Joplin Plan" allows a teacher to work with one reading level and to increase the time that a teacher can work with a group of students. Thus, many of the teachers in a school are teaching reading at the same time. In addition, adult tutors are used as teachers to further reduce class size.

The program emphasizes systematic study of print-to-sound correspondences, as students use auditory and visual skills to associate letters and sounds and to blend sounds to form words. As letters are learned, students read "little books" that contain phonetically regular language. Often, the reading of the "mini-books" takes place when pairs of students work together or during the 20 minutes of required reading at home assigned every night. An example of a *Success for All* lesson in the letter-sound correspondence for **Qq**-/**q**/ follows:[5]

A. **Reading review**. A story that has been previously read is reviewed by the entire group or in pairs.

B. **Letter review**. The teacher then reviews letters introduced previously. Students trace the letters in the air, repeating a "cue phrase" that the students have come to associate with the letter.

C. **New material**.

  1. *Alphabet song.*

  2. *Tongue twister.* The teacher says, "A lot of words start with the sound /**q**/. Listen to this. "The queen quickly poured the quacking duck some Quaker Oats." The teacher pronounces each word that starts with /**q**/, and students repeat each word.

  3. *Introduce /**q**/ pictures and objects.* A picture or object beginning with /**q**/ is pulled from "Alphie's" box. Students name the objects. The objects are shown a second time, and students pronounce the sound they hear at the beginning of each word.

  4. *Make the /**q**/ sound.* Students make the sound and attend to its "feel." The teacher shows students that /**q**/ is actually a blend of /**k**/ and /**w**/.

  5. *Introduce the letter Qq.* Write the names of the objects on the board and confirm that the words do indeed begin with **Qq**.

  6. *Write the letter Qq.* Write both upper-case and lower-case forms, discussing the similarities and differences. Students trace **Qq** in the air as they say the cue phrase, "Circle left, up, down, hook right." They write the letter on paper, trace it on a peer's arm, etc. They then add the phrase, "The sound for **Qq** is /**kw**/." The teacher also explains that **Qq**

---

[5]Slavin, R.E., Madden, N.A., Karweit, N.L., Dolan, L.J., and Wasik, B.A. (1992). *Success For All.* Alexandria, VA: Educational Research Service, 92-104.

is very shy and seldom goes anywhere without **Uu**: "Never a **q** without a **u**."

7. *Games*. Several games follow to help students associate the letter and sound.

D. **Working with words.** Practice is provided in reading words that begin with /**qu**/.

E. **Reading practice.** Practice is provided in reading sight words beginning with /**qu**/. Students pronounce the word, use it in a sentence, and clap when they pronounce the target words.

F. **Shared story reading**. The teacher introduces a shared story that includes many examples of /**qu**/ words, such as "The Duck in the Pond." The teacher begins by previewing the story with background questions.

1. *Reading aloud*. The teacher reads the story aloud. A discussion follows regarding the story's meaning.

2. *Words*. Phonetically regular and sight words are introduced. Students blend the sounds of the phonetically regular words (i.e. *quack*), provide a sentence for the word, and define the word. Sight words are presented on flashcards, pronounced, used in sentences, and spelled until students can identify them.

3. *Guided group reading*. The teacher uses a "teacher script" that offers an elaborated story line and questions and the students read a "student script." The teacher reads the "teacher script" first, followed by the "student script." Then, in unison, the students read their script.

4. *Partner reading*. Pairs of students reread the story to each other. Two comprehension questions follow partner reading. When the group reassembles, each pair responds to the questions. The teacher writes answers to the questions on the board to model the linking of spelling to sound. As students master stories, they are encouraged to read them to other peers or to take the stories home to read with their families.

In Chapter 1 programs using *Success for All*, assessment occurs every eight weeks. Students who are falling behind receive one-to-one tutoring from certified teachers.   Chapter 1 resources are used for tutors—a critical component of the program.   The program emphasizes prevention of academic failure by linking preschool and kindergarten instruction, which emphasizes language development and academic readiness, to the elementary program of intensive reading and writing instruction for grades 1 to 5.   The program's explicit instruction in reading and writing, illustrated by the **Qq** lesson-plan (p. 169, above), is enhanced further by low teacher-student ratios, ungraded instruction in reading, and involvement of families in the achievement of literacy.

Reading Recovery.   A commitment that "early school failure is fundamentally preventable" (Slavin et al., 1993, p. 17) is also shared by Reading Recovery (Allington, 1992; Clay, 1993b; Deford et al., 1991; Hill & Hale, 1991; Pinnell et al., 1994).   Reading Recovery aims to help "at-risk" first-grade children achieve success.   Developed by Marie Clay in New Zealand, the approach utilizes certified teachers who work intensively with individual students.

After a preliminary screening, the first graders who appear to need additional support receive 30 minutes per day of one-to-one tutoring.   The focus of the tutoring is on the development of self-monitoring reading strategies.   On average, students receive tutoring for 12-to-14 weeks.   Thereafter, those who are successful continue to make progress consistent with the average performance of the class.   Reading Recovery points to long-term reductions in retention and special education placements as an indication of the success of the program.

One strength of Reading Recovery is its emphasis on reading simple texts.   Short, simple books that facilitate instruction and encourage success are selected using criteria such as memorability of language patterns, the number of language patterns used, variations in sentence patterns, the extent to which illustrations support the main ideas on each page of the text or the overall text meaning, the length of stories, and the complexity of the story structure.

Each Reading Recovery lesson begins with the rereading of a book that has become easy-to-read from earlier lessons.   The student then has an opportunity to attempt to read independently a book that had been introduced the previous day.   As the student reads, the teacher observes and records the reading performance.   These "running records" are analyzed to determine how effectively the student is monitoring the reading of the story.

A portion of each session is devoted to direct instruction on specific monitoring strategies such as self-correction, rereading, the use of context to crosscheck decoding, and the application of print-to-sound correspondences. Daily opportunities to learn print-to-sound correspondences or decoding by analogy are also provided. In all, approximately 75% of the 30 minute tutorial is devoted to reading, talking about books, or specific skills and strategies. The balance of the session focuses on writing. Each day, the student writes a simple story of perhaps one or two sentences. These sentences are cut-up into words, reassembled by the student, and read. See Chapter 3, pp. 124-125, for greater detail concerning Reading Recovery lessons.

In a program evaluation of Reading Recovery (Pinnell et al., 1994), an effort was made to determine the characteristics of the program that contribute to its success. The researchers suggest that what may be most important in preventing reading failure is the ability of the teacher to match instruction to the needs of the student and to make the instructional steps small enough to ensure that the child will be successful.

Conclusion

Stage 1 of the reading process is a time when students are learning word recognition strategies that will help them decode print to understand text. Learning to recognize words requires a direct, systematic approach in which learners focus on the correspondence of letters to sound. Stage 1 learners need to practice decoding strategies with letters, words, and during the reading and writing of simple, meaningful text. Students achieve the paramount outcome of Stage 1 when they can read unfamiliar books composed predominantly of one-syllable words, with adequate comprehension.

References

Adams, M.J. (1990; 1994). *Beginning to read: Thinking and learning about print.* Cambridge, MA: MIT Press. A summary of this text was prepared by S. Stahl, J. Osborn & F. Lehr (1990) and was published by the Center for the Study of Reading, University of Illinois, Urbana-Champaign.

Allington, R.L. (1992). How to get information on several proven programs for accelerating the progress of low-achieving children. *The Reading Teacher, 46*(3), 246-248.

Anderson, R.C., Hiebert, E.H., Scott, J.A., & Wilkinson, I.A.G. (1985). *Becoming a nation of readers: The report of the Commission on Reading.* Champaign, IL: Center for the Study of Reading, University of Illinois at Urbana-Champaign.

Bader, L.A., & Wiesendanger, K. (1994). *Bader Reading and Language Inventory (2nd ed.)* NY: Macmillan.

Bang, M. (1976). *Wiley and the hairy man.* NY: Macmillan.

Barr, R., & Johnson, B. (1991). *Teaching reading in elementary classrooms.* White Plains, NY: Longman.

Barr, R., Sadow, M., & Blachowicz, C. (1990). *Reading diagnosis for teachers (2nd ed.).* White Plains, NY: Longman.

Blishen, E. (1984). *The Oxford book of poetry for children.* NY: Peter Bedrick Books.

Bloomfield, L., Barnhart, C.L., & Barnhart, R. K. (1965). *Let's read.* Cambridge, MA: Educators Publishing Service.

Brown, M. (1982). *Wings on things.* NY: Beginner Books.

Burns, P.C., Roe, B.D., & Ross, E.P. (1992). *Teaching reading in today's elementary schools (5th ed.).* Boston: Houghton Mifflin.

Burns & Roe, P.C. (1993). *Burns/Roe Informal Reading Inventory (4th ed.).* Boston: Houghton Mifflin.

Calfee, R.C., & Wadleigh, C. (1992). How Project READ builds inquiring schools. Educational Leadership, September, 28-32.

Chall, J.S. (1967). *Learning to read: The great debate.* NY: McGraw-Hill.

Chall, J.S. (1983a). *Stages of reading development.* NY: McGraw-Hill.

Chall, J.S. (1983b). *Learning to read: The great debate (2nd ed.).* NY: McGraw-Hill.

Clay, M.M. (1993a). *An observation survey of early literacy achievement.* Portsmouth, NH: Heinemann.

Clay, M.M. (1993b). *Reading Recovery: A guidebook for teachers in training.* Portsmouth, NH: Heinemann.

Cowley, J. (1990). *Painting.* Bothel, WA: The Wight Group.

Cunningham, P.H., Hall, D.P., & Defee, M. (1991). Non-ability-grouped, multilevel instruction: A year in a first-grade classroom. *The Reading Teacher, 44*(8), 566-571.

Dale, E., & Chall, J.S. (1948). A formula for predicting readability and instructions. *Educational Research Bulletin, 27,* 11-20; 37-54.

DeFord, D.E., Lyons, C.A., & Pinnell, G.S. (1991). Bridges to literacy: Learning from Reading Recovery. Portsmouth, NH: Heinemann.

174

Duffy, G.G., & Roehler, L.R. (1987, January). Teaching reading skills as strategies. *The Reading Teacher*, 414-418.

Ehri, L.C., & Robbins, C. (1992). Beginners need some decoding skill to read words by analogy. *Reading Research Quarterly*, 27(1), 13-26.

Enfield, M.L. (1987). A cost effective classroom alternative to 'pull-out' programs. *Intimacy with language: A forgotten basic in teacher education*, 45-46.

Flesch, R. (1955). *Why Johnny can't read*. NY: Harper and Row.

Gattegno, C. (1968). *Words in color*. NY: Educational Solutions, Inc.

Gaskins, R.W., Gaskins, J.C., & Gaskins, I.W. (March, 1991). A decoding program for poor readers - And the rest of the class, too! *Language Arts*, 68, 213-225.

Geisel, T.S. (1960). *Green eggs and ham*. NY: Beginner Books.

Geisel, T.S. (1991a). *Dr. Seuss's ABC*. [Renewed copyright]. NY: Random House.

Geisel, T.S. (1991b). *Hop on pop by Dr. Seuss*. [Renewed copyright]. NY: Random House.

Golden Step Ahead. (1989). Racine, WI: Western Publishing.

Goodman, Y.M., Watson, D.J., & Burke, C. (1987). *Reading Miscue Inventory: Alternative procedures*. NY: Richard C. Owen.

Goswami, U., & Mead, F. (1992). Onset and rime awareness and analogies in reading. *Reading Research Quarterly*, 27(2), 153-162.

Greene, T., & Enfield, M.L. (1986). *Project READ phonics guide (rev. ed.)*. Bloomington, MN: Language Circle Enterprise.

Gregorich, B., & Henkel, A. (no date). *The big phonics book*. Grand Haven, MI: School Zone Publishing.

Harp, B. (Ed.). (1993). *Assessment and evaluation in whole language programs (abridged ed.)*. Norwood, MA: Christopher-Gordon Publishers.

Heilman, A W. (1993). *Phonics in proper perspective (7th ed.)*. Columbus, OH: Merrill.

Hill, L.B., & Hale, M.G. (1991). Reading recovery: Questions classroom teachers ask. *The Reading Teacher*, 44(7), 480-483.

Hoban, R. (1970). *A bargain for Frances*. NY: Harper & Row.

Hopfenberg, W.S., Levin, H.M., and Associates (1993). *The accelerated schools*. San Francisco: Jossey-Bass.

Hull, M. A. (1993). *Phonics for the teacher of reading (6th ed.)*. Columbus, OH: Merrill/Macmillan.

Karweit, N.L. (1993). *Preventing early school failure: Research on effective strategies*. Boston: Allyn & Bacon.

Lapp, D., & Flood, J. (1992). *Teaching reading to every child (3rd ed.)*. NY: Macmillan.

Leslie, L., & Caldwell, J. (1990). *Qualitative Reading Inventory*. Glenview, IL: Scott, Foresman.

Leeuwen, J. (1979). *Tales of Oliver Frog*. NY: Puffin.

Lobel, A. (1981). *On market street*. NY: Greenwillow.

Lobel, A. (1970). *Frog and Toad are friends*. NY: Harper & Row.

Madden, N.A., Slavin, R.E., Karweit, N.L., Dolan, L, and Wasik, B. (1991). Success for All. *Phi Delta Kappan*, April, 593-599.

Mann, H. (1842/1844/1965). Teaching young children to read, Vol IV., Method of teaching young children on their first entering school, Vol VI *The Common School Journal*. Boston: William B. Fowle and N. Capen. In Smith, N.B. (1965), *American reading instruction*. Newark DE: International Reading Association.

Martin, B. (1984). *Brown bear, brown bear, what do you see?* NY: Holt, Rinehart, Winston.

Miller, W. H. (1993). *Complete reading disabilities handbook*. NY: Center for Applied Research in Education.

Mills, H., O'Keefe, T., & Stephens, D. (1992). *Looking closely: Exploring the role of phonics in one whole language classroom*. Urbana, IL: National Council of Teachers of English.

Minarik, M. (1957). *Little bear*. NY: Harper Trophy.

Norton, D.E. (1991). *Through the eyes of a child: An introduction to children's literature*. NY: Merrill/Macmillan.

Paterson, K. (1991). *The smallest cow in the world*. NY: Harper Trophy.

Pinnell, G.S., Lyons, C.A., Deford, D.E., Bryk, A.S., & Seltzer, M. (1994). Comparing instructional models for the literacy education of high-risk first graders. *Reading Research Quarterly*, *29*(1), 8-39.

Rhodes, L.K. (1993). *Literacy assessment: A handbook of instruments*. Portsmouth, NH: Heinemann.

Rhodes, L.K., & Shanklin, N. (1993). *Windows into literacy*. Portsmouth, NH: Heinemann.

Roskos, K., & Walker, B. J. (1993). *Understanding reading diagnosis*. NY: Merrill.

Roswell, F., & Chall, J. (1991). *Diagnostic Assessment of Reading with Trial Teaching Strategies*. Chicago: Riverside Publishing Company.

Routman, R. (1988). *Transitions*. Portsmouth, NH: Heinemann.

Routman, R. (1991). *Invitations: Changing as teachers and learners K-12*. Portsmouth, NH: Heinemann.

Seuss, Dr. (1957). *The cat in the hat*. NY: Random House.

Seuss, Dr. (1960). *One fish, two fish, red fish, blue fish*. NY: Beginner Books.

Silverstein, S. (1974). *Where the sidewalk ends*. NY: Harper and Row.

Slavin, R.E., Karweit, N.L., & Wasik, B.A. (1993). Preventing early school failure: What works? *Educational Leadership*, January, 10-17.

Slavin, R.E., Madden, N.A., Karweit, N.L., Dolan, L.J., & Wasik, B.A. (1991). Success for All: Ending reading failure from the beginning. *Language Arts*, *68*, 404-409.

Slavin, R.E., Madden, N.A., Karweit, N.L., Dolan, L.J., & Wasik, B.A. (1992). *Success For All*. Arlington, VA: Educational Research Service.

176

Smith, N.B. (1985). *American reading instruction (2nd ed.)*. Newark, DE: International Reading Association.

Smith, N.B. (1986). *American reading instruction (3rd ed.)*. Newark, DE: International Reading Association.

Spiegel, D.L. (1992). Blending whole language and systematic direct instruction. *The Reading Teacher, 46*(1).

Stahl, S.A. (1992). Saying the "P" word: Nine guidelines for exemplary phonics instruction. *The Reading Teacher, 45*(8), 618-625.

Stanovich, K. (1994). Romance and reality. *The Reading Teacher, 47*(4), 280-292.

Sulzby, E. (1985). Children's emergent reading of favorite storybooks: A developmental study. *Reading Research Quarterly, 20*, 458-481.

Tierney, R. J. (1991). *Portfolio assessment in the reading-writing classroom*. Norwood, MA: Christopher-Gordon.

Trachtenburg, P. (1990). Using children's literature to enhance phonics instruction. *The Reading Teacher, 43*, 648-654.

Vacca, J.L., Vacca, R.T., & Gove, M.K. (1993). *Reading and learning to read (4th ed.)*. NY: Harper Collins.

Wasik, Barbara A., & Slavin, Robert E. (1993). Preventing early reading failure with one-to-one tutoring: A review of five programs. *Reading Research Quarterly, 28*(2), 178-200.

Wildsmith, B. (1962). *Brian Wildsmith's ABC*. NY: Watts.

Woods, M.L., & Moe, A.J. (1989). *Analytical Reading Inventory (4th ed.)*. Columbus, OH: Merrill.

Chapter 5: Advanced Decoding and Fluency: Assuring Security and Confidence

Linda W. Kemper, PhD
Rivier College

Readers enter Stage 2 when they consistently apply phonetic skills to monosyllabic words, use a somewhat considerable sight vocabulary, and sound out simple stories (Chall, 1983). In order to develop **fluency**, Stage 2 readers engage in extensive reading of familiar stories while receiving instruction in advanced decoding skills.   Together, these activities generally lead to automaticity—immediate recognition of simple words, swift recognition of longer, more complex words, and rapid, nearly flawless decoding of connected text.   Such automaticity generally enables readers to shift their attention from decoding to meaning in order to enjoy literature and understand expository text.

As with any automatic skill, reading fluency develops through extensive practice. Readers who possess effective word-identification strategies, and who read regularly, tend to engage in a cycle of becoming better, more avid readers, through reading. This cycle develops ever stronger vocabulary and background knowledge, increases understanding of syntax and semantics, and enhances understanding of the printed word. Consequently, exposure to print is a crucial factor in predicting long-term development of reading and other verbal skills (Stanovich, 1986). Teachers encourage reading and the desire to interact with books by helping their students acquire the fluency that stimulates reading pleasure and success.

This chapter discusses the development of reading fluency among Stage 2 readers. It begins by exploring two aspects that contribute to decoding automaticity: reading practice, and the learning of advanced decoding skills. Next, comprehension issues are examined, particularly among children with limited exposure to literature. Finally, reading fluency is considered by exploring the process of integrating automatic decoding and comprehension to produce smooth reading with understanding. Instructional suggestions are offered for readers in elementary classrooms who typically enter Stage 2 in second or third grade. In addition, techniques are recommended for older learners who experience difficulty in making the transition to fluent reading when they lack advanced decoding skills and sufficient reading practice.

Decoding Automaticity

It was once believed that skilled readers use context clues to facilitate word recognition. However, extensive research reported by Stanovich (1994), indicates that "...word recognition processes of the skilled reader [are] so rapid and automatic that they [do] not need to rely on contextual information" (p. 282). Automatic word recognition, achieved through swift and accurate decoding, frees readers' cognitive resources to concentrate on local and global meaning. All attention can focus on comprehension for the purpose of schema construction without the drain of identifying single words. In contrast, less-skilled readers rely heavily on context for word identification; this leads to slow, and sometimes labored, reading (Stanovich, 1984; Stanovich & West, 1981; 1983; Stanovich, West, & Feeman, 1981).

During mature reading, eye movement is rapid and sequential with the reader's eyes resting on words in linear order. In contrast, the use of context for word identification often requires less-skilled readers to study a complete sentence then return to a challenging word, a process that is reflected in recursive eye movements. Until readers develop automatic decoding skills, their reliance on contextual information to identify words redirects eye movement, slows word recognition rate and, in turn, impedes the process of comprehension (Just & Carpenter, 1981; 1987).

Since readers who lack decoding automaticity need to focus most of their attention on consciously identifying individual words, their attention is drawn away from developing a schema of the story. Whether non-automatic word identification is attempted through use of letter-by-letter decoding, the use of rhyming families, or efforts to guess single words from context clues, the process draws attention away from the more advanced work of schema construction (Bloom, 1986; Perfetti, 1985).

Effective teachers provide instruction in advanced decoding strategies by offering lessons that present specific word-generalizations as well as by discussing these generalizations as they arise during reading of connected text, for practice and pleasure. Sometimes instruction begins with the presentation of a specific generalization. Students then practice reading connected text that includes many examples of the target generalization. Other times, teachers begin with the reading of a story and then pause, when a challenging word appears, to present an advanced decoding generalization.

The following discussion examines strategies for enhancing automaticity. To simplify presentation, separate sections are used to describe the reading of connected text and the teaching of advanced decoding skills. However, effective instruction typically combines strategies from each section within a single reading lesson.

PRACTICE WITH CONNECTED TEXT

Stage 2 readers develop automaticity with newly gained decoding skills through plenty of reading practice during broad exposure to connected text. As confidence develops, readers move from word lists and controlled texts to simple literature and expository materials. To help learners feel comfortable with reading, teachers provide a wealth of interesting books that match a variety of independent reading levels. When they practice often with such materials, students generally "figure out" unfamiliar words with ease, and enjoy spending a great deal of time reading.

As learners begin their wide reading to develop automaticity, text with natural language and familiar content encourages them to continue reading (Adams, 1994; Chall, 1983). The familiar language confirms that material was decoded accurately; and, in turn, accurate decoding develops students' confidence. As students engage in reading, books provide models of proper and natural syntax, a wide range of vocabulary, and motivation to continue reading to experience the pleasure of engaging with a variety of interesting topics and genres.

The more time learners spend practicing with familiar material at this level, the more likely they are to move smoothly to Stage 3 where they read to learn about unfamiliar topics. A variety of instructional strategies encourage Stage 2 learners to read often and widely in order to develop decoding automaticity. The suggestions offered below synthesize many techniques appearing in journals, basals, and reading texts and have been reported as useful by classroom teachers during informal observation and discussion (Cooper, 1993; Heilman, 1993; Leu & Kinzer, 1991; Routman, 1991; Savage, 1994; Tunnell & Jacobs,1989).

Select appropriate materials. An environment in which many books are available encourages students to read (Chall, 1983). Appropriate reading materials match learners' interests and are varied in subject and genre. Books that invite reading facilitate independent practice. During early practice with connected text, beginners use short passages that allow them to experience progress as they read slowly to concentrate on each word. Shorter passages at the beginning provide readers with the confirmation that comes with understanding a meaningful piece of text within a brief time span.

Picture books with repetitive patterns (sometimes referred to as "predictable books") are appropriate for younger readers. These books present interesting stories using repetition of ideas and words to reinforce understanding and boost confidence in word recognition skills. Teachers sometimes create short passages that use controlled vocabulary to support fledgling readers. At times, students and teachers create a short story together that can be read many times until it is read fluently (Clay, 1993; Leu & Kinzer, 1991; Morrow; 1993).

Older students who need to develop automaticity also begin with short readings in which sentence and word length are adjusted to match their reading level. Materials for older students are written in one-page passages that begin as single paragraphs and expand as reading ability and confidence increase. Appropriate content of short passages for older students may include topics such as current events, sports, nature, exploration, or the experiences of characters who draw on inner strength to overcome adversity. Collections of passages at increasing levels of difficulty are available from educational publishers such as Educators Publishing Service, Jamestown Publishers, LARC Publishing, New Readers' Press, Readers' Digest, Scholastic, and Steck-Vaughn. Or, if sufficient scaffolding is provided by the teacher, students can practice reading paragraphs from newspapers, magazines, or class textbooks (Brody, 1987).

Check and adjust passage difficulty frequently. Diverse needs exist within any classroom. Some students in the early elementary grades have substantial, successful experience with language and books. They eagerly approach books and tackle print enthusiastically. These students progress easily in a solid Stage 2 developmental reading program that provides ample reading materials, adequate time for reading, along with ongoing instruction, encouragement, and appreciation from a teacher who supports their progress.

Other learners, whose exposure to print may be limited, feel less comfortable with books. Since reading does not come as easily for them, they need additional support and encouragement to increase the likelihood that they will practice reading often. In order to develop fluency, these students need to spend more time reading texts that are written with short words and simple sentences before taking on texts that present longer words and complex sentences.

Teachers ensure that students practice for fluency at their highest comfort-level by checking reading progress frequently. Careful monitoring, through informal records of oral reading accuracies and errors along with notes concerning quality of intonation, expression, attention to punctuation, and grasp of content, assures that each reader progresses to the next level as soon as possible (Leu & Kinzer, 1991). When students demonstrate proficiency in materials at one level, the length of stories or passages, as well as word and content difficulty, are adjusted. (For sample teacher-made reading inventory to assess reading level, turn to Appendix, p. 195.)

Allocate independent reading time. Many classrooms and schools allocate time each day to independent reading through silent reading programs such as Drop Everything And Read (D.E.A.R.) or Sustained Silent Reading (S.S.R.) (Savage, 1994; Vacca, Vacca, & Gove, 1991). Such programs set aside time for reading independently on a regular basis. Although reading material is selected by students, teachers provide guidelines when needed.

Generally, a fifteen-to-twenty minute segment of each day is allocated to this independent silent reading. Some teachers begin the day with S.S.R. or D.E.A.R. in order to set a positive tone for the day and to stress the importance of reading. Others select a later, but consistent, block of time each day. On occasion, an entire school implements a program of independent reading and notifies the community of the routine. All school personnel—secretaries, custodians, principals, cafeteria workers, and librarians—engage in reading during the dedicated block in order to serve as role models who communicate the importance of reading to the students and the community.

Multiple rereadings of recorded stories. Repetition of recorded stories offers a consistent model to make reading practice enjoyable and motivating. Chomsky (1978) formalized the strategy as a means of assisting students who possess basic phonics skills yet need further support to develop reading fluency. Chomsky's approach guides readers to "shift their focus from the individual word to connected discourse and to integrate their somewhat fragmented knowledge" (p. 18). She draws on recorded readings, followed by student/teacher interactions, to teach children about the richness of language and the nature of its structure.

In Chomsky's approach, readers choose books from a large set preselected by the teacher. The students listen to recordings of their books every day, using headphones, while following along with the printed text. Students replay parts of their tapes often, while rereading sections of their books, many times. As sections of the story are practiced, learners read along with the master tape or record their reading onto another tape. In addition, learners use notebooks to write or draw about their readings. Further, individualized phonics instruction, for any challenging words, is offered in the meaningful context of the increasingly familiar story that highlights its relevance. Children's progress is checked weekly by adults who listen to the students read as much of their stories as they are ready to share.

The approach was researched in a third-grade classroom over four months. During the study, children began to select reading as a preferred activity, to write more often, and to transfer their newfound knowledge to unfamiliar stories with enhanced confidence (Chomsky, 1978).

Classroom teachers can implement **recorded reading** in the following way. First develop a collection of matching tapes and books by gathering together existing sets and by working with volunteers to make tapes of favorite, short books that are already in the classroom. Next, package the tapes and books in sets to save time when students are searching for materials. Display the sets in a prominent spot in the classroom. Arrange one area of the room with comfortable seating (stuffed chairs or cushions on the floor) near cassette players with headphones.

Encourage children to select books from a larger set organized into appropriate reading levels. Set up times each day for children to listen to their selected tapes while following along in their books. Also provide opportunities for students to record themselves and listen to their own reading in order to help them notice their increasing fluency. During the process, check daily with students to encourage reading. Arrange opportunities for students to read aloud with an adult: a teacher, aide, volunteer, custodian, secretary, or school principal. Some teachers arrange a special class party at which children read to favorite stuffed animals.

Some children draw pictures or write stories related to their readings to confirm and enhance comprehension. These productions are often retellings of the stories that can be collected in binders as a record of their developing understanding of story-sequence and literary conventions. In addition, writing reinforces and applies words from the stories and enriches learners' reading and speaking vocabularies.

Oral recitation. Oral recitation lessons (ORL) offer another approach to develop fluency (Hoffman, 1985). ORL involves three "routines" or segments used in succession. First, during a direct instruction segment, the teacher introduces a story, reads it aloud as a model, discusses it with students, and helps students summarize it. Next, students read the story chorally, as a group, with teacher assistance as needed. Finally, students take turns reading sections orally to the class. In a study with second graders, students taught with this method demonstrated improved fluency and comprehension (Reutzel & Hollingsworth, 1993).

Paired reading. Reading with a peer or another adult offers another form of repeated practice (Reutzel & Cooter, 1992; Vacca, Vacca, & Gove, 1991). When students pair with an adult, the adult reads first to provide a model. Then student and adult take turns reading, discussing, and rereading each part of the story or passage until it is read fluently by the student.

In order to initiate paired reading activities among peers, a teacher introduces a story by reading it aloud while discussing challenging vocabulary to clarify decoding, word meaning, and story content. After hearing the story and participating in the discussion, peers read stories to each other many times. By engaging in this activity, students enhance their reading fluency. During paired reading, the teacher circulates to help with pronunciation and to assess when children are ready for more challenging text. The teacher also encourages students to sound out difficult words rather than passing over them to finish quickly. When students have practiced sufficiently in pairs to read their stories fluently, they read to different adults, volunteers, friends, people at home, or to younger children.

Read aloud often. Whatever the strategy, activities designed to develop fluency include a model of fluent reading, opportunities for plenty of practice, and exposure to interesting materials that motivate students to ever more reading practice (Samuels, Schermer, & Reinking, 1992). Generally, teachers and students select books or passages in which the majority of the individual words can be read independently, while fluent reading of the selection, as a whole, remains a challenge. The teacher's reading of the passage is used to model expression, articulation, and fluency. During and after reading, the content is discussed to develop comprehension, work through troublesome words, and clarify word meanings. Students practice reading and rereading in order to develop automaticity with the target passage as well as to transfer automaticity to other materials.

Summary of practice with connected text. The old adage, "Practice makes perfect," summarizes the focus of instruction designed to improve automaticity. When students read often, they become more comfortable with reading and begin to read in many settings. Broader practice leads to greater speed and accuracy in word recognition. By engaging in a positive, self-perpetuating cycle, readers develop confidence, read more often, increase their vocabulary, and develop greater understanding (Stanovich, 1986).

ADVANCED DECODING STRATEGIES

As students develop automaticity and confidence in reading simple text, they venture to attempt more advanced material. In their wider reading, students encounter polysyllabic words that cannot be identified with only the basic strategies of letter-sound correspondences, rhyme generalizations, sight vocabulary, and context clues. For example, we, as fluent readers, have forgotten the challenges presented to Stage 2 readers who attempt to decode sentences such as, "Pollution is important for us to consider." Without the additional knowledge of syllabication strategies and common suffixes, sentences that rely on the decoding and understanding of polysyllabic words can discourage readers whose decoding skills are limited.

As they progress in Stage 2, readers need additional strategies to consistently figure out longer, less-familiar words. Advanced decoding instruction teaches readers to recognize inflectional endings, compound words, affixes, root words, contractions, and syllabic patterns. These **structural analysis** skills allow readers to analyze a word's construction and sound out its familiar parts. By learning the common letter-cluster patterns, readers increase their ability to recognize unfamiliar words (Brody, 1985; 1986; Roswell & Chall, 1994).

Since Stage 2 readers vary in their knowledge of word elements, effective teaching needs to match instruction with individuals' levels of achievement. Direct instruction is appropriate for teaching unfamiliar decoding elements. Direct and guided practice develop familiarity with elements that are known but not recognized with confidence. In addition, independent reading encourages progress from familiarity to automaticity. The discussion that follows describes advanced decoding elements and suggests a variety of strategies for their instruction.

Inflectional endings. Students encounter common inflectional endings during Stage 1 and Stage 2 reading. Readers who do not recognize them readily need direct instruction and practice in noticing *-s, -ed, -ing, -ly, -er,* and *-est* (Brody, 1987). These inflectional endings often are introduced by writing a known word (such as *bat*) on the board and asking students to say the word. The inflectional ending *-s* is added and the teacher states that the word now means "more than one." Students read the new word. After this process is repeated with many words and the same inflection, a target word with multiple inflections is used to teach changes in endings.

Some students have difficulty not only in differentiating among inflectional endings but also in noticing **whether** an ending is present. These students often read only the first syllable or first few letters of a word and then guess the rest from context. Learning to read all parts of a word, rather than guessing the ending, can develop when students practice with word lists or flash cards in which the base word remains constant and only the inflectional **endings** change. After reading words on lists, students practice noticing endings of words in context by reading sentences composed of target words along with their various inflectional endings. In addition, students can practice by responding to oral or written sentences by filling in blanks with the target words, with or without inflectional endings. For example:

(dog, dogs)   Five _____ ran through my yard.
    My _____, Shep, ate his dinner.

Compound words. While mastering basic inflections, students also begin to encounter compound words. Teachers foster students' awareness of compound words by asking students to notice small words within larger words. For example, they point out that a *firefighter* is a *fighter* who puts out a *fire*.

Many compound words are introduced in the primary grades, or during Stage 2 reading for older students; some of these include: *into, outside, inside, within, mailman, fisherman, landlady, upon, something, baseball, sailboat, roadway, moonlight, airplane, waterfall, notebook, herself,* and *anyone* (Heilman, 1993).

Many beginning readers are unaware of compound words and need instruction that goes beyond encouragement to look for compound words or to divide longer words into their component parts. Teachers can introduce the concept of compound words by beginning with familiar words. First the compound word is presented (either in text, on the chalkboard, or on a card) and students are asked to find the two small words in the larger word. As students identify them, the teacher circles the two words and explains that the two words were "put together" to form one

compound word. Additional compound words are presented and students are asked to identify the small words within the word. Again, the smaller words are circled to note them clearly. Compound words can also be presented on separate cards with each smaller word written in a different color to aid students in discriminating and attending to the separate words.

Students can practice building and segmenting compound words by playing a matching game in which they select two small word-cards to form one compound word. For example, a game card for *baseball* is made by writing the word on an index card in large print and cutting the card in half between *base* and *ball*. *Baseball* is written on the back of each half-card to allow for self-checking. Separate pieces of several compound words are placed on a table and students search for two halves that form a compound word. They look on the back of each half to check their accuracy and engage in additional practice in reading the parts and reading the whole word. Cards also can be cut in varied shapes to let the puzzle configurations assist younger readers in self-checking.

Affixes and base words. Stage 2 readers often need direct instruction to notice **affixes**, the prefixes and suffixes added to base words to alter their meanings. When teaching affixes, it is important to discuss meaning as well as decoding of the words. Common **prefixes** include: *after-, dis-, extra-, counter-, inter-, mid-, mini-, mis-, non-, post-, pre-, re-, sub-, super-,* and *un-*. Common **suffixes** include: *-able, -ance, -tion, -less, -ness, -ful, -ment,* and *-able* (Brody, 1984; Heilman, 1993).

Prefixes and suffixes are introduced separately. The teacher begins by presenting a base word such as *pay* and reviewing its meaning. Next a prefix, such as *re-* is added, and students are asked to pronounce the new word. The change in meaning is discussed to convey that each affix carries meaning and that *repay* means to pay again. In order to help students understand the meaning of the prefix, other examples are provided using the same prefix, but different base words. Suffixes are introduced in the same way.

Students need to use their knowledge of affixes when reading connected text. When readers hesitate at a word with an affix, teachers can remind them, "This is a word with a suffix (prefix)," and then direct the student to, "Find the base word." This procedure guides students to help themselves by using affixes as part of the decoding process while reading for pleasure.

To provide additional awareness and practice in identifying common affixes, teachers and students can create prefix and suffix charts and display them in the classroom. Such charts include common affixes, their meanings, and examples of words constructed from the affixes as shown in Figure 5.a, below.

Many words constructed with prefixes and suffixes are part of most Stage 2 readers' speaking and listening vocabularies. As readers learn to recognize common affixes during advanced decoding instruction and practice, they more easily identify additional words from their listening vocabularies when they appear in print. Practice in identifying words by reading their affixes leads to greater automaticity during reading of more advanced material.

PREFIXES		
Prefix	**Meaning**	**Examples**
re-	to do again	repay, redo, remake, retell
un-	not	unfair, unlike, unbelievable
pre-	to do before	prepay, prejudge

SUFFIXES		
Suffix	**Meaning**	**Examples**
-less	without	hopeless, careless, homeless
-ness	quality or state of	happiness, playfulness
-ful	full of	hopeful, cheerful, gleeful

Figure 5.a. Prefix and suffix charts.

Complex base words and affixes. It is convenient and effective to introduce affixes and **base words** simultaneously. Although students often recognize simple combinations, many readers need direct instruction to master the more complex constructions. Lessons in the analysis of words such as *disagreeable, reconstruction, imperfection, displacement,* and *uncomfortable* help prepare students to decode the challenging words in advanced textbooks with accuracy.

Analysis of complex polysyllabic words can be taught with the following steps. First, several such words are listed on the board, on cards, or on charts. The teacher selects the first word (for example, *disagreeable*) and asks a student to identify and read its base by dropping the prefix and suffix. The teacher assists by circling the prefix and suffix, as needed, so that the student can identify *agree* as the base. Next, the teacher asks the student to read the prefix (*dis*), and the suffix (*able*). Finally, the student is asked to "put the word together" by reading each part in order. The process is continued with other words on the list. Then students read a small text selection that incorporates several of the words under study.

When a brief introduction is insufficient, it is helpful to introduce many words of similar construction in order to help students identify specific affixes automatically (Brody, 1987). For example, students may study a list of words ending in *tion*, then a list of words ending in *ous*, and next a list of words ending in *able*. Again, reading of the words on lists is followed by reading a small text selection that incorporates the base or affix pattern. Opportunities to construct complex words from base words and affixes are also helpful (Heilman, 1993; Steere, Peck, & Kahn, 1971), as in the following exercise:

> *Select from the prefixes and suffixes below to construct a word that replaces the underlined word(s).*
>
> **Prefixes:** *dis, un, re, pre*
> **Suffixes:** *ful, ment, ness, less, able*
>
> 1. My friend and I <u>do not agree</u> on which movie to see.
>   (_____agree)
>
> 2. I had to <u>pay</u> the bill <u>again</u>.
>   (_____pay).
>
> 3. The ache in my tooth is <u>giving me pain</u>.
>   (pain_____)

Contractions. Some students need many exposures in order to recognize contractions, while other learners generalize easily from a few examples. When presenting contractions, explain that they are words formed from two words, by omitting one or more letters, and inserting an apostrophe. Point out that contractions have the same meaning as the two original words. Model contractions by writing several sets of words on the board, erasing the appropriate letters, and filling in an apostrophe. At the same time, ask students to follow the model on their own papers.

Some students need the additional support of learning common contractions one set at a time. The chart in Figure 5.b, below, can be posted in an elementary classroom or copied into the writing notebook of an older student as a ready reference.

not n't		will 'll	is 's	are 're
does not doesn't	cannot can't	you will you'll	he is he's	we are we're
did not didn't	would not wouldn't	she will she'll	she is she's	you are you're
is not isn't	could not couldn't	he will he'll	it is it's	they are they're
has not hasn't	should not shouldn't	they will they'll		

Figure 5.b. Chart of common contractions.

Syllabic patterns. Another approach to analysis of polysyllabic words teaches students to read longer words in small, manageable parts by dividing the words into syllable-sized chunks and identifying the sounds of these smaller units. Students read each segment, then blend the segments to read a whole word. Readers use word lists or word cards to practice identifying common syllabic patterns. Teachers encourage students to divide words in small segments that approximate syllabic patterns, rather than striving for precise dictionary divisions. This enables students to use the strategy with ease and independence. In addition to word-list practice, students use the strategy when polysyllabic words appear in passages, news articles, and texts. Further practice occurs during writing activities (Brody, 1984).

Programs that teach identification of words through segmentation-by-syllables generally teach six common syllablic types. The markings and names for the syllables vary, but the patterns remain the same across programs since they reflect the syllabic structure of English words. For example, Brody (1987) uses the pattern names that appear in Figure 5.c, on the following page.

Common Syllable Patterns (Brody, 1984)

VC -   a single vowel (short) followed by a consonant,
as in *cat* or *is*.

VR -   a single vowel followed by the consonant *r*,
as in *car* or *her*.

V -   a single vowel (long) ending a syllable,
as in *me* or *go*.

VV -   two adjacent vowels giving one vowel sound,
as in *boat* or *seen*.

VCe -   a single vowel (long) followed by a consonant and
silent *e*, as in *like* or *fame*.

CLe -   a consonant followed by the letter *l* and silent *e*,
as in *uncle* or *apple*.

Figure 5.c. Chart of common syllable patterns.

Summary of advanced decoding skills. Stage 2 learners practice decoding strategies and read widely in connected text in order to develop automaticity. Identification of polysyllabic words is enhanced by knowledge of word-analysis strategies such as recognition of inflections, compound words, affixes and base words, contractions, and syllabic patterns. As students learn word analysis techniques, they read literature or expository text written at a level that reinforces their decoding skills and lets them increase their automaticity. Effective teachers adjust the amount of instruction in word-analysis skills to match the needs of individual students. Good instruction provides time for plenty of practice and application during reading of interesting literature and expository text.

Comprehension

In addition to accurate and speedy decoding, reading fluency depends on rapid recognition of common literary and expository forms at the sentence, paragraph, and story level (Spiegel & Whaley, 1980; Stanovich, 1986). Students who have been read to often, by others, are more likely to recognize simple literary conventions such as repeated refrains, rhyming words, and dialogue patterns. When these students read to themselves, knowledge of literary conventions enables them to check that they have decoded accurately and that they have interpreted the text content meaningfully. Such confirmation is reassuring and encourages further reading.

Research indicates that there is a direct relationship between readers' listening comprehension and their reading comprehension (deLone, 1990; Stanovich, 1993). Teachers can assess students' listening comprehension level by asking questions related to a story read to them or by asking students to retell a story (Bembridge, 1994; Brown & Cambourne, 1987; Glazer, 1992). DeFina (1992) offers a helpful checklist for assessing comprehension through retelling. When students' hearing is adequate, and there are no external or internal issues distracting them from listening to a story, the teacher can tentatively assume that, as these students develop sufficient decoding skills, their reading comprehension will come to match their listening comprehension.

Students who come to Stage 2 with a solid background in literary language need only to develop automaticity with decoding. Their understanding of stories, developed during earlier listening experiences, prepares them to comprehend any materials that they can decode (Chall, 1983). These students have developed an understanding of story syntax and discourse through their past involvement in listening to and discussing stories (Irwin, 1986).

These students possess **syntactic** knowledge—awareness of "word order rules that determine meaning within sentences" (Leu & Kinzer, 1991, p. 100). Although students may not understand the terms *noun* and *verb*, they can select a word of correct, syntactic form to complete sentences. A solid base of syntactic knowledge enables readers to anticipate and confirm when words have been read correctly within a sentence.

Students with substantial syntactic knowledge also make use of **discourse knowledge**, an understanding of various types of writing (newspapers, fairy tales, fiction, nonfiction, mysteries, etc.). Discourse knowledge helps readers form a framework within which to understand the text they are reading. For example, when a story begins with, "Once upon a time..." readers with knowledge of literary discourse recognize that a fairy tale is beginning. These readers anticipate a fairy tale, frame their schemata of the story as a fairy tale, and expect elements of a fairy tale to emerge.

When students listen to stories often, they learn to recognize the discourse elements of character, plot, setting, problem, and resolution. They build this understanding during listening and discussion of many and varied stories. These better-prepared readers also become familiar with cause and effect in stories (if Goldilocks eats the porridge, they expect that the bears will be upset). Such readers understand story sequence (*first*, Goldilocks sits in the chairs, *next*, she eats the porridge, *then*, she sleeps in the beds). When students are familiar with common story elements, their understanding of common structures confirms that readings have been decoded and comprehended with accuracy.

Increasing familiarity with literary language. Students who have had little exposure to print need to learn the basic conventions of literary language in addition to learning to decode print. They need to hear stories read aloud, listen to discussions of stories, and state their own understandings. In order to help students increase their understanding of literary conventions, teachers read to their students often and encourage them to read stories from books that can be decoded with relative ease.

During reading, teachers stop occasionally to ask relevant questions regarding literal and inferential comprehension. Literal questions, which seek specific information written in the text, tend to be easier for students to answer. When literal answers elude readers, teachers encourage them to reread a pertinent section of text and, if necessary, point to the exact words in which the answer is located. Students then reread the sentence that contains the answer. Finally, they state the answer in their own words.

Inferential questions, which ask for information not specifically stated in the text, are also asked during or after reading. These questions are more difficult for students with limited knowledge of literary conventions since answers often depend on an understanding of what is implied or anticipated by the convention. For example, if asked what Goldilocks will do next after lying on Mama Bear's bed, a reader who knows the repetition convention suspects that she will head for Baby Bear's bed, while a student who is unfamiliar with the convention is unsure. In order to expand readers' understanding of story pattern, the teacher and students look back in the story to note how Goldilocks has gone from one chair to another, then one porridge to another, and then to the beds.

During reading, teachers ask questions concerning main characters, and discuss the story's setting. They also prepare students for the story line by asking them to watch for a problem that will arise in the story. When students read about the problem, the teacher stops the reading to ask students to describe it. If they did not recognize it, the teacher helps them return to that section of text in order to reread the relevant material and engage in discussion for clarification. After the story is finished, the teacher encourages students to discuss how the problem was solved and to summarize the story briefly.

In summary, instruction in literary conventions is provided to enhance comprehension among students who lack knowledge of common story structures. In turn, comprehension of simple stories facilitates enjoyment of reading, confirms decoding accuracy, and encourages students to read common stories more often as a means of developing decoding automaticity.

Attention

When a reader begins Stage 2, "the combined attention demands of decoding and comprehension are greater than the reader's attention resources [can handle]," (Samuels, et al., 1992, p. 130). Until advanced decoding is automatic and literary conventions are well understood, readers may experience difficulty in shifting attention between decoding and meaning. As these abilities develop, readers generally enter a more sophisticated level of reading. No longer do they attend only to decoding or only to content. Instead, they integrate these elements to read fluently and with understanding.

When decoding becomes automatic, most readers unconsciously shift their attention to comprehension. In turn, clear comprehension confirms the accuracy of students' automatic decoding and encourages readers to remain attentive to meaning as they move smoothly through text. When mismatches arise between decoding and comprehension, misunderstandings unconsciously signal readers to double-check their decoding for accuracy. When appropriate repairs are made, readers' text schemata, solidly based in common literary conventions, help with a seamless return of attention to comprehension.

Some readers learn to shift between decoding and meaning with relative ease; others need specific instruction to develop the ability. Readers with learning disabilities sometimes experience particular difficulty in switching attention between decoding and comprehension (Denckla, 1983). Two types of instruction are offered in an effort to enhance these students' attention-switching capacities. As discussed earlier in detail, reading practice is provided, and advanced decoding skills are taught, in order to develop automaticity and free attention for comprehension. For those who need it, teachers can also consciously cue attention switches during oral and silent reading.

When directly teaching attention-switching through cuing, teachers begin a lesson by asking a question that sets a purpose for reading in order to focus attention on meaning. When an unknown word is encountered, the teacher prompts students to "sound it out" as a cue for students to shift attention to decoding. Once a word is identified, a request for students to summarize the earlier reading, or a brief summary provided by the teacher, guides readers to return their attention to meaning. When the story schema, up to the point of interruption, is reestablished, the teacher asks another question to focus attention on the portion about to be read. The process involves: 1) asking questions to focus on meaning; 2) providing cues to switch to decoding when confusing errors arise; 3) reminders of the schema of the text already read to scaffold a shift back to meaning; and, 4) asking a question to focus on the next section of text to resume reading. Much practice is needed before students with attention difficulties can focus as deeply as they must on decoding or meaning while also providing these cues for themselves.

Summary. At times, providing plenty of practice in decoding of word-lists and connected text develops automaticity that, by its very nature, leads students to shift attention effortlessly between decoding and meaning. However, some students need extensive practice with explicit cues from a teacher in order to develop fluency in making decoding-meaning shifts. In either case, teachers need to provide plenty of reading practice, and, when shifts do not occur independently, offer the scaffold of immediate cues to focus attention where needed.

Conclusion

Fluent readers move through text smoothly while closely understanding the author's meaning and attending to decoding aspects of reading, as needed. Mastery of decoding and familiarity with common literary conventions contribute to readers' ability to distribute attention to read fluently and with understanding. Readers develop fluency by reading connected text, practicing advanced word-analysis strategies, and reading, listening to, and discussing stories and expository passages that follow familiar text structures. When learners read text that is at an appropriate level, they experience confirmation and success that, in turn, stimulate an ongoing cycle of reading to learn, and of enhancing their reading ability, by reading.

Appendix: Informal oral reading inventory prepared by Barbara Goebel,
LD Specialist, Thorntons Ferry School, Merrimack, NH.

Informal Oral Reading Inventory

Student's Name_____ Reviewed by_____

Date_____ Book or passage selection_____

Accuracy (Note ability with phonetically regular words, glue words, unfamiliar words.)

Errors

Quality of Intonation

Expression/Fluency

Attention to Punctuation

Grasp of Content

Passage Level (Note sentence complexity, word length, and word meaning difficulty.)

General Comments:

References

Adams, M.J. (1994). *Beginning to read: Thinking and learning about print.* Cambridge: MIT Press.

Bembridge, T. (1994). A multilayered assessment package. In S.W. Valencia, E.H. Hiebert, & P.P. Afflerbach (Eds.) *Authentic reading assessment.* Newark DE: International Reading Association.

Bloom, B.S. (1986). Automaticity: "The hands and feet of genius." *Educational Leadership, 43,* 70-77.

Brody, S. (1984). *Patterning: Reading becomes easy.* Milford, NH: LARC Publishing.

Brody, S. (1985). Patterning: Reading becomes possible, In *Resource Papers, NH Task Force on Secondary Special Education.* Concord, NH: NH Department of Education.

Brody, S. (1986). The Brody reading method: A successful approach to reading and written-language skills for at risk students. Paper presented at the Annual Meeting of the Association for Children and Adults with Learning Disabilities (23rd, NY, NY, March 12-15). ERIC ED275 103.

Brody, (1987). *The Brody reading manual: An implementation guide for teachers.* Milford, NH: LARC Publishing.

Brown, H., & Cambourne, B. (1987). *Read and retell.* Portsmouth, NH: Heinemann.

Chall, J.S. (1983). *Stages of reading development.* New York: Mc-Graw Hill.

Chomsky, C. (1978). When you still can't read in third grade: After decoding what? In S.J. Samuels (Ed.), *What research has to say about reading instruction (1st ed.).* Newark, DE: International Reading Association.

Clay, M.M. (1993). *Reading Recovery: A guidebook for teachers in training.* Portsmouth, NH: Heinemann.

Cooper, J.D. (1993). *Literacy: Helping children construct meaning.* Boston: Houghton-Mifflin.

DeFina, A.A. (1992). *Portfolio assessment: Getting started.* NY: Scholastic.

deLone, H.T. (1988). *Reading skills and metacognition of fourth grade students.* Unpublished Doctoral Dissertation, Harvard Graduate School of Education.

Denckla, M.B. (1983). Learning for language and language for learning. In U. Kirk (Ed.), *Neuropsychology of language, reading and spelling,* 33-43. NY: Academic Press.

Glazer, S.M. (1992). *Reading comprehension.* NY: Scholastic.

Heilman, A.W. (1993). *Phonics in proper perspective.* New York: Macmillan.

Hoffman, J.V. (1985). *The oral recitation lesson: A teacher's guide.* Austin, TX: Academic Resource Consultants.

Irwin, J.W. (1986). *Teaching reading comprehension processes.* Englewood Cliffs, NJ: Prentice Hall.

Just, M.A., & Carpenter, P.A. (1981). Cognitive processes in reading: Models based on readers' eye fixations. In A.M. Lesgold & C.A. Perfetti (Eds.), *Interactive processes in reading.* Hillsdale, NJ: Lawrence Erlbaum. 177-213.

Just, M.A., & Carpenter, P.A. (1987). *The psychology of reading and language comprehension.* Needham Heights, MA: Allyn & Bacon.

Leu, D.J., Jr., & Kinzer, C.K., (1991). *Effective reading instruction, K-8 (2nd ed.).* New York: Macmillan.

Morrow, L.M. (1993). *Literacy development in the early years: Helping children reading and write (2nd ed.).* Boston, Allyn & Bacon.

Perfetti, C.A. (1985). *Reading ability.* NY: Oxford University Press.

Reutzel, D.R., & Cooter, R.B. (1992). *Teaching children to read: From basals to books.* NY: Merrill.

Reutzel, D.R., & Hollingsworth, P.M. (1993). Effects of fluency training on second graders' reading comprehension. *Journal of Educational Research, 86*(6), 325-331.

Roswell, F.G., & Chall, J.S. (1994). *Creating successful readers: A practical guide to testing and teaching at all levels.* Chicago: Riverside Publishing Co.

Routman, R. (1991). *Invitations: Changing as teachers and learners, K-12.* Portsmouth, NH: Heinemann.

Samuels, S.J., Schermer, N., & Reinking, D. (1992). Reading fluency: Techniques for making decoding automatic. In S.J. Samuels & A.E. Farstrup (Eds.), *What research has to say about reading instruction (2nd ed.).* Newark, DE: International Reading Association.

Savage, J.F. (1994). *Teaching reading using literature.* Madison, WI: Brown & Benchmark.

Spiegel, D.L., & Whaley, J.F. (1980). Elevating comprehension skills by sensitizing students to structural aspects of narratives. Paper presented at the Annual Meeting of the National Reading Conference (30th, San Diego, CA, December 3-6). ED199 634.

Stanovich, K.E. (1984). The interactive-compensatory model of reading: A confluence of developmental, experimental, and educational psychology. *Remedial and Special Education, 15*, 11-19.

Stanovich, K.E. (1986). Matthew effects in reading: Some consequences of individual differences in the acquisition of literacy. *Reading Research Quarterly, 21*(4), 360-407.

Stanovich, K.E. (1993). The construct validity of discrepancy definitions of reading disability. In G.R. Lyon, D.B. Gray, J.F. Kavanagh, & N.A. Krasnegor (Eds.), *Better understanding of learning disabilities.* Baltimore, MD: Brookes Publishing Co.

Stanovich, K.E. (1994). Romance and reality. *The Reading Teacher, 47*(4), 280-291.

Stanovich, K.E., & West, R.F. (1981). The effect of sentence context on ongoing word recognition: Tests of a two-process theory. *Journal of Experimental Psychology: Human Perception and Performance, 7*, 658-672.

Stanovich, K.E., & West, R.F. (1983). On priming by a sentence context. *Journal of Experimental Psychology: General, 112*, 1-36.

Stanovich, K.E., West, R.F., & Feeman, D.J. (1981). A longitudinal study of sentence context effects in second-grade children: Tests of an interactive-compensatory model. *Journal of Experimental Child Psychology, 32*, 185-199.

198

Steere, A., Peck, C.Z., & Kahn, L. (1971). *Solving language difficulties*. Cambridge, MA: Educators Publishing Service.

Tunnell, M.O., & Jacobs, J.S. (1989). Using "real" books: Research findings on literature based reading instruction. *The Reading Teacher, 42*, 470-477.

Vacca, J.L., Vacca, R.T., & Gove, M.K. (1991). *Reading and learning to read (2nd ed.)*. NY: Harper Collins.

Chapter 6. Spelling: A Window on Linguistic Development[1]

Louisa Cook Moats, EdD
St. Michaels College
Upper Valley Associates

In 1967, Johnson and Myklebust characterized spelling as a complex entity, requiring more simultaneous perceptual discrimination, memory, sequentialization, and analysis and synthesis of linguistic information than any other academic skill. In the intervening 25 years, research has confirmed their viewpoint and deepened our understanding of why this apparently simple form of language output presents so much difficulty for so many.

Far from being "mechanical," spelling has been shown to be a multifaceted linguistic skill that integrates and depends upon several layers of language knowledge: *phonological* awareness of speech sounds in words; *morphological* awareness of the meaningful parts that make up words; *semantic* knowledge of word meanings and word relationships; and *orthographic* knowledge of the letter sequences and patterns that are used to spell words (Ehri, 1989; Fischer, Shankweiler, & Liberman, 1985; Frith, 1980; Henderson,1990; Hodges, 1981; Read, 1986).

---

[1]Much of the material in this chapter will appear in a forthcoming book by Louisa Cook Moats entitled *Spelling: Development and Disability*, Baltimore: York Press.

Reading and spelling are two sides of the same coin—the mental processing of print as language. The study of one enhances the study of the other. Most commonly, individuals who are instructed systematically in spelling become better readers and expand their word knowledge. Nevertheless, many people are good readers but poor spellers (Sweeney & Rourke, 1985).

Learning to spell English is inherently difficult: the average adult in our society attains the equivalent of only an eighth grade spelling level (Jastak & Wilkinson, 1984). Spelling disabilities are ubiquitous among individuals with learning problems and usually coexist with disorders of oral language, reading, motor skills, and attention. Individuals with the specific reading disability, dyslexia, often can improve their decoding and reading comprehension after appropriate intervention, yet usually continue to be less-than-exemplary spellers (Bruck, 1987; Finucci, Gottfredson, & Childs, 1985; Moats, in press).

Good spellers do not simply have better visual memory for letters. They also have been shown to be more sensitive to language structure, more able to think about and manipulate language, and more able to learn linguistic complexities than individuals who are poor spellers. Spelling is a visible record of language processing, a window through which to view development of orthographic knowledge, phonological development, and understanding of word structure.

This chapter will consider the complex process of spelling. First, the nature of regularity in the English spelling system is reviewed. Next, the stage-like progression in which spelling is generally learned is explored. Then, principles for helping able and less-able spellers are proposed. Finally, a recommended order of instruction is examined along with specific strategies for reducing spelling problems.

The Regularity of English Spelling

English orthography is often maligned as unpredictable. On the contrary, although there are complexities and irregularities, English orthography is a structured and predictable system in which spellings for phonemes, syllables, and morphemes are rule-governed or explainable according to a word's historical origins, meaning, and sound structure (Chomsky, 1970; Henry, 1988; Venezky, 1967; 1970).

Hanna, Hanna, Hodges, and Rudorf's (1966) computer-based analysis of English orthography tested the predictability of sound-symbol correspondences in English, and documented that one-half the words in English could be spelled accurately and another 37% could be spelled with one error using phoneme-grapheme correspondence rules alone. Hanna et al.'s estimate of predictability took into account the fact that many graphemes or spellings for phonemes involve more than one letter (for example, *igh*, *ay*, *dge*, *tch*). A variety of additional factors, described below, influence the nature of predictable patterns of English spelling.

Phonemic context. Many spellings for sounds are influenced by the phonemes that come before or after them, or by their phonemic context. For example, the sound /f/ is spelled *ff* at the ends of words following a short vowel (*fluff, off*), *ph* after an /s/ (*sphere, sphynx*), or *gh* at the ends of a small set of Anglo-Saxon words (*tough, laugh, rough, cough, enough, trough, slough*).

Stress patterns. In addition, spellings are determined in part by stress patterns. For example, the speech sound /j/ is spelled *dge* at the ends of syllables with stressed short vowels (*dodge, fudge, wedge, badger, ridge*) but is spelled *ge* after long vowels or unaccented vowels (*college, village, stooge, wage*). Because stress can be difficult for writers with learning disabilities to discriminate, it is not surprising that they have difficulty with such spellings despite their regularity.

Orthographic rules. English spelling is also determined by purely orthographic rules that specify what letter sequences are allowed and what letters can be used to spell speech sounds in certain contexts (Venezky, 1970). For example, no word in English ends in the letter *v*; words ending in /v/ use a marker letter *e* to prevent *v* from ending a word (*love, mauve, shove, above*). Because of orthographic constraints, many of the letter sequences that make up words are redundant or repetitious, and we learn the probabilities of these constraints unconsciously through exposure to print. Readers know, for example, that the names *Nkruma*, *Rajiv*, and *Khrushchev* are not English spellings, although they may not be able to explain exactly why without more language study.

Lexical relationships. English spelling is also determined by the meaningful parts that comprise words (Chomsky, 1970; Moats & Smith, 1992). In fact, meaning often takes precedence over sound in spelling because lexical roots, base words, and affixes are usually spelled consistently in spite of pronunciation changes, as in *preside - president; define - definition*. Consonant shifts in pronunciation occur in *social - society; precocious - precocity; medic - medical - medicine*, and vowel shifts occur in words such as *divine - divinity; obscene - obscenity; compete - competition*. One of the reasons that English orthography is not a simple phonetic transcription system is that lexical relationships are preserved in our spelling to communicate meaning consistently even when pronunciation changes in words that are derived from one another.

Other spelling consistencies preserve lexical relationships in the presence of silent letters: *sign - signal - signature; muscle - muscular; hymn - hymnal*. Still others involve phonological and orthographic assimilation rules so that prefixes are compatible with the root: *in-* is assimilated in *irregular, illegitimate,* and *immortal* by changing the *n* to match the first consonant of the base word. Similarly, *ad-* is changed in *affix, approach, arrest, attend*.

Anglo-Saxon exceptions. Many common words of Anglo-Saxon origin are exception words, or words that do not follow common spelling patterns (see Table 6.1, below). About 350 of the 500 most often used words in English have odd spellings, according to Horn (1969), who was a strong advocate of memorization techniques in spelling instruction. The words most commonly misspelled by children with spelling disabilities tend to be those oddities, words such as *done, because, again, buy, some, their, were, would, where, of* and *who* (Moats, in press).

Table 6.1. The 100 Most Often Used Words in Writing, by Frequency.

The 100 Most Often Used Words in Writing, By Frequency					
I	on	like	do	now	school
and	would	went	about	or	little
the	me	them	some	know	into
a	for	she	her	your	who
to	but	out	him	home	after
was	have	at	could	house	no
in	up	are	as	an	am
it	had	just	get	around	well
of	there	because	got	see	two
my	with	what	came	think	put
he	one	if	time	down	man
is	be	day	back	over	didn't
you	so	his	will	by	us
that	all	this	can	did	things
we	said	not	people	mother	too
when	were	very	from	our	
they	then	go	saw	don't	

From Hillerich (1978), courtesy of Charles C. Thomas, Publisher, Springfield, Illinois

Phonological rules. The relationship between speech and spelling is complex, indirect, and multifaceted. Even words that seem to use straightforward, predictable spellings can present problems to novices. For example, short or lax vowels that precede the voiced consonant /g/ are changed slightly in pronunciation, by phonological rule, so that the vowel in *big* is closer to long *e* than the vowel in *bit*; the vowel in *egg* is closer to long *a* than the vowel in *bed*; the vowel in *bag* is pronounced as a diphthong with two parts, unlike the vowel in *back*. The /t/ phoneme in words like *little* and *attitude* is reduced to tongue flap /D/ in such spoken words, and is affricated in the /tr/ blend in *train*.

These distinctions might seem picky or irrelevant to those of us who can spell already, but the child learning to spell must learn to ignore such phonetic detail and treat the phoneme as an abstraction that can vary in pronunciation. Spelling is not a literal phonetic transcription of speech such as a linguist would accomplish with a phonetic alphabet. Therefore, children can progress only so far with "invented" spelling, or guessing at a phonetic transcription.

The Course of Spelling Development

Spelling develops in a broadly predictable sequence between kindergarten and about sixth grade, even among children who have had different instructional experiences. Much work during the past twenty years has been directed toward defining this stage-like progression (Bissex, 1980; Ehri, 1987; Henderson, 1990; Read, 1971, 1986; Templeton, 1992; Treiman, 1993), and although there is some disagreement among researchers, a common framework has been constructed (see Table 6.2, following page).

Phonetic stage. After a prephonetic stage, in which letter-like forms are made without regard to alphabetic speech representation, children begin economically and rulefully to produce syllabic representations of the salient consonants and vowels in words, often using letter name strategies. With practice and instruction, children later learn to represent all of the prominent phonemes of the word, including the vowel nucleus.

In both early and late phonetic spelling, children often use their knowledge of alphabet letter names creatively. They will derive short vowel spellings from the letter name articulated in similar position (/E/ derived from *a*; /I/ derived from *e*; /U/ derived from *o*, for example, BAD/bed; FES/fish; OP/up). Long vowels are often represented with one letter, as in FET/feet, NIT/, night, or SA/say.

Table 6.2. Stages of Spelling Development.

Stages of Spelling Development

1. **Preliterate Stage**
   a) idiosyncratic symbols used
   b) letters and numerals combined
   c) no use of a phoneme-grapheme correspondence system
   d) may or may not go left to right
   e) only the child can read the message back

2. **Semiphonetic or Prephonetic Stage (Early Letter Name)**
   a) growing awareness of left to right
   b) incomplete or abbreviated spellings
   c) use of single letters for whole syllables
   d) use of letter names for sounds
   e) salient consonants represented
   > Examples: RUDF? IWILGEVUAKNOPENR
   > (Are you deaf? I will give you a can opener.)

3. **Later Phonetic Stage**
   a) systematic representation of all sounds
   b) surface phonetic features represented
   c) systematic and principled, based on awareness of what
   mouth is doing
   d) not aware of correct spellings for sounds
   Examples: a) tense (long) vowels: DA - day, KAM - came, FEL - feel
   > b) lax (short) vowels: derived from letter name close in articulation
   > SAD (said)   WEL (will)   KIT (cut)
   c) preconsonantal nasals omitted:
   > JUP (jump)   AD (and)   BAK (bank) ED (end)
   d) syllabic consonants m, n, l, r:
   > LITL (little) BIGR (bigger) SOGR (sugar)
   e) inflected endings spelled phonetically (ed, s):
   > WAKT (walked)   ARIVD (arrived)   HALPT (helped)
   f) vowel spellings show phonetic detail:
   > SOWN (soon) GOWT (goat) BOE (boy) POWLEOW (polio)
   g) affrication of tr and dr:
   > CHRA (tray)   CHRIBLS (troubles)   JRADL (dreidel)
   h) intervocalic flaps shown as D:
   > LADR (letter)   WODR (water)   BEDR (better)
   i) letter names Y for /w/ and H for /ch/:
   > YOH (watch)   YL (will)   HRH (church)

4. **Transitional or Syllable Juncture Stage and Beyond**
   a) awareness of syllable patterns
   b) nasals are represented
   c) no more syllabic l, r, m, n
   d) use of silent letters such as "e"
   e) visual awareness of letter groups
   f) awareness of vowel teams
   g) automatic spelling of sight words
   h) rules over-generalized
   > Examples: EIGHTE(eighty)   YOUNITED(united)   TAOD(toad)

Diphthongs and back vowels are often spelled in a way that expresses phonetic detail, such as PIYL (pile), BOE (boy) and BOWT (boat). Phonetic features are represented, such as the affrication on the initial blends *tr* and *dr* (CHRAN/train; JRS/dress), and the reduction of /t/ to tongue flap [D] (LEDR/letter). Syllabic segments [l], [r], [m], and [n] are usually represented with one letter (LIDL/little; METN/mitten; NHR/nature).

Children who succeed with inventive, phonetic spelling have achieved an essential milestone toward mastery of decoding in reading. As discussed in Chapter 3, the ability to spell phonetically is a powerful predictor of early reading success, and a powerful measure of early reading progress, because phonological awareness, alphabet knowledge, and realization of the alphabetic principle are necessary for both early spelling and early decoding (Mann, Tobin, & Wilson, 1987; Rubin, in press; Tangel & Blachman, 1991). Phonological awareness and phonological processing permit and facilitate the connection between phonemes and graphemes in memory, and are the foundation for acquisition of specific word knowledge.

Transition to standard spelling. To make the transition to standard spelling, children must absorb many concepts and facts about English orthography, and accumulate a store of knowledge in the orthographic memory system. After phonetic spelling is achieved, children must learn the actual graphemes that spell syllable parts and the ways in which syllables are joined. Henderson (1990) and his colleagues (Gentry, 1978; Templeton, 1992) have labeled these stages "within word pattern" and "syllable juncture" according to the primary orthographic content to be learned at each level.

For example, children must realize that many vowels are spelled with letter combinations, some letters can be doubled, spellings change when endings are added, and much phonetic detail is not represented in spelling. Further, children must learn the constancy of many morpheme spellings and consider sound, pattern, meaning, and even syntax to spell correctly. The teacher's interpretation of spelling errors must be informed by awareness of these developmental principles. Otherwise, errors that, in fact, are developmentally common and stage-appropriate will be viewed as pathological (Cook, 1981; Invernizzi & Worthy, 1989; Moats, 1983).

Development when spelling disabilities are present. Children with reading and spelling disabilities, who usually have related difficulties with language processing, follow the normal course of spelling development more slowly (Invernizzi & Worthy,1989) and with ultimate limits on their achievement (Moats, in press a). Most dyslexic students with average verbal intelligence achieve gross phonetic accuracy in their misspellings after sufficient instruction (Bailet, 1990; Bruck, 1988; Carlisle, 1987; Moats, 1983; Nelson, 1980; Pennington et al., 1986).

However, there are certain phoneme-grapheme correspondences, aspects of word structure, and specific word spellings that appear to be insurmountably difficult for many poor spellers to learn, and students with phonological processing deficits often remain stuck at about a fifth grade level of spelling accuracy even though they may learn to read close to grade level in adolescence (Moats, in press). The growing disparity between reading and spelling in the remediated dyslexic appears to be a consequence of the much greater precision in word memory that is required for spelling than is needed for word recognition (Bruck, 1988; Ehri, 1989; Frith, 1980).

What is difficult for the person with spelling disability. In the past, researchers and test makers have focused on whether children were better or worse at spelling "predictable" or "unpredictable" words in order to characterize a disability. This approach has very limited value. More recently, it has been shown that error patterns in the misspellings of both good and poor spellers may be influenced by at least four factors.

First, individual phoneme characteristics, such as the presence or absence of voicing or aspiration in a consonant, or the place of articulation of a vowel, may influence the accuracy with which it is spelled (Hoffman & Norris, 1989). Second, the phonological characteristics of spoken syllables, such as their stress and whether they contain a liquid (/l/, /r/) or a nasal (/n/, /m/, /ng/) after a vowel are related to spelling difficulty (Moats, 1993; in press; Read & Ruyter, 1985; Treiman, 1993).

Third, morphophonemic aspects of word structure, such as the presence of an inflected ending (-ed,-s, -er, -ing) or the distance between a root and a derivation, determine the likelihood of correct spelling (Bailet, 1990; Carlisle, 1987; Fischer, Shankweiler, & Liberman, 1985; Henry, 1988; Sterling, 1983).

Finally, orthographic structure itself is related to difficulty, such as the presence of doubled letters (Henry, 1988; Schlagal, 1986). Words whose spellings represent complex relationships between morphology, phonology, and orthography are in general the hardest to recall. Poor spellers usually are stymied by certain linguistic constructions as well as specific, irregular words, and their ultimate level of success with spelling depends in large part on the intactness of their phonological processing capabilities.

Principles of Spelling Instruction

Through the twentieth century, spelling instruction research has considered several major questions: Should word lists be grouped according to word frequency or word pattern? What kind and what amount of practice will result in the most efficient and generalizable learning? What role should tests play in word study? How can teachers ensure that word study generalizes to writing? Although studies of spelling instruction usually have not defined or grouped their subjects according to their spelling level or their cognitive characteristics, several findings have emerged consistently in spelling research since the 1920s.

The following principles of instruction have been shown to be useful in classroom-based instruction of spelling that is aimed at helping the average child at or near grade level (Fitzsimmons & Loomer, 1977; Hillerich, 1985; Horn, 1969):

1. The test-study-test method is desirable, especially if students immediately correct their pretests themselves and use the information to focus their study.

2. Ten to fifteen minutes per day is sufficient for most students to master a week's spelling lesson of twenty words.

3. Words should be grouped by both frequency and spelling pattern.

4. Practice should include frequent writing of the unknown words, since spelling improves most when children are asked to write often.

5. Active study rather than "looking the words over" or oral spelling gets the best results.

If even this much were practiced from one grade to another, within an organized, consistent plan for skill development, spelling might not be the cause for concern that it has become for many children. Unfortunately, within popular philosophies, *component skill* development often takes the back seat (indeed, the rumble seat) in many classrooms. Systematic, structured, and sequential spelling practice is discouraged because it is considered less meaningful than integrated written expression.

Further, many teachers have been led to believe that isolated practice of component skills is a waste of students' time. In such a climate, children with dyslexia or spelling disability are often ignored. A few may be assigned to a learning specialist who is often asked to teach language skills, including spelling, with little reinforcement from the classroom teacher. In addition, many children with typical learning abilities miss the opportunity to learn and practice accurate spelling, instead practicing and remembering invented spellings during writing activities that provide little or no corrective feedback.

INSTRUCTION FOR GOOD SPELLERS

Some children learn to spell rather effortlessly; nevertheless, they do need instruction. Such children easily remember orthographic patterns as they encounter them in print. They also do well on tests of phonological processing, as the ability to discriminate and analyze speech sounds is a prerequisite for spelling competence as well as decoding proficiency. Children with good spelling memories can learn by almost any method, as long as some type of systematic practice is present, and the spelling list is at the appropriate developmental level. Henderson's Qualitative Inventory of Spelling Development can be used to determine developmental spelling level (Table 6.3, following page), as described in Henderson's (1990) excellent text, *Teaching Spelling*. This text is a rich source of activities for teaching children in classroom spelling groups.

Basal programs, designed for use by grade level with large classes of students, vary considerably from one another and need to be used with caution. Many contain information that is not linguistically accurate, and many provide no valid rationale for including words on lists. Sometimes they oversimplify, or explain poorly, the complexities of sound-symbol correspondence. Because they are designed for the average child at a given grade level, the instructional level and unique needs of less-able learners (and the most able learners) typically are not met. Too many words and too many concepts are presented at once; too many confusing stimuli are offered in one lesson; and not enough review and practice of previously learned material is offered for the poor speller. Further, basal texts often fail to give the linguistic or historical reasons concerning why English words are spelled the way they are, when such information might help spelling make sense.

Basal texts can be useful if the level of difficulty is matched to the students' developmental spelling level, using a developmental assessment (Table 6.3, following page) and if the teacher follows the research-supported steps listed above. Within any typical classroom, at least three levels of spelling ability require instruction at any one time. One of the most critical factors in the success of such an approach is the teacher's ability to direct students' attention to various aspects of word structure. Teachers must therefore be devoted students of language study themselves.

Table 6.3. Qualitative Inventory of Spelling Development. (From Edmund Henderson, *Teaching Spelling* (2nd ed.), copyright © 1990 by Houghton Mifflin Company. Reprinted with permission.)

I	II	III	IV	V	VI
girl	traded	send	force	lunar	satisfied
want	cool	gift	nature	population	abundance
plane	beaches	rule	slammed	bushel	mental
drop	center	trust	curl	joint	violence
when	short	soap	preparing	compare	impolite
trap	trapped	batter	pebble	explosion	musician
wish	thick	knee	cellar	delivered	hostility
cut	plant	mind	market	normal	illustrate
bike	dress	scream	popped	justice	acknowledge
trip	carry	sight	harvest	dismiss	prosperity
flat	stuff	chain	doctor	decide	accustom
ship	try	count	stocked	suffering	patriotic
drive	crop	knock	gunner	stunned	impossible
fill	yard	caught	badge	lately	correspond
sister	chore	noise	cattle	peace	admission
bump	angry	careful	gazed	amusing	wreckage
plate	chase	stepping	cabbage	reduction	commotion
mud	queen	chasing	plastic	preserve	sensible
chop	wise	straw	maple	settlement	dredge
bed	drove	nerve	stared	measure	conceive
	cloud	thirsty	gravel	protective	profitable
	grabbed	baseball	traffic	regular	replying
	train	circus	honey	offered	admitted
	shopping	handle	cable	division	introduction
	float	sudden	scurry	needle	operating
			camel	expression	decision
			silent	complete	combination
			cozy	honorable	declaration
			graceful	baggage	connect
			checked	television	patient

INSTRUCTION FOR POOR SPELLERS

What can be done for the person who spells poorly? Too often, the poor speller in the elementary grades is deemed not ready for instruction; the poor speller in the intermediate grades is deemed unresponsive to instruction; and the poor speller in high school or beyond is viewed as a hopeless case. When such attitudes prevail, it is not surprising that poor spellers often remain untaught. Although research on general classroom instruction of spelling is plentiful, research on spelling instruction for the student with well-defined spelling disability is much more limited.

Spelling improvement can occur in poor spellers if it is carried out systematically over a long period of time. Very poor spellers seldom progress in spelling as fast as they can improve in reading. Although the ultimate gains may be modest, they provide a basis for simple written communication. An effective instructional program for poor spellers, according to criteria of the National Teacher Education Initiative Task Force of the Orton Dyslexia Society, will be integrated with other language instruction and will include the following components:

- direct teaching with teacher-student interaction
- simultaneous, multisensory methodology
- systematic, sequential, and cumulative emphasis on phonology
- synthetic-analytic phonics progressing from part to whole
- systematic morphology for spelling and usage

Teacher-directed, systematic practice with controlled amounts of new information. Systematic teaching regulates the amount of information presented to the learner at one time, the number of concepts or patterns (amount of redundancy) present in the stimuli, and the amount of practice that occurs with new and old information. The teacher assumes that students will forget, even as they study, and that forgetting will make new learning difficult to establish. It is necessary to be systematic due to the exact nature of spelling. Children who cannot spell well obviously do not remember words from incidental exposure to print. Spelling requires explicit and precise recall of orthographic sequences. The correspondence system is less predictable for spelling than it is for reading, so that greater demands are placed on word-specific orthographic memory in spelling. In addition, many of the most commonly used words in English are of Anglo-Saxon origin and have retained low frequency or odd spellings that also must be memorized (Table 6.1, p. 202).

Regardless of the content domain, people with learning disabilities generally learn better when the amount to be learned is controlled, the amount of practice is monitored, and reinforcement theory is applied deliberately by the teacher (Lyon & Moats, 1988). To build up word images in memory and to ensure that words are so well learned that they can be recalled without delay or extra attention, a great deal of practice of a few elements at a time is required. A good rule of thumb is 80% old information, 20% new information in a lesson plan designed for a person who spells poorly. Fernald (1943) showed that some children require up to 40 opportunities to write a word correctly before they remember it.

Limit number of words. The number of words presented at one time also needs to be limited for poor spellers. Rieth et al. (1974) found that poor spellers recalled more words by the end of the week if they learned five or six a day and were tested on those daily. Good spellers, however, learned well with all twenty words given on Monday. Bryant, Drabin, and Gettinger (1981) found that students with severe spelling disabilities did best with only three new words a day. This data is most applicable to situations when students are trying to *memorize specific words*.

When students are being taught a concept, rule, or generalization about sound-symbol correspondence, such as the "f, l, s doubling rule," only one concept or pattern should be taught at a time. However, ample practice with 30 or more examples in one lesson is often necessary for the redundant pattern to be internalized. Children learn patterns through repeated exposure to many examples. Poor spellers need more experience with print and more focus and repetition during that experience than good spellers.

Modeling and immediate feedback. With poor spellers, effective teaching also entails direct teaching and much interaction between student and teacher. Passive activities such as worksheets and telling a student to look over words are ineffective. Teachers will get the best results if they give students immediate corrective feedback when they make errors and if they model active study strategies for students. One strategy that has been validated with students with learning disabilities is error imitation and modeling (Nulman & Gerber, 1984). The teacher reproduces the child's error and then corrects it, highlighting the difference between the incorrect and correct words, before asking the student to write the word correctly.

Multisensory instruction. The term *multisensory* refers to the simultaneous engagement of hearing, seeing, saying, and feeling during spelling practice. The initials VAKT - visual, auditory, kinesthetic, tactile - refer to multisensory instruction. Children might be asked to say a word while writing it with fingers on a rough surface, or might be asked to say a word slowly, analyze its sounds, say the letters that correspond to sounds, and write them, for example. Although it is not entirely clear from research why multisensory techniques are most efficacious with dyslexic children, experienced remedial teachers have recommended it for decades (e.g., Fernald, 1943; Gillingham & Stillman, 1960; King, 1984) and it has been shown experimentally to produce better results than unisensory techniques with naive or dyslexic children (Bryant & Bradley, 1985; Thomson, 1991).

One likely reason for the efficacy of the multisensory approach is that it encourages the child to externalize and focus upon the phonemic elements of the word by saying it slowly and deliberately, noticing how each phoneme is represented. This activity facilitates the "comparator function" viewed as central to spelling by

Lindamood, Bell, and Lindamood (1992)—the differentiation of similar word forms and conscious matching of sound to symbol. Moreover, more attention is deployed when several sensory modalities are engaged simultaneously, probably resulting in increased brain activation levels and increased chances for information storage.

Organized and sequential instruction. Children who are poor spellers are insensitive to the structure of spoken and written language. They need much more practice than good spellers to remember sound-symbol associations, and do not spontaneously perceive the semantic, phonological, or orthographic relationships among words derived from one another. When the correspondences, syllable patterns, and other redundancies of the language are presented one at a time in a logical sequence, the elements are differentiated, brought into focus, and related to one another. All the elements are not equally difficult, and repetition of the hardest concepts and associations can be built into lessons as needed.

Components of Spelling Instruction

Whether there is an ideal sequence for teaching spelling is open to debate. However, there seems to be substantial commonality in the basic scope and sequence of most spelling programs. The sequence seems to represent a natural order of word learning that corresponds to phonological, reading, and vocabulary development (see Table 6.4, following page). Such a sequence allows for orderly introduction of redundant elements and a systematic exploration of their relationships.

The components of spelling instruction described on the following pages reflect the general sequence of Figure 6.a (below), but are not intended to be used in a lock-step manner. Teaching should be recursive. New concepts can be introduced while others are being mastered and automatized through varied practice.

Sequence of Spelling Instruction

Explicit Practice with Phonological Analysis
Basic Sound-symbol Correspondences
One-syllable Patterns
Inflections
Conditional Word and Syllable Patterns
Homophones
Syllable Patterns and Syllable Junctures
Latin and Greek Morpheme Patterns
Ending Rules

Figure 6.a. Sequence of spelling instruction.

Table 6.4. Spelling scope and sequence chart. (Developed by L.C. Moats in collaboration with G. Giveans and teachers from Dresden School District, Hanover, New Hampshire.)

Grade Level	1	2	3	4	5	6	7	8
Beginning Consonants	b c d f g h j k l m n p r s t v w y z		qu	c: cent g: gent				
Ending Consonants	b d g m n p t	x ff ll ss zz			ck-k ge-dge			
Beginning Blends		bl cl fl gl pl sl br cr dr fr gr pr tr sc sk sl sm sn sp st sw	scr spr spl str squ	shr thr		sch		
Ending Blends		mp nd ft lt nt lf st nk ng						
Digraphs		ch sh th	wh-	ph	ch-tch	ch: ache chorus		
Silent Letters			ck lk	wr kn	gn			
Vowels	short a e i o u	long a-e e-e i-e o-e u-e	y as long i: sky	y as long e: happy		ie ei schwa (ə)	y as short i: system eigh augh ough	
Vowel Digraphs		ai ee oa ea	au aw oo: boot ew	oo: foot				
Diphthongs			ou ow oi oy					
r- control			ar er ir or ur	air ear				
Prefixes				un- re-	pre- en- dis- mis- ex- in-	con- per- com- a-	bi- mal- circum- inter- intra- super- trans-	Derivational doubling: immature irregular
Grammatical Endings		No base change -s -ed -ing	Double final consonant Drop final e -ed -ing	Change y to i -ed -ing -er -est			Double final consonant of accepted syllable: regretted	
Suffixes				-ly -ful -ness -less	-tion -sion -teen	-ment -en	Adjective suffixes: -ous -able -ible -ic -al	Noun suffixes: -tion -sion -al -ment -ian -ance -ence -tious -cial -ture
Syllables: open and closed		Concept of syllable	Divide compound words sail/boat	Divide words with prefixes and suffixes: re/turn sad/ly	Divide cvc words: mo/ment Divide vccv words: trum/pet	Suffix -le takes preceding consonant: ta/ble	Vowel digraphs and diphthongs remain undivided in syllables: com/pound	
Contractions			I'm he's she's it's	'll: he'll n't: aren't	'd: we'd 're: you're 've: they've			
Sample Words	lap run flop yet big	sniff stamp chops made load	quitting striding why snoop smart	rice shrilly unhook hurried phone	gnat prediction token napkin judge	school receive neither noble compartment	submitting humorous destructive horizontal agreeable	accord funeral version librarian spacial

EXPLICIT PRACTICE WITH PHONOLOGICAL ANALYSIS

Because accurate spelling is facilitated by an accurate internal representation of a word's phonemic structure, phonological awareness activities should be incorporated into spelling lessons for children who cannot represent words phonetically. Awareness can be developed through a variety of games and activities that are brief, fun, and interspersed with activities throughout the day (Rubin, in press); also see Chapter 3 of this volume.

Introductory phoneme awareness activities.

a) Create silly words, such as names for puppets, animals, and characters, using rhyme and alliteration (Bino the Rhino).

b) Point out that known names begin with certain sounds.

c) Contrast words that differ only in one sound (goal - gold).

d) Have children purchase store items or play guessing games by saying a "little bit" of a word or getting ready to say a word and producing the first sound only.

e) Select a target sound for the day, and reward the student for noticing when the sound occurs in names.

More explicit forms of word analysis.

a) Identify initial phonemes in words through analysis of rhymes. Using blocks or other counters, show children how a rhyme is formed by changing the initial phoneme. Say, "Your name is Jason. Now, if I take off the /j/ and add an /m/, I can make a rhyme—Mason! Now you try it.

b) Identify an initial phoneme in words while moving a block or counter. Use continuant phonemes (/f/, /s/, /m/, /n/, /l/, /r/, /th/, /v/, /z/) rather than stops, such as /t/, /k/, /p/, because it is easier to blend a continuant than a stop.

c) Identify the phonemes in a consonant-vowel combination (Sue, moo, new, shoe), moving a block for each sound and blending the sounds together. Then change the vowel and show with the counters what happened (Sue, see, say, so).

d) Add a final consonant to consonant-vowel combinations and represent each phoneme with a block (su + p = sup).

e) Use Ball and Blachman's (1991) "Say It and Move It" procedure, modeled after Elkonin (1973): The child is presented with a line drawing of an object she can name. Below the picture is a rectangle divided into sections that correspond to the number of phonemes in a word. The teacher models, then the child puts a counter in a section while saying the word slowly. Then the child says the blended word fast.

After playing this game with many different words, the child can be given chips of different colors to represent the consonants and the vowels. Later, letter tiles can be substituted for chips and beginning spelling can occur. (Ambiguous vowels, diphthongs, r-controlled vowels, and consonant blends should be avoided at this stage.) Beginning awareness of inflections such as plural /s/ can be developed at this stage.

f) Play sound deletion games after Rosner's (1973) auditory analysis activities:
1. syllable deletion from a compound (say "sunshine" without the "sun")
2. syllable deletion (say "cucumber" without the "cu")
3. initial consonant deletion ("part"without the /p/)
4. final consonant deletion ("seat" without the /t/)
5. initial phoneme in a blend ("stake" without the /s/)
6. final phoneme in a blend ("past" without the /t/)
7. second consonant in an initial blend ("stake" without the /t/)

g) Coding with colored blocks (after *Auditory Discrimination in Depth*, Lindamood & Lindamood,1975): The child uses colored blocks to represent sounds and shows changes where they occur in spoken syllables by changing the color of a block, adding a block, or taking a block away. If sounds are the same, the same color should represent them; if sounds are different, different colors should be used. An order for level of difficulty is as follows:
1. add a sound (if this says /i/, show me /i+p/)
2. delete a sound (if this says /kap/, show me /ap/)
3. change a consonant (if this says /slap/ show me /snap/)
4. change a vowel: (if this says /slap/, show me /slop/)
5. change the order of sounds (pats to past)
6. duplicate a sound already in the word (art to tart)

Once skill is developed with colored blocks, then letter tiles can be gradually substituted for them.

Additional phonological awareness activities suitable for older students:
a) With one-syllable words, have the student say each word slowly, separating the phonemes, and marking each sound on a finger. Model this as often as necessary.

b) Given an array of counters that correspond to the phonemes in longer words such as *silver*, ask the student which counter corresponds to /l/ or some other sound.

c) If the student has difficulty representing a vowel, be sure the reader has identified the vowel in the syllable correctly by saying it in isolation and giving a cue word beginning with the vowel.

d) Deliberately contrast prefixes and words that have subtle differences in pronunciation, such as *pre*, *per*, and *pro; migrate* and *migraine*, by dictating these slowly and having the student spell them with letter tiles.

e) Words in a student's writing vocabulary can be categorized by sound. For example, awareness of confusing blends such as *fr* and *fl* can be enhanced by grouping words such as *flagrant* and *fragrant* with others beginning with the same clusters.

TEACHING BASIC SOUND-SYMBOL CORRESPONDENCES

The most basic multisensory drill advocated by Gillingham and Stillman (1960) and other programs based on similar principles (Clark, 1988) includes viewing a letter form on a card, saying the letter name, saying a key word, and then saying the target phoneme in isolation ("*i*, itchy, /I/") The letter form is traced on a rough surface as the student recites.

To spell, the order of drill is changed to saying the sound, the key word, and the letter that makes it, and then writing the letter. The Orton-Gillingham approach stresses automatic learning of these associations, and even after longer words are being spelled successfully, the student is asked to repeat the drill at the beginning of each lesson. As associations are learned, words are spelled using the Gillingham Simultaneous-Oral-Spelling (S.O.S.) technique, described below (Gillingham & Stillman, 1960), to establish reliance on a phonetic encoding strategy:

1) The teacher pronounces the word.

2) The child hears the word and repeats the word. (He is hearing his own voice and feeling the articulation.)

3) The child says the word sound by sound. After identifying each phoneme, the child says the name of the letter that represents the sound, and writes the letter as it is being named.

4) The child reads orally the word that was written.

Many older children are not sure of all the alphabet letter names or forms even though they have been in school for several years. Some of the most confusing letters are *u*, *y*, and *w*, because their names, sounds, and forms relate in misleading ways to one another.

Choice of an unambiguous key word containing each phoneme is critically important in the basic sound-symbol drill. For example, desirable key words to associate with the short vowel phonemes would avoid nasalized vowels, r-controlled vowels, or vowels that are distorted by the following consonant. Suggested key words are as follows:

Vowel	Key Word	Words to Avoid
/ă/	at, apple	ant, bag, air
/ĕ/	Ed, Eddy	egg, elephant
/ĭ/	it, icky	igloo, Indian, ink
/ŏ/	ox, octopus	on, off
/ŭ/	up, us	umbrella, uncle

If students are severely learning disabled and affected by severe deficits in phonological processing, they must be taught speech sound awareness before and during sound-symbol instruction. Methods such as *Auditory Discrimination in Depth* (Lindamood & Lindamood, 1975) that emphasize the place, manner, and contrasts of phoneme production in the throat and mouth can be effective where others fail, (Alexander et al. 1991; Ehri & Sweet 1991; Howard 1982; Torgesen & Morgan, in press). Vowel discrimination and memory for vowel correspondences can be enhanced when the articulatory placement of vowels is associated with their most reliable spellings (see Figure 6.b, following page).

A practice of the Lindamood and Gillingham approaches that should be incorporated into any remedial spelling program is the explicit and correct definition of linguistic concepts. Vowels are a set of speech sounds; digraphs are different

218

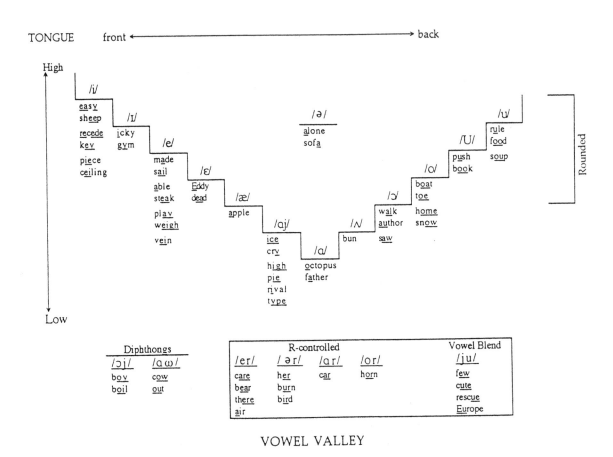

Figure 6.b. Vowel correspondences by vowel placement.

from blends; schwa is the unaccented vowel, and so forth. Even young children can learn this terminology. It serves to clarify, not confuse, but of course the teacher must be well informed about language to teach these concepts.

Persistent letter confusions and letter reversals can usually be corrected with a multisensory drill, and daily practice reading and writing words with the confusing letters. Immediate corrective feedback must be available at first until the student internalizes a self-checking strategy. Reference to a mnemonic image, such as a bed for *b* and *d*, is often very helpful.

TEACHING REGULAR ONE-SYLLABLE PATTERNS

The basic units of spelling should be presented and learned in an order progressing from high frequency, high regularity units to complex, more unusual units that operate within several constraints. For example, Forbes (1968) organized her word lists into those that could be "sounded out," those that could be "sounded out and thought out," and those that required memorization or thorough knowledge of complex rules and probabilities.

The first level of practice occurs with predictable short-vowel word families or recurring syllable patterns. Initial presentation of a new pattern should ask the student to actively reorganize, compare, contrast, and sort word lists by their initial consonant(s) and by their rime. Lists of words sharing rime features should be kept for later reference (e.g., *mass, grass, compass*) and for adding new words as they are encountered. Comparison, sorting, and classification are much more effective than rule recitation for learning about patterns, although ample practice writing words will be necessary to reinforce their automatic recall.

Vowel spellings, again, are the most varied and require the most practice. At first, the single letter and vowel-consonant-e patterns should be taught, then the vowel digraphs and diphthongs, one at a time. Vowels followed by /l/, /r/, and nasals /m/ and /n/ will be the most challenging for students because the presence and identity of the consonant as separate from the vowel is difficult for dyslexic students to realize. These constructions are phonologically ambiguous or obscure. In addition, the spellings in *hurt, bird, learn, were, her,* and *favor* all map to the same indistinct vowel plus /r/, and the word *fire* sounds as if it has two syllables, as in *higher*. Many poor spellers never quite master these complexities, so repeated practice with different patterns should be ongoing even when more advanced polysyllabic words are being studied.

Corrective feedback should take into account the reason for a child's confusion about spelling. Very often, the phonological ambiguity of the words themselves will be the cause of a misspelling. For example, if the child spells BAG for *beg*, the student could be taught that the vowel in *beg* is in fact pronounced like a "long a," but that this distortion in speaking is ignored in writing, and the word is to be grouped with the family that includes *leg, keg, Meg,* and *egg*.

EARLY INTRODUCTION OF INFLECTIONS

As soon as students are reading and writing verb forms, they are ready to be introduced to the past tense *-ed* morpheme. As soon as they are reading and writing noun forms, they are ready to learn the plural /s/ spelling. Learning that these morphemes are spelled consistently in spite of variations in pronunciation is the first step to realizing that spelling represents meaning, often in preference to sound. Explicit teaching of the past tense necessitates identification of the /d/, /t/, or /ed/ that ends words such as *begged, walked,* and *wanted,* before words are written to dictation. Inflectional spellings should be reviewed and practiced often for many years. It is insufficient to present one lesson on each and expect the learning to be internalized.

CONDITIONAL WORD AND SYLLABLE PATTERNS

Many patterns and generalizations are predictable but conditional. They include the spellings of *tall, annoy, glue, glove,* and *most*. In these cases, the student can either be asked to understand a pattern from examples (inductive learning) or to apply a given rule or principle to examples (deductive learning). The inductive approach is a powerful tool with bright students who enjoy solving puzzles. It is illustrated by the following exercise to teach the *ch, tch* generalization:

Given this list of words,

inch	catch	bunch	kitchen
starch	pouch	fetch	butcher
pitch	march	ranch	pinch
hatchet	pooch	botch	stitch,

students state when *tch* is used to spell /ch/ at the ends of words or syllables. They may realize there are a few exceptions, including *rich, much, such, which, attach, sandwich,* and *bachelor*, and these should be presented as atypical. The "word sort" activity (after Sulzby, 1980) is helpful in discovering principles and can be carried out with words on cards or with lists of words that the student generates.

If the inductive approach is confusing or ineffective with students because they are unable to see the patterns in the examples, then a deductive approach must be taken. A deductive approach calls for the teacher to state the rule and ask the student(s) to apply it to examples. With the word list above, the teacher might state, "A one-syllable word ending in /ch/ is spelled with *tch* after an accented short vowel. In all other cases, /ch/ is spelled *ch.*" Then words could be grouped, read, and spelled to dictation.

HOMOPHONES

Their, there, and *they're; you're* and *your; its* and *it's* are among the most often misspelled words in the language. Other spellings of words that sound the same but differ in meaning and spelling, such as *course* and *coarse, knight* and *night, prophet* and *profit* are commonly confused by children who cannot rely on letter memory. The best one can hope for in cases of very poor spellers is to clarify confusions among words they use most often, because practice of these words **in context** is what eventually develops the correct word habit.

Teachers often claim it takes an entire year of repeated practice to straighten out the *there/their/they're* confusion in older children. Matching games in which spelling and meaning are paired are helpful, at least in sensitizing the writer to what must be looked up, along with dictated phrases given regularly. Spell checkers on computers do not catch such errors and they can be embarrassing (like the letter from the ski coach who asked parents to learn the *coarse* before *gait*-keeping).

A comprehensive list of homophones can be found in *Spellmaster* (Greenbaum, 1987); another is published in the *New Reading Teacher's Book of Lists* (Fry, Fountoukidis, & Polk, 1985). Recall is facilitated when the words are placed in meaningful contexts repeatedly, including phrases, sentences, cloze exercises, analogies, jokes, cartoons, and puns. Homophones should be taught a few at a time; however, only the most able learners can work with the long lists that often appear in workbooks.

SYLLABLE PATTERNS AND SYLLABLE JUNCTURE

The syllable should be defined as a pronounceable unit that always contains a vowel sound and vowel letter (exceptions *rhythm*; *-ism*). Children with spelling difficulties benefit from learning the six syllable types (see Table 6.5, following page). One reason for teaching syllables is that redundant patterns in longer words can be much more quickly discerned; another is that the rules for adding endings to words and the way in which syllables are combined into longer words depend on the type of syllable(s) in the word; and finally, spellings become more predictable when the type of syllable is taken into account. For example, the most common spelling of "long a" in an open syllable within a polysyllabic word (*radio, vacation, stable*) is simply the letter *a*, and not the other seven alternatives.

Table 6.5. Syllable Types.

Syllable Type	Characteristics
Closed *rabbit* *racket* *picnicking*	These syllables contain a short vowel followed by a consonant. In a polysyllabic word, a short vowel is usually protected from an adjacent vowel by two consonants. Thus, if a short vowel is heard in the first syllable, there are most likely two consonants between it and the next vowel.
Open *moment* *radar* *decide*	The long vowel in an open syllable is usually separated from the next syllable with only one consonant letter or no consonant, because an open syllable ends with a vowel.
R-Controlled *bird* *berth* *absurd*	When a vowel is followed by /r/, the vowel loses its identity as long or short, and is coarticulated with the /r/. A similar phenomenon occurs when /l/ follows a vowel. Students must learn that syllabic /r/ and r-controlled vowels are spelled with a vowel letter plus the letter *r*.
Vowel Team *boat* *see* *boil* *draw*	Many long vowels are spelled with two vowel letters including *ai, ay, ee, ea, ie, oa*. Diphthongs are also spelled with two vowel letters such as *oi, oy, ou*. In addition, the letter *w* can act as a vowel in a team, as in *ow, aw*. These teams, which are difficult for many poor spellers, can appear at the middle or end of words or before certain consonants (e.g. *aw* before *n* and *l*).
Vowel-e *write* *pace* *bake*	In the vowel-consonant-silent *e* pattern, the first vowel is long and the *e* is silent. The silent *e* can be removed when adding endings provided another vowel takes its place to keep the first vowel long: *writing, pacer*.
Consonant-le *juggle* *rifle* *table*	When the syllabic /l/ occurs at the ends of spoken words, it is often preceded by a consonant that is part of that last syllable. Thus the word *bugle* has an open first syllable while *little* has a first syllable closed by the first *t*. The sound of the vowel in the first syllable determines whether two consonants are needed.

If one knows about syllable types, one can remember more easily that *accommodate* has two *m's*—because the second vowel is short it most likely is followed by two consonants, one ending the closed "com" syllable, the other beginning the open "mo" syllable. The word *little* has two *t*'s because the first syllable is closed and the last syllable is a standard consonant-le configuration. A double *n* is necessary in words like *beginning* because the second syllable is closed and double letter protects the "short i" vowel sound. There are many excellent programs for teaching syllable structure, including the Brody Reading Method (Brody, 1987), *Words* (Henry, 1990), *Megawords* (Johnson & Bayrd, 1983), *Solving*

Language Difficulties (Steere, Peck & Kahn, 1971), and the game *Syllable Plus* (Stoner, 1985).

LATIN AND GREEK MORPHEME PATTERNS

Latin patterns. Latin-based words are usually taught after basic Anglo-Saxon vocabulary has been learned (Henry, 1993). In some ways, Latin-based words are easier to spell than Anglo-Saxon words. They do not use the problematic digraphs so common in Anglo-Saxon spellings, and because many spellings are meaning-based prefixes, roots, and suffixes, they tend to be constant even though many are reduced to /ə/ when they are unaccented. If students learn to recognize those meaningful units, many spellings will seem more logical. For example, *recommend* would not have two *c*'s, because the prefix *re* is added to the root *commend*.

There is ample evidence from cognitive psychology that words sharing derivational relationships should be taught together (Moats & Smith, 1992; Templeton, 1992). Many roots of Latin origin have consonants whose phonetic form changes in derived words such as the *t*, *c*, and *s* that appear in *partial, magician, confusion*. In addition, reduced vowels can be ambiguous in various derived forms (*confidence, sedative, competition*). In many words with ambiguous vowels or chameleon consonants, the correct spelling of a base word or derivation can be recovered more easily if it is learned in partnership with a word sharing the same root and more transparent pronunciation (Henry, 1993; Hodges, 1982; Templeton, 1992).

On any list of "hard to spell" words, there are some that can be taught so that root-derivative relationships are made clear: *differ, different; favor, favorite; child, children; autumn, autumnal; sign, signal, resign, resignation; vacate, vacation; athlete, athletic; theater, theatrical; magic, magician.*

Many other words that turn up on "hard to spell" lists are rule-based or comprise affix-root constructions that make the spelling make sense. There is no reason why *beneficial, advice, attend,* or *misspell* should be learned in isolation as sight words, when all have prefixes. The method for teaching such words should call attention to the word's structure at the levels of sound, syllable, and meaningful parts.

Greek patterns. Words of Greek origin comprise a large segment of our scientific vocabulary, and are best studied in the context of science and math. The spellings of *y* for /I/ (*gym, sphynx, krypton*), *ph* for /f/ (*photo, sphere, graph*) and *ch* for /k/ (*chorus, chameleon, ache*) signify a Greek derivative. Greek words combine morphemes but assign them equal status, like English compounds (*stratosphere, phonograph, thermometer*). The spellings tend to be very consistent and phonically transparent, and thus easier than words from other languages. Programs that address these include *Words* (Henry, 1990) and *Classical Roots*.

The word *mnemonic* might seem obscure and difficult to spell until one considers its Greek origin and the related forms that have entered English. Mnemosyne was the Greek goddess of memory. The words *amnesia* (without memory) and *amnesty* (literally, forgetting a transgression) are cousins of *mnemonic*. Such knowledge helps clarify for most people that the other phonetically confusing Greek root, *pneumo* (*pneumatic, pneumonia*) is an altogether different form having to do with air. Memory and air, are, we hope, dissociated.

ABOUT ENDING RULES

The three major rules requiring an orthographic change when endings are added to words seem daunting for students to learn and frustrating for teachers to teach (see Table 6.6, following page).

The only hope for teaching these rules is to present them at intervals over several years, along with repeated reinforcement when corrective feedback about spelling is given. Consistent practice is needed rather than one or two lessons in sixth grade. Furthermore, these rules should be introduced after students have the conceptual underpinnings: a firm grasp of single-syllable spellings; the concepts of consonant, vowel, and syllable; and the ability to read multiple examples.

Most people begin to internalize the patterns for spelling word endings through repeated exposure to them in print. A good speller can produce a rule-based construction without necessarily stating the rule accurately, although knowledge of the rules helps clarify what is right when specific word memory fails. Individuals with mild spelling difficulties profit from practice with rules because their attention can be focused on the entire letter sequence in words such as *beginning* and *easier* when the spelling makes sense.

The internalization of orthographic change rules is very difficult for many poor spellers. Very often, students with spelling disabilities will fail to recognize when a rule needs to be applied, even if they know the rule (Carlisle, 1987; Liberman, Rubin, Duques, & Carlisle, 1985). Spelling research suggests that poor spellers will often recall specific word spellings without evidence that they have internalized or automated the rule that governs them.

Table 6.6. Orthographic Change Rules for Adding Endings.

Rule	Characteristics
Doubling Rule *running* *wettest*	When a one-syllable word with one vowel ends in one consonant, double the final consonant before adding a suffix beginning with a vowel.
Advanced Doubling *conferring* *occurred*	When a word has more than one syllable, double the final consonant when adding an ending beginning with a vowel *if* the final syllable is accented and has one vowel followed by one consonant.
Silent-e *confining* *wasteful*	When a root word ends in a silent *e*, drop the *e* when adding a suffix beginning with a vowel. Keep the *e* before a suffix beginning with a consonant.
y *studied* *studying* *monkeys*	When a root word ends in a y-preceded-by-a-consonant, change the *y* to *i* then add any suffix but *ing*. When adding *ing*, or when the root word ends in y-preceded-by-a-vowel, make no change and add the suffix.

Instructional Strategies Across the Sequence

MEMORIZING WORDS AS WHOLES

Multisensory techniques can be applied to the memorization of individual words. Even Horn (1969), who was generally hostile to linguistic or rule-based spelling instruction, notes that word study was more effective when several sensory images were stimulated simultaneously. His word study method follows:

1) look at the word
2) pronounce the word
3) say the letter names
4) recall how the word looks with the eyes closed
5) look back at the word and check
6) write the word
7) check and repeat if necessary

This particular method, however, avoids explicit analysis of speech sounds and their representations. The Fitzgerald method (Fitzgerald, 1951) places more emphasis on linking meaning with spelling, and remains an effective multisensory technique for memorizing words with somewhat unpredictable or complex spelling patterns:

1) *Meaning and pronunciation.* Have the child look at the word, pronounce it, and use it in a sentence.

2) *Imagery*. Ask the child to see the word and say the word. Have the child say the word by syllable, spell the word orally, and trace over the word with a finger or write it in the air.

3) *Recall*. Ask the child to look at the word and then close her eyes to see the word in her mind's eye. Have her spell the word orally with her eyes closed. Ask her to open her eyes and see if the spelling was correct.

4) *Write the word*. The child writes the word from memory, and then checks against the original.

5) *Mastery*. The child covers the word and writes it. If she is correct, she should cover it and write it two more times.

The Fernald (1943) technique is similar to the above, but the whole word is traced repeatedly with the index and middle fingers on a rough tactile surface until the child can write it from memory. The learned word is then placed in the context of a meaningful sentence. There is no concern for grouping words by phonic pattern in Fernald's approach.

Such techniques foster the recall of whole word images for words that a student must commit to memory. They should accompany explicit instruction in the patterns and logic of the spelling system to facilitate the whole word learning process. There is some evidence (Vaughn, Schumm, & Gordon, 1993) that a variety of motoric conditions can be used for multisensory practice of spelling words—writing, tracing, or typing on a computer—and each of these is equally beneficial.

PROMOTING THE USE OF ACTIVE RECALL STRATEGIES
Although many programs offer suggestions for mnemonic devices that will aid spelling recall, the most effective mnemonics are those that students make up themselves. Because more active mental processing is necessary to create an idea than to listen to one, the self-generated strategy is the one most likely to be used. Gerber (1984) and others also have shown that children's word recall could be enhanced if they were taught to identify which words they were unsure of and to write plausible alternatives.

PLANNED GENERALIZATION OF SKILL
Most children who spell poorly can learn some words in lists with sufficient practice, yet they regress to old habits during spontaneous writing. Instruction is not worthwhile unless it generalizes. Regular dictation exercises, personal spelling

dictionaries with words listed alphabetically, and proofreading practice can strengthen the bridge between spelling skill development and its automatic use. Furthermore, overlearning basic sound-symbol associations and syllable patterns, and rehearsing words using multisensory drills prior to writing them in text facilitates generalization.

For example, Brody (1987) suggests that informal classroom use of syllabication and multiple word writing improves spelling. Her steps include:
1. Student says words in syllables.
2. Student writes word in syllables (separating with spaces, not lines).
3. Student writes word as whole.
4. Words are written repeatedly, 5 times each, in syllables, over 3 - 5 days.

INTEGRATED LESSON PLANNING

A systematic teacher plans the major elements of a lesson according to a predefined sequence of skills, and keeps an informal record of a student's responses to instruction. Although the plan can always be adjusted, it serves as a guide by which good teaching principles are implemented. Such a plan includes a choice of appropriate examples, sufficient review and practice, and application of skills to meaningful writing. On the basis of detailed record keeping, the next lesson can be tailor-made. *Spellmaster* (Greenbaum, 1987) is a system for individualizing instruction for a class group. An individual progress record and data sheet for recording the specific spelling patterns each student has mastered accompany a detailed set of word lists and instructional activities.

Systematic spelling instruction usually occurs in coordination with reading and vocabulary instruction. A remedial lesson plan within a multisensory, linguistic approach might be similar to this:
1. phonogram drill
   a) sound-symbol
   b) symbol-sound

2. writing to dictation and immediate correction of errors by reference to logic or known words; review of previously learned material

3. sight word practice using multisensory writing-saying technique

4. introduction of new concept using inductive method or deductive method, as appropriate; exploration of phonological, orthographic, and etymological facts about the concept

5. writing nonsense and real words to dictation

6. sentence writing activity using new words

INDIVIDUAL DIFFERENCES AND FLEXIBLE TEACHING

Various strategies work for different types of words and different types of children. All of the specific suggestions offered here may be useful at some point, with some students. For example, some learners need quick integration of basic patterns into advanced vocabulary (*patch, dispatch, dispatcher; cent, century, percent, centennial*), but other learners might be overwhelmed by exposure to the harder words or words not in their speaking vocabulary. It is essential to have available a comprehensive word list that includes examples of each sound-symbol correspondence, syllable type, spelling pattern, rule, or generalization (e.g., Forbes, 1968; Greenbaum, 1987; Henderson, 1990) and to use it with discretion.

As Stanback (1980) concluded after reviewing the historical literature on teaching spelling, there is no one right way to represent word structure for children or to help them remember this information. Techniques for making word structure memorable should vary according to the words under study. These strategies should match the properties of the target word presented as well as the learner's capabilities.

Additional Strategies to Aid Memorization

Several additional strategies for spelling instruction can be helpful when employed selectively and sensibly:

1. *Invoke a "spelling pronunciation."* This works well for words with silent letters, and foreign or irregular spellings that do not match pronunciation, such as *Wednesday, was,* and *antique.*

2. *Group words with like, but unusual, spelling-meaning patterns.*

two	one	there	their
twenty	once	here	heir
twelve	only	where	

3. *Employ mnemonic devices (association links):*
He **mean**t to be **mean**. There's **a rat** in sep**arat**e. Knights would **die** val**i**antly in me**die**val times. **Loose** as a **goose**. It's hard to **lose** your **nose**. **Sally** finall**y** came home.

4. *Highlight visual-orthographic features of words.* People with poor orthographic memory may store and retrieve word images more readily if novelty or contrast is used to highlight letter sequences. Techniques that may be useful include: color coding (to contrast vowels and consonants); underlining; using different fonts on a word processor; or writing letters in different sizes. The effectiveness of such manipulations is not well researched at present, however.

SPECIAL CONSIDERATIONS FOR TEACHING ADOLESCENTS

Adolescents and adults often view themselves as hopeless cases if they have spelling disabilities, especially if prior instruction has been haphazard or linguistically uninformed. Many of them, however, can make significant improvement if their disabilities are worked with systematically, sequentially, and logically over a sustained period of time. When instruction is aimed at their developmental level of word knowledge (see Table 6.3, p. 209), adolescents can develop confidence that language makes sense and that many spelling problems can be solved with knowledge of language structure.

Adolescents often know many individual words but do not understand spelling principles or word relationships. They have a much larger oral vocabulary to draw upon, so that rimes and other syllable units can be applied immediately to many examples. Their vocabulary can be used to build understanding of redundant language patterns. Goals for accuracy must be modest and realistic. Instruction should be aimed at improving the person's chances to communicate clearly and recognize the need to check a spelling.

Conclusion

The teacher of spelling who knows language intimately can clarify the patterns of English for the learner. When a teacher understands the course of spelling development and the meaning of various error patterns, the level of instruction can be matched to the instructional level of each learner. Individual variation in spelling is extremely wide in any classroom, and a knowledgeable teacher is able to survey the developmental levels of the students and provide meaningful practice at those levels. Effective instruction and practice will depend upon the nature of the vocabulary to be learned, the developmental level of the learner, and the presence of any learning disability. Successful teaching will net more than improved spelling; it will also strengthen the learner's knowledge of language structure and vocabulary, and result in more proficient decoding skills.

230

References

Alexander, A., Andersen, H., Heilman, P., Voeller, K., & Torgesen, J. (1991). Phonological awareness training and remediation of analytic decoding deficits in a group of severe dyslexics. *Annals of Dyslexia, 41,* 193-206.

Bailet, L.L. (1990). Spelling rule usage among students with learning disabilities and normally achieving students. *Journal of Learning Disabilities, 23,* 121-128.

Ball, E., & Blachman, B. (1991). Does phoneme awareness training in kindergarten make a difference in early word recognition and developmental spelling? *Reading Research Quarterly, 26,* 49-66.

Bissex, G. (1980). *Gnys at wrk: A child learns to write and read.* Cambridge, MA: Harvard University Press.

Boder, E. (1973). Developmental dyslexia: A developmental approach based on three atypical reading-spelling patterns. *Developmental Medicine and Child Neurology, 15,* 663-687.

Brody, S. (1987). *The Brody reading manual: An implementation guide for teachers.* Milford, NH: LARC Publishing.

Bruck, M. (1987). The adult outcomes of children with learning disabilities. *Annals of Dyslexia, 37,* 252-263.

Bruck, M. (1988). The word recognition and spelling of dyslexic children. *Reading Research Quarterly, 23 ,*51-69.

Bryant, N.D., Drabin, I.R., & Gettinger, M. (1981). Effects of varying unit size on spelling achievement in learning disabled children. *Journal of Learning Disabilities, 14,* 200-203.

Bryant, P.E., & Bradley, L. (1985). *Children's reading problems.* Oxford: Blackwell.

Carlisle, J.F. (1987). The use of morphological knowledge in spelling derived forms by learning-disabled and normal students. *Annals of Dyslexia, 37,* 90-108.

Chomsky, C. (1970). Reading, spelling, and phonology. *Harvard Educational Review, 40,* 287-309.

Clark, D.B. (1988). *Dyslexia: Theory and practice of remediation.* Baltimore: York Press.

Cook, L. (1981). Misspelling analysis in dyslexia: Observation of developmental strategy shifts. *Bulletin of the Orton Dyslexia Society, 31,* 123-134.

Ehri, L.C. (1987). Learning to read and spell words. *Journal of Reading Behavior, 19,* 5-31.

Ehri, L.C. (1989). The development of spelling knowledge and its role in reading acquisition and reading disability. *Journal of Learning Disabilities, 224,* 349-364.

Ehri, L.C., & Robbins, C. (1992). Beginners need some decoding skill to read words by analogy. *Reading Research Quarterly, 27,* 13-26.

Ehri, L.C., & Sweet, J.(1991). Finger-point reading of memorized text: What enables beginners to process print? *Reading Research Quarterly, 26,* 442-462.

Ehri, L.C., Wilce, L.S., & Taylor, B.B. (1987). Children's categorization of short vowels in words and the influence of spellings. *Merrill Palmer Quarterly, 33,* 393-421.

Elkonin, D.B. (1973). USSR. In J. Downing (Ed.), *Comparative reading.* NY: Macmillan.

Felton, R.H., & Wood, F.B. (1989). Cognitive deficits in reading disability and attention deficit disorder. *Journal of Learning Disabilities, 1,* 3-13.

Fernald, G. (1943). *Remedial techniques in basic school subjects.* New York: McGraw Hill.

Finucci, J., Gottfredson, L.S., & Childs, B. (1985). A follow-up study of dyslexic boys. *Annals of Dyslexia, 35*, 117-136.

Fischer, F.W., Shankweiler, D., & Liberman, I.Y. (1985). Spelling proficiency and sensitivity to word structure. *Journal of Memory and Language, 24*, 423-441.

Fitzgerald, J.A. (1951). *A basic life spelling vocabulary.* Bruce.

Fitzsimmons, R.J., & Loomer, B.M. (1977). *Excerpts from spelling, learning and instruction - research and practice.* Iowa State Department of Public Instruction and the University of Iowa, Iowa City.

Forbes, C.T. (1968). *Graded and classified spelling lists for teachers grades 2-8.* Cambridge, MA: Educators Publishing Service.

Frauenheim, J.G., & Heckerl, J.R. (1983). A longitudinal study of psychological and achievement test performance in severe dyslexic adults. *Journal of Learning Disabilities, 16*, 339-347.

Frith, U. (1980). Unexpected spelling problems. In U. Frith (Ed.), *Cognitive processes in spelling* (pp.495-515). New York: Academic Press.

Fry, E., Fountoukidis, D.L., & Polk, J.K. (1985). *The new reading teacher's book of lists.* Englewood Cliffs, NJ: Prentice Hall.

Gentry, J.R. (1978). Early spelling strategies. *The Elementary School Journal, 79*, 88-92.

Gerber, M. (1984). Techniques to teach generalizable spelling skills. *Academic Therapy, 20*, 49-58.

Gillingham, A., & Stillman, B. (1960). *Remedial training for children with specific disability in reading, spelling, and penmanship.* Cambridge, MA: Educators Publishing Service.

Goswami, U., & Bryant, P. (1990). *Phonological skills and learning to read.* East Sussex, U.K.: Lawrence Erlbaum.

Greenbaum, C.R. (1987). *Spellmaster.* Austin, TX: Pro-Ed.

Hanna, P.R., Hanna, J.S., Hodges, R.E., & Rudorf, E.H. (1966). *Phoneme-grapheme correspondences as cues to spelling improvement.* Washington, D.C.: U.S. Government Printing Office, U.S. Office of Education.

Henderson, E. (1990). *Teaching spelling (2nd ed.).* Boston: Houghton Mifflin.

Henry, M. (1988). Beyond phonics: Integrated decoding and spelling instruction based on word origin and structure. *Annals of Dyslexia, 38*, 258-275.

Henry, M. (1990). *Words.* Los Gatos, CA: Lex Press.

Henry, M. (1993). Morphological structure: Latin and Greek roots and affixes as upper grade code strategies. *Reading and Writing: An Interdisciplinary Journal, 5*, 227-241.

Hillerich, R.L. (1978). *A writing vocabulary of elementary children.* Springfield, IL: Charles C. Thomas.

Hillerich, R.L. (1985). *Teaching children to write, K-8: A complete guide to developing writing skills.* Englewood Cliffs, NJ: Prentice Hall.

Hodges, R.E. (1981). *Learning to spell.* Urbana, IL: National Council for Teachers of English.

Hoffman, P.R., & Norris, J.A. (1989). On the nature of phonological development: Evidence from normal children's spelling errors. *Journal of Speech and Hearing Research, 32,* 787-794.

Horn, E. (1969). Spelling. In C. W. Harris (Ed.), *Encyclopedia of Educational Research* (pp. 1282-1299). New York: Macmillan.

Howard, M. (1982). Utilizing oral-motor feedback in auditory conceptualization. *Journal of Educational Neuropsychology, 2,* 24-35.

Invernizzi, M., & Worthy, M.J.(1989). An orthographic-specific comparison of the spelling errors of learning disabled and normal children across four grade levels of spelling achievement. *Reading Psychology: An International Quarterly, 10,* 173-188.

Jastak, S., & Wilkinson, G.S. (1984). *Wide Range Achievement Test manual.* Wilmington, DE: Jastak Associates.

Johnson, D. (1986). Remediation for dyslexic adults. In G.T. Pavlidis & D.F. Fisher (Eds.), *Dyslexia: Its neuropsychology and treatment* (pp. 249-262). Chichester, England: J. Wiley and Sons.

Johnson, D., & Myklebust, H.R. (1967). *Learning disabilities: Educational principles and practices.* New York: Grune & Stratton.

Johnson, K., & Bayrd, P. (1983). *Megawords.* Cambridge, MA: Educators Publishing Service.

Kent, R.D. (1992). The biology of phonological development. In C. A. Ferguson, L. Menn, and C. Stoel-Gammon (Eds.), *Phonological development: Models, research, implications.* Timonium, MD: York Press.

King, D. (1984). *Teaching written expression to adolescents.* Cambridge, MA: Educators Publishing Service.

Liberman, I.Y., Rubin, H., Duques, S., & Carlisle, J. (1985). Linguistic abilities and spelling proficiency in kindergartners and adult poor spellers. In D.B. Gray & J.F. Kavanaugh (Eds.), *Biobehavioral measures of dyslexia* (pp. 163-176). Parkton, MD: York Press.

Liberman, I.Y., & Shankweiler, D. (1985). Phonology and the problems of learning to read and write. *Remedial and Special Education, 6,* 8-17.

Liberman, I.Y., Shankweiler, D., & Liberman, A.M. (1989). The alphabetic principle and learning to read. In D. Shankweiler and I.Y. Liberman (Eds.), *Phonology and reading disability: Solving the reading puzzle.* Ann Arbor: University of Michigan Press.

Lindamood, P.C., Bell, N., & Lindamood, P. (1992). Issues in phonological awareness assessment. *Annals of Dyslexia, 42,* 242-259.

Lindamood, C., & Lindamood, P. (1975). *The A.D.D. Program: Auditory discrimination in depth (2nd ed.).* Allen, TX: DLM, Inc.

Lyon, G. R., & Moats, L.C. (1988). Critical issues in the instruction of the learning disabled. *Journal of Consulting and Clinical Psychology, 56,* 830-835.

Mann, V.A., Tobin, P., & Wilson, R. (1987). Measuring phonological awareness through the invented spellings of kindergarten children. *Merrill Palmer Quarterly, 33,* 365-391.

Moats, L.C. (1983). A comparison of the spelling errors of older dyslexics and second-grade normal children. *Annals of Dyslexia, 33,* 121-139.

Moats, L.C. (1993). Spelling error interpretation: Beyond the phonetic/dysphonetic dichotomy. *Annals of Dyslexia, 43*, 174-185.

Moats, L.C. (in press). Phonological spelling errors in the writing of dyslexic adolescents. *Reading and Writing: An Interdisciplinary Journal.*

Moats, L.C., & Smith, C. (1992). Derivational morphology: Why it should be included in assessment and instruction. *Language, Speech and Hearing in the Schools, 23*, 312-319.

Nelson, H.E. (1980). Analysis of spelling errors in normal and dyslexic children. In U. Frith (Ed.), *Cognitive processes in spelling* (pp. 475-493). London: Academic Press.

Nulman, J.H., & Gerber, M.M. (1984). Improving spelling performance by imitating a child's errors. *Journal of Learning Disabilities, 17*, 328-333.

Orton, S. (1937). *Reading, writing, and speech problems in children.* New York: W.W. Norton and Co.

Pennington, B.F., McCabe, L.L., Smith, S.D., Lefly, D.L., Bookman, M.O, Kimberling, W.J., & Lubs, H.A. (1986). Spelling errors in adults with a form of familial dyslexia. *Child Development, 57*, 1001-1013.

Rack, J.P., Snowling, M., & Olson, R.K. (1992). The non-word reading deficit in dyslexia: A review. *Reading Research Quarterly, 27*, 28-53.

Read, C. (1971). Preschool children's knowledge of English phonology. *Harvard Educational Review, 41*, 1-34.

Read, C. (1986). *Children's creative spelling.* London: Routledge and Kegan Paul.

Read, C., & Ruyter, L. (1985). Reading and spelling skills in adults of low literacy. *Remedial and Special Education, 6*, 43-52.

Reith, H., Axelrod, S., Anderson, R., Hathaway, F., Wood, K., & Fitzgerald, C. (1974). Influence of distributed practice and daily testing on weekly spelling tests. *Journal of Educational Research, 68*, 73-77.

Rosner, J. (1973). *The perceptual skills curriculum.* New York: Walker Educational Book Co.

Rubin, H. (in press). *Reading and Writing: An Interdisciplinary Journal.*

Schlagal, R.C. (1986). Informal and qualitative assessment of spelling. *The Pointer, 2*, 37-41.

Snowling, M.J. (1981). Phonemic deficits in developmental dyslexia. *Psychological Research, 43*, 219-234.

Stanback, M. (1980). *Teaching spelling to learning disabled children: Traditional and remedial approaches to spelling instruction. Research Review Series 1979-1980, Volume 3.* Research Institute for the Study of Learning Disabilities, Teachers College, Columbia University.

Steere, A., Peck, C.Z., & Kahn, L. (1971). *Solving language difficulties.* Cambridge, MA: Educators Publishing Service.

Sterling, C.M. (1983). Spelling errors in context. *British Journal of Psychology, 74*, 353-364.

Stoner, J. (1985). *Syllable plus.* Cambridge, MA: Educators Publishing Service.

Sulzby, E. (1980). Word concept development activities. In E.H. Henderson and J. W. Beers (Eds.), *Developmental and cognitive aspects of learning to spell.* (pp. 127-137) Newark, DE: International Reading Association.

234

Sweeney, J.E., & Rourke, B.P. (1985). Spelling disability subtypes. In B.P. Rourke (Ed.), *Neuropsychology of learning disabilities: Essentials of subtype analysis* (pp. 147-166). New York: Guilford Press.

Tangel, D.M., & Blachman, B.A. (1992). Effect of phoneme awareness instruction on kindergarten children's invented spelling. *Journal of Reading Behavior, 24*, 233-261.

Templeton, S. (1992). Theory, nature, and pedagogy of higher-order orthographic development in older students. In S. Templeton and D. R. Bear (Eds.), *Development of orthographic knowledge and the foundations of literacy: A memorial Festschrift for Edmund H. Henderson.* (pp. 253-277). Hillsdale, NJ: Erlbaum.

Thomson, M. (1991). The teaching of spelling using techniques of simultaneous oral spelling and visual inspection. In M. Snowling and M. Thomson (Eds.), *Dyslexia: Integrating theory and practice.* (pp. 244-250). London: Whurr Publishers.

Torgesen, J., & Morgan, S. (in press) The effects of two types of phonological awareness training on word learning in kindergarten children. *Journal of Experimental Psychology.*

Treiman, R.(1993). Beginning to spell: *A study of first grade children.* New York: Oxford.

Vaughn, S.V., Schumm, J.S., & Gordon, J. (1993). Which motoric condition is most effective for teaching spelling to students with and without learning disabilities? *Journal of Learning Disabilities, 26*, 191-198.

Vellutino, F. R., & Scanlon, D.(1987). Phonological coding, phonological awareness, and reading ability: Evidence from a longitudinal and experimental study. *Merrill Palmer Quarterly, 33*, 321-364.

Venezky, R. (1967). English orthography: Its graphical structure and its relation to sound. *Reading Research Quarterly, 2*, 75-105.

Venezky, R. (1970). *The structure of English orthography.* The Hague: Mouton.

Viise, N.M. (1992). A comparison of child and adult spelling development. Doctoral Dissertation, University of Virginia, Curry School of Education.

IV. THOUGHT

Chapter 7. Comprehension: Gathering Information and Constructing Understanding

Sara Brody, EdD
Rivier College

When students enter Stage 3, they read fluently—with speed, accuracy, and comprehension (Chall, 1983).[1] During Stage 3, students learn how to process unfamiliar information and develop understanding while reading. With guidance, they begin to use reading as a highly versatile problem-solving tool. They rapidly discover that reading enables them to gather ideas and useful details from sources as diverse as the information superhighway and their own shopping lists. Further, some students turn to reading for the pleasure of fantastic adventure, enthralling romance, or a close-up encounter with the thoughts of a respected role model.

As they progress through Stage 3, students use reading itself, along with relevant instruction, as a means to enrich their vocabulary, broaden their background,

---

[1]As in earlier chapters of this volume, this selection draws heavily on Jeanne Chall's work that clarifies the nature of reading development, in this case, Stage 3 reading comprehension. For further detail please see *Stages of Reading Development* (Chall, 1983; in press).

and increase their agility in developing clear understanding of unfamiliar concepts. As they build their background resources and continue in their cognitive maturation, successful students later use reading as a process that lets them synthesize and share deep understanding concerning complex systems of thoughts, concepts, and structures.

Teachers enhance comprehension development among Stage 3 readers through instruction that facilitates reading to learn and deeply understand specialized information. As students mature toward Stages 4 and 5, teachers can provide scaffolds that help advanced readers become adept at gathering information from multiple sources in order to construct new understanding while reading challenging text.

Research suggests that during Stage 3, effective instruction needs to draw on the skills emphasized in classic instructional techniques while providing enhancement with more recent experimental approaches. In particular, until the 1980s, reading comprehension activities generally focused on teaching students the skills needed to determine the main idea and details of a selection, along with how to compare and contrast concepts, identify cause and effect, and draw inferences and conclusions. Such activities foster Stage 3 reading—using text to learn new concepts, information, thoughts, feelings, relationships, etc. These activities remain central to constructing a clear understanding of text (Vacca & Vacca, 1993).

In addition, during the last few decades, researchers and educators began exploring means of facilitating Stage 4 and 5 reading—gathering information from multiple perspectives to actively construct new knowledge—by teaching a variety of metacognitive strategies. As a whole, studies of these strategies yielded rather mixed findings among 4th and 5th graders who were at the stage of learning to gather specialized content from text (Brody, 1989; Haller, Child, & Walberg, 1988). The mixed findings mirror the experiences reported to me informally by reading specialists and teachers who have found inconsistent results in their own classrooms. Teachers often indicate that strategy effectiveness is related to students' needs, abilities, and background, with skilled readers generally performing well on comprehension tasks no matter which strategy is employed.

It is tempting to conclude that teachers must rely solely on experimentation in order to find activities that can be used during classroom instruction to meet the individual needs of both advanced and less-skilled learners. However, it seems that instructional planning can be enriched by a guiding framework if it delineates the effective elements of Stage 3 instruction, profiles additional elements that facilitate higher level comprehension, and specifies when and how these elements may be integrated effectively.

In order to seek such guidelines, I sifted through the mixed findings in the literature concerning Stage 3 reading comprehension instruction. First, I reviewed and synthesized dozens of research studies, from the 1980s to '90s, concerned with classroom reading comprehension instruction of 4th and 5th graders—readers beginning the process of gathering specialized information from print (Brody, 1989; 1991; 1993). Then, I examined these practices and findings along with the findings from similar studies conducted with older students (Flood & Lapp, 1990; Graves, Cooke, & LaBerge, 1983; Hayes, 1989; Palincsar & Brown, 1984; Slater, Graves, & Piche, 1985).

The review indicated that, across the age range, certain underlying elements were **present** when *any* method exhibited a comprehension advantage over a comparison procedure. In addition, when any method found effective in one study exhibited *no advantage* in another study, these core underlying elements appeared to be **lacking** when the instructional procedure was used during the latter study.

This chapter draws on these studies to consider the nature of effective reading instruction, particularly at Stage 3. First, underlying **core elements** related to comprehension among Stage 3 readers are identified. Next, these elements are examined by considering factors that contribute to their effectiveness, along with instructional approaches in which they are incorporated during classroom reading instruction. This is followed by a review of strategies that are commonly recommended to facilitate higher levels of reading comprehension. Finally, the chapter describes a process that integrates core elements of Stage 3 instruction with strategies that facilitate preparation for Stage 4 and 5 reading.

Core Elements and Comprehension Instruction

The core instructional elements that continually reappear when Stage 3 reading comprehension methods appear effective seem almost too common-sense to study or consider. And yet, it is the presence or absence of these elements that seems consistently related to strategy effectiveness. The core elements are summarized below:

1) assure that students are able to read the words in which the material is written (introduce specialized polysyllabic words

before assigning reading to **enhance decoding fluency**, or use text written at readers' decoding competency level);

2) provide multiple exposures to the meanings of unfamiliar words, or assure that readers possess the necessary background from which to **develop knowledge of word meanings** while reading (teach word meanings before and during reading along with teaching the background concepts needed to infer word meanings from context);

3) **pose questions** that develop an organizing focus and purpose for reading and continuing to read (use questions, before and during reading, that prime readers to process what they read);

4) assure that readers possess crucial background knowledge that is needed in order to grasp the concepts in the material under study (**explain background** needed to form inferences);

5) provide many exposures to unfamiliar ideas in the reading, and offer many opportunities to organize and express these concepts (arrange **plenty of practice and application** of unfamiliar concepts).

Validation. The effectiveness of the core elements in facilitating reading comprehension is corroborated in two ways. As discussed above, these elements commonly appear as an integral part of instruction when any reading comprehension approach is found effective. In addition, research concerning the habits of skilled readers indicates that "strategic" readers *use these same elements* in their own self-directed reading processes (Flood & Lapp, 1990).

Flood & Lapp (1990) report that skilled readers slow down, when needed, to **decode unfamiliar words**; use various strategies to **determine the meanings** of unknown words; **ask questions** of themselves to focus on relevant concepts in the reading; search through their prior knowledge to **seek background** that will let them form appropriate inferences; and engage in **repeated rehearsal and review** of a text under study as a means of developing meaningful and complete schemata.

The match is quite close between the behaviors of skilled readers and the instructional elements that assist less-skilled readers. This match suggests that when instruction incorporates these core elements, it serves as a scaffold that enhances less-skilled readers' comprehension until they develop the rich background and ability needed to use "strategic" habits independently.

It appears that various instructional strategies are likely to enhance the comprehension of Stage 3 readers *provided* that the methods include the effective elements noted above. This section presents core elements in detail in order to clarify how and why these "active ingredients" help readers comprehend text. Several elements are discussed in separate chapters of their own and are mentioned only briefly in this section. (See Chapter 8 concerning background concepts; Chapter 9 concerning vocabulary concepts; and Chapter 10 related to multiple exposures and expression through writing.)

Element One: Develop Decoding Fluency Before and During Reading

As discussed in Chapter 5, decoding fluency sets a reader's mind free to focus on comprehension of the information and concepts relayed by text (Bloom, 1986; Samuels, Schermer, & Reinking, 1992; Stanovich, 1994). The research of the 1980s generally examined strategies designed to foster inference formation rather than decoding competency. However, through the nature of their research designs, most researchers acknowledge that decoding fluency is a prerequisite to the use of a variety of reading comprehension strategies whether applied to literature or content texts.

For example, researchers design their comprehension studies to avoid limited decoding competency by selecting only students whose decoding skills are at grade level, or students otherwise judged to be competent decoders (Anstey & Freebody, 1987; Palincsar & Brown, 1984). Other times, studies use reading materials that are written well below the grade level of the students in the study as a means of assuring that all subjects can decode the study materials with fluency (Hansen & Pearson, 1983; Spiegel & Whaley, 1980).

Several studies of the 1980s provide evidence to substantiate the positive influence of decoding fluency on reading comprehension in the upper elementary grades (e.g., Durkin, 1984; Sadoski & Page, 1984). They compare decoding error rates with reading comprehension scores and find a significant correlation. Occasionally, researchers speculate that a strategy under study is not as effective as expected because the metacognitive requirements of the strategy are overwhelming when accompanied by the demands of less-than-fluent decoding among less-skilled readers (Gordon & Pearson, 1983).

One study, comparing silent and oral reading, found that upper-elementary grade readers with limited decoding competency understood text no better whether reading silently or orally. During silent reading, these students completed the assigned reading task more quickly, by skipping over unfamiliar words, but this did not enhance their understanding of what was read (Juel & Holmes, 1980).

The procedures used by researchers to rule out decoding limitations during research activities are not available routinely to classroom teachers. Consequently, several alternatives are suggested below.

Develop decoding fluency with unfamiliar content words. Many readers beyond the primary years generally decode fluently but stumble on long words that convey unfamiliar content in tradebooks or textbooks. Teachers can ease the burden of decoding long words by introducing them before assigning independent reading. The introduction can follow these steps:

Teacher:
- write the word on the board
- say the word
- break the word into syllables and say syllables while pointing to them
- tell word meaning if unknown

Students:
- repeat the above activities following the teacher's model.

The approach can be combined with a variety of prereading strategies such as text-structure frames, focus questions, or reading previews (described later in this chapter). Whatever strategy is in use, referring to the activity as a vocabulary procedure reduces embarrassment that may accompany explicit recognition of limited decoding competency. This prereading practice showed promise during informal research in elementary, middle, and high school classes (Brody, 1986; 1987a).

Teachers who recognize the burden of less-than-fluent decoding skills respond willingly to students' requests for assistance in reading unknown words. This scaffold lets learners get on with the project of reading the passage. Since readers need to build efficient visual-phonological-lexical links through extensive, **accurate** repetition (Perfetti, 1985), teachers need to provide correct pronunciation, when asked, rather than encouraging students to "get by" with many inaccurate guesses (Adams, 1994). Providing pronunciation will **not** deprive students of an opportunity to identify a word through context since students tend to ask for help only when they feel that the strategies they possess have failed.

Compensate with alternatives to reading. The great diversity in students' reading abilities presents a particular challenge during instruction in the content areas. When decoding limitations lie deeper than a lack of fluency with a few specialized content words, students risk falling far behind in background knowledge development (Stanovich, 1986; 1994). In order to convey important content concepts, teachers can provide alternative exposures through oral language presentations accompanied by visual materials such as pictures, graphs, videos, and experiences. Class lectures, discussions, and group projects allow opportunities for multiple non-print exposures to the central concepts of a lesson. In order to assure that the **language** for expressing these concepts is learned as well, teachers need to accompany visual and experiential instruction with **oral descriptions** and **discussion** (Brody, 1993).

At the same time, it is important to offer many reading opportunities for students who *can* decode, since proficient reading may provide a broader range of information than may be available from listening to a single source. These opportunities capitalize on the apparent advantage of reading as a means of developing vast stores of background knowledge (Stanovich & Cunningham, 1993).

Ensure that oral activities remain on topic and sequential. Students with limited decoding competency need to experience rich, oral exposure by engaging in fruitful discussions concerning the topic under study. These students lose the opportunity to learn when class discussions wander aimlessly or in multiple directions that scramble topics and issues with irrelevant trivia (Mangano, 1983).

Discussions that enhance comprehension focus on central points as well as clearly illustrate the connections between secondary issues and main concepts (Manzo & Manzo, 1990). In this way, class discussion can serve as an effective vehicle for sharing concepts with students who lack decoding ability. Discussion also needs to be focused in order to effectively confirm and clarify the important aspects of what was read by efficient decoders. (See Chapter 10 concerning the use of writing to facilitate discussion, application, and deep conceptual understanding.)

Element Two: Knowledge of Word Meanings

Readers need to possess sufficient knowledge of the meanings of the words in a passage in order to "get the meaning from context" when unfamiliar words are encountered (McKeown, 1985). Readers who lack this competency sometimes can be identified by their ability to read with deep comprehension in subject areas that are familiar to them, but with little or no understanding concerning unfamiliar subjects. It is as if someone had deleted nearly every content word and left the reader to glean meaning only from the short "glue" words in the paragraphs.

This comprehension problem can plague readers whose learning disabilities have limited their vocabulary development, or it may afflict readers who have not been read to by others, or who have not read widely to themselves (Chall, Jacobs, & Baldwin, 1991). Reading and oral language comprehension strategies need to provide multiple exposures to unfamiliar words by defining, explaining, clarifying, or demonstrating the meanings of words that appear in text (McKeown, 1985; 1993).

Some students seem more "motivated" to read material on a familiar favorite topic than to read about an unfamiliar concept. By consistently providing adequate vocabulary exposure when *introducing* a unit, teachers can enhance motivation and encourage readers to explore unfamiliar concepts. Engagement in broad reading, in turn, extends readers' knowledge of word meanings and background concepts (Chall, 1987; Chomsky, 1972; Stanovich, 1986; Stanovich & Cunningham, 1993). (See Chapter 9 concerning vocabulary development.)

Element Three: Use Questions to Organize Focus Before and During Reading

Readers need to identify and sequence what is important in text and sort it from what is extraneous. Some students can understand expository or narrative text that is well organized or "considerate," but experience difficulty when text is scattered and "inconsiderate" (Armbruster, 1984; 1991). For example, some readers become confused when reading a story that employs flashbacks or shifts in author's voice. Similarly, readers may be confused when the running text of a social studies book is broken by insertions of fictionalized historical accounts or reproductions of authentic artifacts such as newspaper articles.

Strategies that assist readers in locating important information and recognizing subordinate material seem to **pose questions**, in some format, to be answered by gathering information from text. Some strategies pose questions directly (Wixson, 1983); other strategies couch questions within a problem to solve or in a framework to complete during reading (Slater et al, 1985). Yet others direct students to develop their own questions (Helfeldt & Henk, 1990). Relevant questions help students focus on important content under study while irrelevant questions lead readers to remember tangential concepts (Wixson, 1983).

The effectiveness of questions as a means of focusing readers' attention on central information is reflected in research on human motivation and our need to make sense of the world.   Humans have a driving need to resolve cognitive dissonance (Csikszentmihalyi, 1990; Festinger, 1957). Teachers can create cognitive dissonance by posing questions that demand focused reading to achieve resolution.

Textbook questions. A great volume of material is crammed into typical classroom textbooks.   Publishers try to accommodate audiences that vary widely across the nation (Chall & Squire, 1991). Consequently, they often include so much information in any one chapter that it is very difficult for an inexperienced reader to sort out the extraneous detail.   Since the publishers could not decide what was pertinent and what could be left out, it is not unreasonable that an inexperienced reader, with limited background concerning the subject, would also have difficulty with that task.   It is important, then, for teachers to determine what material should be read and what ignored.   These decisions can be communicated, to some extent, through questions that accompany the reading (Santa, 1986).

When asked questions before reading, learners typically remember question-related information and forget information that was not related to a question (Wixson, 1983).   Thus questions give readers a way to recognize what is important and what is less important.   In addition, as questions are answered, they offer students concrete evidence that progress has been made in understanding what was to be learned.

Sometimes teachers are dismayed that students have a tendency to read assigned questions *before* reading the related text.   However, students who are learning how to learn-from-text have not yet mastered the art of differentiating important and unimportant, or central and supporting, concepts.   They preview questions to assist themselves with this differentiation (and to finish the assignment quickly). Teachers can capitalize on their students' tactic by providing questions that draw together the relevant information.   Such questions help students construct meaningful schemata while reading to find answers to specific questions.   If important or sufficient information is not highlighted by questions printed in the text, teachers can develop and assign alternative or additional questions of their own.

During reading of content texts or literature, much of the cognitive process of arranging lexical units to form a schema seems to be an unconscious questioning of whether information is making sense in a particular arrangement and whether the information is important enough to include in the schema (Perfetti & Curtis, 1986). In a sense, readers form a text schema to answer the question, "What is this all about?" As readers make their way through text, answering questions may confirm that relevant schemata are being formed.

Cue questions. When developing questions, teachers can use several strategies that lead to particularly effective study. Carefully worded questions subtly preteach or reteach relevant background. Such questions are phrased to include relevant background that clarifies the focus expected in the answer. For example, rather than asking the very broad question, "Why is sexism a problem?" teachers prepare students to seek the issue of relevance by asking, "Given that women generally earn less than men when working at the same job with equal or better efficiency, and given that the nation's poor are predominantly women and children, why is sexism a problem and what steps might decrease its influence?"

As a general rule, questions should follow the sequence of the text. This practice helps students develop cohesive schemata composed of relevant points. When literature or expository texts are assigned, less-skilled readers may attempt the material, if they are given the scaffold of questions that include (in parentheses) the page number and paragraph heading in which an answer is located. Less-skilled readers also may be aided by varied spacing, between questions, that indicates the size of the answer that is anticipated. For example, one line of space would appear under a question asking for the date of an event, while a quarter or third of a page would appear under a question that requires an answer listing several points.

Questions to facilitate pleasure reading. The effectiveness of posing questions to guide reading is well established (Wixson, 1983). Questions encourage independent pleasure reading when they appear in book-report or reading-record formats to be completed for bonus credit.

Reading-record formats include questions such as: What is the story title? Where is the setting? Describe the main characters. What five major events occurred (plot)? What is the author's message about life (theme)? How can you apply the author's lesson to your life or the life of a friend (application and transfer)? Or, with expository text: What are three interesting concepts presented? Describe several aspects of each concept. How do these concepts affect our society?

Questions that stimulate problem-solving. Problem-solving offers an alternate form of posing questions. Perkins (1986) and Perkins & Salomon (1988) propose that problem-solving facilitates the learning of information as "active" (accessible and applicable) knowledge rather than as an "inert" collection of facts that cannot be recalled or applied to appropriate situations.

Csikszentmihalyi (1990) suggests that the greatest challenge in creative work is defining the problem to be solved. He proposes that once the problem is found—the question framed—a paradigm is formed and material can take shape as a meaningful and cohesive set of concepts. In essence, problem-solving is completed when one gathers and arranges information into a meaningful and cohesive sequence (schema).

Problem Types. Several types of problems can engage readers with text.

Type One. Type One problems focus on the problem of completing an assignment. Some students enjoy solving the problem of completing work, checking it off, and handing it in on time.

While this aspect of problem-solving develops important organizational skills, it can lead to erroneous understanding since it **does not** assure meaningful engagement with reading material. (A student could check off a Type One problem after **in**accurately completing an assignment.) While assignment-completing behaviors are crucial, they do not assure that unfamiliar concepts are learned.

Type Two. Another, more effective, type of problem assures direct engagement with the content of a specific passage under study. Perkins (1986, p. 101-106) suggests a variety of ways to frame text-specific problems. A few of his approaches, paraphrased below, adapt easily to assignments related to literature or content area texts:

> **develop a definition**—identify a class of cases important in a situation, or a statement of the conditions under which something occurs. (What is a setting? What are bacteria?)

> **explain**—account for what is known to be fact. (Why did the character act sheepishly? How does mitosis occur?)

> **classify**—make order out of a chaos of information by developing a structure or a set of rules for sorting the material. (What factors differentiate two genres of fiction? Why are some living things classified as plants and others as animals?)

Solutions to these Type Two problems emerge through reading and clarifying information found in text.

Type Three. A third type of problem is related to the community or environment (Dahlberg, 1990). Readers use texts and literature as references while solving real-life problems. (Students may read from a text to find information on pollution while they develop an answer to solve a community recycling problem. Or they may read relevant poetry in order to locate quotations for a recycling flyer.)

Question-Text-Organize-Practice-Share (Q-TOPS). This strategy illustrates a means of implementing Type Two problem-solving. During my informal research with middle and high school students, the approach seemed to provide motivation, focus, and understanding of concepts under study. A teacher using **Q-TOPS** follows these steps:

- **Question.** When preparing for class, select several topics from a study-unit and develop questions that pose a problem that requires construction of a definition, explanation, or classification. (See examples on previous page.)

- **Text.** Begin class by dividing students into small groups; assign one problem to each group. Distribute reading materials that will enable a group to answer questions that solve the problem. For example, when studying protists, groups may be assigned to define protists, to explain how bacteria are helpful and harmful, or to classify forms of life. Reading materials that span mixed abilities could come from the grade-level science text, junior library books, introductory or advanced science magazines, and even a simple summary written by the teacher.

  Allocate 10 to 20 minutes for students to search for data relevant to their group problem. Suggest that each student jot at least five brief notes concerning related information. Circulate during reading to assist less-skilled readers in finding information.

- **Organize.** When most students have written five informative notes, ask each group to pool its findings into a group list and organize the material into a coherent answer.

- **Practice.** When group lists seem to be in order, ask students within the group to break into pairs or triplets to rehearse the information with each other.

- **Share.** Ask each group to share its solution with the class. Students record these solutions in their notebooks while the teacher writes them on the board. During this process, engage the class in discussion to clarify and refine the solutions.

Teachers can stimulate Stage 4 reading and multiple-viewpoint thinking by providing a variety of source materials and by eliciting applications to other contexts during a discussion that enhances and elaborates on the concept.

Pose questions to fill in frameworks while reading. A variety of strategies for developing and filling in frameworks were proposed during the 1980s to '90s. These strategies were devised with the intent of sensitizing students to text structure and its value as a framework upon which to form a schema (Armbruster, Anderson, & Ostertag, 1989; Jones, Pierce, & Hunter, 1989).

For example, students might be asked to fill in a framework or flow chart related to a piece of literature or expository text that follows the structure of cause-reactions-effect, or a temporal sequence such as first-next-finally. Research concerning framework strategies yielded mixed results. Typically, skilled readers remember relevant information requested by the frame, while less-skilled readers tend to remember a mix of relevant and irrelevant information (Alvermann & Boothby, 1986; Armbruster, Anderson, & Ostertag, 1987; Gordon & Pearson, 1983).

Less-skilled readers' inability to sort and focus on relevant information could arise from not understanding the language of the structures, such as cause-effect, enumeration, etc. Or, it could reflect that readers lack sufficient background to recognize which concepts are relevant. In their confusion, less-skilled readers might view frame completion as a Type One Problem and focus on simply filling the frame.

This difficulty can be circumvented with study guides, such as those recommended by Slater et al. (1985), Santa (1986), or Armbruster (1991), that guide students in sorting the important from the unimportant. These study guides offer specific questions that elicit answers to fill in the framework. When completing frames while guided by carefully phrased questions, students learn how to use textbooks, trade books, and other resources to gather needed information.

As readers become familiar with this process, some of the questions and structures that form a study guide can be withdrawn slowly, at a rate that allows students to continue to experience success. Some students are ready sooner than others to have parts of the frame withdrawn. Eventually, many students construct their own frames, and develop questions to fill the frames (Santa, 1986), while others continue to need a full study guide indefinitely.

Conclusions concerning questioning techniques. Questions appear in effective comprehension strategies for Stage 3 readers whether presented as cues to guide the use of frameworks that reflect text structure, as problems in need of solutions, or as probes to gather, sequence, summarize, and synthesize relevant information. Effective questions lead students to focus on relevant and important concepts in text. Appropriate questions assist readers in organizing information into a meaningful understanding.

Element Four: *Provide* crucial background from which to form inferences.

Readers need to possess **sufficient, accurate, background knowledge** in order to form inferences and understand unfamiliar text. When there are too many gaps in readers' background knowledge, they are unable to form cohesive schemata that accurately represent the concepts expressed in narrative or expository text. Without broad and deep background knowledge, readers lack building blocks from which to develop new understanding (August, Flavell, & Clift, 1984; Barnitz & Morgan, 1983; Lipson, 1984; McKeown, 1985; Wilson & Anderson, 1986).

Activities that provide or review accurate and relevant background can assist readers in better comprehending the major points and subtle nuances of unfamiliar material (Brody, 1991; Dole, Valencia, Greer, & Wardrop, 1991; Graves et al., 1983). (A discussion of effective strategies and teachers' crucial roles in building readers' background knowledge appears in Chapter 8.)

Element Five: Offer *Multiple Opportunities* to Absorb, Process, Rehearse, and Express Unfamiliar Material Under Study

Readers need to **process and express unfamiliar concepts** in order to expand their fluent use of knowledge in an area of study. Lack of automaticity with language that expresses a concept is indicated when readers successfully choose among several possible answers proposed to them, but have difficulty wording an answer independently (Bloom, 1986; Curtis & Glaser, 1983).

Skilled readers rehearse and repeat unfamiliar information for themselves (Flood & Lapp, 1990). In preparation for Stage 4 and 5 reading, students seem to need multiple exposures to unfamiliar concepts. These exposures may help them access neural representations of reviewed concepts with confidence and fluency. Extensive practice seems to lead to automatic retrieval, selection, and sequencing of concepts. As agility develops in retrieving a broad array of lexical units, readers seem to begin experiencing the fluency of thought that will let them eventually progress to Stage 4 and 5 reading, perhaps during high school or college.

Depth and breadth. Provide enriched depth and breadth by layering multiple meanings, nuances of meaning, and varied applications of a concept (McKeown et al., 1985). Schema theory suggests that this richness of understanding fosters multifaceted neural connections. Multiple exposures range from simple repetition to varied activities centered on one concept.

At times, students need repetitive practice to master complex concepts (Bloom, 1986; Just & Carpenter, 1987). After a concept is understood from one perspective, exposures in multiple contexts, with varied activities, increase its accessibility for use in other contexts during further reading, thinking, and problem-solving (Perkins & Salomon, 1988).

Multiple exposures develop the precise meaning and nature of a concept. Such clarity assists in its appropriate retrieval and use. For example, if students learn that *explicit* means clear, they may try to describe a blue sky on a clear day as *explicit*. Guided and varied exposures offer opportunities to repair misconceptions.

Activities. Teachers and students can express concepts through explanations, oral reports, or class discussions. Writing, reading-and-retelling what was read, or summarizing subtopics during reading also offer opportunities for students to absorb and express unfamiliar concepts (Flood & Lapp, 1990; Hayes, 1989; Manzo & Manzo, 1990). Book reports, vocabulary study, and outlining-while-reading are other assignments that encourage multiple exposures and expression (Brody, 1987b). (See Chapter 10 for suggestions concerning multiple exposures and written expression.)

It is important to differentiate whether a strategy provides **students**, or their **teacher**, with multiple exposures and opportunities to express a concept. A **teacher** engages with a concept when using strategies that require the teacher to repeat or demonstrate the same concept. **Students** engage with a concept when using strategies that require a teacher to model the concept followed by a variety of activities in which **students** say, read, write, observe, or demonstrate the concept.

This does not imply that teachers remain silent while students flounder. Instead, teachers provide initial models along with supports such as alternative explanations and confirmations of comprehension accuracy. However, each time that a teacher needs to provide an alternative explanation, students need multiple opportunities to express the concept as well.

Students can practice stating unfamiliar concepts by explaining them to other classmates during group activities. Classmates' questions generate careful reconsideration and restatement of the content (Palincsar, 1986; Palincsar & Brown, 1984). Students and teachers can prepare to present unfamiliar concepts by reading a text, a secondary source, a fictionalized account, or technical support material, as well as through seeing a video, hearing a lecture, or conducting an experiment.

Strategies Proposed to
Elicit Higher Level Comprehension

Teachers who know a variety of strategies possess a convenient means of keeping themselves alert and fresh as well as a means of continuing to use the element of surprise that can engage students in the ongoing challenge of learning (Keller, 1983). In order to assure that students continue to expand their reading comprehension while engaging in novel activities, teachers need to check that their strategies amply incorporate one or more of the core elements of Stage 3 comprehension instruction.

Students need to allocate some of their attentional resources to understanding an unfamiliar strategy, and this draws concentration away from text comprehension. Consequently, teachers should use caution when switching among strategies. Some teachers like to develop a small range of strategies that they use consistently in order to offer variety as well as familiarity with several methods.

Following are descriptions of various activities designed to teach higher level reading comprehension. The discussion highlights those features of the activities that implement some of the basic elements of effective comprehension instruction. In addition, the description suggests adjustments that may enhance the effectiveness of strategies that did not appear to be particularly effective during classroom studies.

Text-structure frames. As discussed earlier (pp. 249-250), classroom research remains mixed on the effectiveness of text frames in aiding reading comprehension. In instances when framing strategies seem to facilitate reading comprehension, the framing is accompanied by detailed note-taking activities (Slater et al., 1985) or specific questions and elaboration that help students focus on text (Santa, 1986). Armbruster (1991) suggests the following process for developing frames to help students understand science text:

1. While preparing a lesson plan, outline the important ideas of the topic and the points contributing to those ideas. Develop a flow chart or grid that includes boxes to record this information as well as **questions** or headings to elicit the information.

2. During the lesson, ask students to fill in the frames by answering the questions while reading the related text.

3. Use the frames as a basis for class discussion during or after reading as well as for writing projects.

4. Encourage students to refer to the frames as questions and answers while studying for tests.

Frames can be used with science and social studies texts to list characteristics, compare types, record a time line, present cause-reactions-effect, etc. (Armbruster, 1991). Readers can use frames with literature to record the problem, climax, and resolution of a story or to note the author, setting, plot, and theme (Brody, 1987b).

Study guides. Teachers use study guides to: ask questions that focus on important concepts; provide a glossary of vocabulary definitions; offer multiple exposures to material under study; and elicit a variety of written responses concerning the content (Just & Carpenter, 1987). Study guides can facilitate higher level comprehension and stimulate self-directed active learning, particularly when direct modeling by the teacher is faded out slowly as the process is mastered (Santa, 1986).

Study guides that encourage two-column note-taking are particularly helpful (Palmatier, 1973; Santa, Havens, & Harrison, 1989). In Column One, readers list main ideas, important vocabulary, and specialized concepts. In Column Two, important details, elaborations, and definitions are listed directly across from their related concepts in Column One. Later, readers can use the material in Column One to elicit the details in Column Two in order to study for a test (Santa, 1986).

Study guides have been used over time to ask questions that elicit literal, inferential, and applied responses. When constructing study guides, teachers can vary both the comprehension level of response desired and the format in which students respond to the questions. Study guides can include activities such as taking notes, defining vocabulary terms, and drawing a diagram of an object or process under study (Tierney, Readence, Dishner, 1985).

Semantic mapping. Semantic maps offer an alternative format for outlining information from text. Rather than organizing information by stating the main idea and listing supporting details beneath, a semantic map or web places the main concept in a box or circle at the center of a page, with supporting or related details springing out as spokes from the main concept. Semantic maps offer variation in how material is presented. Vocabulary acquisition studies indicate that semantic maps are as effective as other means of teaching a concept and its definition provided that they offer **multiple exposures** to the word, its *correct* meaning, and its use in **multiple contexts** (McKeown et al., 1985).

Questioning techniques. Approaches such as Reciprocal Questioning (Palincsar & Brown, 1984) or ReQuest (Flood & Lapp, 1990; Manzo, 1969) teach students to ask their own questions while reading. (See Chapter 10 of this volume as well.) To initiate these activities, teachers model how to pose relevant questions that draw on important concepts and their elaborations. This is followed by students asking questions. Questions are asked while the text is read in small segments, sentence-by-sentence or paragraph-by-paragraph, silently or aloud.

When working in a one-on-one setting, the teacher and student take turns asking questions, with the teacher modeling and shaping the quality of questions. Within a group, students as well as the teacher respond to questions and comment on how to improve the effectiveness of questions. Eliciting questions from students seems to stimulate active involvement in reading. Forming teams to ask questions may also heighten motivation (Helfeldt & Henk, 1990; Vacca & Vacca, 1993).

Lesson formats. Classic approaches such as the Directed Reading Activity (Betts, 1946) provide an instructional process that introduces, studies, reviews, and applies concepts encountered in literature or content texts. When using the Directed Reading Activity (DRA), the teacher introduces a reading by sharing relevant background information and unfamiliar vocabulary meanings and pronunciation, along with posing guiding questions. Students read a section of text silently then take part in clarifying their comprehension through questions and discussion. Next, students reread the text orally for further understanding. Finally, students apply what they have learned during follow-up activities.

Guided Reading Procedure (GRP) (Manzo, 1975; Ruddell, 1993) is introduced similarly to DRA. However, after initial silent reading, students close their books and state all that they can recall, while the teacher writes their responses on the board. This is followed by students checking the passage to add or correct any concepts that were missed or recorded inaccurately. Next, the teacher guides students to organize the material that they have gathered from the text, and facilitates discussion that lets them link what they are learning with other concepts that are familiar. Finally, students are tested on the reading.

Over the years, elements of DRA and GRP have appeared commonly in basal and content area reading texts. These strategies include many of the core elements of effective comprehension instruction presented earlier in this chapter. Since they include these elements in their design, it is understandable that newer strategies do *not* consistently outperform basal activities such as DRA or GRP.

Synthesizing Core Elements and Advanced Comprehension Strategies to Optimize Understanding

Recent theories of cognitive development suggest that when learners perform relatively simple activities at one stage nearly independently, they are ready to practice the activities within a set of more complex demands that constitute a higher stage *if* they are supported with **sufficient** scaffolding (Case, 1980; Fischer, 1980).

Several studies discussed earlier suggest that such scaffolding may be helpful in the transition from Stage 3 to Stage 4 and 5 reading. Palincsar & Brown (1984) found that 7th and 8th grade students could learn to ask focus questions of themselves when teachers first provided a model and plenty of scaffolding. Santa (1986) found that high school students, who were Stage 3 readers, could learn to construct their own study guides when teachers provided models and questions that were slowly withdrawn when the supports were no longer needed. In addition, Slater et al. (1985) report that text-structure organizers, when used in conjunction with note-taking, were beneficial to ninth-grade students' comprehension of expository text.

These studies suggest that teachers can expose readers to activities associated with advanced critical thinking and construction of new knowledge while teaching Stage 3 competencies. It seems that such exposure may be helpful *if* teachers carefully include core elements to scaffold more advanced reading. In addition, when working with younger readers, teachers need to monitor when advanced strategies place too great a stress on beginners' attention and simplify activities until core elements are handled successfully (Gordon & Pearson, 1983).

In short, as we continue to search for ways to improve readers' comprehension, we need to include, and use plentifully, the core elements that seem to facilitate Stage 3 comprehension. At the same time, we can draw on newer strategies to provide elaboration, active questioning, application to real problems, and frameworks that arrange concepts into meaningful schemata. In heterogeneous classrooms, such instruction can enable Stage 3 readers to engage with core elements of comprehension instruction while at the same time enabling more advanced readers to engage with higher level strategies.

Building Effective Elements into Teacher-Designed Strategies

Teachers can use a checklist (Table 7.1, below) to review any practices under consideration for adoption from a journal or by requirement of a school district. Alternatively, teachers can develop strategies of their own by assuring that their plans include many of the elements appearing on the checklist. Strategies that focus on the core elements recorded on the checklist are likely to assist students in developing reading comprehension ability. When strategies lack these elements, teachers can use the checklist as a guide to develop adaptations that can enhance instruction.

Table 7.1. Checklist of Core Comprehension Elements.

Strategy Name:		
Core Elements	**Yes/No**	**Plans that Add Element**
1. Teaches accurate decoding of unfamiliar words.		
2. Provides **unfamiliar** word meanings before and during reading.		
3. Poses **relevant** questions concerning the text under study.		
4. Teaches **accurate** and **crucial** text-related background concepts.		
5. Offers **multiple** opportunities to **study** and **express** unfamiliar concepts.		

Below is an example of a comprehension strategy that was developed to incorporate some of the checklist elements.

Spell-Vocabulary-Schema (SVS). Stage 3 readers sometimes have difficulty forming appropriate schemata. They may be hampered by limited decoding fluency, insufficient vocabulary knowledge, or difficulty processing textual material in their own words. SVS was developed and informally researched in order to help students engage with challenging concepts while reading unfamiliar text selections (Brody, 1986; 1987a). This strategy previews the decoding and meaning of difficult content words from the assigned text, then provides opportunities for readers to articulate their understanding as they read. By answering text-related questions that lead them to state their learnings as they read, students share their schema-building process, during construction, and receive scaffolding as needed.

Spelling: List potentially difficult words on the board before a selection is read. Introduce each word by clearly pronouncing it while pointing to its syllables. Blend the sounds of the syllables to say the whole word and ask the class to segment, blend, and say the word. Post these words in a highly visible spot for the remainder of the unit, and encourage students to refer to them for accurate spelling during related writing assignments.

Vocabulary: Follow the pronouncing of a word by presenting its meaning. Offer several sentences that illustrate the meaning of the word. Ask students to generate additional sentences. Students write the words, and their use in meaningful sentences, in notebooks.

Schema: Students read from a content text or a short story while pausing after a paragraph, or short section, to enumerate important details by answering questions such as, "What is one thing you learned?" or "What is one important thing that happened?" After discussing details, readers also articulate a brief schema that relates the details to the main idea by answering questions such as, "So what is the main point?" or, "How does this tie in with what happened earlier?" As needed, teachers provide scaffolding that assists in locating and forming relevant responses. The frequency of pauses should be planned to assure that readers construct accurate schemata by thinking over what has been read, looking back and clarifying any confusions, and describing central concepts in their own words.

SVS draws on many core elements. In addition, teachers can scaffold Stage 4 reading from multiple viewpoints by using SVS when students read and discuss several related passages written from varied points of view. The strategy shows promise for elementary, middle, and high school classrooms among students who are beginning Stage 3 reading (Brody, 1986; 1987b).

Conclusion

As students read widely in literature and content texts to gather information and develop understanding during Stage 3, teachers can support them with a variety of strategies that incorporate "active ingredients" of effective instruction. Such instruction assists with the decoding and meaning aspects of unfamiliar words, uses questions to provide a guiding focus, offers crucial background concepts required to form inferences and understand the reading, and creates multiple opportunities to absorb, process, and express the material under study.

In addition, teachers can encourage middle grade and high school students as they begin the transition to higher level comprehension and application by arranging for scaffolded use of strategies such as: solving problems and applying the findings to several contexts; completing text-structure frames by answering accompanying questions; organizing information with semantic maps; or engaging students in self-questioning during reading.

When used consistently during the reading of content texts and engaging literature, core comprehension elements can assist students in becoming confident Stage 3 readers who possess broad and deep background that prepares them for Stage 4 and 5 critical thinking, wide reading, and synthesis. With teachers' scaffolding, Stage 3 readers can begin to apply concepts to multiple contexts while participating in shared efforts to construct new knowledge.

References

Adams, M.J. (1994). *Beginning to read: Thinking and learning about print.* Cambridge, MA: MIT Press.

Alvermann, D.E. & Boothby, P.R. (1986). Children's transfer of graphic organizer instruction. *Reading Psychology* 7(2), 87-100.

Anstey, M.M. & Freebody, P. (1987). The effects of various pre-reading activities on children's literal and inferential comprehension. *Reading Psychology*, 8(3), 189-209.

Armbruster, B.B. (1984). The problem of "inconsiderate text." In G.G. Duffy, L.R. Roehler, & J. Mason (Eds.), *Comprehension instruction.* New York: Longman.

Armbruster, B.B. (1991). Framing: A technique for improving learning from science texts. In C.M. Santa & D.W. Alvermann (Eds.), *Science learning: Process and applications.* Newark DE: IRA.

Armbruster, B.B., Anderson, T.H. & Ostertag, J. (1987). Does text structure/summarization instruction facilitate learning from expository text? *Reading Research Quarterly*, 22(3).

Armbruster, B.B., Anderson, T.H. & Ostertag, J. (1989). Teaching text structure to improve reading and writing. *The Reading Teacher, 43*(2), 130-137.

August, D.L., Flavell, J.H. & Clift, R. (1984). Comparison of comprehension monitoring of skilled and less skilled readers. *Reading Research Quarterly*, Fall, 20(1), 39-48.

Barnitz, J.G. & Morgan, A.L. (1983). Aspects of schemata and syntax in fifth grade children's inferential reading comprehension of causal relations. *Reading Psychology*, 4(3), 337-348.

Betts, E.A. (1946). *Foundations of reading instruction.* New York: American Book Co.

Bloom, B.S. (1986). "The hands and feet of genius" Automaticity. *Educational Leadership.* February.

Brody, S. (1986). The Brody Reading Method: A successful approach to reading and written-language skills for at risk students. Paper presented at the Annual Meeting of the Association for Children and Adults with Learning Disabilities (23rd, NY, NY, March 12 - 15). ERIC ED275 103.

Brody, S. (1987a). *The Brody reading manual: An implementation guide for teachers.* Milford, NH: LARC Publishing.

Brody, S. (1987b). *Study Skills: Teaching and learning strategies for mainstream and specialized settings.* Milford, NH: LARC Publishing.

Brody, S. (1989). Elements of effective reading instruction in grades 4 and 5: Lessons from recent research. Unpublished Qualifying Paper, Harvard Graduate School of Education.

Brody, S. (1991). *Clarifying the role of prereading instruction in 4th graders' comprehension of social studies text.* Unpublished Doctoral Dissertation, Harvard Graduate School of Education.

Brody, S. (1993). Developing background knowledge: A context enrichment strategy that may provide more consistent results than activation of prior knowledge. *Proceedings: UKRA '94 Annual Conference*, United Kingdom Reading Association, Exeter, England.

Case, R. (1980). The underlying mechanism of intellectual development. In *Cognition, development, and instruction.* Academic Press.

Chall, J.S. (1983). *Stages of reading development*. NY: McGraw-Hill.

Chall, J.S. (1987). Two vocabularies for reading: Recognition and meaning. In M.G. McKeown & M.E. Curtis (Eds.), *The nature of vocabulary acquisition*. Hillsdale, NJ: Lawrence Erlbaum.

Chall, J.S. (in press). *Stages of reading development (2nd ed.)*.

Chall, J.S., Jacobs, V.A., & Baldwin, L.E. (1991). *Why poor children fall behind in reading: What schools can do about it*. Cambridge, MA: Harvard University Press.

Chall, J.S. & Squire, J.R. (1991). The publishing industry and textbooks. In R. Barr, M.L. Kamil, P. Mosenthal, & P.D. Pearson (Eds.), *Handbook of reading research, volume II*. NY: Longman.

Chomsky, C. (1972). Stages in language development and reading exposure. *Harvard Educational Review*, 42(1).

Csikszentmihalyi, M. (1990). *Flow: The psychology of optimal experience*. NY: Harper.

Curtis, M.E. & Glaser, R. (1983). Reading theory and the assessment of reading achievement. *Journal of Educational Measurement*, 20(2).

Dahlberg, L.A. (1990). Teaching for the information age. *Journal of Reading* 34(1).

Dole, J.A., Valencia, S.W., Greer, E.A., & Wardrop, J.L. (1991). Effects of two types of prereading instruction on the comprehension of narrative and expository text, *Reading Research Quarterly*, 26(2), 142-159.

Durkin, D. (1984). The decoding ability of elementary school students. Reading Education Report No. 49. Bolt, Beranek and Newman, Inc., Cambridge, MA. Illinois University, Urbana. Center for the Study of Reading. (ERIC Document Reproduction Service No. ED 244 228)

Festinger, L. (1957). *A theory of cognitive dissonance*. White Plains, NY: Row, Peterson and Company.

Fischer, K.W. (1980). A theory of cognitive development: The control and construction of hierarchies of skills. *Psychological Review*, 87(6), 115-169.

Flood, J. & Lapp, D. (1990). Reading comprehension instruction for at-risk students: Research-based practices that can make a difference. *Journal of Reading, 33*(7), 490-496.

Gordon, C.J. & Pearson, P.D. (1983). The effects of instruction in metacomprehension and inferencing on children's comprehension abilities. Technical Report No. 277. Bolt, Beranek and Newman, Inc., Cambridge, MA. Illinois University, Urbana. Center for the Study of Reading. (ERIC Document Reproduction Service No. ED 232 132)

Graves, M.F., Cooke, C.L., & LaBerge, M.J. (1983). Effects of previewing difficult short stories on low ability junior high school students' comprehension, recall, and attitudes. *Reading Research Quarterly*, 20(2).

Haller, E.P., Child, D.A., & Walberg, H.J. (1988). Can comprehension be taught? A quantitative synthesis of "metacognitive" studies. *Educational Researcher, 17*(9), 5-8.

Hansen, J. & Pearson, P.D. (1983). An instructional study: Improving the inferential comprehension of good and poor fourth-grade readers. *Journal of Educational Psychology*, 75(6), 821-29.

Hayes, D.A. (1989). Helping students GRASP the knack of writing summaries. *Journal of Reading, 33*(2), 96-101.

Helfeldt, J.P. & Henk, W.A. (1990). Reciprocal question-answer relationships: An instructional technique for at-risk readers. *Journal of Reading, 33*(7), 509-515.

Jones, B.F., Pierce, J., & Hunter, B. (1989). Teaching students to construct graphic representations. *Educational Leadership*, December 88/January 89.

Juel, C. & Holmes (1980). Comparison of processing strategies in oral and silent reading by good and poor readers. Paper presented at the Annual Meeting of the American Educational Research Association (Boston, MA, April 7-11). ERIC Document Reproduction Service No. ED 192 289)

Just, M.A. & Carpenter, P.A. (1987). *The psychology of reading and language comprehension*. Boston: Allyn & Bacon.

Keller, J.M. (1983). Motivational design of instruction. In C.M. Reigeluth (Ed.), *Instructional-design theories and models: An overview of their current status*. Hillsdale, NJ: Lawrence Erlbaum.

Lipson, M.Y. (1984). Some unexpected issues in prior knowledge and comprehension. *Reading Teacher*, 37(8), 760-764.

Mangano, N.G. (1983). The effects of teacher explanation and questioning patterns on fourth grade students during basal reading instruction. Paper presented at the Annual Meeting of the National Reading Conference (33rd Austin, TX, Nov. 29-Dec. 3). (ERIC Document Reproduction Service No. ED240 502)

Manzo, A.V. (1969). The request procedure. *Journal of Reading*, 11, 123-126.

Manzo, A.V. (1975). Guided reading procedure. *Journal of Reading*, 18, 287-291.

Manzo, A.V. & Manzo, U.C. (1990). Note cue: A comprehension and participation training strategy. *Journal of Reading*. May.

McKeown, M.G. (1985). The acquisition of word meaning from context by children of high and low ability. *Reading Research Quarterly*, 20(4), 482-496.

McKeown, M.G. (1993). Creating effective definitions for young word learners. *Reading Research Quarterly*, 28(1), 16-30.

McKeown, M.G., Beck, I.L., Omanson, R.C., & Pople, M.T. (1985). Some effects of the nature and frequency of vocabulary instruction on the knowledge and use of words. *Reading Research Quarterly*, 20(5), 522-35, Fall.

Palincsar, A.S. (1986). The role of dialogue in providing scaffolded instruction. *Educational Psychologist*, 21(1-2), 73-98.

Palincsar, A.S. & Brown, A.L. (1984). Reciprocal teaching of comprehension-fostering and comprehension-monitoring activities. *Cognition and Instruction*. 1(2), 117-175.

Palmatier, R.A. (1973). A notetaking system for learning. *Journal of Reading*, October.

Perfetti, C.A. (1985). *Reading ability*. New York: Oxford University Press.

Perfetti, C.A. & Curtis, M.E. (1986). Reading. In R.F. Dillon & R.J. Sternberg (Eds.) *Cognition and instruction*. Academic Press.

Perkins, D.N. (1986). *Knowledge as design*. Hillsdale, NJ: Lawrence Erlbaum.

Perkins, D.N. & Salomon, G. (1988). Teaching for transfer. *Educational Leadership, 46*(1), 22-33.

Ruddell, M.R. (1993). *Teaching content reading and writing*. Boston: Allyn and Bacon.

Sadoski, M. & Page, W.D. (1984). Miscue combination scores and reading comprehension: Analysis and comparison. *Reading World*, 24(1), 43-53.

Samuels, S.J., Schermer, D.R., & Reinking (1992). Reading fluency: Techniques for making decoding automatic. In S.J. Samuels & A.E. Farstrup (Eds.), *What research has to say about reading instruction (2nd ed.)*. Newark DE: International Reading Association.

Santa, C. (1986). Content reading in secondary schools. In J. Orasanu (Ed.). *Reading comprehension: From research to practice*. Hillsdale, NJ: Lawrence Erlbaum.

Santa, C. Havens, L. & Harrison, S. (1989). Teaching secondary science through reading, writing, studying, and problem solving. In D. Lapp, J. Flood, N. Farnam, (Eds.), *Content area reading and learning: Instructional strategies*. Englewood Cliffs, NJ: Prentice Hall.

Slater, W.H., Graves, M.F. & Piche, G.L. (1985). Effects of structural organizers on ninth-grade students' comprehension and recall of four patterns of expository text. *Reading Research Quarterly* 20(2).

Spiegel, D.L. & Whaley, J.F. (1980). Elevating comprehension skills by sensitizing students to structural aspects of narratives. Paper presented at the Annual Meeting of the National Reading Conference (30th, San Diego, CA, December 3-6). (ERIC Document Reproduction Service No. ED199 634)

Stanovich, K.E. (1986). Matthew effects in reading: Some consequences of individual differences in the acquisition of literacy. *Reading Research Quarterly*, 21(4), 360-406.

Stanovich, K.E. (1994). Romance and reality. *Reading Teacher,* 47(4).

Stanovich, K.E. & Cunningham, A.E. (1993). Where does knowledge come from? Specific associations between print exposure and information acquisition. *Journal of Educational Psychology* 85(2), 211-229.

Tierney, R.J., Readence, J.E. & Dishner, E.K (1985). *Reading strategies and practices: A compendium (2nd ed.)*. Boston: Allyn & Bacon.

Vacca, R.T. & Vacca, J.A.L. (1993). *Content area reading (4th ed.)*. NY: Harper Collins.

Wilson, P.T. & Anderson, R.C. (1986). What they don't know will hurt them: The role of prior knowledge in comprehension. In J. Orasanu (Ed.), *Reading comprehension: From research to practice*. Hillsdale, NJ: Lawrence Erlbaum.

Wixson, K.K. (1983). Questions about a text: What you ask about is what children learn. *The Reading Teacher* 37, 287-294.

Chapter 8. Previews: Learning Pertinent Background and Text Concepts[1]

Sara Brody, EdD
Rivier College

Readers understand text more completely and with greater ease when they possess broad and deep background knowledge. Such knowledge develops during a lifetime of exposure to a vast array of learning experiences. When these experiences are understood and stored with the use of language, they become available for later processing or recall during language-dependent activities such as reading, writing, and speaking. In addition to developing language-based background by interpreting and storing experiences linguistically, learners who can understand unfamiliar text enhance their background knowledge by reading.

Rich background knowledge enables learners to supply missing details to infer a text's meaning when an author's explanation is incomplete. At times, the problem

---

[1]This chapter expands concepts presented in Brody, S. (1993). Developing background knowledge: A context enrichment strategy that may provide more consistent results than activation of prior knowledge. In D. Wray (Ed.), *Proceedings: 1992 United Kingdom Reading Association Annual Conference*, Exeter, England: UKRA.

of insufficient background may be avoided by selecting a text that matches the background possessed by a reader. Otherwise, crucial background knowledge needs to be developed through instruction. Even less adept readers can increase their background knowledge by reading, when they receive the support needed to learn new concepts with accuracy.

Readers in the upper elementary grades and beyond generally possess the intellectual ability to comprehend specialized concepts (Chall, 1983; Gazzaniga, 1992; Inhelder & Piaget, 1958). However, when science and social studies lessons present unfamiliar and specialized topics, many Stage 3 readers need assistance in order to understand their texts. The issue is not one of waiting for readers to mature sufficiently to become able to learn new material, but rather one of providing instructional activities that assure sufficient background knowledge to promote the learning of unfamiliar information.

This chapter examines the nature of background knowledge and its instruction during Stage 3 reading development. First, the role of background in readers' understanding of text is considered. Next, evidence from classroom research related to background knowledge is explored. Finally, teaching strategies that appear to enhance the availability and use of appropriate background knowledge during reading are presented.

The Role of Background in Text Comprehension

A note on terminology. In this chapter, **background knowledge** refers to concepts, experiences, information, and text structures that are relevant to a text under study. These concepts *may or may not be known by the reader*. However, knowledge of them would be useful to a reader who is trying to fully comprehend a text. In contrast, the reading literature generally uses the term **prior knowledge** to refer to background knowledge that a reader *actually possesses* when beginning to read a text. This knowledge is stored in a reader's memory in a form that is accessible through written or spoken language. Thus, background knowledge is the broader term, encompassing relevant knowledge known or not known by the reader; and prior knowledge is a reader-specific term, since the experiences, exposures, and memory of the reader define its parameters.

Interaction of text and prior knowledge. Theorists postulate that a reader's prior knowledge plays an important role in the comprehension of text. As discussed in Chapter 1, recent reading theory suggests that comprehension occurs when a reader constructs a schema (an understanding of the text) by combining the information presented in a text with knowledge the reader already possesses. Schema theory suggests that it is this interaction of what is in print and what is in the reader's mind that produces what is finally understood or misunderstood (Adams, 1994; Perfetti & Curtis, 1986).

Readers' comprehension of text is influenced by the related prior knowledge that they bring to their reading as well as by how clearly a writer states relevant and crucial concepts. In addition, comprehension is influenced by the misconceptions and preconceived misunderstandings that readers possess before beginning to read a passage. When readers' prior knowledge conflicts with material written in a text, readers tend to misread the text to make it fit their previously formed schemata, whether they are accurate or not (Lipson, 1984; Wilson & Anderson, 1986).

National assessments of educational progress suggest that reading comprehension is related positively to the amount of time students spend reading (Mullis, Campbell, & Farstrup, 1993). Further, a preliminary study suggests that, among college students, spending time reading enhances general background knowledge (Stanovich & Cunningham, 1993). During Stage 3 reading and beyond, learners who engage in extensive reading generally increase their store of background knowledge—concepts, vocabulary, experiences, and text patterns (Chall, 1983; Stanovich, 1994). As their background knowledge broadens and deepens, these readers appear to develop lexical resources that allow them to select for relevance and appropriateness, quickly and effectively, when engaging with varied materials that express multiple points of view concerning an area of interest.

Related Research

A variety of studies concerning background knowledge were conducted during the 1980s and early 1990s. Some explored whether comprehension would be enhanced by "activating" prior knowledge—encouraging readers to recall whatever they knew related to a topic before reading (Anstey & Freebody, 1987; Hansen & Pearson, 1983). Others explored the effects of teaching relevant and related background during prereading activities (Brody, 1991; Dole, Valencia, Greer, & Wardrop, 1991; Graves & Cooke, 1980; Graves, Cooke, & Laberge, 1983; Graves, Prenn, & Cooke, 1985).

"Activation" studies. Several classroom studies drew on theoretical models of reading comprehension as justification for developing instruction that would "activate" a reader's prior knowledge. Researchers postulated that the possession of activated prior knowledge, along with the strategy of making conscious use of prior knowledge, would lead a reader to form a schema of a text more easily. Although results with such approaches were mixed, activation of prior knowledge is often recommended as a means of making the reader's background more available to contribute to reading comprehension.

For example, if a text on farming in Switzerland were assigned, a teacher might probe to activate students' prior knowledge by asking students what they think people do to produce milk and milk products. A related approach teaches the strategy of consciously using one's knowledge to make sense of text when a difficult section is encountered during reading. For example, if a passage concerning Swiss grazing practices were confusing, students would be prompted to think about what they know about farming in general. They would be encouraged to use their knowledge as a context within which to interpret the confusing text.

Potential problems related to the strategy of activating prior knowledge. The knowledge that readers possess before they begin to read is very powerful. People tend to remember and rely on what they already know when new information that they see, hear, or read contradicts what they know. Even when readers' prior knowledge is inaccurate, it often overrides the accurate information read in a text (Wilson & Anderson, 1986). Lipson (1984) describes several studies in which elementary students with no prior knowledge concerning a topic understood a related passage better than students with related but inaccurate prior knowledge. This is congruent with neurological research that suggests "the human capacity to hang on to our beliefs in the presence of confounding data is astounding" (Gazzaniga, 1992, p. 136).

For example, based on their inaccurate prior knowledge, readers may continue to think that whales are fish, not mammals, even after reading a text that explains that they are warm blooded, need to surface for air every 10 to 30 minutes, and nurse their young. Even though the text presents explanatory information, the reader's prior knowledge may still override what is in print. Consequently, it seems that the strategy of activating prior knowledge inadvertently may lead to a *misunderstanding* of text by refreshing readers' misconceptions before reading, by raising inaccurate predictions before reading, or by sharing students' misconceptions with others before reading.

During prereading activities that encourage readers to recall their prior knowledge, teachers often ask students to discuss their thoughts and experiences related to a topic to be studied. The usefulness of information learned during these activities depends upon the accuracy and relevance of the prior knowledge that classmates share during prereading activation. For example, prereading instruction concerning a passage about whales may begin by asking students to tell their ideas about whales. If students indicate that whales are fish because they swim, this may reinforce misinformation or provide misinformation to students who knew nothing about whales.

Even when readers work independently, if their knowledge concerning a topic under study is limited, recalling that knowledge may not offer a sufficiently rich context to support the reading of unfamiliar text. In such instances, an activation approach does not account for readers who need to learn unfamiliar concepts for which they *lack* any relevant prior knowledge. Computers provide a helpful analogy. We can do many applications and innovative projects using the software already in our computers. However, for some projects, we may need to expand our versatility by installing completely new programs. If we were to insist that all our work and applications derive only from one, beginning program, we would limit our potential to develop breadth of knowledge. Similarly, strategies designed to activate the knowledge that readers already possess, before coming to a text, may not compensate sufficiently for the limited, or inaccurate, prior knowledge that many young readers possess as they begin to read unfamiliar and specialized text.

Classroom studies of prior knowledge activation strategies. The issue of instruction in activation of prior knowledge has been particularly confusing since early, mixed results were considered encouraging. In order to clarify why the findings were mixed, several studies comparing activation strategies with other methods of instruction, conducted with 10 to 12 year olds, are reviewed below.

One study (Hansen & Pearson, 1983) finds mixed results, sometimes favoring an activation strategy, other times favoring a brief introduction of the topic and several pertinent points, but finding little difference between approaches overall. It appears that when the prior knowledge activation was more effective, the strategy also generally conveyed some of the pertinent and central concepts of the text under study while the comparison approach gave only cursory introduction to the topic. In this study, the activation approach previewed relevant text concepts during an activity in which the teacher used specific information taken from the text, while modeling how to use text information, and prior knowledge, to form inferences.

A later study (Anstey & Freebody, 1987) found somewhat similar results. In this study, several approaches designed to activate prior knowledge were compared. One activation approach provided exposure, through a picture, to the central concept of a text before reading. In this approach, students wrote their ideas concerning the content of a passage while viewing a picture that depicted the main concept of the story. In two comparison activation approaches, no direct exposure to the central text concept was provided. Instead, students wrote free associations either from the story title or from questions related to the topic to be read. In this study, only the strategy of exposing the main story concept (with a picture) was related to an advantage over reading the passage without any prereading instruction. These findings suggest that students may have benefitted from exposure to pertinent concepts or information before the reading of unfamiliar text rather than from activation of prior knowledge.

Directly teaching relevant background knowledge. Several studies examine the role of background knowledge by directly providing readers with accurate background before reading, through instruction in crucial related concepts. The findings from these studies consistently suggest that directly providing upper-elementary and secondary-school students with accurate and relevant background before reading literature or social studies passages seems to be related to enhanced reading comprehension of the passage under study (Brody, 1991; Dole et al., 1991; Graves & Cooke, 1980; Graves, et al., 1983; 1985).

Two of these studies (Brody, 1991; Dole et al., 1991) explore further the questions raised by classroom activation studies. They examine whether it is the activation of prior knowledge or, instead, the teaching of pertinent and important background concepts that is related to enhanced comprehension of a text among upper-elementary school students. These studies compare methods that teach central background concepts and information related to upcoming text with approaches that ask students to recall knowledge that they already possess. These strategies are also compared with the reading of a passage after no prereading instruction at all.

The results of these studies (Brody, 1991; Dole et al., 1991) indicate an advantage associated with the teaching of background information related to the text under study when compared with either activation or with no prereading instruction at all. These findings lend further evidence suggesting that reading comprehension of an assigned text is enhanced when the teacher directly conveys relevant background knowledge and important concepts before reading. Further, they suggest that drawing out prior knowledge does not seem to be associated with enhanced comprehension of a passage.

Teaching Strategies

The following discussion describes several strategies researched in the classroom studies noted above.

Present crucial concepts before reading. Teachers can present crucial concepts related to the text that students are about to read by following several steps that require very little change from directions given in teachers' manuals, yet that are related to a marked increase in students' understanding of text (Brody, 1991). First, during planning, the teacher selects several concepts crucial to understanding of the text and develops clear 3- to 5-sentence explanations of each. When a complex concept needs longer explanation, the teacher breaks the concept into smaller elements in order to present each smaller element in a 3- to 5-sentence explanation. Developing these brief presentations ensures that students will attend during presentation rather than getting lost in a lecture and drifting from the content. When preparing the lesson, teachers may draw on class texts, parallel texts, encyclopedias, trade books, visual media, or other resources to enhance their own background.

To begin the lesson, the teacher tells, reads, or demonstrates one concept by using the 3-5 sentence explanation. Next, the teacher asks questions that lead students to explain and apply what they have learned from the teacher's presentation. When a student's response to a question is accurate, the teacher confirms the response and sometimes repeats it in similar words to reinforce the concept for all the class.

Alternatively, when a student's response is inaccurate, the teacher says, "Actually, ..." and then explains the information again using other wording and perhaps a diagram or picture as well. In this case, the teacher would ask additional questions that draw out further explanation or application from students in order to assure that the clarification was understood.

Concepts are introduced in small steps, one-at-a-time. The process of first presenting a concept, then asking questions that require explanation and application, and finally confirming or reiterating the concept, is repeated several times. The number of concepts presented will vary with the background of the class. The teacher needs to present sufficient background concepts to provide a rich context from which to read the text. Introduction of 2 to 4 concepts crucial to understanding a section of text may take no more than 5 to 10 minutes, since the teacher keeps the class focused on pertinent material through brief instruction, questions that elicit explanation and application, and statements that confirm or clarify responses.

For example, students could be presented with an explanation of the concept "irrigation" by the teacher. Then they could be asked to tell how it is used to solve a problem, or how irrigation works, in order that they might actively apply the concept in their own words. If a student's answer indicates a misunderstanding of irrigation, the teacher would acknowledge the student's response by saying, "Actually, irrigation is used in this way..." The teacher then asks the same student the question again, in order to provide an opportunity for the student to experience success and in order to be sure that the teacher's revised explanation was understood.

Such a strategy can be used along with the materials and manuals that teachers already have in their classrooms. The only adjustment necessary is to **begin** by providing students with information concerning a concept and to **follow** with questions that encourage students to discuss the concept. This is in contrast to beginning as well as ending the prereading lesson by encouraging students to discuss a concept without first receiving accurate information to use in developing thoughts and responses. The approach can be used in whole class, small group, or individual instruction. The crucial elements appear to be: 1) accurate presentation of relevant concepts by the teacher; 2) an opportunity for students to express their understanding of each concept, as soon as it is presented, through the answering of questions that require an explanation or application of the concept; and, 3) immediate confirmation or else clarification by the teacher when the student's response suggests a misunderstanding of the concept (Brody, 1991).

Previews. Graves et al. (1980; 1983; 1985) suggest that teachers frame prereading instruction as a preview similar to that for a movie. Students are given an overview of a story that introduces its main characters and setting. In addition, the preview offers background that leads to, but does not reveal, the story climax. In this procedure, students are given an opportunity to discuss the preview information, and have their misunderstandings clarified, before reading. Graves et al. indicate that learners found these previews helpful in understanding where to focus attention during reading and that their understanding of the text was fuller when given such previews. Informal questioning of students in the study suggests that previews contribute to understanding without detracting from motivation, suspense, or interest.

Preteaching Background for Active Learning

Direct teacher contribution of background knowledge is sometimes viewed as a more traditional approach to instruction when compared with expecting students to activate their prior knowledge to figure out meaning independently. However, preteaching of accurate background differs from rote-learning, since it is accompanied by opportunities for students to actively apply the concepts. When properly implemented, presentation of background knowledge engages students in meaningful processing of accurate concepts rather than in spinning inappropriate and inapplicable schemata (Brody, 1993).

This practice is compatible as well with educational reform efforts that strive to implement school-based experiences that reflect community-based applications. For example, in the workplace, if an employee is to learn a new process, the manager would teach the unfamiliar practice before asking an employee to use it with customers or in a costly production routine. Similarly, medical students are not encouraged to make their first surgical incisions by drawing inferences from their related prior knowledge. Instead, they are shown precisely where and how to cut. Much later, when the concept of how and where to make a particular incision is embedded in their prior knowledge of medical practice, they can innovate in unusual circumstances.

Direct instruction and creativity. Many educators fear that children's creativity will be stifled unless they are left to develop understanding completely on their own from their prior knowledge, without the interference of adults' formalized background knowledge. However, research suggests that creative expression seems to unfold in a stage-like progression similar to the development of reading and language (Gardner, 1982).

Howard Gardner's studies (1982) suggest that young, artistic children take great delight in creating from what they know, with little concern for adult conventions during the early years. This is somewhat parallel to the pretend reading and language development play of Stage 0. As artistic children mature, they develop an intense desire to learn the conventions of perspective and other techniques that will allow them to make their drawings appear "real." They are pleased to be shown how to make objects in the picture plane come forward or recede and how to turn a line to make a familiar figure. Although their drawings at this stage do not seem as "creative" as earlier productions, this stage appears to lead to enhanced creative expression. As young artists practice their drawing, they use conventional techniques as convenient tools that let them go on, in the high school years and beyond, to create their personal style and expression with a sense of control and power rather than happenstance.

Promoting creativity, active learning, and self-confidence. Active integration and application of concepts are integral elements of strategies that directly develop background knowledge. In these strategies, the concepts presented by the teacher are immediately applied by students. Such application occurs through discussions that are stimulated by asking readers to answer questions by explaining or describing the concepts under study. These opportunities for thoughtful explanation and application of relevant background to text-related contexts contrast greatly with the practice of rote repetition without understanding.

For example, students could be presented with a description of the concept "pollination" by the teacher. Then they could be asked to explain the concept in their own words by describing how farmers plant their crops to increase pollination. The offering of information by the teacher does not replace active involvement in learning; instead it offers students rich and accurate background knowledge to use while developing and articulating their thoughts. Further, students may be able to use the information, while reading, to understand the text more clearly. Rather than coming to the process of constructing meaning with inaccurate background, students enter the process with a context of pertinent and enriched background. As suggested by the results of the studies reviewed above, this seems to assist students in constructing accurate schemata that let them comprehend unfamiliar texts more fully.

Whatever the strategy in use, the crucial elements to include when developing background involve directly presenting students with accurate concepts while providing opportunities for students to apply those accurate concepts to relevant situations or examples. When misconceptions emerge during discussion, the teacher corrects or clarifies them to assure that they do not persist during reading of the text.

Conclusions

Compatibility with schema theory. Schema theory suggests that readers comprehend text by integrating what they read with what they know in order to construct text schemata. Studies suggest that literal and inferential comprehension are associated positively with prereading instruction in which teachers accurately present text related concepts in order to develop enriched background knowledge (Brody, 1991; Dole et al., 1991; Graves et al., 1983; 1985). This research suggests that effective instruction develops accurate and relevant background knowledge, and thereby facilitates the forming of a meaningful text schema. This conforms with the findings of earlier studies in which readers who possess accurate and relevant knowledge concerning a new text understand it better than those who possess inaccurate or tangential knowledge (Barnitz & Morgan, 1983; Lipson, 1984; Wilson & Anderson, 1986).

Instruction. Recent studies suggest that teachers can prepare students to read and learn about the unfamiliar by presenting and clarifying pertinent concepts before reading, rather than by prompting students to recall what they know concerning the unfamiliar or specialized topic. Teachers can adapt their lessons and manuals to include this strategy by teaching relevant concepts and background before carrying out prereading discussions that ask students their thoughts about a topic.

Further research. There is a need for research to expand our understanding concerning the nature and number of background exposures needed to optimize learning from literature, science, and social studies texts. Further research could clarify how best to integrate teacher instruction in pertinent concepts with student application in order to maximize the richness, relevance, and accuracy of the context that students bring to text.

Additional research is needed to examine the notion that educators encourage learning and self-esteem by responding **without** corrections to **in**accurate views expressed by students. This practice may leave students feeling insecure and unsure. Readers may sense when they lack the background knowledge needed to understand a concept and may recognize when their understanding of unfamiliar information is unclear and vague. We need to respond to inaccurate statements sensitively while injecting accurate background that lets readers clarify misconceptions. Research may suggest additional methods that let this occur while neither alienating learners through a gesture of rejection nor binding learners to continued confusion through condescending, though well-intentioned, acceptance of inaccurate responses.

Summary. Relevant background knowledge appears crucial to understanding of unfamiliar and specialized text. Comprehension appears to be enhanced when prereading instruction provides learners with accurate information and concepts, along with opportunities to discuss and clarify understanding of such concepts. Such instruction seems to fill in gaps in prior knowledge and to provide opportunities for students to express their newly developing understanding in their own words. Such instruction is provided through previews of relevant concepts followed by the posing of questions that encourage students to reformulate and apply the previewed concepts and background. With such preparation, students seem to experience enhanced comprehension when reading unfamiliar and specialized text. This success may lead them to view reading as an opportunity for constructive interaction with new concepts and ideas rather than as an exercise in frustration and confusion.

274

References

Adams, M.J. (1994). *Beginning to read: Thinking and learning about print.* Cambridge: MIT Press.

Anstey, M.M. & Freebody, P. (1987). The effects of various pre-reading activities on children's literal and inferential comprehension. *Reading Psychology, 8*(3), 189-209.

Barnitz, J.C. & Morgan, A.L. (1983). Aspects of schemata and syntax in fifth grade children's inferential reading comprehension of causal relations. *Reading Psychology, 4*(3), 337-48.

Brody, S. (1991). *Clarifying the role of prereading instruction in 4th graders' comprehension of social studies text.* Unpublished Doctoral Dissertation, Harvard Graduate School of Education, Cambridge, MA.

Brody, S. (1993). Developing background knowledge: A context enrichment strategy that may provide more consistent results than activation of prior knowledge. In D. Wray (Ed.), *Proceedings: 1994 United Kingdom Reading Association Annual Conference,* Exeter, England: UKRA.

Chall, J.S. (1983). *Stages of reading development.* New York: McGraw-Hill.

Dole, J.A., Valencia, S.W., Greer, E.A., & Wardrop, J.L. (1991). Effects of two types of prereading instruction on the comprehension of narrative and expository text. *Reading Research Quarterly, 26*(2), 142-159.

Gardner, H. (1982). *Art, mind, and brain: A cognitive approach to creativity.* New York: Basic Books.

Gazzaniga, M.S. (1992). *Nature's mind: The biological roots of thinking, emotions, sexuality, language, and intelligence.* New York: Basic Books.

Graves, M.F., & Cooke, C.L., (1980). Effects of previewing difficult short stories for high school students. *Research on Reading in Secondary Schools, 6,* 38-54.

Graves, M.F., Cooke, C.L., & Laberge, M.J. (1983). Effects of previewing difficult short stories on low ability junior high school students' comprehension, recall, and attitudes. *Reading Research Quarterly, 18*(3) 262-276.

Graves, M.F., Prenn, M.C., & Cooke, C.L. (1985). The coming attraction: Previewing short stories. *Journal of Reading, 28*(7), 594-598.

Hansen, J. & Pearson, P.D. (1983). An instructional study: Improving the inferential comprehension of good and poor fourth-grade readers. *Journal of Educational Psychology, 75*(6), 821-29.

Inhelder, B., & Piaget, J. (1958). *The growth of logical thinking from childhood to adolescence.* NY: Basic Books.

Lipson, M.Y. (1984). Some unexpected issues in prior knowledge and comprehension. *Reading Teacher, 37*(8), 760-764.

Mullis, I.V., Campbell, J.R., & Farstrup, A.E. (1993). *Reading report card for the nation and the states.* Washington, DC: United States Government Printing Office.

Perfetti, C.A. & Curtis, M.E. (1986). Reading. In R.F. Dillon & R.J. Sternberg (Eds.), *Cognition and instruction.* NY: Academic Press.

Stanovich, K.E. (1994). Romance and reality. *The Reading Teacher, 47*(4), 280-291.

Stanovich, K.E., & Cunningham, A.E. (1993). Where does knowledge come from? Specific associations between print exposure and information acquisition. *Journal of Educational Psychology, 85*(2).

Wilson, P.T. & Anderson, R.C. (1986). What they don't know will hurt them: The role of prior knowledge in comprehension. In J. Orasanu (Ed.), *Reading comprehension: From research to practice*. Hillsdale, NJ: Lawrence Erlbaum.

Chapter 9. Vocabulary: Teaching Words and Their Meanings

Paula H. Sable, EdD
Bradford College

Reading is greatly enhanced when learners possess substantial vocabulary knowledge. Extensive knowledge of word meanings offers a solid underpinning as readers peruse text to understand an author's message. Such background assists readers in forming inferences more accurately and efficiently and also contributes to a sense of confidence that the author's meaning is understood. A range of knowledge contributes to an extensive vocabulary. Recognition of the multiple elements that constitute vocabulary understanding can enhance vocabulary instruction.

This chapter examines the nature of rich reading vocabulary and its development. First, the types of vocabulary knowledge that readers use are described. Next, issues related to direct and indirect instruction are considered. And, finally, strategies used to increase word knowledge are presented.

Types of Vocabulary Knowledge

A reader's lexicon, or mental dictionary, is composed of what the person knows about words and their meanings. The term **vocabulary** refers to one's lexical understanding; this is the case whether words represent tangible items, abstract ideas, or concepts. Lexical knowledge includes both meaning—purely semantic aspects of words—and the syntactic or technical elements of words, such as word endings that signify tense or possession. Together, semantic and syntactic knowledge constitute a reader's lexicon. This body of information can be drawn on to understand and engage in linguistic thought. What readers know *about* words, as well as the words readers know, influences the clarity with which learners understand a range of spoken and written language.

The act of reading draws heavily on an understanding of word meanings. Proficient readers connect printed words to their meanings with ease. In addition, they negotiate meanings of unfamiliar words by drawing on text content and prior knowledge of syntax, semantics, and synonyms. In order to consider thoroughly the contribution of vocabulary knowledge to reading, it is helpful to explore the kinds of "vocabularies" readers possess and the extent to which they understand these words.

Depth and breadth. By the time learners develop reading fluency, one of the primary functions of instruction is the extension of their substantial lexicon in order to enhance the development of both depth and breadth of vocabulary knowledge. Readers encounter a variety of words (breadth); they also learn that some words have meanings that vary by context (depth).

These multiple meaning words are especially important when learners study in different disciplines. For example, readers may know that the term *cabinet* describes a particular type of furniture. When readers learn about forms of government, the term *cabinet* indicates a body of people with a specific governmental function. The learning of such multiple-meaning terms becomes an important focus for the development of vocabulary depth, especially when reading within the academic content areas.

Denotation and connotation. Vocabulary development reflects an additional dimension as well. Not only are unfamiliar words and/or meanings encountered, but denotative and connotative aspects of meaning are explored. Although individual words may have very specific denotations, or definitions, they may also convey very different connotations, or suggested meanings, when used in unusual situations.

With instruction, practice, and wide reading, students learn to clarify a word's connotative meanings in relation to the words surrounding it. Such clarification occurs very quickly when fluent readers, with strong vocabularies, engage with well structured text. However, the process requires careful instruction for readers who lack a range of background that can aid in negotiating an author's intended meaning. The following example illustrates how a reader may draw on both semantic and syntactic knowledge to learn a connotative meaning:

Samantha knows that *unique* means one of a kind. She can identify a unique object when asked to select it from several others.

Samantha also knows that *circumstances* is used to identify situations. If presented with two situations, Samantha can select the unique one.

However, Samantha must draw on syntactic, as well as semantic, knowledge when she encounters the following sentence: *When the unique circumstances occurred repeatedly, policy changed.*

In order to fully comprehend this sentence, Samantha draws on her syntactic knowledge of the suffix *ly* in order to be aware that what has been unique is now occurring, not one time, but often. She makes use of semantic knowledge as well. By knowing that policy is promulgated to reflect common circumstances, Samantha more fully comprehends the sentence.

In addition, connotation alone can affect word meaning. Compare the implications of these two sentences.

The students described their teacher as very patient.

The students described their teacher as very meek.

In these two syntactically similar sentences, the words *patient* and *meek*, though quite close in meaning, represent very different personalities. Such connotations can only be understood when the reader possesses considerable semantic knowledge.

Oral and literary language. A writer's or speaker's choice of words varies to match the context in which the words are used. For example, when sharing information concerning vocabulary in an educational column of a local newspaper, one's choice of wording and phrasing would differ from that used when writing a paper to present at a research convention. To accommodate these differences in level of formality, we need to develop a broad vocabulary that enhances communicative flexibility.

Learners who have experienced very little exposure to books or conversations in which literary language is used tend to rely primarily on informal expressions. In contrast, avid readers and those regularly exposed to conversations that draw on literary conventions tend to possess broader vocabularies. This breadth reflects both exposure to literary language and exposure to informal, oral language through daily experience and wide reading in which both formal and informal vocabulary is encountered. Learners who begin Stage 3 reading with both formal and informal language exposure tend to increase their reading ability with greater ease (Chall, 1987; Stanovich, 1986).

Receptive and productive vocabulary. When listening to another person talking, or when reading, students rely on their stored knowledge of words in order to comprehend the content. These words make up their receptive vocabulary. When readers' receptive vocabulary is weak, they search to bridge their knowledge gaps in one of several ways. They may try to discern a meaning in relation to the context of a topic or sentence, or seek help from another source, such as a dictionary or another person.

Often, readers with limited vocabulary lack sufficient receptive word knowledge to fill in, from context, and understand with accuracy (McKeown, 1985). In addition, their weak receptive vocabulary makes it difficult to comprehend dictionary meaning (McKeown, 1993) and may leave them too self-conscious to ask for help. If these students are to learn from reading, teachers need to preview vocabulary related to assigned text. This preview, coupled with subsequent, active engagement with the word, while reading it in multiple contexts, helps to insert the words into the memory bank of receptive vocabulary.

Productive, or expressive, vocabulary refers to those words used during speech or writing. Students transfer a word from receptive to expressive vocabulary when they know its meaning well and feel comfortable or competent using it actively (Graves, 1987). Words that are part of receptive vocabulary do not necessarily become part of productive vocabulary, or may require a considerable number of encounters before transfer. Consequently, receptive vocabulary is usually more expansive than productive vocabulary. One of the tasks of good vocabulary instruction is to enhance students' productive vocabulary in order to facilitate independence in active, linguistic processing of unfamiliar concepts.

Completeness. Completeness of word knowledge can be described in terms of various developmental schemes. The one presented here was introduced by Edgar Dale (1965) and its usefulness further expanded by Mary E. Curtis (1987). It delineates four states of word knowledge that reflect a word's increasing accessibility in receptive and/or productive vocabulary.

Unknown Words. Dale describes the earliest level of word knowledge as no knowledge—words to which one cannot attach meaning. Dale describes a student's response at this stage as, "I never saw it before." Learners may not even be sure that a word in this stage is a real word, as has been demonstrated when they have been asked to identify "real" words from a list of real and nonsense words (Curtis, 1987).

Vague Knowledge. At this level of word knowledge, a student may respond, "I've heard of it, but I don't know what it means." A student at this stage is aware of a term but has not yet associated clear meaning with it. Such a word cannot be part of the student's productive vocabulary since no meaning is available to initiate its use. Further, the word is of little value in the reader's receptive vocabulary since it can only elicit quizzical looks or awareness that it would be wise to consult a dictionary or other reference source.

Partial Knowledge. Dale indicates that a reader with partial knowledge would have a general association of a word within a specific context. Thus, a response would be, "It has something to do with...." Words in receptive vocabulary are often initially those for which partial understanding is held. Usually, such words require additional encounters, within several contexts, before a reader feels confident that the meaning is perceived accurately. Still further exposure is needed before learners attempt to use these words in speaking or writing. Thus, these words are tentatively embedded in receptive vocabulary, and unlikely to be part of productive vocabulary.

Deep Knowledge. Curtis describes this level of vocabulary as that at which a reader can define a word without tying it to a specific context (1987, p. 43). In order to do this, the reader must possess sufficient understanding to relate the word to synonyms, use it in differing contexts, and explain its meaning in some detail. Since such knowledge is necessary to allow use in productive vocabulary, it is worth teaching toward this level.

Partial knowledge of words is often sufficient to recognize meaning when context is explicit. Curtis (1987) found such knowledge adequate to produce correct responses on multiple choice vocabulary tests. But partial knowledge is troublesome when it leads students to misunderstand what they read. Further, problems arise when partial understanding leads teachers to assume that students have developed a greater depth than is actually the case (Sable, 1992).

When selecting words for instruction, teachers may pass over words for which students possess partial knowledge. The importance of instruction in such words becomes evident during productive use or when content is less explicit. Many teachers who have asked students to look up word meanings in the dictionary, then use these words in sentences, have encountered examples of partial understanding. Miller and Gildea (1987) illustrate with this example:

A fifth grader, having read in the dictionary that *meticulous* means being very careful about details, wrote the following sentence: *I was meticulous about falling off the cliff* (p. 98).

Deep knowledge of word meanings is particularly important when readers add technical and specialized words to their productive vocabulary during Stage 3 reading and beyond. Such words carry a great deal of the content load. Fluent use of the words allows readers to think about material under study and to use language to actively apply content to a variety of contexts and circumstances. This processing aids in remembering the material and in understanding its relevance (Perkins & Salomon, 1988). In addition, such use enables readers to communicate the content to others during discussion or in writing.

Teachers need to recognize the importance of developing deep understanding of words as a goal of vocabulary instruction. Since their students generally perform well on multiple choice or matching quizzes with only partial knowledge of word meanings (Curtis, 1987), teachers may not recognize the limitations imposed by knowledge developed only to the level of exposure. Insufficient knowledge of word meanings may persist when teachers provide only brief exposure to vocabulary, in expectation that mastery of meanings will come later, through other means (Sable, 1992).

Direct and Indirect Vocabulary Instruction

Vocabulary is acquired through direct instruction and incidental exposure. Both types of learning contribute to the development of a rich and varied vocabulary (Chall, 1987). Since both instruction and exposure enhance word knowledge, teachers need to assist students in developing vocabulary through each of these means.

Prior to schooling, very young children develop an understanding of words through instruction by parents who point to objects while saying their names, and through repeated labeling of actions and ideas during daily routines. This occurs primarily during speaking, being spoken to, and listening to others. Language development and vocabulary acquisition are further enhanced by exposure to print, as occurs when adults read aloud. (See Chapter 2, of this volume, concerning language development.)

Children continue to expand their vocabulary through these avenues when they enter school. At this point, opportunities expand with exposure to unfamiliar activities and routines. In addition, as children develop reading proficiency, they enhance their capability to learn word meanings from printed context. The rate of such learning is quite varied since some children select and read books and other materials avidly, while others read little or not at all.

Independent reading can provide a positive opportunity for expansive development of vocabulary among children who are avid readers (Nagy, Herman, & Anderson 1985). The more these children read, the more they encounter new words. Extensive vocabulary expansion can occur as a result of this exposure. Consequently, many educators suggest that an important contribution to vocabulary instruction lies in turning children loose with books and encouraging them to read, read, read (Green, 1984; Nagy & Herman, 1987).

However, simply exposing children to books does not develop vocabulary sufficiently in the upper elementary grades and beyond (Beck & McKeown, 1983; Chall, 1987; Graves, 1987). Learners at these levels need to comprehend unfamiliar information in a variety of subject areas but do not gain sufficient exposure to all areas of knowledge through independent reading alone.

Numerous studies attest to the need for an instructional approach that includes direct, systematic instruction as well as encouragement to read frequently and broadly (Mezynski, 1983; Nagy, 1988; Stahl & Fairbanks, 1986). The need for direct instruction becomes especially evident when considering the learning characteristics of the readers described below:

Infrequent Readers. Many students lack the habit of frequent and independent reading (Mullis, Campbell, & Farstrup, 1993). These readers are exposed to words through context less frequently than their peers who read often. Consequently, they require direct instruction in order to develop depth and breadth of vocabulary. In turn, this word knowledge can support greater understanding during reading and perhaps promote greater reading frequency among some students.

Readers from Limited-literacy Backgrounds. Much research has examined the relationship between reading development and family/situational backgrounds (Chall, Jacobs, & Baldwin, 1990; Chall & Snow, 1982; Feitelson, Kita, & Goldstein, 1986). This research demonstrates that children who have little reading material available in their homes are less likely to read frequently. When children come to school with limited exposure to print and literary language, direct instruction in words and their meanings particularly enhances recognition of a broad variety of words and their meanings in literary discourse and expository text.

Readers from Varied Cultural Perspectives. The teacher's role, and the way learning is perceived and achieved, differs among cultures. Since students' expectations often influence how they learn (Heath, 1983), children who look to the teacher to initiate instruction will benefit from direct instruction (Delpit, 1986; 1988).

Readers who Lack Extensive Vocabulary. As readers enter the upper elementary grades, they need to draw on broad and deep vocabulary to help them determine word meanings accurately from context (McKeown, 1985). Lack of such knowledge affects skilled readers, as well as those less skilled, when they try to understand text that was written with many specialized words. Direct instruction provides meanings of crucial content words as a foundation from which to develop accurate word meanings from context (Graves, 1984).

Less-Skilled Readers. Research comparing the practices of skilled and less-skilled readers (Golinkoff, 1975-76; Sullivan, 1978) indicates that less-skilled readers rely on fewer strategies for negotiating meaning. In order to learn unfamiliar words through the exposure of independent reading, students need to recognize whether they understand a word or concept. Research on metacognition indicates that some readers, particularly those who are younger or less skilled, lack this awareness; consequently, they do not know when to seek an unknown definition (Paris & Lindauer, 1982). These learners need direct instruction to develop sufficient vocabulary knowledge to recognize whether they know words.

Risk-avoiding Readers. Reading often requires learners to take risks. Skilled readers usually take risks. When one strategy fails, they try another (Sullivan, 1978). In contrast, less-secure readers tend to be more rigid and to give up easily when a first attempt at meaning fails (Bransford, Vye, & Stein, 1984). These students need direct instruction in word meanings to build their vocabulary as a means of bolstering their confidence during independent reading.

Independent Readers. Even skilled readers in the elementary grades experience difficulty in learning the meanings of specialized content words solely from context or context-with-dictionary-support. They need some direct instruction for assistance, since most dictionary meanings are too broad to define specific concepts clearly (McKeown, 1993).

Readers come to Stage 3 with a variety of learning characteristics that contribute to their need for focused vocabulary instruction. Such instruction teaches words directly through multiple exposures to words, their meanings, and synonyms; it also provides many opportunities for independent reading (Chall 1987; Mezynski, 1983; Stahl & Fairbanks, 1986).

Vocabulary Instruction

Classroom research suggests that effective vocabulary instruction integrates four components: a clear statement of, and focus on, the definition of unfamiliar words; multiple opportunities to use words under study in spoken and written contexts; the association of words under study with related words and concepts; and use of activities that require reasoning about word meanings and their relationships with other words (Beck, McKeown, & Omanson 1987; Beck, Perfetti, & McKeown, 1982; Mezynski, 1983; Sable, 1988; Stahl & Fairbanks, 1986). The following discussion offers guidelines concerning how to select words for direct instruction and then suggests a variety of instructional strategies that incorporate the four components described above.

SELECTING WORDS FOR DIRECT INSTRUCTION

Teachers need to select words for instruction carefully since time allows only a limited number of words to be taught directly. Some research suggests that lessons involving 10 - 12 words seem appropriate for most students in the intermediate grades (Beck et al., 1982; McKeown, Beck, Omanson, & Pople, 1985; Wixson, 1986; Wysocki & Jenkins, 1987). In the primary grades, or with less-skilled readers, five or six words per lesson seem to be more effective (Gipe, 1979; Pany & Jenkins, 1977). Vocabulary lessons in commercial materials sometimes exceed these numbers; however, these materials often include many words that students already know (Sable, 1988). Maria (1990) and Graves, Slater, & White (1989) offer helpful criteria for selecting words to study. These are described below:

Relevant Words. Words for study should be taken from material that students will actually read, such as textbooks and trade or story books used in the classroom. These establish a functional basis for inclusion.

Unfamiliar Words Not Easily Inferred from Context. Words that students are not likely to know, or to figure out from context, should be selected. Teachers can focus instruction on these words by choosing carefully among lists of words recommended in commercial programs (Sable, 1988) or by previewing reading materials and selecting those words likely to pose an undue challenge.

Maria (1990) advises that words whose meanings may be easily inferred from context should not be selected for instruction. For such words, a brief query during the actual reading of the text with repeated use during post-reading discussion may ensure comprehension and word learning.

When text includes more words requiring instruction than can fit a lesson, Maria (1990) and Graves (1987) suggest the following additional criteria to narrow word selection:

Words Essential to Comprehension. Since only a limited number of words can be taught, content words most essential to understanding should be selected. Klein (1988) refers to these as "enabling" words.

Words that Foster Strategic Skill Development. In addition to essential words, it is also useful to select words that provide opportunities to develop word-learning strategies. For example, sometimes several words in the text have the same affix or root word. Part of the lesson can focus on the common element in these words to provide a strategy for identifying other similar words.

Words of General Utility. Select essential words that appear often in other contexts as well. When a text contains several unusual words, they may be defined briefly **during actual reading** to reserve vocabulary lesson time for higher frequency words that can influence reading comprehension more broadly. For example, in a science lesson on bacteria, appropriate vocabulary words may include *chloroplast, flagella,* and *cilia*, while brief instruction during reading would suffice for a passing reference to *trypanosoma*.

Words that Pique Interest. Maria also suggests selecting words of particular interest. She cites educators (e.g., Richek, 1988) who demonstrate that focus on words of interest can increase word knowledge and interest in the study of words.

These criteria offer guidelines to consider when choosing words for direct instruction. By culling words selectively, teachers maximize the extent that vocabulary lessons increase students' knowledge of word meanings along with their skill in determining meaning independently.

When selecting words to teach, it is helpful to consider the type of knowledge that students need to develop concerning each target word. Graves, Slater, & White (1989) describe six specific word-learning skills that may be needed to enhance receptive or productive vocabulary. Their classification system is delineated below:

Type One: Recognition of Known Words. The most basic word learning task is learning to decode words whose meanings are already known. By learning to "crack the code," learners can recognize, in print, words that they already possess in their listening vocabulary. (See Chapters 3, 4, and 5 of this volume for a detailed description of instruction.)

Type Two: Polysemous Words. The second word type described by Graves et al. is recognition that a word's meaning may differ when the context is changed. Instruction of polysemous, or multiple-meaning words, occurs especially in relation to various content areas. Devine (1986) indicates that there are two kinds of polysemous words. One includes common words for which a variety of meanings are already known, such as *stop, store, ice.* The other includes words whose meanings vary in different disciplines such as *charged* used in war, finance, and electronics.

Type Three: Unfamiliar Words for Familiar Concepts. Readers need to learn unfamiliar words that represent well known concepts. For example, students may not know the word *antimacassar*, but readily recognize the concept that it represents—small lace (or paper) cloth pieces set on an airplane seatback or large livingroom chair to protect the upholstery from hair oils. Unfamiliar synonyms can be linked with a concept that is already understood by providing a simple explanation of the meaning, coupled with examples that associate the word with the reader's existing schema.

Type Four: Unfamiliar Words for Unfamiliar Concepts. Perhaps the most difficult vocabulary task is learning unfamiliar words for unknown concepts. Such words appear frequently in content area reading. Terms such as *entropy, isolationism* or *imaginary number* often require conceptual development before they can be fully understood. Johnson and Pearson (1984), suggest that students learn unfamiliar concepts through multiple experiences with central and related information in similar and varied contexts.

Type Five: Depth and Precision of Word Meaning. Another vocabulary development task described by Graves et al. is "clarifying and enriching the meanings of known words" (1989, p. 216). Such instruction helps students increase depth of understanding and use greater precision in word usage as in clarifying the difference between *assertive* and *aggressive*.

Type Six: Moving Words to Productive Vocabulary. The final, ongoing, task described by Graves et al. involves the expansion of productive vocabulary. Since most individuals comprehend more words than they speak or write, expanding productive vocabulary tends to require additional instruction. A variety of strategies foster habits of vocabulary awareness, interest in words, and the use of new words.

The classifications provided by Graves et al. underscore the importance of the vocabulary word selection process and the need to vary teaching rate to accommodate the kinds of words under study. A fifteen-minute lesson may introduce effectively six or more synonyms for familiar concepts; however, at least that time may be needed to introduce one unfamiliar word and its related unfamiliar concept.

Developing the meanings of unfamiliar words that express unfamiliar concepts requires more time than teaching synonyms for familiar concepts.

INSTRUCTIONAL STRATEGIES

Whether learning a Type One or a Type Six word, a crucial element of effective instruction is the provision of multiple and varied exposures to the word and its meaning. This exposure includes explanation and demonstration by the teacher as well as opportunities for students to use the word many times in many contexts to assure clear understanding and transfer to productive vocabulary. The following strategies can be effective in vocabulary instruction:

Concrete examples. The critical factor in teaching polysemous words is knowing the appropriate match between meaning and context. When the meaning is already known, instruction simply needs to teach explicitly the match between the word and its unfamiliar context. This can be done by providing students with the unfamiliar usage and several concrete examples, prior to encounter in print. For example, the teacher might turn on a flashlight with a dead battery, then replace it with a *charged* battery before students read about electricity. The demonstration could be followed by asking students to describe other gadgets that require charged batteries.

Linking unfamiliar synonyms with familiar meanings. Graves et al. (1989), Sable (1988), Curtis (1986), Johnson & Pearson (1984), and Beck & McKeown (1983) discuss a variety of ways to link synonyms with existing schemata. When used in combination, such strategies effectively provide multiple exposures to words and their meanings. These activities include:
- Provide the definition of a word orally.
- Offer a definition and use the word orally in a context laden sentence.
- Ask students to look up the word in a dictionary or glossary.
- Offer multiple examples by using a word in several contexts, followed by asking students to deduce word meaning.
- Engage students in adapted card games such as Concentration.
- Develop semantic maps of the word and its synonyms.

Presentation and discussion of words in multiple contexts. Discussion of the definitions and use of a word in multiple contexts can enhance memory of the word and understanding of its meaning (Stahl & Vancil, 1986). Group discussion of sentences and meaning offer opportunities for associations among words as well as opportunities for students to use the words themselves in unfamiliar ways. Throughout the discussion, it is crucial that the teacher directly confirm accurate usage and correct inaccuracies to assure that students embed the term appropriately in their lexicon. Whatever the strategies used, as with all types of vocabulary words, they will be learned and remembered best if students are given many exposures to the word and its meaning (Beck et al., 1983).

Word maps. Word mapping, developed by Schwartz (1988), assists students in learning unfamiliar concepts and their related words. This activity, which may be completed with a text frame (see Chapter 7), provides a framework that teaches a concept by noting its class, distinguishing characteristics that separate it from other members of its class, and several examples of the concept in use. Schwartz recommends that the following questions be used during instruction:
- What is it? (categorize by class)
- What is it like? (compare with similar concepts or describe attributes)
- What are some examples? (demonstrate understanding)

For example, when defining the term *republic*, students would answer questions to fill in a word map with responses such as:
- What is it? *form of government*
- What is it like? *citizens vote for representatives, head is elected*
- What are some examples? *U.S.A., Canada*

Clarifying meaning by example and non-example. Research suggests that work with semantically related words clarifies and deepens word knowledge (Beck & McKeown, 1983; Johnson & Pearson, 1984; Marzano & Marzano, 1988). Graves et al. (1989) and Frayer, Frederick, & Klausmeier (1969) offer a strategy that clarifies word meaning by comparing familiar and unfamiliar terms.

To use this approach, teachers first introduce a target word, its meaning, and its attributes. Next, they compare the target word to similar, but different, words while noting similarities and distinctions. Then, they provide examples of appropriate use of the target word. This is followed by demonstrating non-examples (related contexts in which a different word needs to be used for accuracy) along with examples (related contexts for which the target word is appropriate). Teachers offer additional examples and non-examples while leading students through a discussion to clarify the concept. Finally, teachers ask students to present their own examples and non-examples. When students do this successfully, they understand the concept.

Semantic maps. Semantic maps, sometimes called word webs, are diagrams that show how words are related to one another (Johnson & Pearson, 1984, p. 12). Semantic maps are developed by noting associations among words. When discussion is guided carefully, it can verify, correct, and expand students' understanding of word meanings (Heimlich & Pittelman, 1986). This process seems especially appropriate for refining depth and precision of word meanings. (See Figure 9.a.)

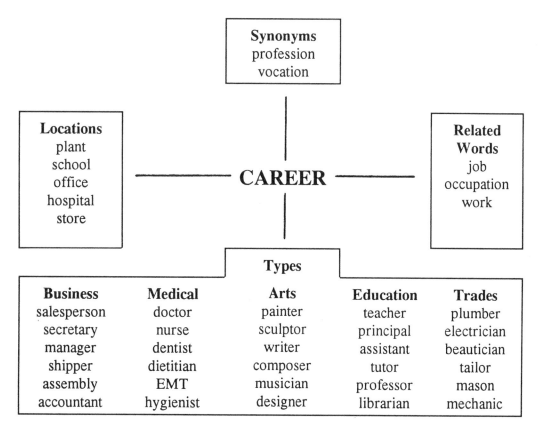

Figure 9.a. Semantic map.

It is helpful to follow a mapping lesson with activities that require students to use words from the map in speaking, reading, and writing. Questions that encourage students to think, respond, and provide reasons for their responses seem particularly effective in the development of depth of word knowledge (Beck et al., 1987). In particular, the additional exposure to target words during such activities reinforces meaning (Beck & McKeown, 1983; Beck et al., 1982).

Semantic feature analysis. Another method of refining word meaning involves a comparison-contrast activity conducted while developing an attribute grid. In this activity, a particular category is selected and target words within the category are listed. These, and a row of attributes, form a matrix. Students identify the attributes of each target word by placing a check or plus/minus in appropriate spaces on the matrix. (See Figure 9.b, below.)

Word	Characteristics				
	Lasting	Pleasant	Food Related	Mild	Strong
aroma	+	+	+/-	+	-
fragrance	+	+	-	+	-
odor	+	-	+/-	?	+
stench	+	-	-	-	+
scent	-	+	?	+	-
whiff	-	+/-	+/-	+	-

Figure 9.b. Semantic feature analysis grid.

Marzano & Marzano (1988) suggest using such matrices in several ways: to develop generalizations concerning related words; to note how few words possess the same attributes; to describe similarities and differences among words; and to develop definitions. As with semantic maps, feature analysis matrices lend themselves to activities that raise questions, analyze meaning, and develop connotative understanding. They may also be used to note terms that are formal and those that are reserved for informal contexts.

Analogies. The completion or construction of analogous relationships is a form of word play that promotes depth of understanding. However, in order for students to engage in this activity, they need to understand the kinds of relationships displayed in analogic equations. Johnson & Pearson (1984) suggest several relationships that are demonstrated by analogy. A few examples of these include:

Characteristics:	Stone is to hard as fur is to soft.
Part/Whole:	Page is to book as spoke is to wheel.
Location:	Clerk is to store as teller is to bank.
Action/Object:	Skate is to ice as cook is to skillet.

Analogies are used to depict relationships, and students clarify their vocabulary understanding by explaining the analogy. Students actively process the words and their meanings through discussion or writing. Once students master the relationships of analogy, teachers can help them develop their own analogies using related words under study.

Vocabulary notebooks. Vocabulary notebooks are especially helpful in expanding productive vocabulary. Marzano & Marzano (1988) suggest that students develop these notebooks arranged by category and concept. For example, under the category "personality traits," the student would list the concept "peevish." Within this format, students list the target word, words that are similar, and a definition (see figure 9.c, below). Since the three-ring notebook is arranged with at least one page per category, students can add words by category without concern for alphabetical order. Activities involving the notebook provide opportunities to note differences among similar words and encourage students to use the words accurately.

Category:	words that convey emotion	
Concepts:	anger, joy, sadness, apathy	
WORD	RELATED WORDS	DEFINITION
ire	anger, wrath, fury	deep anger
dejection	sadness, misery, melancholy	depression
ecstatic	overjoyed, delighted, blissful	full of happiness

Figure 9.c. Vocabulary notebook page arranged by category and concept.

Klein (1988) recommends the use of vocabulary notebooks when teaching theme-related words, particularly in content-area learning. He suggests that students use notebooks to record times and places where unfamiliar words are heard or used both in school and other settings. He cautions that the notebooks must be coupled with brief, daily discussion if entries are to be mastered. In a similar program, Word Wizard (Beck & McKeown, 1983), students earn points by sharing, in class, target words seen, heard, or used outside of class.

Etymology. Interest in expanding productive vocabulary can be sparked through lessons that explore the origin of words and their meanings. Etymology, the history of words, can intrigue students when properly presented. A focus on etymology is particularly appropriate for learners at or beyond Stage 3 reading development since a rudimentary facility with dictionaries and basic research skills is helpful. Klein (1988) suggests that lessons can focus on word evolution by noting semantic changes, word formation, and dialect.

Students are often interested in how new words are formed. Even at very young ages, children experiment with new names for objects and play at developing their own words. (See Chapter 2 for detail.) Discussion of word formation enhances this curiosity and offers specific knowledge as well. The following examples describe a variety of ways in which words are formed:

Acronyms are developed by shortening longer titles or phrases to the initial letter of each word in the descriptor as in *SCUBA* (self-contained underwater breathing apparatus; or, *EMT* (emergency medical technician).

Abbreviations evolve from longer words through deletion as in *gym* (gymnasium).

Blends develop from two or more existing words as in *smog* (smoke and fog).

Coined words express a concept in a new field as in *interface* (coined to describe connectors that let various computer accessories work together).

Role shifts occur when words used as one part of speech are used in another, as in *service* (a noun used as a verb to explain that *the car was serviced*).

Whatever teaching strategy is selected, teachers can facilitate the learning of unfamiliar words by assuring that instruction defines words clearly and offers students multiple opportunities to use the words appropriately in a variety of contexts. Such instruction aids in the learning of unfamiliar words and in moving words from receptive to productive vocabulary (Beck et al., 1982; 1987).

Conclusion

Comprehension of literature and expository text is enhanced by broad and deep vocabulary knowledge that lets a reader fully understand word meanings. Mastery of word meaning requires frequent exposure to words in a variety of contexts. Word knowledge is enhanced by a program of consistent instruction that includes systematic review of word meanings, and encouragement to use these words during oral communication (Sable, 1988).

In addition, maintaining a learning atmosphere where students are comfortable exploring the use of words is a crucial instructional goal. Effective programs teach sets of semantically-related words; offer daily practice that involves semantic association, connotation, and production of definitions; and create opportunities for students to use the words often when writing or speaking.

296

References

Beck, I.L., & McKeown, M.G. (1983). Learning words well: A program to enhance vocabulary and comprehension. *Reading Teacher, 36,* 622-625.

Beck, I.L., McKeown, M.G., & Omanson, R.C. (1987). The effects and uses of diverse vocabulary instructional techniques. In M.G. McKeown & M.E. Curtis (Eds.), *The nature of vocabulary acquisition*. Hillsdale, NJ: Erlbaum.

Beck, I.L., Perfetti, C.A., & McKeown, M.G. (1982). Effects of long-term vocabulary instruction on lexical access and reading comprehension. *Journal of Educational Psychology, 74,* 506-521.

Bransford, J.D., Vye, N.J. & Stein, B.S. (1984). A comparison of successful and less successful learners: Can we enhance comprehension and mastery skills? In J. Flood (Ed.), *Promoting reading comprehension*. Newark, DE: International Reading Association.

Chall, J.S. (1987). Two vocabularies for reading: Recognition and meaning. In M.G. McKeown & M.E. Curtis (Eds.), *The nature of vocabulary acquisition*. Hillsdale, NJ: Erlbaum.

Chall, J.S., Jacobs, V.J., & Baldwin, L.E. (1990). *The reading crisis: Why poor children fall behind*. Cambridge, MA: Harvard University Press.

Chall, J.S., & Snow, C. (1982). *Families and literacy*. NIE Report.

Curtis, M.E. (1986). The best kind of vocabulary instruction. *Massachusetts Primer, 15,* 5-9.

Curtis, M.E. (1987). Vocabulary testing and vocabulary instruction. In M.G. McKeown & M.E. Curtis (Eds.), *The nature of vocabulary acquisition*. Hillsdale, NJ: Erlbaum.

Dale, E. (1965). Vocabulary measurement: Techniques and major findings. *Elementary English, 42,* 895-901; 948.

Delpit, L.D. (1986). Skills and other dilemmas of a progressive black educator. *Harvard Educational Review, 56,* 379-385.

Delpit, L.D. (1988). The silenced dialogue: Power and pedagogy in educating other people's children. *Harvard Education Review, 58,* 280-298.

Devine, T. G. (1986). *Teaching reading comprehension: From theory to practice*. Needham, MA: Allyn & Bacon.

Feitelson, D., Kita, B., & Goldstein, Z. (1986). Effects of listening to series stories on first graders' comprehension and use of language. *Research in the Teaching of English, 20,* 339-356.

Frayer, D.A., Frederick, W.C., & Klausmeier, H.J. (1969). *A schema for testing the level of concept mastery*. (Working Paper Number 16.) Madison, WI: Wisconsin Research and Development Center for Cognitive Learning.

Gipe, J. (1979). Investigating techniques for teaching word meanings. *Reading Research Quarterly, 14,* 625-644.

Golinkoff, R.M. (1975-76). A comparison of reading comprehension processes in good and poor comprehenders. *Reading Research Quarterly, 11,* 623-659.

Graves, M. (1984). Selecting vocabulary to teach in the intermediate and secondary grades. In J. Flood (Ed.), *Promoting reading comprehension*. Newark, DE: International Reading Association.

Graves, M. (1987). The role of instruction in fostering vocabulary development. In M.G. McKeown & M.E. Curtis (Eds.), *The nature of vocabulary acquisition*. Hillsdale, NJ: Erlbaum.

Graves, M., Slater, W., & White, T. (1989). Teaching content area vocabulary. In D. Lapp, J. Flood, and N. Farnam (Eds.), *Content area reading and learning: Instructional strategies*. Englewood Cliffs, NJ: Prentice-Hall.

Green, G. (1984). On the appropriateness of adaptations in primary level basal readers: Reactions to remarks by Bertram Bruce. In R. Anderson, J. Osborn, & R. Tierney (Eds.), *Learning to read in American schools*. Hillsdale, NJ: Erlbaum.

Heath, S.B. (1983). *Ways with words: Language, life, and work in communities and classrooms*. Cambridge: Cambridge University Press.

Heimlich, J.E., & Pittelman, S.D. (1986). *Semantic mapping: Classroom applications*. Newark, DE: International Reading Association.

Johnson, D.D., & Pearson, P.D. (1984). *Teaching reading vocabulary, (2nd ed.)*. New York: Holt, Rinehart, & Winston.

Klein, M.L. (1988). *Teaching reading comprehension and vocabulary: A guide for teachers*. Englewood Cliffs, NJ: Prentice-Hall.

Maria, K. (1990). *Reading comprehension instruction: Issues and strategies*. Parkton, MD: York Press.

Marzano, R.J., & Marzano, J.S. (1988). *A cluster approach to elementary vocabulary instruction*. Newark, DE: International Reading Association.

McKeown, M.G. (1985). *The acquisition of word meaning from context by children of high and low ability*. (Outstanding Dissertation Monograph, 1985). Newark, DE: International Reading Association.

McKeown, M.G. (1993). Creating effective definitions for young word learners. *Reading Research Quarterly, 28*, 16-31.

McKeown, M.G., Beck, I.L., Omanson, R.C., & Pople, M.T. (1985). Some effects of the nature and frequency of vocabulary instruction on the knowledge and use of words. *Reading Research Quarterly, 20*, 522-535.

Mezynski, K. (1983). Issues concerning the acquisition of knowledge: Effects of vocabulary training on reading comprehension. *Review of Educational Research, 53*, 253-279.

Miller, G.A., & Gildea, P.M. (1987). How children learn words. *Scientific American, September*, 94-99.

Mullis, I.V., Campbell, J.R., & Farstrup, A.E. (1993). *Reading report card for the nation and the states*. Washington, DC: United States Printing Office.

Nagy, W.E. (1988). *Teaching vocabulary to improve reading comprehension*. Newark, DE: International Reading Association.

Nagy, W.E., & Herman, P.A. (1987). Breadth and depth of vocabulary knowledge: Implications for acquisition and instruction. In M.G. McKeown & M.E. Curtis (Eds.), *The nature of vocabulary acquisition*. Hillsdale, NJ: Erlbaum.

Nagy, W.E., Herman, P. A., & Anderson, R.C. (1985). *Learning word meanings from context: How broadly generalizable?* (Technical Report Number 347.) Urbana-Champaign: University of Illinois, Center for the Study of Reading.

Pany, D., & Jenkins, J.R. (1977). *Learning word meanings: A comparison of instructional procedures and effects on measures of reading comprehension with learning disabled students*. (Technical Report Number 25.) Urbana-Champaign: University of Illinois, Center for the Study of Reading.

298

Paris, S.G., & Lindauer, B.K. (1982). The development of cognitive skills during childhood. In B. Wolman, (Ed.), *Handbook of developmental psychology*. Englewood Cliffs, NJ: Prentice-Hall.

Perkins, D.N., & Salomon G. (1988). Teaching for transfer. *Educational Leadership, 46*(1), 22-33.

Richeck, M.A. (1988). Relating vocabulary learning to world knowledge. *Journal of Reading, 32*, 262-267.

Sable, P.H. (1988). *Vocabulary instruction in basal readers: Does it reflect research?* Unpublished qualifying paper, Harvard Graduate School of Education.

Sable, P.H. (1992). *Vocabulary instruction in fourth and fifth grades: What teachers say they do.* Unpublished doctoral dissertation, Harvard Graduate School of Education.

Schwartz, R. M. (1988). Learning to learn vocabulary in content area textbooks. *Journal of Reading, 38*, 108-118.

Stahl, S.M., & Fairbanks, M.M. (1986). The effects of vocabulary instruction: A model-based meta-analysis. *Review of Educational Research, 56*, 72-110.

Stahl, S.M., & Vancil, S.J. (1986). Discussion is what makes semantic maps work in vocabulary instruction. *Reading Teacher, 40*, 62-67.

Stanovich, K.E. (1986). Matthew effects in reading: Some consequences of individual differences in the acquisition of literacy. *Reading Research Quarterly, 21*(4), 360-406.

Sullivan, J. (1978). Comparing strategies of good and poor comprehenders. *Journal of Reading, 21*, 710-715.

Wixson, K.K. (1986). Vocabulary instruction and children's comprehension of basal stories. *Reading Research Quarterly, 21*, 316-329.

Wysocki, K., & Jenkins, J.R. (1987). Deriving word meanings through morphological generalization. *Reading Research Quarterly, 22*, 66-81.

Chapter 10. Writing: The Royal Road to Reading Comprehension

Sandra Stotsky, EdD
Harvard Graduate School of Education

Over a decade ago, I published an article (Stotsky, 1982) describing a number of writing activities that might enhance students' reading comprehension. The activities I discussed were dictation, paraphrasing, summary writing, sentence combining, outlining, copying, and the reproduction exercise. Although they were all potentially useful for developing a variety of reading (and listening) skills, some had never been the direct focus of research. However, there was support from related if not direct research for using all of them. In addition, many of these activities had been used for years if not centuries, in this country and elsewhere, as a regular feature of language instruction.

As I suggested at the time, these strategies generally provide a vehicle for encouraging students to engage actively with a text whether that text is presented orally or in writing. And as writing researchers and teachers have long observed, writing is an active learning process that focuses attention and demands thinking if sensible written expression is to emerge. It seemed reasonable to conclude that when students are asked to manipulate new information and ideas in some form of purposeful and meaningful writing, they must engage in active thinking and hence are likely to improve their comprehension of these new ideas and information.

Two years later, Anderson and Armbruster (1984) reviewed the research on a number of cognitive strategies—activities that were once referred to as the study skills. The studies that they critiqued focused on underlining, mapping, outlining, notetaking, networking, summary writing, self-generated questioning, and responding to attention-focusing questions interspersed throughout an instructional text. The review was not able to comment on academic journal writing because research on it had only just begun. Although there was still little research on summary writing and self-generated questioning, Anderson and Armbruster were able to conclude from the limited results they reviewed that any strategy could be useful if its use was appropriate to the task demanded of the student. However, they noted that some strategies, such as mapping or outlining, seemed to have more potential than others for promoting the processing of new information at deep conceptual levels.

And they believed, on the basis of the research that had been done, that students could benefit from using these strategies if they were taught their use, if they were helped to improve their use of these strategies, and if, in addition, they were taught metacognitive skills, that is, taught to make judgments about when a strategy might or might not be used most fruitfully or when understanding was or was not adequate. As the research suggested, students needed to be taught *how* to use and improve their use of study strategies that required them to recall, restate, reorganize, integrate, elaborate upon, or identify relationships among ideas. Without such instruction, students generally were not able to benefit from using them. If a student could not use a strategy to process informational material at a deep level, then the strategy was no more effective than just reading the text and reviewing it, or repetitive reading. And if a student could not use a mind-intensive strategy appropriately and efficiently on his or her own, then, as Anderson and Armbruster suggested, the student might not be willing to expend effort to use it at all.

It seems clear from my article, and from Anderson and Armbruster's review, that all students should be taught how to use cognitive strategies effectively, especially if they entail writing. Moreover, although much depends on the student's age, ability, and metacognitive skills, strategies that require both thinking and writing would seem to have educational value in the literature class as well as in the content area class.

In this chapter, I focus on four writing techniques that can be used productively in both settings: self-generated questioning, academic journal writing, summary writing, and dictation. I have chosen the first three because of their potential for developing higher level reading skills and because the research on self-generated questioning and summary writing, which grew markedly in the 1980s, seems to support their usefulness fairly consistently. I have chosen dictation because it is an exercise that can affect the learning of a number of lower level reading skills and it thus provides a useful balance to the other three strategies, even though students cannot engage in a dictation exercise independently of a teacher (or capable student) who must read the material that is being dictated. While dictation is not a study technique and is a very circumscribed writing activity in comparison to the other three, I believe it has much untapped potential for enhancing the learning of lower level skills in an integrated way and should be used more frequently than it is by both reading and writing teachers. Interested readers can refer to my 1982 article for details on copying, paraphrasing, sentence-combining, and the exercise in reproduction or recall. For an update on the results of research on the effects of sentence combining practice on reading comprehension, readers may refer to the succinct synthesis of the research literature in Wilkinson & Patty (1993).

Self-Generated Questioning

Self-generated questioning may be the single most important intellectual process in which students engage for developing understanding of idea-centered prose. Indeed, it seems to be an effective study technique in almost every study in which it is examined. According to Brown et al. (1983) and Palincsar & Brown (1984), asking and answering their own high-level questions as part of their learning seem to facilitate students' comprehension by inducing such cognitive activities as focusing attention, organizing the new material, and integrating the new information with existing knowledge. Further, as King (1992) suggests in a comparison of self-questioning, summarizing, and notetaking-review as strategies for learning from lectures, self-questioning provides learners with a way to test themselves; that is, it helps them to check how well they are comprehending what they are studying. And this is one kind of metacognitive skill many students need to develop. Indeed, King's own study found that self-questioning seemed to be even more effective than summarizing for long-term retention of the material.

As I have suggested in an earlier article on student-generated questioning (Stotsky, 1986) the ability to ask appropriate and substantive questions about ideas may be the essential component in critical thinking. For students who have been accustomed only to answering questions—and answering them in the way in which they think their teachers want them to be answered—learning how to ask questions may be a difficult learning experience. But it is a necessary one in view of the fact that asking questions does not seem to be a "natural" activity for students in school. According to reviews of research on question-asking behavior in the elementary school, children rarely ask questions in school (Dodl, 1965; Floyd, 1960), and when the quality of the few questions they ask is examined, they are usually judged to be extremely low-order ones that produce yes/no or single word answers concerning literal features of the material they are studying (Gallagher, 1965; Guszak, 1966).

One possible reason for the failure of teachers to encourage question-asking by their students is the seeming obsession in educational research with the questions the teacher asks. A great deal of effort has also focused on teaching students at all levels of education how to answer not only their teachers' questions and the questions that appear in their textbooks but also the questions that appear on standardized tests. However, there appears to be little research on how to teach students to ask intelligent, perceptive questions. This gap in the research is particularly surprising in view of the fact that most, if not all, textbooks on the teaching of reading recommend a technique for studying in the content areas called SQ3R—Survey, Question, Read, Recite, and Review. It is apparently assumed that students know how to ask questions, as I can find no helpful discussions in these texts on how to help students learn to ask the kinds of questions that will initiate genuine in-depth involvement with a particular subject. At best, these texts suggest that students invert the boldface section headings in their informational material into questions. While this is useful to do, this suggestion tends to make the students' questions completely textbased. Students' questions should also go beyond the text at hand.

How questions are formulated. What happens when children or adults try to formulate a question? First, in order to formulate any relevant question at all about a given topic, they focus on the subject under discussion, think about what it is or could be, and consider what questions could be directed to it. Then, as I have discovered in talking to teachers in workshop sessions over the years, questioners do several things, although not necessarily in the same order. They may try to classify the new subject with known subjects judged to be similar in nature so that questions that are appropriate for the known subject can be used for the new topic. I have called that "a transfer of knowledge-based categories." For example, the kinds of knowledge that most of us in this country are apt to have about the beliefs and practices of Judaism or Christianity are easily turned into questions for learning about a relatively unknown religion such as Buddhism or Islam. I have regularly seen participants at question-storming sessions ask if there are holy books, holy places, or places of worship for the new religion they are hypothetically about to study because they know that these exist for Christianity and Judaism.

Questioners may also search through their minds for what is known about the new subject, connecting ideas in some way. This kind of thinking—to recall to mind what is already known about a subject—can serve two purposes. First, it helps the questioner begin with the more obvious questions; these ease initiation into the activity of questioning. It also helps learners discover questions at the edge of their knowledge of the subject, particularly after the more obvious questions have been formulated and less obvious ones are being sought. These kinds of questions are extremely important for they can often turn the learner's attention to completely new areas to explore. In this way, asking questions not only requires thinking, it develops thinking.

Enhancing question formulation. Students at all educational levels seem to need some guidance in learning how to generate their own questions about a topic they have been asked to read or that they have chosen to explore. Students need to learn both how to ask questions and how to ask "good" questions. The first hurdle is getting students to ask questions at all. They can probably learn best how to generate questions by participating in question-generating sessions with their peers in preparation for reading about a particular topic in a content-area textbook. These question-storming sessions might well be considered one kind of collaborative learning. The opportunity to hear the kind of questions their peers raise is beneficial to all students and encourages even reluctant students to ask questions. And by accepting almost any question offered so long as it is at all relevant, the teacher provides a non-threatening environment for students to learn how to ask good questions.

For example, suppose students are to read an essay about national holidays. The teacher can start them off by asking students to come up with questions that they would expect to see answered or would like to see answered in this essay. Phrasing the directions in this way stimulates both prediction (what do they expect to see answered) and self-interest (what would they like to see answered). As they call out their questions, the teacher should be writing them on the chalkboard. Students might come up with such questions as:

> What is a national holiday?
> What are our national holidays?
> How do we celebrate a national holiday?
> Do we go to school on any national holiday?
> How does a national holiday get to be one?
> Who decides?

Why do we have national holidays?
Are they like other countries' national holidays?
Have we recently added or taken away any national holidays?
Has the way in which holidays are celebrated changed over time?

What is happening is that students are learning what specific questions are possible to raise about a particular subject. Moreover, every question that is put on the chalkboard may stimulate several others. This kind of cross-fertilization causes students to become aware of the many potentially critical attributes of the subject under discussion. It also helps students to learn different ways of forming questions.

The second hurdle is helping students appreciate the worth of self-generated questioning. Once a large number of questions have been generated, students can be asked to read the essay. They are apt to discover that their interest in the text material was piqued by the questions, and that material that addressed the questions became salient as they read through the chapter. They may also come to realize the value of non-textbased questions, as they will undoubtedly discover that many of their questions have not been answered by the chapter. Students could be asked to discuss how reasonable it was to expect information to answer these questions and what could account for the lack of information addressing them. The absence of information that one hopes to find in a particular source is often as informative as the information itself.

The third hurdle is helping students improve the quality or usefulness of their questions. Students can be helped to judge the quality of their questions in several ways. First, the teacher can show how questions can be divided into two general classes, open and closed. Closed questions are those that can be answered simply by yes or no or with one or two words or simple phrases, such as "When are the holidays?" Open questions are those that elicit a great deal of material, such as "Why do we have national holidays?" Even though closed questions lead to much more limited information, both kinds of questions are useful, and students should learn that they need to generate and explore both open and closed questions. Second, the teacher can ask students to judge for themselves which questions would seem to elicit more interesting or useful material, and which do not. It is important for the teacher to let students use their own judgment, and to encourage them to evaluate and prioritize any sets of questions they might generate on their own.

Although the goal of all this is to help students learn how to generate and write down their own questions as a regular study strategy before they undertake reading on their own, a number of sessions of group question-storming is invaluable for helping students discover the range of questions that can be generated about any topic. It also helps students learn how to set their own purposes for reading informational material, even if the material has been assigned by the teacher because it is part of the curriculum.

Contexts for question formulation. Once students have begun to learn how to ask their own questions about a variety of topics, there are many pedagogical contexts for the activity. The doing of the research paper is a chief one. Evaluation of self-generated questions is most useful when students are about to undertake a research paper. Before plunging into reference books and other sources of information, students should be guided to generate and evaluate a series of questions that could get them into their material most productively. Students who are not guided initially by their own questions as they begin to investigate a topic either take voluminous notes on everything they find on their topic or copy large sections of the texts they find because they have no specific focus for their reading. Researchers usually pursue questions of their own in their reading of the literature on a subject rather than read through everything they can find on a topic in order to discover a question. Student researchers need to be taught a similar way of proceeding so that their focus is narrowed to something manageable.

The literature class provides a very different but equally appropriate context for self-generated questioning. Jane Schaffer, a high school English teacher (1989), describes the way in which she uses student-generated questions to guide discussion after a literary text has been read. She asks students to generate three interpretive questions each in advance of class discussion, and she then selects the best ones to use for initiating discussion. Having all students write down their own questions before class discussion is also useful for ensuring that all students engage in some critical thinking about the text they have just read. Class discussions are so often dominated by a small number of students that such an activity makes sure that all students have to do some thinking of their own.

In another article on questioning by a high school English teacher, Valerie Hobbs (1988) describes how she developed and used "question" journals. Students had to formulate a number of "good" questions in a response journal as they proceeded on their own through an assigned informational or literary text. Afterwards, they had to work out a more formal piece of writing in response to the one they judged was the best. Over the course of the year, her students developed a number of criteria for a "good" question. A "good" question was one that:
> we all wanted the answer to,
> wasn't boring,
> would help us understand the whole chapter/book,
> made us want to answer it,

couldn't be found at the end of the chapter,
made us think,
couldn't be answered easily or forever,
helped us learn/understand something about life that we didn't know before,
made us ask more questions,
and, encouraged lots of answers.

As wonderful as this all sounds, Hobbs notes that at the end of the year some students reported that "thinking is just 'too hard'" and that they "prefer to write to assigned topics...rather than write their way into their own." For many students, "it is 'just too confusing' and, besides, there are too many questions that will never be answered" (p. 12). Such comments tell us about the current needs of our students and the critical importance of Hobbs' pedagogy.

Academic Journal Writing

The "question" journal that Hobbs evolved for use with her students is an excellent illustration of the way in which two useful study strategies have been intertwined. Just a few decades ago, it would have been difficult to find teachers who even tried to use journals for academic learning; at that time the journal was considered chiefly a repository of the writer's intimate thoughts on personal concerns, like a diary. But this situation was dramatically changed by teachers' responses to the views expressed by the authors of a study on the development of writing abilities from 11-18 carried out in England in the early 1970s and first published in 1975. After analyzing the kinds of writing assignments that British teachers gave their secondary students, James Britton and his associates concluded that most teachers tended to overemphasize, if not focus exclusively on, formal writing.

They did not give their students the opportunity to use more informal writing—"expressive" writing, as they termed it—for exploring and developing their ideas before shaping them in "transactional" writing—writing to convey knowledge or information to an external audience. Because these ideas seemed to make a lot of sense to teachers, the use of informal journal writing—or writing-to-learn activities, as they later came to be called—mushroomed throughout all areas of the curriculum, far beyond the composition class: in the literature class, this informal writing became known as the response journal; in other academic subjects, it was called the reading log, the learning log, or the academic journal. Students were not prevented from writing about their own experiences or making connections between their personal lives and what they were learning about. But the primary purpose of these journals was to encourage students to see writing as a way to elaborate and reflect on their own thinking about the ideas they were attempting to understand in their school subjects.   They were to do so without concern for genre conventions, the requirements of the written code, and textual coherence, all of which are entailed by formal writing to others—whether the teacher or another reader.

In-class journal writes. Teachers have found many ways in which to work in brief episodes of informal writing during on going classroom work. They may introduce a discussion class with a five-minute journal-write, using the journal to bridge the gap between the previous day's discussion and the focus of the current discussion. Or teachers may ask students to respond briefly to a quotation from a reading assignment as a way to get them to focus their attention on the subject and to compose their thoughts. Teachers may also end a class with a brief journal-write. Students may be asked to pull together information or ideas that they have learned during the class or write down questions that remain unanswered. As a way to refocus students during a rambling class discussion, teachers may interrupt the discussion and ask students to write about what the class is trying to explain and have them restate some of the main points of the argument. Simply as a change in pace during a lecture, teachers may ask students to write down briefly what is being discussed and any confusions or questions they may have.

Journal assignments for homework.   In contrast to these examples of in-class journal writing, teachers may assign it as homework. Students may be asked to record their thoughts and questions as they read an assigned chapter in a literature class or a content area class, or to maintain a record of and response to a current issue that they may be following in the media. Some teachers provide students with starter questions or sentence beginnings to get them going. Part of the purpose in doing so is to make sure that students approach their writing from a variety of perspectives.   For example, one list of sentence-beginnings I have seen used successfully by a science teacher to assist her students in writing journal entries on a regular basis includes:

> I realized…
> I noticed…
> I think…
> I was reminded of…
> I'm surprised that…
> I'd like to know…
> I'm not sure…
> Although it seems…
> I don't understand….

As an illustration, after reading and discussing rheumatoid arthritis in a health and disease class at the community college level, a student used several sentence beginnings to write the following as a homework assignment:

> I was surprised to find out that rest is recommended to someone with rheumatoid arthritis. I thought exercise would help so that the joints would not become stiff. I realized that there is no cure for rheumatoid arthritis but perhaps if early detection through a blood test treatment with anti-inflammatory drugs can begin.

> I was reminded that simply by being my age and gender, I am prone to yet another disorder in which I have no control. Also that every time I give blood I might get a little card in the mail telling me that my blood is no good because they ran a test on it which revealed some factor that no one else wants.

> I was surprised that x-rays showed rheumatoid arthritis. Too bad the joints have to be eroded away in order for it to be clear, other than the obvious soft tissue swelling. I'd like to know if stress has been directly linked to rheumatoid arthritis. Because I'm not sure if rheumatoid arthritis is the body's turning on itself in response to continual stimulants, as suggested by a few people.

For another journal entry, this time in a radiography class at the community college level, a student answered the teacher's question: What did you learn about producing radiographs from today's lab?

> Some new things that I learned was for one how to operate the x-ray machine. I also learned about setting the dials on the controller. I also learned how to develop an x-ray, but it is not that new to me because I work in a dental office and make x-rays all the time and I also develop them and somewhat understand how they work because I am in charge of cleaning the machines. I think it helped me to understand what I am doing. I also learned about the dosimeter which measures the amount of radiation the object is receiving.

The basic question posed by these writing assignments—what new things did you learn?—can be asked of students in any class at any level after any piece of informational reading. As can be seen, what these students have done through their informal journal entries is to recall and summarize the main points of their recent learning experiences.

Application in science class. Learning logs can be used productively in the science class and even by young children. In the elementary grades, students can be asked to keep a science journal in which they must simply write a page-long entry once or twice a week. The entry can be their own free writing based on a science observation or what they have read in a science book, or it can be a page of interesting facts they have copied verbatim. Just the activity of thinking about and writing down the information they find of interest to themselves is useful for vocabulary development and comprehension.

Learning logs can also be used in the science class to help students pull together what they have learned and to stimulate their curiosity for further information or observation. The teacher can ask the students simply to write down (1) what they learned, (2) what they didn't understand, and (3) what questions they want the answers to after they have completed a lesson or an observation. Or the teacher can ask students to fill out regularly on a response form the "answers" to the three following sentence beginnings after each science lesson:

Today in science I learned…
I don't understand…
I'd like to know more about…

One first grader, after a lesson on the sun and the moon, wrote down in answer to the first stem "that the sun lite reflects off the moon. And I learned that the earth turns like a spinning ball." Another child wrote "about the world. At the Surprise Center we are using the globe. We shine the flashlight on the earth and it goes to the moon." In response to the third stem the first child wrote "I would like to know more about the sun and the moon," while the second child wrote "the world and how the moon reflects onto the ground." As can be seen from these responses, further benefit of journal writing in the science class is that it provides students with the opportunity to use the vocabulary they are learning in meaningful writing, whether they write just phrases or complete sentences.

As these examples suggest, journal entries can be totally uncontrolled and unstructured by the teacher, as in an assignment to respond to a particular reading selection in whatever way the student wishes. Or they can be completely teacher-directed and teacher-structured, as in an assignment to summarize a particular reading selection or class discussion. These differences in use reflect the teacher's judgment as to what will benefit the students most, a judgment that is based largely on the needs of a particular discipline, the teacher's goals for a particular lesson, and the student's ability level. Some journals have become the opportunity for a written dialogue between the student and the teacher, with the teacher responding to a few of the student's entries with comments or questions. The size of the class and the time that the teacher is willing to give these assignments are critical factors in the decision to turn journal entries into a dialogue between teacher and student.

Cautions concerning journal use. Teachers need to know that despite the voluminous literature that now exists on writing across the curriculum and on writing to learn, there is little empirical literature to support the values claimed for academic journal writing. Anson & Beach (1990) did a study of their own at the college level after reviewing the research literature, and reported that the kinds of thinking encouraged by journal writing had little to do with the students' learning as measured on the objective tests given in the course. They also found that how much students wrote in their journals had little or no bearing on the kinds of entries they wrote. Although they acknowledged that the ways in which thinking and learning were measured in their study might not have been the best measures, nevertheless they noted that teachers need to monitor their use carefully and remain alert to what seem to be productive and unproductive ways in which students might use them.

A number of other cautions are in order for teachers who wish to use informal journal writing as a regular study strategy. First, beware of overuse. Any new idea is prone to overkill, and journal writing has become one of them. Students who are asked to keep journals in almost every subject are apt to develop an intense dislike of writing in any of them. Journal writing needs to be coordinated across the curriculum if it is a regular assignment. Second, avoid romanticizing them. Journals are not the magic strategy that will naturally lead to a high level of learning for all students. Much depends on the effort students are willing to put in. Even if there were a great deal of research evidence supporting the use of journal writing, no one technique can entail the exercise of all the intellectual processes that students must use for in-depth comprehension of any topic. Third, as with all strategies, many students need to look at a range of models that suggest the sorts of entries a teacher thinks might be appropriate. Fourth, as with all writing assignments, journals should be read through occasionally by the teacher and graded. Although journal writing should remain unevaluated writing from a compositional perspective, fluency and cogency should be rewarded as part of the students' final grade.

Summary Writing

Summary writing is an exercise in reading comprehension par excellence; it is also, according to Hood (1967), an exercise in vocabulary building, in sentence construction, and in clear, concise expression. Although students are frequently asked to summarize material they have read or heard, it is not clear how frequently or how well they are given instruction in summarizing. Summarizing entails a specific set of skills in its own right and should not be assigned (or expected in journal entries) with the assumption that students can compress ideas and information into at least one-third of their original bulk easily and without instruction. Summary writing needs to be taught and can be taught to students in the upper elementary grades as well as to secondary or postsecondary students. When a specified number of words is required, summary writing is called precis writing.

The basic tasks confronting the student in summary or precis writing are the selection of important facts, the rejection of unimportant ones, the brief restatement of key ideas by means of generalization, and determination of the controlling idea. Many researchers and educators have offered their ideas on how to teach summary writing (e.g., Brown & Day, 1983). However, I will draw heavily here on Karen D'Angelo's article (1983) on teaching summary writing to fourth grade students because it is the best I have seen for young students and can easily be adapted for older students.

According to D'Angelo, students must remember three things to help them write an accurate summary: they must identify topic sentences, rephrase material in their own words, and keep the order of the text, at least in the beginning. To help them with these tasks, she recommends lessons in each of the following: selecting topic sentences, identifying paragraph shapes, using synonyms, and rephrasing. D'Angelo points out that identifying the main ideas of paragraphs is often difficult but students must be able to locate them before beginning to write a summary.

To help students learn how to identify the main ideas in each paragraph of the materials they are learning to summarize, D'Angelo suggests that students first should be taught that there are four possible locations for a topic sentence in a paragraph (at the beginning, at the end, at both the beginning and the end, and within the paragraph) and that sometimes the topic sentence is not stated. Then they should be given practice selecting topic sentences and rejecting sentences that contain unimportant ideas in all these paragraph types. For help in finding the topic sentence, they should look for the most general and inclusive sentence in the paragraph. Students should also discuss their reasons for selecting a certain topic sentence. To help students use their own words to paraphrase important ideas in a text, students should be asked to supply synonyms for key words, if possible, using a dictionary or thesaurus if necessary.

D'Angelo recommends giving students many opportunities to practice these steps as a group so that they can discuss their choices and develop oral skill in rephrasing. As with the initial teaching of self-generated questioning, D'Angelo believes that students should learn to write group summaries as part of a group lesson before trying to write summaries on their own.

D'Angelo does not discuss how students can determine the controlling idea of the whole article when, as can happen, it is not simply the topic sentence of the opening paragraph. Colleen Rae (1986), a college teacher, recommends that students try to determine the author's main idea only after they have read through each paragraph and written the topic sentence or a one-sentence summary of each one. Then, she suggests, students should go through these topic sentences to try to come up with a word or short phrase that suggests what the author's focus is for the whole work. Most likely the controlling idea contains the key words in the article, whose importance can be determined by their frequency throughout the article but especially in its opening and closing paragraphs.

Dictation

Dictation has generally been used in this country only for teaching and testing in foreign language classes. However, it has long been used in many other countries as a regular part of their native language teaching. By dictation, I do not mean the dictation of isolated spelling words or sentences using those words. I mean the dictation of well-written, interesting, and complete passages from literature or non-literary informational prose for students to transcribe. At a surface level, it is a way to teach spelling, punctuation, capitalization, grammar, and handwriting in a meaningful context. At a deeper level, it is a highly structured way to give students practice in listening to, writing, and then reading worthwhile vocabulary and ideas or information in complete sentences in connected discourse. Thus, it is an exercise that contextualizes important skill work and integrates listening, writing, and reading.

In addition to providing contextualized practice for handwriting and spelling, regular dictation practice can enlarge a student's vocabulary. It clearly provides structured but active practice in listening to and writing words in context and, as research by Gipe (1978-1979) and Wolfe (1975) suggests, reading and studying new words in context seems to be the most effective method for developing vocabulary. It may also be a way of helping students incorporate part of their reading vocabulary into their writing vocabulary.

Finally, dictation gives students regular practice in proofreading, a skill and a habit that is rarely fully developed even by high school age. Structured proofreading practice may help them to proofread their own free writing more effectively.

Preparation for dictation. Well-written passages for dictation can easily be found in the unadapted literary and non-literary informational selections that are in the student's regular curriculum. It is important that the reading level of a passage be close to the students' reading level so that its ideas and vocabulary are within their reach. Unless the whole class can benefit from the same dictation passages, dictation groups might be similar to reading groups.

As I have discussed in an earlier article (Stotsky, 1983), the length of the passage depends upon the grade level and capability of the students. It is better, generally speaking, to begin with short passages of about three to four sentences in order to work out a smooth procedure for regular use. It is also best not to use passages with dialogue, as the language of dialogue is not usually enriching; third-person narrated passages or informational passages are much more satisfactory. Before a passage is given, it should be marked off in syntactic groups appropriate for the students' span of attention. Before the first dictation is given, the teacher should explain clearly what procedures he or she will use. If students are asked to skip every other line on their papers, it will be easier for them to insert omitted words and correct misspellings when these are discovered.

Dictation procedures. In traditional dictation, the passage is read aloud three times. The first reading acquaints students with the meaning of the selection, but students should not write. Difficult proper nouns and long words with unfamiliar spellings may be written on the chalkboard so that they do not serve as obstacles to fluent writing. Then the entire passage should be read slowly according to the syntactic phrases that have been marked off, with a pause after each one while the students write. There should be no repetitions. This is critical for developing their span of attention. Of course, the pace of reading and the length of the phrases should be adjusted for different ability groups, but students should be warned in advance that no repetition is allowed during the second reading. (If necessary, students with serious learning disabilities may need to have the second reading presented one-word-at-a-time at first in order to achieve success.) Punctuation may or may not be given orally depending on the learning focus of the dictation. In the earliest grades, telling the students "end of sentence" when the end of a sentence has been reached may be helpful and should automatically clue them into capitalizing the next word. For the third reading, the passage should be read at normal speed while students check for omitted or superfluous words.

To make the dictation a learning experience, not a testing session, students must make their own corrections by proofreading from the original passage. The passage can be either on the chalkboard (covered up during the dictation) or in their textbooks. Students will have a powerful incentive to improve their handwriting and to proofread carefully if they are graded only on the number of errors they do not find themselves. In this way, only unwillingness to proofread carefully is penalized, and no student is penalized for lack of spelling ability. Needless to say, when students have to read their own writing regularly to find their own errors, the care they take to make the dictation legible increases automatically. A dictation corrected by the student can also be given several days later as a test. Students can also be given the option of studying a passage as homework the night before a dictation lesson or a dictation test. Although teachers may collect the corrected dictations to give them a grade based on the number of errors the student did not find, they may also have students exchange papers and let them determine how many errors their peer failed to correct. Doing this reduces the amount of student work the teacher must grade herself, making the dictation exercise a more welcome addition to classroom practice.

After the dictation lesson has been completed, the dictation passage can be used as the basis for a vocabulary or grammar lesson or even as free writing. There are many ways to use a good piece of writing, and each passage will suggest a different focus.

Outcomes of using dictation. Although we have as yet no research on the benefits of frequent dictation practice, dictation exercises may be useful at all grade levels and for all kinds of students. It may be particularly beneficial for bilingual, learning disabled, and other special-needs students. As Pappas (1977) notes, dictation is a simple technique for developing the power of concentrated listening, for increasing the span of attention for phrases and sentences, and for developing facility in recording words exactly. It is obvious that students must pay attention in order to reproduce the dictated passage, and an immediate writing activity reinforces what the student has comprehended orally.

Moreover, dictation of syntactic phrases in increasingly larger units may be an effective way to develop students' span of attention for reading and writing in longer and longer phrases; as Amble's (1967) research found, training in phrase reading improved elementary school students' reading comprehension. And, finally, training in recording accurately the exact words of a passage may be important for limited English-speaking students who need to become more familiar with the variety of inflectional and derivational endings in English words in order to develop a better understanding of their semantic and syntactic uses. Frequent practice in writing exactly the vocabulary of informational prose in an interesting context may be far more effective for these students than simply reading it in context—or filling in blanks in multiple-choice exercises. In addition, regular practice in writing complete well-written sentences may help them develop a stable sense of English sentence structure and the sense of a complete sentence.

Concluding Remarks

One thing we should try to avoid as much as possible is teaching study strategies or writing exercises in isolation from each other. As Valerie Hobbs' "question" journal demonstrated, useful pedagogical techniques often reflect integration of several strategies. But that is not the only kind of integration that is useful. Teachers can also coordinate different thinking and writing activities across a series of lessons concerning one reading selection to allow for accumulated learning.

To show how one thoughtful teacher coordinated several activities for a series of lessons with some sixth and seventh grade students in a Chapter One program, I present the outline of her lessons and the summary that one of the students produced. The teacher first read the short opening paragraph of a six-paragraph selection about the Loch Ness Monster to her students. She then asked her students to raise as many questions as they could about what they thought the rest of the selection might tell them or what they wanted to know about. Next she read the story aloud, discussed it, and answered questions about it. She asked them to write down the main idea for the whole story and then write down the main idea for each paragraph and form a summary. She next dictated the opening paragraph and had students proofread for errors. Finally, she discussed with them the use of the comma in the first sentence to separate a word from an explanation of the word and had students punctuate similar types of sentences. The following is the summary produced by one of her students, with spelling and punctuation corrected.

> People believe that the Loch Ness monster exists, but other people don't believe it. Loch Ness is a lake in Scotland where they say there is a monster that exists in the lake. They call it Nessie. People say they have seen the Lock Ness monster at night. Other people say that they are imagining things. Robert Rines, a scientist, went to Loch Ness. He came from Boston. He set up a trap that the monster would come close to the cameras so they can take pictures of it. After a few weeks the monsters came towards them and they took pictures of it. It seems to be a picture of two monsters not just one. There might be two monsters not just one. But

some people still don't believe the pictures are enough. Some scientists are trying to take more pictures. People believe that the monster came in by an inlet and there was an avalanche that cut off the ocean from the lake.

I believe this teacher's lesson outline represents a fine effort to create a meaningful sequence of learning activities. I also think the student's summary reflects an excellent response.

As most teachers know from experience, we must try to avoid assumptive teaching. We cannot assume students know how to use study strategies—or how to use them well. It may be self-defeating to ask students to summarize material or to generate their own questions or outlines without teaching them how to do so and without giving them opportunities to learn how to improve their use of these strategies. We cannot teach reading comprehension explicitly in the sense that we teach students exactly how to construe something. But we can give them instruction and practice in using study techniques that require them to make connections between prior experience or knowledge and new information. Such instruction will show them how to construct their own understanding of something as well as give them practice in how to go about constructing an understanding of new information and ideas when they read on their own.

There is another, perhaps more important reason for us to give this kind of instruction regularly. Students need to learn that quality comprehension (or composition) requires hard work—and steady work. Neither reading well, nor writing well, comes easily and quickly to most people. To read (or write) effectively requires much mental effort as well as regular reading and writing. There are no magic pedagogical bullets that, if fired, turn students into good readers and writers. We do a grave disservice to our students if we let them think that there are shortcuts or substitutes for regular and thoughtful reading and writing. The rewards for active thinking are there, but they are intangible and internal. The intellectual and emotional satisfaction that results from having used one's mind well is the reward for the effort. The supreme challenge for teachers today is how to convince more students that the satisfaction they will gain from using their minds well is worth the effort.

References

Amble, B. (1967). Reading by phrases. *California Journal of Educational Research, 18*, 116-24.

Anderson, T., & Armbruster, B. (1984). In P. D. Pearson (Ed.), *Handbook of reading research*. NY: Longman, Inc. 657-679.

Anson, C., & Beach, R. (1990). *Research on writing to learn: The interesting case of academic journals.* Unpublished paper presented at the Conference on College Composition and Communication, Chicago, Illinois.

Brown, A.L., & Day, J. D. (1983). Macrorules for summarizing texts: The development of expertise. *Journal of Verbal Learning and Verbal Behavior, 22*, 1-14.

Brown, A.L., Bransford, J.D., Ferrara, R.A., & Campione, J.C. (1983). Learning, remembering and understanding. In J.H. Flavell and E.M. Markman, (Eds.), *Handbook of Child Psychology. Vol. III: Cognitive Development* (77-166). NY: Wiley.

Britton, J., Burges, T., Martin, N., McLeaod, A., & Rosen, H. (1975). *The development of writing abilities* (11-18). Great Britain: Macmillan Education Ltd.

D'Angelo, K. (1983). Precis writing: promoting vocabulary development and comprehension. *Journal of Reading,* March, 534-539.

Dodl, N. (1965). *Pupil questioning behavior in the context of classroom interaction.* Unpublished doctoral dissertation, Stanford University.

Floyd, W.D. (1960). *An analysis of the oral questioning activity in selected Colorado primary classrooms.* Unpublished doctoral dissertation, Colorado State College.

Gallagher, J. (1965). Expressive thought by gifted children in the classroom. *Elementary English, 42*, 559-569.

Gipe, J. (1978-1979). Investigating techniques for teaching word meaning. *Reading Research Quarterly, 14*, 624-644.

Guszak, F. (1966). *A study of teacher solicitation and student response interaction about reading content in selected second, fourth and sixth grades.* Unpublished doctoral dissertation, University of Wisconsin, 1966.

Hobbs, Valerie. (1988). Collective survival: Using question journals in the classroom. *The Quarterly of the National Writing Project and the Center for the Study of Writing, 10*, 9-12.

Hood, R. (1967). *Precis writing practice.* Cambridge, MA: Educators Publishing Service.

King, A. (1992). Comparison of self-questioning, summarizing, and notetaking-review as strategies for learning from lectures. *American Educational Research Journal, 29*, 303-323.

Palincsar, A., & Brown, A.L. (1984). Reciprocal teaching of comprehension fostering and monitoring activities. *Cognition and Instruction, 1*, 117-175.

Pappas, G. (1977). You mean you still give dictation? *Language Arts, 54*, 401-402.

Rae, C. (1986). Before the outline--the writing wheel. *College Teaching, 34*, 99-102.

Schaffer, J. (1989). Improving discussion questions: Is anyone out there listening? *English Journal,* April, 40-42.

Stotsky, S. (1982) The role of writing in developmental reading. *Journal of Reading, 25*(4), 330-341.

318

Stotsky, S. (1983). Dictation: Building listening, reading, and writing skills together. (1983). *The Leaflet*, Spring, *82*, 6-12.

Stotsky, S. (1986). Asking questions about ideas: A critical component in critical thinking. *The Leaflet*. Fall, *85*, 39-47.

Wilkinson, P., & Patty, D. (1993). The effects of sentence combining on the reading comprehension of fourth grade students. *Research in the Teaching of English, 27*, 104-125.

Wolfe, R. (1975). *An examination of the effects of teaching and reading vocabulary upon writing vocabulary in student composition*. Unpublished doctoral dissertation, University of Maryland. ED 114 818.

V. ASSESSMENT & APPLICATION

Chapter 11. Diagnosis: Developing Informed Reading Assessments and Interpretations

John O. Willis, EdD
Rivier College

The goal of an assessment of reading skills should ordinarily be to help determine an instructional program for a student in reading. The assessment should help decide what should be taught and how it should be taught. Sometimes an assessment of reading skills is conducted for other purposes. Students may be tested in connection with research projects or simply to classify the students in various categories of educational disability defined by state departments of education.

Some authorities also recommend the testing of skills other than reading. For example, some authors (e.g., Hynd & Cohen, 1983) insist that nothing less than a profound understanding of underlying neurological processes will permit an adequate assessment of reading. Often, too, testing is used to trace reading difficulties back to weaknesses in oral language or fundamental auditory skills. Acuity of vision and hearing certainly contribute to reading. Social and emotional issues can also play parts in the drama of a student's reading abilities.

Nonetheless, a reading assessment is generally most productive when it focuses on the determination of what aspects of reading abilities are in need of instruction (Chall & Curtis, 1990). Consequently, the process of identifying areas in need of reading instruction is the focus of this chapter.

CHAPTER ORGANIZATION

The assessment of reading is an extremely broad topic. This chapter concentrates primarily on issues concerned with how to provide a comprehensive assessment of a student's reading skills. The assumption underlying most of the discussion below is that the evaluator will work individually with the student for an hour or more and spend that time assessing the student's reading skills.

Specific reading tests. Specific tests are discussed in this chapter as examples that illustrate various points, but several caveats are in order. First, the mention of a test does not indicate endorsement of that test, in some cases quite the opposite. The absence of a test does not necessarily indicate disapproval. New tests and revisions of old ones are being published every day. Some of the citations of specific tests will be outdated before the chapter is printed. In most cases, revisions of tests are improvements, but this is not always true. Occasionally, the Yiddish term, *farpochket*, applies, referring to something that is damaged or destroyed in a misguided effort to fix or improve it.

The reader will also note that I seldom, if ever, recommend using only one test or approve all aspects of one test. I have yet to find one test that evaluates all important aspects of reading. Furthermore, the needs of some students dictate assessment of underlying skills as well as actual reading skills, so their evaluations must go beyond the scope of "reading" tests. In addition, sometimes the more skills that a single test battery attempts to cover, the less depth it gives to any skill. A point of diminishing returns can be reached where each subtest becomes so brief that reliability becomes unacceptably low.

A note on terminology. Although this chapter is generally written in standard English, some technical terminology and jargon (such as "reliability" in the paragraph above) have inevitably crept in. Because different readers will be familiar with different terms, most of the definitions will be found in the Glossary rather than within the text. Throughout the chapter, I refer to the person assessing reading as the "examiner" and the person whose reading is being assessed as the "student."

Assessment of reading is not possible without an understanding of the processes of reading, and it is not likely to be of much value without an understanding of approaches to instruction that might be recommended. This chapter assumes an understanding of reading competencies and instructional approaches presented earlier in this book. The chapter begins by placing reading assessment in the context of other assessments, such as intellectual testing. Here, "IQ" tests and what they do and do not contribute to reading assessments are discussed. Next, a section titled "Planning the Assessment" carries the examiner through the initial steps of planning.

These introductory sections are followed by discussion of various reading components: Passage Comprehension, Reading Vocabulary, Oral Vocabulary, Oral Reading of Passages, Oral Reading Decoding, and Auditory Skills and Phonemic Awareness. Each of these subsections examines some specific tests and attempts to highlight their strengths and weaknesses for various purposes. The hope is that the sometimes-detailed discussion will provide enough background to allow the examiner to understand, evaluate, and select tests and subtests currently available or available in the future, and to interpret test results intelligently.

The chapter closes with guidelines for conducting an assessment. These include suggestions for introducing and concluding an evaluation, along with "Some Rules for Testing Reading," a bluntly prescriptive list of procedures for planning and implementing an assessment. (See Figure 11.a below.)

READING ASSESSMENTS AND OTHER ASSESSMENTS

PLANNING THE ASSESSMENT

TESTING READING AND ITS SUBSKILLS
Passage Comprehension
Vocabulary Tested Through Reading
Vocabulary Tested Orally
Fluency and Accuracy in Oral Reading of Passages
Oral Decoding of Words
Auditory Skills and Phonemic Awareness

INTERACTIONS WITH THE STUDENT

SOME RULES FOR TESTING READING

CONCLUSIONS

Figure 11.a. Format of Chapter 11.

Reading Assessments and Other Assessments

Often, a student with reading difficulties is referred to a reading specialist who is asked to perform a reading assessment and report on the student's reading skills and needs. In many other instances, the reading assessment is part of a broader evaluation, such as a psychological, psychoeducational, neuropsychological, neurological, speech and language, or vocational evaluation. Regardless of its context, the reading assessment should be thorough and valid. Otherwise, it may do more harm than good by generating incorrect information and plans. Brief and careless "screenings" are not benign; they often lead to bad decisions about students' programs.

IQ AND READING

There can be considerable value to a thorough, comprehensive intellectual assessment that includes a thoughtful interpretation of intelligence testing. However, the relationship between tested IQ scores and reading is much weaker than is supposed. In fact, it is so weak that examiners interested primarily in testing reading might do best to ignore the student's IQ score.

For example, Hammill and McNutt (1981) collected all of the studies they could find, over a period of 30 years in 25 major journals, that compared Wechsler IQ scores and reading test scores. The median correlation between Full Scale Wechsler IQs and total scores on various reading tests was only 0.44. This means that only 19% (0.44 x 0.44 = 0.19) of the variance in total reading scores was attributable to Full Scale Wechsler IQ scores. The remaining 81% of the variance in total reading scores was attributable to other, unknown factors, such as, perhaps, number of books in the home, parental education, or auditory discrimination ability.

Even more surprising was Hammill and NcNutt's examination of correlations between individual Wechsler subtests and total reading scores. The subtest with the highest correlation with reading was not, for example, Vocabulary, general Information, or verbal Comprehension. It was Arithmetic. Arithmetic is the Wechsler subtest that, at least for children, is most like an achievement test and least like an IQ test. Achievement tests correlate better with each other than they do with IQ tests.

Classroom evidence further indicates that students with low IQ scores can learn to read. Fuller (1983) invented the Ball-Stick-Bird method of reading instruction and reported relatively little difficulty teaching not only reading decoding, but reading comprehension skills through a sixth grade level, to students with IQ scores lower than 60. Ursula Willis (1971) and many other teachers have taught elementary reading skills to students classified as moderately intellectually challenged ("moderately mentally retarded").

In short, the correlation between reading and IQ test scores is very modest; much of that small correlation comes from the achievement-test aspect of the IQ tests; and direct efforts to teach reading skills to intellectually challenged students are often successful. Furthermore, modern IQ test scores cannot be converted into mental ages. Consequently, there remains no justification whatsoever for computing potential reading levels from IQ test scores. The practice should simply be abolished without regret.[1]

In addition, IQ test score should never, under any circumstances, be used to terminate reading instruction. No matter how well or how badly a student might be reading, and no matter how intellectually challenged or gifted that student might be, it is always possible for that student to learn one more sight word or one more letter sound or one more phonetic or structural pattern. If so, then the student must be able to learn one more after that. The goal of a reading assessment should be to determine **how**—NOT whether—**the student can be taught to read better**.

THE ACID PROFILE

At least as far back as Altus (1953), researchers have attempted to find patterns of Wechsler (1949; 1974; 1991) subtest scores that are associated with reading difficulty. The most famous and most enduring is Altus's (1953) ACID profile: low scores on **A**rithmetic, **C**oding, **I**nformation, and **D**igit Span. The mental Arithmetic test and oral questions of general Information are, of course, at least as much achievement tests as intelligence tests, so low scores for weak readers on those

---

[1]These facts knock most of the supports out from beneath the various formulae that purport to predict reading ability levels from IQ test "mental ages." The final support collapses when we reflect that modern IQ test scores are not even based on mental ages. Until 1949 (Wechsler, 1949), children's IQ test scores were ratios between a "mental age" score and the child's actual age. They were literally intelligence "quotients." The abbreviation, IQ, has endured long beyond the concept. Since 1949, the now essentially universal trend has been toward "deviation IQs" based on the relationship of the child's score to the average and the variability of scores of other children the same age. "Mental ages," if they are used at all, are computed from the child's raw scores on the test or subtests, independently of the IQ scores. One simply cannot compute a "mental age" directly from the IQ score on a modern test.

tests are hardly surprising. Both tests also require considerable receptive language ability, some expressive language, auditory discrimination, and auditory memory, among other abilities.

Digit Span asks the student to repeat increasingly long series of digits dictated by the examiner and to repeat additional series in correct, reversed order. Weaknesses in rote, short-term, auditory, sequential concentration and memory, in auditory discrimination, or in hearing acuity might be expected to impair beginning reading progress.

The Coding subtest, for children of ages eight and over, asks the child to mark rows of randomly sequenced, printed digits with certain symbols according to a digit-symbol code at the top of the page. The score is the number marked correctly in two minutes. The Coding subtest requires, among other abilities, sequential organization, facile learning of written symbols, left-to-right organization, sustained concentration for two minutes, and willingness to work hard on an apparently pointless task simply because a teacher said to do it.

The ACID profile makes sense and is supported by research findings. However, there is less there than meets the eye. When students are referred for testing **because** of reading difficulty, the ACID profile sometimes does and sometimes does **not** reveal low scores. Either way, the students still exhibit reading difficulty.[2]

---

[2]There are many books and pamphlets that offer varying degrees of misinformation about the Wechsler IQ test subtests and what each subtest is alleged to "measure," an idea harking back to the "faculty psychology" of the 19th century, which enjoyed its special education heyday in the 1960s and 1970s, when students with learning disabilities were subjected by my colleagues and me to grueling exercises with balance beams, tether balls, and dittoed mazes in the forlorn hope of "remediating" deficiencies in "basic processes" to provide a foundation for academic progress. Myriad instruments were designed to "pretest" and "posttest" these "basic processes," and the Wechsler scales were also pressed into service for this, a purpose never anticipated by the author. The most striking aspects of these published lists of "abilities" allegedly measured by Wechsler subtests is that the lists almost never cite "intelligence" as one of the abilities required for success on any or all of the subtests of these instruments, which were developed explicitly to measure intelligence. Much of the material in most of these handbooks is a waste of time. Some of it may be actively harmful.

CONCLUSION

The best way to assess reading is by testing, observing, and listening to the student's reading. If the examiner suspects, from the reading assessment, that weaknesses in basic processes underlie the student's reading difficulty, those processes can be assessed further by methods designed for those purposes. Such methods include tests of hearing acuity, visual acuity, auditory discrimination, and memory. Intelligence testing is an essential part of a comprehensive assessment of a student's total intellectual functioning. In conjunction with a reading assessment, it can provide the valuable context of a more complete understanding of a student's cognitive functioning. It is not, even with well-designed instruments that yield fascinating profiles of scores, such as the various Wechsler scales, a very efficient or thorough means of directly assessing reading abilities and needs. A simple, uninterpreted IQ score by itself offers no contribution to a reading assessment.

Planning the Assessment

INITIAL STEPS

A good reading assessment should be a planned process directed toward a goal. It should attempt to answer specific questions. It should not be the blind application of a standard battery of tests.

Given this philosophy, the reading assessment must begin by collecting questions and concerns from teachers and, at least for minor students, from parents. The student's own questions are also essential, but must await the first meeting between the student and examiner. The examiner needs to know the specific reasons someone thinks there is a reading problem, such as difficulty understanding questions on science tests, apparent boredom with grade-level reading material that seems to be too easy, or failure to master the beginning, first-grade instruction in letter sounds.

Some observations may be in conflict; for example, there may be disagreements among various parents and teachers about how well or badly the student reads. One party may be deeply concerned and another not at all. The student's reading behavior may really vary among different settings. Various observers may have different standards or may be using different reference groups, such as classmates or older siblings. All of this information is important and should be catalogued by the examiner. Questionnaires, interviews, or telephone calls may be needed to clarify and refine questions, concerns, and observations.

The concerns and observations should be summarized in writing before the assessment begins, and the refined questions should be written so that they can be quoted and answered in the report. It is wise, almost essential, to write each portion of the report as soon as the information is available. The report will be written better and sooner than if it is postponed to a single burst of creative writing during some future weekend, based on long-forgotten events and sketchy notes.

The examiner must also review previous testing, including group tests, and previous report cards and progress reports. Limited knowledge of phonetic rules has a very different meaning for a student who has been exposed to only "whole language" than for one who has been receiving intensive training in phonics. A table of report card marks and a chronological report of comments are not very creative, but they convey the information clearly.

ORDER OF ASSESSMENT
The examiner is now ready to plan the initial stages of the assessment. Certain skills will certainly need to be evaluated. The first stage of the evaluation may suggest other areas that need to be explored as well. A good strategy is to begin with higher-order skills and work down until a floor of solid competence in more basic skills is reached. This approach usually requires less time and effort than beginning with the most basic, underlying skills and working up toward higher-order ones. The top-down approach also lowers the likelihood of chasing after red herrings: apparent weaknesses in basic skills that are no longer relevant at the student's present reading level or for which the student really is successfully compensating. Pursuit of such red herrings not only wastes time, but may result in recommendations that are grossly inappropriate.

Testing Reading and its Subskills

This section examines assessment practices and instruments by starting with broad comprehension skills, next moving to reading vocabulary, then to oral vocabulary, followed by oral decoding and finally phonemic awareness. This order reflects the hierarchy of broad to basic skills that a planned assessment might follow. When planning an assessment, this order should be applied with some thoughtful flexibility. For example, if a student is known to have very limited broad comprehension, extensive oral vocabulary, but difficulty with decoding, the assessment might take one measure of reading comprehension as a benchmark then focus more on identifying subskills of decoding in need of instruction rather than on broad comprehension.

In contrast, if a student is known to decode fluently, but to exhibit reading comprehension weaknesses, the assessment might examine comprehension and knowledge of word meanings from multiple vantage points and pick up a benchmark of decoding efficiency while testing comprehension of passages read orally. The reader may find it helpful to refer to Table 11.1 (following page) as an organizing framework while reading the following descriptions of various tests and subtests.

PASSAGE COMPREHENSION

Reading comprehension is a complex process that involves the interaction of many abilities. These include, but are not limited to, language, decoding, thinking, remembering, checking, and synthesizing. Efforts to measure this activity have produced many tests of reading comprehension arrayed in a vast number of formats.

There is a danger that these very different tests will be considered interchangeable measures of a monolithic skill of "reading comprehension." Yet no single test of reading comprehension even begins to test all of the major components of reading comprehension, and each test of reading comprehension is unavoidably flawed by compromises among various constraints and mutually exclusive objectives. The examiner's goal, therefore, cannot be to select THE correct reading comprehension test, or even THE correct reading comprehension test for a particular student. Instead, the examiner must select one, or probably more than one, reading comprehension test and use it or them with a lively awareness of the limitations of each test.

The following discussion of several popular reading comprehension tests is intended to give the examiner a few examples of the many available instruments, some insight into major strengths and weaknesses of those instruments and, especially, to provide a model of the type of analysis that the examiner should apply when selecting and interpreting any reading comprehension test. The tests used for examples below are grouped by format.

Read and answer. The traditional measure of reading comprehension is a test in which the student reads a passage and answers questions about the passage. Even this single procedure offers several variations, some examples of which follow.

Most items on the Kaufman Test of Educational Achievement, Comprehensive Form (K-TEA) (Kaufman & Kaufman, 1985) ask the student to read a brief passage and orally respond to one or two written questions at the end of the passage. The format is straightforward and appealing in its simplicity. Sometimes the student has more difficulty with the wording of the questions than with the passage itself, which is not a problem in the scoring, because this difficulty is part of the standardization and norming of the test. However, particular difficulty with the questions would be

Table 11.1. Subtests of a Few Reading Tests. (Test inclusion, exclusion, or order of appearance does not reflect test quality or usefulness. Use blank rows to add others.)

Test	Passage Comprehension	Reading Vocabulary	Oral Vocabulary	Oral Passages	Oral Word Decoding	Phonemic Awareness	Spelling
Diagnostic Assessment of Reading with Trial Teaching Strategies	S		L	O	O		W
Woodcock Reading Mastery Tests-R	S	O			O		
Kaufman Test of Educational Achievement - Comprehensive Form	S				O		W
Peabody Individual Achievement Test-R	S,M				O		M
Wechsler Individual Achievement Test	S				O		W
Gates-MacGinitie Reading Tests, 3rd ed.	S,M	S,M					
Gray Oral Reading Test-3	O,M			O			
Diagnostic Reading Scales-81	O,S			O	O	L	
Wide Range Achievement Test-R					O		W
Slosson Oral Reading Test-R					O		
Goldman-Fristoe-Woodcock Auditory Skills Test Battery					O	L	W

Key: S = silent reading　　O = oral reading　　M = multiple choice　　W = written response　　L = listen and respond orally a valuable observation worth pursuing with additional assessment, since following written directions is an important skill for school work (see Brody, 1987). The student's answers to the test questions, spontaneous comments, and replies to an examiner's inquiries can sometimes suggest whether there is more difficulty with the level of the vocabulary or with the complexity of the language of the passages.

The K-TEA offers a diagnostic analysis that classifies each question as factual or inferential comprehension along with norms to indicate whether the student showed a strength or weakness in each area compared to other students in the same grade who reached the same ceiling item on the test. This diagnostic analysis must be used with great caution because, for example, the student might miss a question, not because of difficulty with factual recall or inferential reasoning, but because the student could not understand any of the long words in the passage. In that case, specific categories of comprehension never came into play. In addition, the use of only one or two questions per passage seems to be a limitation.

The Wechsler Individual Achievement Test (WIAT) (Wechsler, 1992) Reading Comprehension test is very similar to that of the K-TEA. The major difference is that the student announces completion of the reading and the examiner then asks the one or two comprehension questions orally. The scoring of answers is extremely strict, and the manual warns the examiner not to deviate from the strict scoring, since this was how the test was standardized and normed.

Both the WIAT and the K-TEA mostly use relatively short passages of one to a few sentences. If a referral question for an older student involves study skills, the ability to sustain attention during long reading assignments, or comprehension of lengthy material in content-area reading (see Chapter 7), a test of brief passages, such as the K-TEA or WIAT, will not be sufficient. Comprehension of brief passages may provide valuable information, but a longer test, such as the Gates-MacGinitie Reading Tests (3rd ed.) (MacGinitie & MacGinitie, 1989), will also be required.

Some tests, such as the Diagnostic Reading Scales-Revised (DRS-81) (Spache, 1981) and the Gray Oral Reading Test—Third Edition (GORT-3) (Wiederholt & Bryant, 1992), ask the student to read passages aloud and then answer oral questions about the passages. On the Spache, the questions are purely oral and open-ended. On the GORT-3, the questions are multiple choice and are both shown to the student in print and simultaneously read aloud. The passages are, at most grade levels, longer than those on the K-TEA or WIAT, but still not long enough to help answer questions about study skills and sustained reading comprehension. Some of the questions, especially on the Spache, have high "blind ratios." Students may be able to answer some of the questions without reading the passage, e.g., "What was the girl's name?" "Where was she going?" "What did she do when she saw the red light?" [Mary, school, stop].

Chall and Curtis (1990) observe that some students do not easily comprehend material that they have read aloud. Such students may need to read silently in order to understand what they have read. The Spache partially addresses this concern by having the student read aloud successively more difficult passages and answer oral questions until the student's oral reading errors exceed a specified criterion. After that criterion is reached, the student continues to read more difficult passages silently and answer oral questions after each one until the student misses a specified number of questions for a passage. However, a student whose comprehension was severely impaired by oral reading might fail more than the allowed number of comprehension questions before making the specified number of oral reading errors. That student would never have a chance to attempt silent reading comprehension.

On the GORT-3, the student earns separate scores for the rate of reading, the number of reading errors, and the comprehension questions. The two oral reading scores are combined into a "passage" score, which has a basal and ceiling separate from the basal and ceiling for the comprehension score. It would seem that comprehension could then, as on the Spache, be measured separately from oral reading once a ceiling for oral reading had been reached. However, no explicit provision is made in the manual for allowing the student to read silently on higher-level passages after reaching a ceiling for oral reading speed and accuracy.

Allowing a student to stop reading aloud would also raise another problem. Just as Chall and Curtis observe that some students do not comprehend well while reading aloud, other students do not read carefully **unless** they read aloud. The latter group of students naturally exhibit limited performance on silent reading comprehension tests. Students who are distractible, tired, bored, unmotivated, resistant, or discouraged may pay attention to what they are reading only when they read aloud. The prudent examiner will include measures of comprehension of material read silently and material read aloud when students exhibit difficulty with silent reading comprehension.

The Spache and the GORT-3 both offer two forms. These are composed of parallel sets of passages of increasing difficulty. The Spache passages are identified by specific grade levels, which seem to be reasonably accurate for criterion-referenced purposes, although the identifications seem to have been arrived at arbitrarily and should not be taken too seriously. The availability of two sets of parallel passages on the Spache allows the examiner to discover those situations in which a student's comprehension of material read silently is very different from the student's comprehension of material read aloud.

The GORT-3 offers "standard scores" (which would be called "scaled scores" on most tests, since they have a mean of ten and a standard deviation of three) and percentile ranks for the reading rate, the reading accuracy, the difficult-to-interpret combined rate-and-accuracy "passage score," the comprehension, and the very-difficult-to-interpret total. Unfortunately, the commendable omission of grade equivalent scores on the earlier GORT-R (Wiederholt & Bryant, 1986) has been lost; the GORT-3 does offer these dangerously misleading statistics which the examiner should eschew in preference for the GORT-3 percentile or standard scores.

The Diagnostic Assessments of Reading with Trial Teaching Strategies (DARTTS) (Roswell & Chall, 1992) completely separates comprehension from oral reading. Comprehension is assessed with oral comprehension questions about a set of reading passages that do not have to be read aloud and which are not scored for reading accuracy, even if the student does choose to read aloud. Oral reading of text is assessed with a second set of passages without any comprehension questions. This is particularly helpful since some students become slow and inaccurate in their oral reading when they realize that they must prepare to be quizzed in comprehension as well.

The DARTTS measures the student's success by specified criteria on each of a series of graded passages. Consequently, the examiner can report both that the student's **oral reading** was acceptable on passages written at or below a certain grade level and that the student's **comprehension** was acceptable on passages written at or below a certain, possibly different, grade level. This use of passages identified by the grade level of the content is a very useful way of reporting reading scores and is very different from statistically deriving a grade equivalent score for a raw score on a test. With the Spache or the DARTTS, the examiner is reporting the highest grade level **of material** that the student could handle successfully. In contrast, tests yielding grade equivalent scores provide only the **average grade placement of students** who obtained the same number of raw score points as this student, even though this student may have struggled and failed on some passages far below that grade level or easily succeeded on others far above it.

The Gates-MacGinitie Reading Tests (3rd ed.) (MacGinitie & MacGinitie, 1989) and many other group tests offer a format of reading a passage and responding by marking answers to printed multiple-choice answers. The disadvantages of this format include the lack of interaction with the student and lack of any way to monitor the student's work until the tests are scored afterwards. The primary advantage is the length of the passages, usually longer than those for individual reading tests, and the total length of the test, which allows a better measure of the kind of sustained reading demanded by middle- and high-school courses. The large number of items and huge norming samples on group tests contribute to highly reliable scores, a virtue offset by the examiner's difficulty in monitoring the student's attention while taking the test.

Read and choose. The Peabody Individual Achievement Test-Revised (PIAT-R) (Dunn & Markwart, 1989) offers the unusual reading comprehension format of having the student read a sentence, turn a page, and, without looking back at the sentence, choose the one of four pictures that best illustrates the previously read sentence. For some reason, I find this odd format a strangely satisfying measure of reading comprehension, directly connecting the printed language with meaning and avoiding contamination by such factors as the student matching isolated words in multiple-choice answers with isolated words in the text. However, the PIAT-R also clearly differs from other reading comprehension tests, and is not measuring the same skills. It additionally puts a premium on memory. These differences imply that, although the PIAT-R correlates well with other reading comprehension tests, it might yield different results with an individual student.

Cloze technique. The Woodcock Reading Mastery Test-Revised (WRMT-R) (Woodcock, 1987) and Woodcock-Johnson Psychoeducational Battery-Revised (WJPB-R) (Woodcock & Johnson, 1989) offer reading comprehension tests with a fill-in-the-blank format, e.g., "'Woof!' said the _____ before biting the hand that fed it." The student tells the examiner the one word needed to complete the sentence. Two-word phrases synonymous with the correct answers are not acceptable, and the student is again asked for a one-word answer. This cloze technique measures grammatical knowledge as well as reading. Students with weak oral grammar are penalized, and students with strong oral grammar may earn inflated scores. There is one item for which the missing word is *such* in the phrase *such as*. Only the most grammatically sophisticated students pass that item since it is marked wrong when a student answers *like*.

I find there are so few reading comprehension items on the WJPB-R that, despite impressive standardization statistics, scores for individuals may be inflated or depressed by one or two lucky or unlucky guesses. Consequently, I am reluctant to use these reading tests.[3]   When I am using the rest of the WJPB-R achievement battery, I substitute the WRMT-R for the WJPB-R reading tests, preserving the format of the WJPB-R tests, but substantially increasing the number of items.

The cognitive battery of the WJPB-R includes a listening comprehension test that is similar format to the WRMT-R.   The student listens to a tape recording of sentences with missing words and tells the examiner the missing word.   This would allow a very precise comparison between listening and reading comprehension with both tests normed on the same sample, except for one difference: the missing word on the listening comprehension test is always the last word in the sentence.   There is still some value to the comparison, since both tests are normed on the same students, but the comparison is not perfect.   When teachers are taught to construct their own examinations, they are urged to write fill-in-the-blank items with missing words only at the end of the sentence because missing words imbedded within sentences are much more confusing and difficult.

Informal reading inventories.   Passage comprehension can also, of course, be assessed by examiner-made or published informal reading inventories (e.g., Ekwall, 1981).   The scope of the assessment is the same as with published, standardized, normed tests.   The examiner-made informal reading inventory has the

---

[3]Consider, for example, a student in the sixth month of grade five (5.6) whose actual reading comprehension ability, as measured by the WJPB-R form A test of naming the missing word in each passage, is precisely at grade 5.6, which is equivalent to a raw score of 24 points. If the student inattentively or impulsively misses two items, the grade equivalent drops a full year to 4.6, and the student's standard score falls from 100 (50th percentile) to 94 (30th percentile). If, instead, the student accidentally passes two additional items, the grade equivalent climbs more than a year to 6.9 for a standard score of 108 (70th percentile). The 68% confidence bands for the lucky and unlucky scores do not even overlap.

The WRMT-R also reflects large changes in scores for small numbers of lucky or unlucky guesses, but the longer tests show less variability than the shorter WJPB-R tests. For example, on the WRMT-R form G, the same student described above would drop from the 50th percentile to the 41st percentile by missing two items, thus remaining in the 5th or average stanine. If the same student scored two lucky guesses on the WRMT-R, the score would increase to the 65th percentile.

Clearly, examiners need to worry about the effects of random errors, even on longer tests. It is always wise to examine the norms tables of tests and perform thought experiments such as the one described above. In general, longer tests are to be preferred over very brief ones. Random errors on brief screening tests are not harmless, since they may precipitate unnecessary further testing or, worse, prevent further testing for a student who really needs it.

advantages of containing the precise material and format that the examiner wishes to use. The examiner-made inventory can also use materials from, or materials similar to those used in, the student's classes, an important consideration as curriculum-based assessment becomes more popular.

The examiner-made or published informal reading inventory should include measures of comprehension of passages read aloud and passages read silently. It should extend low enough to include a student's level of solid comprehension and high enough to include the student's level of very limited comprehension. Ideally, it should include material similar to what the student will encounter in science, social studies, English, and other classes. It should include passages as long as the longer passages that the student would be expected to read for classes. Except, perhaps, with very shy and inhibited youngsters who could write answers better than they could explain them orally, the comprehension questions should ordinarily be oral so that reading the questions and writing the answers do not become confounding variables clouding the assessment of reading comprehension. The questions should require both factual information and understanding that exceeds recall. In addition, students should not be able to answer the questions without reading the passage.

It is best to avoid placing undue emphasis on memory. When designing an inventory, distinguish between questions the student can answer immediately, from memory, and those the student can answer after re-reading part of the passage. The inventory should include questions calling for recall or location of important, factual information, for inferences from information given, and for predictions. When creating an inventory, try it out on students, who do not have reading difficulty, at various grade levels in the local school system. Even though materials were selected from the local curricula, there still could be questions that are much too easy or much too difficult for average readers.

The major limitation of examiner-made and published informal reading inventories is the lack of trustworthy norms. Such instruments may be thoroughly "standardized," that is, equipped with a standardized set of instructions so that they are always given precisely the same way under the same circumstances. However, they either are not "normed" at all or are normed very casually—little or no effort has been made to select a stratified, random, national sample of students who form a microcosm of the United States student population, nor to use the scores of such a sample as the yardstick for measuring the performance of other students.

If an evaluation/placement team is mindlessly using precise, numerical scores to make important decisions about students—a practice I find insupportable on logical, psychometric, and moral grounds—then precise norming becomes a paramount concern. For instance, one cannot compare reading results from an informal reading inventory to results from a normed intelligence test. However, in other situations, it may be far more useful to concentrate on information gleaned from an informal assessment. For example, it can be helpful to examine the social studies text that a student is expected to read; such a review could indicate that the text would present a problem for the student and require appropriate instruction.

VOCABULARY TESTED THROUGH READING

As discussed in Chapter 9, knowledge of word meanings is one of the essential foundations of reading. If a student has difficulty understanding a reading passage, one possible reason would be a limited reading vocabulary. In this instance, I am referring to understanding the meaning of printed words rather than the ability to decode words with or without understanding their meanings.

There are a great many kinds of reading vocabulary tests and a great many examples of each kind. As with the passage comprehension tests, each type of reading vocabulary test has advantages and disadvantages that the examiner must keep in mind when selecting, interpreting, and reporting results. Few characteristics of vocabulary tests are absolutely bad, but any of them can render an assessment inappropriate or invalid or misleading for a particular student. The following discussion of vocabulary tests describes their features, some aspects of what they measure, and how their construction may influence findings.

Oral synonyms and antonyms. The Woodcock Reading Mastery Tests-Revised (WRMT-R) (Woodcock, 1987) and the Woodcock-Johnson Psychoeducational Battery-Revised (WJPB-R) (Woodcock & Johnson, 1989) offer tests on which the student reads a word and states a synonym or antonym for the printed word. This is sometimes a useful technique, but it has its limitations. Thinking of synonyms and antonyms requires, besides knowledge of the meaning of the given word, specific types of verbal reasoning and also the ability to think of or "retrieve" a wanted word quickly. Problems with this "word-finding" ability are common among students identified as having specific learning disabilities (especially "language-based" specific learning disabilities) and speech/ language disabilities. As with the cloze technique discussed above, students with word-finding difficulties may understand the material on the test, but not be able to retrieve the single word needed for a correct answer. As on the cloze-technique tests, phrases are not acceptable for the WRMT-R antonyms and synonyms tests. If the student complains, "I know the word, but I can't think of the answer," ask the student what the printed word means. If the student is able to define several of the words without being able to think of synonyms or antonyms for them, this test is not a valid measure of reading vocabulary for that student.

Some students also have difficulty shifting between the synonyms and antonyms subtests. These students may need an intervening activity and some warm-up before beginning the second subtest, just as wine tasters clear their palates with cheese between wines.

Multiple-choice synonyms and antonyms. Many of the group achievement tests, such as the Gates-MacGinitie Reading Tests (3rd ed.) (MacGinitie & MacGinitie, 1989), offer multiple-choice tests asking for synonyms or antonyms for written words. These tests have the advantages of avoiding the word-finding problem and of providing a large number of words in a fairly narrow range of reading levels, since the group tests offer several different forms for different grade levels. They are also normed on vast numbers of students. However, the examiner has difficulty monitoring the student's care and attention, even if the test is administered individually.

Also, if the test is administered in a group, and if it has both synonym and antonym sections (as on the California Achievement Test), there is the danger of the student continuing to select synonyms when taking an antonym section. If the student's item analysis from a group test shows a much higher score for the first of two synonym and antonym sections, the student probably failed to make the change or failed to adhere to it.

Analogies. The WRMT-R measures reading vocabulary with a test of completing printed analogies, e.g., pig:domestic::aardvark:____" Once again, this test is contaminated by verbal reasoning and by word-finding abilities, so that students with strong verbal reasoning abilities who do not have word-finding difficulty will earn inflated scores, higher than simple reading vocabulary knowledge, and students with weak verbal reasoning skills or with word-finding difficulties will earn scores lower than their simple reading vocabularies.

Verbal reasoning abilities are important for reading, and word-finding difficulties are often related to reading disabilities. It is valuable to know about a student's verbal reasoning and about any word-finding difficulties the student may have. However, it is also important not to let these issues confound measurement of reading vocabulary. The examiner must be clear about what is being measured and reported.

The WRMT-R classifies each word in the reading vocabulary tests as General Reading, Science-Math, Social Studies, or Humanities. A numerical score is not offered for the number of items correctly responded to in each category, but the totals can be plotted on the Diagnostic Comprehension Profile on p. 15 of the WRMT-R Test Record and compared visually to one another.[4]

Oral definitions. Many oral vocabulary tests use the straight-forward approach of simply presenting a word for the student to define orally. Oddly enough, to the best of my knowledge, there are no silent reading vocabulary tests using this obvious approach. The Test of Written Language (2nd ed.) (TOWL-2) (Hammill & Larsen, 1988) has a written vocabulary subtest on which the student writes definitions of printed words, but this method deliberately adds assessment of writing skills to assessment of reading vocabulary.

Picture vocabulary tests. The lowest levels of some of the group reading tests, e.g., Gates-MacGinitie Reading Tests (3rd ed.) (MacGinitie & MacGinitie, 1989), provide reading vocabulary tests on which students match a picture to one of several printed words in a multiple-choice format. Sadly, to the best of my knowledge, none of these tests extends this format beyond early primary reading levels.

Informal reading vocabulary inventories. Here is an opportunity for an informal reading inventory to fill a gap in the offerings of existing normed tests. The examiner could take words from reading materials in the local curricula, present them in printed form, and ask the student what the words mean. Ambiguous responses should be questioned, neutrally—without "leading questions"—until the student's meaning is clear. General definitions that could apply to a great many words should also be questioned. The student should be given credit for any response that makes it clear that the student recognizes the printed word and knows what it means. If words were placed in separate lists from various curriculum materials, the examiner

---

[4]If further information is desired, the scores could also be compared to the oral science, social studies, and humanities knowledge tests on the older Woodcock-Johnson Psychoeducational Battery WJPB (Woodcock & Johnson, 1977). The older WJPB also offers oral tests of synonyms and antonyms and of completing analogies. It can be valuable to compare a student's performance on the written and oral versions of these tests. The results of these oral tests can be plotted on the WRMT-R Diagnostic Comprehension Profile of the WRMT-R to allow a direct comparison between analogous measures of oral and reading vocabularies.

could estimate the student's highest grade level of solid reading vocabulary in each subject area.

Another approach involves follow-up questioning after informal passage comprehension inventories. The examiner can ask in general if the words were difficult and can specifically ask for the meanings of some of the more challenging words in the passages with which the student had difficulty. This approach would not yield a score, but might shed some light on the source of the student's difficulty with passage comprehension.

VOCABULARY TESTED ORALLY

In-depth assessment of oral meaning vocabulary is beyond the scope of this chapter, but it provides a means of measuring knowledge of word meanings when a student's decoding skills are too limited to permit vocabulary assessment through a reading measure. It is particularly important not to confuse a meaning deficit for a decoding weakness or vice versa since vocabulary knowledge is essential to successful reading, as discussed above in chapters 2 and 9. For example, some oral reading errors, such as "hyperbowl" for "hyperbole," make it clear that the student's problem is with meaning vocabulary, not with decoding. Complaints such as, "I don't know what these words mean," can be another indication of difficulty with meaning vocabulary. As suggested above, the examiner can also question the student about the meaning of key words in a difficult informal inventory reading passage. If the student cannot decode a word, the examiner can tell the student the word and again ask about the meaning.

If the examiner begins to suspect that limitations of oral meaning vocabulary are contributing to the student's reading difficulty, there must be further investigation. It would be futile to continue teaching higher-level decoding skills alone without also teaching the definitions of words whose meanings are unfamiliar.

The Diagnostic Assessments of Reading with Trial Teaching Strategies (DARTTS) (Roswell & Chall, 1992) includes a test of oral meaning vocabulary. Like most of the other parts of this assessment, the DARTTS oral vocabulary test is organized by grade levels, so that the examiner reports that the student correctly defined acceptable numbers of words up through a given grade level and not beyond it. The test is much less sophisticated than the oral vocabulary tests used in speech/language, educational, and psychological assessments, but it provides some indication of the student's oral vocabulary. It can suggest whether limitations of oral vocabulary interfere with the student's reading progress or whether a strength in oral vocabulary could be exploited to support reading instruction.

If there appears to be a problem with oral vocabulary, the student should have a thorough and accurate assessment of it and probably of other oral language abilities as well. Such assessments are usually performed by speech/language pathologists, specialists in the assessment of intellectual functioning, and psychologists. The findings of the additional assessment should be **integrated** with the reading assessment report to create a more comprehensive picture of the student's academic functioning. These additional assessments should not be presented simply as separate packages integrated only by a staple.

When present, limitations of oral language should be ameliorated through work on oral language as part of the student's reading instruction or Individualized Education Program. Such limitations must never be taken as an excuse for giving up on instruction in reading nor as an indication that the student is already reading at maximum capacity.

FLUENCY AND ACCURACY IN ORAL READING OF PASSAGES

Above, we discussed assessment of **comprehension** during oral reading of passages. This section discusses assessment of **decoding fluency and accuracy** during oral reading of passages. As described in Chapter 5, fluent decoding enables a student to engage in reading for meaning more attentively. The tests described below provide some means of measuring the extent that students have achieved the automaticity in decoding connected text that will let them shift attention to meaning.

Many reading tests include oral reading of connected material. Some, such as the DARTTS (Roswell & Chall, 1992), completely separate the oral reading from comprehension. Most, such as the Diagnostic Reading Scales (Spache, 1981) and the GORT-3 (Wiederholt & Bryant, 1991) ask comprehension questions about material read aloud. The Diagnostic Reading Scales also include comprehension questions on passages read silently above the student's highest level of successful oral reading. The criteria for successful oral reading of the passages are based on the ratio of errors ("deviations from print" on the GORT-3) to the total number of words in the passage.

Each test of oral reading of connected material offers its own system of recording errors on the examiner's copy of the reading passage. Examiners may wish to adopt or adapt one of these systems and use it for all oral reading tests rather than continually changing systems from instrument to instrument. As suggested below, it would be wise and necessary to record a personal notation system so that, if asked, the examiner could demonstrate that it contains all of the information covered by the system published with a particular test in use. A more important point is that the examiner absolutely must adhere to the penalty system used with each test. Some tests penalize a student for errors even if the student spontaneously corrects them. Others do not. Some tests penalize a student for repetition of a single word, some for repetitions of more than one word, and others do not penalize at all for simple repetitions. An examiner needs to review the penalty rules when switching among oral reading tests.

The examiner must make a verbatim transcript of the student's reading, at least according to the errors "counted" by the test. It is good to maintain an accurate and complete record and notes that would permit later reading of the passage aloud exactly the way the student did, including pauses, repetitions (whether scored or not), and intonation. General characteristics of the student's reading should be noted while or immediately after the student reads, before the examiner begins to forget, for example, whether the student read word-by-word or in phrases, whether the student acknowledged punctuation (I cross out and insert punctuation marks to show how the student read aloud), and how much expression the student gave to the reading (interrogation and exclamation points may help with recording expression).

Grade-level designations of passage difficulty. The Diagnostic Assessments of Reading with Trial Teaching Strategies (DARTTS) (Roswell & Chall, 1992), Diagnostic Reading Scales (Spache, 1981), and published informal reading inventories identify each reading passage by its readability grade level and report a passing or non-passing performance for oral reading at each passage level. This is a useful way of looking at oral reading performance, so long as the examiner is careful to note situations in which a particular type of penalty rule depressed or inflated the student's reading score beyond reason.

The designation of the highest difficulty level of a passage read by a student is very different from a grade equivalent derived from the number of raw score points earned. The examiner is reporting that the student read satisfactorily from passages written up to a certain difficulty level, but not beyond that level. However, this designation still does not tell whether the student's performance was within, near, or far from the average range for the student's age or grade. Reading skills vary a good deal within any grade, so the successful reading of passages at levels one or two grades below or above grade placement may not deviate dramatically from the norm for that grade.

Within-group comparisons. The GORT-3 provides percentile ranks and "standard scores" (which would be called "scaled scores" on most tests, since they have a mean of 10 and a standard deviation of 3) for the rate (number of seconds to read the passage) and for the accuracy (number of "deviations from print") of the student's oral reading of a series of successively more difficult passages. There is also a "passage score" that combines the rate and accuracy measures in an odd and, to me, useless mixture. The standard score tells how far away the student's score is from the average for the student's age group, and the percentile rank tells the percent of students in the same age group whose scores this student tied or exceeded. These scores do not tell the highest grade level at which the student demonstrated acceptable oral reading accuracy. The grade equivalent score on the GORT-3 merely lists the average grade placement of other students who earned the same number of points for reading rate, reading accuracy, or the combined "passage" score. Grade equivalent scores may differ dramatically from the grade level of reading material that the student can read aloud, and those grade equivalent scores should **not** be used.

Informal inventories of oral reading. For the examiner who wishes to use them, there are published informal reading inventories that include measures of oral reading. Examiners can also make their own oral reading tests, using local curriculum materials (e.g. see Chapter 5 Appendix, p. 195). A rigorous recording system should, of course, be employed as described above. Even in high school, oral reading of connected material can allow an examiner to determine whether work on oral reading fluency would help improve the student's overall reading skills and whether teachers should be encouraged to have the student read aloud in class or should be discouraged from doing so.

ORAL DECODING OF WORDS

Most reading tests include measures of oral reading of words. This valuable exercise helps the examiner assess a student's ability to decode a word without using cues from the context in which the word may appear. Reading in context is a much more "natural" process and a major portion of mature reading. However, in order to advance to the level of mature reading, the student must first be able to figure out what the words say. Chapters 4 and 5 discuss in depth the processes of learning to decode words. Assessment of reading of less skilled readers needs to include a measure of reading single words aloud.

Recording responses. When testing oral reading of words, examiners should record verbatim the student's preliminary attempts at reading a word, some indication of the length of time before starting to pronounce the word, the length of any pauses before the student finishes with the word, and the final pronunciation of the word. This can be accomplished by marking any mispronunciations on the examiner's sheet followed by "sc" (for self-correct) to indicate that the word was finally read accurately. The subsequent analysis of the transcript may be the most valuable aspect of this part of the assessment.

Untimed word lists. Many oral reading tests, such as those of the WRMT-R (Woodcock, 1987), K-TEA (Kaufman & Kaufman, 1985), and WIAT (Wechsler, 1992), ask the student to read words aloud from lists of unrelated, increasingly difficult words. The student is allowed to take the necessary time to attempt each word, and the student's final decision is accepted. These are "power" tests that permit the student to use recall of "sight" words as well as phonetic and structural analysis skills. The examiner's verbatim transcript, including latencies—time from initial encounter to final reading of a word—helps distinguish sight words from words that were analyzed.

Timed word lists. Other tests, such as the SORT-R (Slosson, 1991) and Diagnostic Reading Scales (Spache, 1981) put a time limit on the student's response to each word. These tests are designed to test "automaticity," or the student's immediate recall of sight vocabulary and instant application of decoding skills. Many examiners are comfortable using an untimed test and determining whether the student read most of the words quickly. Other examiners prefer to use both a timed and an untimed oral reading test. The disadvantage of the first approach is that the distinction between automatic and non-automatic words is determined subjectively and may not be accurate. The disadvantage of the second approach is that the norming samples of the different reading tests are radically different, and it is not always safe to compare scores on different reading tests. Schultz (1988) compared nine popular reading tests and reported extraordinarily different scores for the same level of skill. In one example, a six-year-old student who could name all letters, but not read any words on a test, would receive standard scores (mean = 100, standard deviation = 15) ranging from 65 to 98 on the various tests!

Timed oral reading tests should always be accompanied by untimed measures as well, since automatic reading of words is one important skill, but phonetic and structural analysis are also essential to comprehension of unfamiliar words and text.

Grade-level word lists. Many tests, such as the DARTTS and the SORT-R, group words into brief lists. Each list is composed of words at a difficulty level typically found at a particular grade level. The DARTTS reports performance in terms of the grade level of the highest list on which the student correctly read the requisite number of words.

Single word lists. Other tests, such as the K-TEA, WIAT, and WRMT-R use a single, increasingly difficult, list with a "ceiling rule" to determine when to stop testing the student after a certain number of errors. The raw score is the number of words read correctly plus any words not tested below the student's "basal" level (a certain number of words read correctly). This raw score is translated into a standard score and percentile rank. In some cases, a grade equivalent is also available, but should not be used.

It would be most helpful to know both the grade level of the highest group of words that a student could read easily and also how that student's performance compared to the scores of other students in the same grade or of the same age. Decisions concerning whether to test both or one are often based on the time available for assessment along with sensitivity to avoid wearing out the student with testing since few tests offer both kinds of information.

Nonsense words and word fragments. Several instruments, such as the Diagnostic Reading Scales and the DARTTS, provide tests of reading aloud parts of words, such as common syllables, vowels, consonants, digraphs, diphthongs, and blends. Such tests are usually criterion-referenced with, at most, a footnote indicating the grade level at which the particular skill is usually taught. There really is little need for normative data on these skills. If, for instance, a student can read most single consonants, some digraphs, and no blends, the instructional implications are clear, regardless of the student's age or grade placement or the performance of other students of the same age or grade. At this point in the assessment process, the question is no longer whether there is a reading problem, but what specific skills need instruction. That question does not require comparison with age or grade peers.

Some tests, such as the Goldman-Fristoe-Woodcock Auditory Skills Test Battery Sound-Symbol Tests (GFW) (Goldman, Fristoe, & Woodcock, 1974) and the WRMT-R use lists of nonsense words, such as "blik" or "slopeck," to test phonetic word attack skills. The GFW also offers a test of written spelling of dictated nonsense words. The Diagnostic Reading Scales use nonsense words as carriers for the sounds being tested. For instance, short vowel sounds might be tested with the list, "bap, bep, bip, bop, bup." Nonsense words are very appealing vehicles for testing phonetic word attack, since they eliminate any confusion with sight vocabulary. However, they must be used with great caution, since the process of reading a nonsense word is very different from that of reading a real word, and some students are confused or even upset by the idea of trying to read words that are not real. I usually use the word "fake" in my introductory discussion with the student before beginning testing, and I explain that the goal is to see how the student can sound out words that the student has never seen before.

The GFW and WRMT-R nonsense word tests offer error inventories that allow the examiner to specify which sounds were read incorrectly. This is a useful analysis, but is not as direct and may not be as effective as the approach used by the DARTTS or Diagnostic Reading Scales of using specific word lists to test particular phonetic word attack skills.

Use of word decoding tests. The oral reading decoding tests have the purpose of analyzing the student's ability to decode individual words in isolation. Consequently, the examiner's verbatim transcriptions of errors and latencies are crucial. The examiner is attempting to determine the level of the student's reliable sight vocabulary, the phonetic and structural analysis skills that the student can apply reliably, and gaps in the student's reading skills that should become instructional goals. The Diagnostic Assessments of Reading with Trial Teaching Strategies (DARTTS) is unique in including a separate set of mini-lessons that the examiner can use with the student to assess the student's ability to learn the missing skills and to evaluate possible methods of instruction.

Informal inventories of word decoding. These goals can also be accomplished through informal inventories. If an oral reading score is going to be used as part of an official determination of need for remedial reading or special education, then a normed test would be necessary, although score cut-offs and formulae should never be used alone to determine eligibility for services. An examiner-made inventory could be tied very closely to reading materials such as reading series, literature, and content-area textbooks in the local school system. However, it is essential that the favored method or methods of reading instruction in the child's school **not** be allowed to limit the skills tested nor the reading methods and materials considered. No single system of reading instruction is going to be effective for all students at all times. There always will need to be exceptions, and one goal of the reading assessment is to identify those exceptions.

AUDITORY SKILLS AND PHONEMIC AWARENESS
If the student is experiencing serious difficulties with oral decoding of single words, it is probable that there is an even more basic weakness in auditory skills and phonemic awareness as discussed in Chapter 3. The student may have difficulty hearing sounds correctly, discriminating between similar sounds, determining the order of sounds in a word, identifying the different sounds in a word, or even realizing that a word is made up of separate sounds. Although these skills are

essential foundations for reading, adequate assessment of them is a highly specialized field and beyond the scope of this chapter.

The following tests may be used to assess phonemic awareness informally. The GFW provides some tests of several aspects of auditory skills, which are easy to administer thanks to tape-recorded test materials, but which are difficult to interpret. Norms for the GFW are old and based on small, poorly defined samples. The Lindamood Auditory Conceptualization Test (revised edition) (LAC) (Lindamood & Lindamood, 1979) offers valuable activities for assessing phonemic awareness. The WJPB-R includes a Sound Blending subtest that is taped and well-normed, but very brief. If the student's single-word decoding skills suggest underlying auditory difficulties, an examiner who is not trained in this area of assessment should seek such training or refer the student to an audiologist, speech/language pathologist, specialist in the assessment of intellectual functioning, psychologist, or reading or learning disabilities specialist who does have the requisite training. It is essential that the fundamental auditory skills be assessed thoroughly and precisely, if there are possible difficulties in this area, since remedial training is likely to be challenging, but effective.

Interactions with the Student

Introducing the assessment. The examiner's first contact with the student will help determine the value of the evaluation. The evaluation should be a pleasant or at least tolerable experience for the student. It should: leave the student with some accurate information about his or her reading skills, enhance or at least not impair the student's self-esteem, and yield recommendations that will be useful for the student's progress in reading.

In introducing the evaluation, it is important to displace the emphasis from the student's possible deficiencies onto the student's reading instructional program. I usually begin by asking what the student knows and suspects about the evaluation, including its purpose and nature. Then I offer a comment such as the following.

> Everyone is better at some things than at others, but it is different things for different people, of course. What I am trying to do is find out which are easier for you—which things you are best at—and which are hardest for you. If your teachers know more about what things you are best at and which you might need more help with, then they should be able to teach you better, so this is mostly to help them. However, to find out these things, I have to ask you to [brief description of planned activities]. Some of the things we do will be too easy. Please don't be insulted. Some of them will be too difficult. They are really

for older students [I often specify a grade level well above the student's, roughly corresponding to the ceiling-level items the student will encounter]. We need those to make sure we don't miss anything you are especially good at. You may not be able to do those since you've not been in [grade X, high school, college, graduate school, etc.] yet. Just do the best you can. On most of the things we do, I am not allowed to tell you if you are right or wrong or tell you the answers. Whenever I can, I will. Don't assume my little comments, like "umhm," mean you are right. I'm just thanking you for answering. If I don't say anything, it just means I didn't say anything. You can always change your answers. After we are all done, I will go over all the results with you. You will be the first to find out what happened. Later, I will [explanation of planned meetings and reports].

I never promise any particular format for reviewing the results. I do not want to promise, for example, numerical test scores and then discover to my horror that the student is reading much worse than I had suspected. Sometimes I do give the student numerical scores. Often I provide a table listing, for example, "Things You Were Best At" and "Things That Were More Difficult For You." I defer the decision on how to report the results until later in the assessment.

After the introduction, I solicit questions, concerns, and observations from the student. After my presentation, the student may have additional responses to my earlier question of what the student knows or suspects about the evaluation.

Examiners differ on how much time to spend introducing an evaluation and establishing rapport. Each examiner needs to find a comfortable style, but remain flexible in adapting it to each student. I find that most students usually remain worried until the testing actually begins and the tests evolve from abstractions into realities. Therefore, after the above introduction and discussion of the student's comments and questions, I generally move right into the first test. I find that additional conversation is more productive after the student has had an opportunity to experience some testing and to get to know me in that context.

During the testing, students often recall the introduction and ask me if a particular, difficult item is at the X grade level. I am usually inclined to agree that it is, since any item is within the broad range of abilities for any grade. I am not saying that the student is working at grade level X or even that the student passed an item at that level, since I am not telling the student whether the response was correct.

It is sometimes necessary to halt testing occasionally to answer further questions. This is usually time well spent, unless the student is making a serious effort to stall. In that case, it can be helpful to remind the student that the length of the evaluation is determined by the material to be covered, not by the time originally planned for the assessment.

The goals of these interactions with the student are to obtain the most valid possible samples of the student's reading and to build the student's legitimate self-confidence about reading. These goals cannot be accomplished mechanically. It is essential to clear your mind of the other pressures of the day and concentrate completely on building this brief, but important relationship as well as you can. You have an opportunity to do some good or a great deal of harm.

Sharing assessment findings with the student. Most tests forbid feedback to the student during the exam, and that rule must be adhered to if the test norms are to be used. However, even though specific feedback about the correctness of responses is forbidden, most tests do allow general encouragement and allow more specific feedback between subtests. One of the obvious virtues of the DARTTS is that it permits much more encouragement of the student than do most standardized reading tests. The examiner would be wise to read the manuals for the DARTTS if for no other reason than to gain an idea of the kinds of encouragement that can be offered to the student. Throughout the assessment, it is important to remind the student of the purpose: finding more effective ways for the student to be taught reading skills. Even if a student obviously has a hopeless struggle with a subtest, the examiner can express satisfaction that the test helped clarify exactly what can be worked on.

It is very important to elicit from the student some idea of the student's own assessment of reading strengths and weaknesses and a detailed picture of the student's interests in and attitudes toward reading. The School Self-Rating Scale (SSRS) (RSEC Staff, 1993) is one vehicle for beginning this assessment of the student's own perceptions, attitudes, and interests.

The concluding interview ("debriefing") with the student should provide specific, concrete information about the student's test results. When results are not promised in any particular form, examiners are free to use a form most appropriate for the particular student and the results obtained. In some cases, I present a table of test scores in stanines. In others, I recall the discussion of "things you are best at and things that are most difficult for you" and give the student two such lists, always including more skills in the first than the second list. The debriefing should include reference to the self-perceptions, attitudes, and interests expressed by the student, and it should focus on the recommended instruction, without promising delivery of services that the examiner cannot guarantee. Above all, the debriefing should end on a truthfully optimistic note.

Some Rules for Testing Reading

Following are some basic testing rules developed from more than a quarter-century of painful mistakes I have made or witnessed in testing reading skills. Since my purpose is to summarize ideas elaborated earlier in this chapter, these rules are presented very bluntly and dogmatically with little explanation. The points are reiterated here to protect you, and therefore your students, from repeating these mistakes. I hope that a brief list will serve as a ready reference for future use.

1. **Do not alter standardized tests**. If the format of the test is uncomfortable for you or inappropriate for your student, do not use that test. **Do not use a norm-referenced, standardized test for informal testing**. This is the reason we have informal reading inventories. If you give a norm-referenced, standardized test, **administer it precisely as instructed**. Do not change the wording of directions at all, although you should read them in a natural, pleasant tone. Treat the directions like the lines in a play, delivered smoothly, naturally, and with expression, but absolutely verbatim.

Obey the basal and ceiling rules, and make sure you have them right, since they vary from test to test. Carefully observe time limits. If you are compelled to "test the limits" after standardized administration, for instance by allowing additional time for pronouncing words on the Slosson Oral Reading Test-Revised (SORT-R) (Slosson, 1991) or the Wide Range Achievement Test-Revised (WRAT-R) (Jastak & Wilkinson, 1984), carefully and blatantly label the results everywhere they appear in your report. When reporting findings that occur with additional time or prompts, avoid giving a specific score, instead simply state that the student performed better when time limits were ignored. Each and every time the result is mentioned or listed, make it abundantly clear once more to your reader that these are not norm-based, but only your experiments. Otherwise, someone will eventually mistake your experiments for valid scores, with dire consequences when the student is re-evaluated. It would, however, be far better to substitute another test that does not require the constraints you find distasteful.

2. **Never report test scores or results that are misleading or untrue**. Simply report that you gave the test and obtained invalid results and explain the reason. **Do not specify the invalid results** because I promise you that someone will

copy the number or classification onto a form where it will haunt you and the student for years to come.

3. **Pay attention to norming samples**. If an examiner cannot resist the seriously risky and unwise compulsion to use a badly normed, standardized test instead of an informal test or a well-normed one for "diagnostic" purposes, the scores from the badly normed test should not be reported under any circumstances.

4. If a skill is worth testing at all, **test with an adequate number of examples** so that random fluctuations in performance do not excessively inflate or depress assessment results. No matter what the published statistics say, a single lucky or unlucky guess on a very brief test can dramatically change a score. Before considering the use of a brief reading test, look at the norms tables to see what would be the effect, for someone the age of your student, of raising or lowering a raw score by two points. If the effect is large, seek an alternative. Misleading data are worse than none at all.

5. **Record the student's oral reading and answers to questions verbatim**. Whenever the student reads aloud, use an expendable copy of the passage or word list that you can mark to reflect precisely the way the student read it, including: long, short, and very long pauses; misplaced stresses; repetitions of sounds, syllables, and words; insertions; omissions; substitutions; and words provided by the examiner. Various reading tests (e.g., Spache, 1981; Wiederholt & Bryant, 1992) offer such editing systems. Most examiners prefer to develop their own systems that they can use consistently on different tests. It would be well to record your own system so that it could be submitted along with the manuals for the tests used and the test record forms if raw data were subpoenaed for a legal action. The record would demonstrate that the personalized system included everything in the systems offered with the various tests used.

6. **When reporting numerical scores, limit the scoring systems used and include a clear explanation of each system** (Willis, 1990, pp. 24-26). Nothing bewilders and antagonizes readers faster than a statistical Tower of Babel with age equivalents, grade equivalents, and age-based and grade-based standard scores, scaled scores, percentiles, percentile ranks, and quotients used apparently interchangeably and without explanation. If the examiner finds it difficult to translate a confusion of scores into a single statistical system, imagine how difficult it must be for many parents and many classroom teachers, who may not have recent, advanced, graduate training in mental-test statistics. When several examiners test the same student, the examiners should agree on a single statistical framework for the student's reports.

Failing such utopian consensus, the team members should at least be punctilious in clearly and graphically defining each statistic they use. The alternative is confusion, misunderstanding, resentment, and bad decisions.

7. **Use nonsense words with caution**. I find them very useful for testing phonics skills, since they guarantee that the student will not be familiar with the test words, unless the student is subjected to frequent re-evaluations with the same form of the same test under a seemingly misguided Individualized Education Program (IEP). However, some students are disturbed by the mere concept of reading words that are not real words, and other students who can accept the idea still cannot resist substituting similar-sounding, real words. Furthermore, there is the danger of false generalizations. The process of sounding out a nonsense word in a list is not quite the same as that of decoding an unfamiliar, real word in a list and is very different from decoding an unfamiliar word in a meaningful reading passage.

8. When tests offer both grade and age norms, always **calculate scores compared to students of the same age *and* compared to students in the same grade**. If the scores are similar by both methods, you can report only one set, better the age-based ones, if other tests are used which offer only age-based scores. If scores are different by the two comparisons, then report both sets, since the complete truth is found in neither alone.

9. **Be cautious with fall-spring or fall-winter-spring norms**. For younger students, the drop in scores overnight from one season to the next can be dramatic (Willis, 1990, p. 73-74).

10. **Be wary of grade-equivalent or other misleading test scores**. Tests which offer grade-equivalent scores corresponding to a number of points earned by a student can be very misleading, e.g., Willis (1977). The same number of points, and therefore the same grade equivalent, might be earned by three students, one of whom read through a sixth grade level very well, but could not read much of anything above that level, another of whom read well only through a third grade level, but accumulated additional points for partial successes to a ninth grade level, and yet another who read with moderate but inconsistent accuracy to an eighth grade level. Labeling all three students as sixth-grade-level readers would be seriously misleading. The International Reading Association (1982) has wisely condemned grade equivalent scores for reading tests.

Likewise, be aware that the "easy" and "difficult" grade-equivalent ratings on the Woodcock Reading Mastery Tests-Revised (WRMT-R) (Woodcock, 1987) are not based on actual passages at certain grade levels which the particular student read easily or with difficulty, but on confidence bands established with the norming sample. Instead of these scores, examiners should report only percentile or standard scores. A grade-level designation of material that a student reads easily, reads with difficulty, or cannot read at all is a different matter and can be very useful information. Tests such as DARTTS (Roswell & Chall, 1992) with graded passages which the student "passes" or "fails" attempt to offer this type of information.

11. **Do not adhere blindly to interpretive categories developed for tests**. If a comprehension question labeled "inference" is missed by a student because the student simply could not decode most of the words in the passage, do not take this as evidence that the student has difficulty making inferences. Even if reading "synecdoche" as "sinnecdoch" is officially listed as a phonetic vowel miscue, report that the problem lies in oral vocabulary. Diagnostic interpretive systems can be very valuable, but they cannot substitute for an examiner's good judgment.

12. **Do not assume that a student's ability in one reading skill predicts a similar level of skill in others**. For example, the Wide Range Achievement Test-Revised (WRAT-R) (Jastak & Wilkinson, 1984) Reading Test involves reading words aloud from an increasingly difficult list. The author's published intent is simply to measure the student's mastery of the reading code system and to ignore comprehension. In fact, the WRAT-R accomplishes even this limited purpose only in part, since the test includes only single, unrelated words and no decoding of connected text. Many examiners inexcusably assume that a student's success on the WRAT-R reading accurately predicts the student's ability in other aspects of reading, even comprehension. This unwarranted and dangerous assumption is the fault of the examiner, not the authors of the test.

13. **Use tests that report different reading skills with separate, differentiated scores**. The ultimate goal of reading instruction is integration of all of the various reading skills into a coherent whole. The goal of reading assessment is the opposite. A thorough reading assessment requires analysis of the student's reading as separate skills so that strengths, weaknesses, and needs can be observed. Therefore, tests that report skills in a single score cause confusion.

For example, the Brief Form of the Kaufman Test of Educational Achievement (K-TEA) (Kaufman & Kaufman, 1985) begins with oral reading from a word list and ends with comprehension questions for brief reading passages, providing a single "reading" score, which gives no information concerning what areas need instruction. The Comprehensive Form of the same test (K-TEA) more appropriately offers separate tests of oral reading from a word list and of reading comprehension.

The comprehension tests for both versions of the K-TEA offer oral questions about reading passages and clever direction-following items similar to "Spin about in your chair, then leap to your feet as if you were startled by the sudden ingress of a threatening presence." The potential value of these comprehension questions is wasted when reported as a combined score that includes performance on oral reading from a word list as happens with the Brief Form.

Similarly, the second edition of the Gray Oral Reading Tests (GORT-R) (Wiederholt & Bryant, 1986) combined oral reading speed and oral reading errors into a single "Passage" score which inextricably confused slow, accurate readers with fast, inaccurate readers and with moderately fast, moderately inaccurate readers. The GORT-3 (Wiederholt & Bryant, 1986) wisely remedied this error by providing separate scores for speed and for accuracy as well as the combined "Passage" score.

14. **Do not assume that comprehension of passages read aloud and of passages read silently are comparable**. Some students seem to need to hear themselves reading before they can make sense of a passage. Others can read aloud or understand, but not both at once. Although they implicitly make the unwarranted assumption that silent reading comprehension will always be as strong as or stronger than comprehension of passages read aloud, the Diagnostic Reading Scales-Revised (DRS-81) (Spache, 1981) have the virtue of including comprehension questions for passages read both silently and aloud. This is a necessary provision for any thorough reading assessment when silent reading comprehension is in question. The DARTTS (Roswell & Chall, 1992) completely separates oral reading from comprehension.

15. **Do not mistake limitations of oral vocabulary for weaknesses in word analysis skills**. If a student pronounces "hyperbole" to sound like a post-season football championship, the fault is not in phonetic and structural analysis. In fact, phonics generalizations were followed; the word and its meaning are unknown. Limitations of oral meaning vocabulary essentially impose a ceiling on reading decoding. After students can decode most of the words that they know orally, further reading progress is enhanced more by development of oral vocabulary than by instruction in basic decoding skills.

16. **Do not assume that all measures of reading comprehension are comparable**. In fact, assume the opposite. Among the common methods for testing reading comprehension are orally supplying missing words in printed sentences (cloze

technique), orally completing printed analogies, and orally supplying synonyms and antonyms for printed words [e.g., Woodcock Reading Mastery Tests-Revised (WRMT-R) (Woodcock, 1987)], multiple-choice tests of synonyms and multiple-choice questions about reading passages [e.g., Gates-MacGinitie Reading Tests, 3rd. ed., (MacGinitie & MacGinitie, 1989)], oral questions about passages read silently or aloud [e.g., Diagnostic Reading Scales Revised (Spache, 1981)], oral, multiple-choice questions about passages read aloud with the questions also presented in print [e.g., GORT-3 (Wiederholt & Bryant, 1992)], and choosing one of four pictures that best conforms to a sentence previously read silently [e.g., Peabody Individual Achievement Test-Revised (PIAT-R) (Dunn & Markwart, 1989)]. Although there are strong correlations among **groups** of students taking some of these tests, individual variation reveals differences in aspects of reading comprehension tested.

17.   While it is important to evaluate everything that is relevant to the particular student's reading, **do not automatically test everything that could be tested**. If, for example, the student easily and accurately pronounces and correctly spells almost all words that are unfamiliar but phonetically regular, there is little need to test auditory discrimination.   Even if the student's auditory discrimination is imperfect, the student is compensating successfully.   Do not fall into the trap of testing for, finding, and recommending "remediation" of problems that do not exist or do not interfere with the student's reading.

18.   Similarly, **it is generally best to test higher-order skills first**.   Begin by having the student attempt to read aloud unfamiliar passages at or above the student's grade level and by having the student answer factual and inferential comprehension questions about grade-level or higher passages.   This will quickly reveal how much, if any, testing is needed for more basic skills, such as auditory discrimination, primary and advanced phonics skills, structural analysis, use of context cues, and sight vocabulary.   In contrast, an assessment that begins with the more basic skills may take a long time in revealing that they did not need to be tested.

19. **Pay attention to referral questions and background information**. You must view the information with informed skepticism, but you must also keep it in mind.   If, for example, one of the referral concerns is the student's allegedly short span of attention, you must include an assessment of the student's comprehension of long reading passages.   A test consisting of only brief passages would miss essential information.   If, for another example, the referral cites special difficulty with reading comprehension in high school science and social studies courses, you need to assess

higher-level reading skills for technical material. You may ultimately determine that the background information or referral question is erroneous, misguided, or misinterpreted—hence the need for skepticism—but always consider the information during the assessment.

20. **If they are not offered, solicit specific referral questions from teachers, the student and, at least for students who are not adults, parents.** Quote each question or concern in your report and reply to each one, even if it is only to say you do not know. Consistent application of this rule will eventually elicit better questions from your referral sources, will increase acceptance of your recommendations, and will ensure that you always pay attention to potentially valuable information.

21. **Pay attention to the student.** Find out how the student assesses her or his own reading ability. Find out how much the student enjoys various kinds of reading. Learn about the student's reading interests and other interests that might be exploited for reading. Solicit complaints about previous and current reading instruction. See if the student has any recommendations for reading instruction.

22. **Carefully consider the student's educational history.** For example, limited phonics skills have very different instructional implications for students who have been taught primarily in whole language programs than for students who have been given intensive instruction in phonics.

23. **Do not allow assessment results to be used as numbers to harm a student.** Focus evaluation reports, team deliberations, recommendations, and instruction on the realities of the student's situation, not on the numerical scores. If reading difficulties are interfering with the student's education, then the student needs help with reading, whatever the numbers from an evaluation.

Conclusion

The process of assessing a student's reading requires much more thought than simply selecting and administering a test battery. At every step in the process, the examiner must exercise cautious judgment and pay close attention to what is really happening. It is not enough only to assess individual skills. Cause-and-effect relationships among the skills must also be examined. The entire process should be undertaken to achieve the goal of determining what needs to be taught and how it might best be taught.

None of the standardized, normed tests covers all the skills that might need to be assessed for a particular student, and none of these tests is without flaw. However, when parts of different tests are combined in one assessment, the examiner must also consider differences among test norms. Does the difference between two test scores reflect a real variation in the student's skills, or just the difference between norms on two different tests?

Informal reading inventories can be tailored specifically to the needs of the assessment of a particular student, but they provide no normative information. Furthermore, an informal inventory that is designed to match the local curricula poses the danger of restricting possible instructional approaches that might be recommended only to those currently in favor. This restriction would seriously penalize any student whose needs did not match the currently popular, local model.

In general, testing should proceed downward from the highest-level skills expected of the student, through more fundamental skills, until solid foundations are reached. At each stage, the examiner should be asking why the student is doing something well or why the student is having difficulty with something else. The *what*s are the beginning of the assessment. The real value lies in the *why*s.

References

Altus, G.T. (1953). WISC patterns of a selective sample of bilingual school children. *The Pedagogical Seminary and Journal of Genetic Psychology. 83,* 241-248.

Brody, S. (1987). *Study skills: Teaching and learning strategies for mainstream and specialized classrooms.* Milford, NH: LARC Publishing.

Chall, J.S. & Curtis, M.E. (1990). Diagnostic achievement testing in reading. In C.R. Reynolds & R. Kamphaus (Eds.), *Handbook of Psychological and Educational Assessment of Children's Intelligence and Achievement.* NY: Guilford Press.

Dunn, L.M. & Markwart, F.C., Jr. (1989). *Peabody Individual Achievement Test-Revised.* Circle Pines, MN: American Guidance Service.

Ekwall, E.E. (1981). *Locating and correcting reading difficulties (3rd ed.).* Columbus, OH: Charles E. Merrill Publishing Co.

Fuller, R. (1983). *In search of the I.Q. correlation.* Stony Brook, NY: Ball-Stick-Bird Publications.

Goldman, R., Fristoe, M. & Woodcock, R.W. (1974). *Goldman-Fristoe-Woodcock Auditory Skills Test Battery.* Circle Pines, MN: American Guidance Service.

Hammill, D.D. & Larsen, S.C. (1988). *Test of Written Language (2nd ed.).* Austin, TX: Pro-ed.

Hammill, D.D. & McNutt, G. (1981). *The correlates of reading: The consensus of thirty years of correlational research.* Austin, TX: Pro-ed.

Hynd, G. & Cohen, M. (1983). *Dyslexia: Neuropsychological theory, research, and clinical differentiation.* Boston: Allyn and Bacon.

International Reading Association. (1982). Misuse of grade equivalents: Resolution passed by the Delegates Assembly of the International Reading Association, April, 1981, *Reading Teacher,* January, p. 464.

Jastak, S. & Wilkinson, G.S. (1984). *Wide Range Achievement Test-Revised.* Wilmington, DE: Jastak Associates.

Lindamood, C., & Lindamood, P. (1979). *Lindamood Auditory Conceptualization Test (rev. ed.).* Allen, TX: DLM Teaching Resource.

Kaufman, A.S. & Kaufman, N.L. (1985). *Kaufman Test of Educational Achievement, Brief Form* and *Comprehensive Form.* Circle Pines, MN: American Guidance Service.

MacGinitie, W.H. & MacGinitie, R.K. (1989). *Gates-MacGinitie Reading Tests (3rd ed.).* Chicago: Riverside Publishing Company.

Roswell, F.G. & Chall, J.S. (1992). *Diagnostic Assessments of Reading with Trial Teaching Strategies.* Chicago: Riverside Publishing Company.

RSEC Staff (1983). *School Self-rating Scale.* Milford, NH: Regional Services and Education Center.

Schultz, M.K. (1988). A comparison of standard scores for commonly used tests of early reading. *Communique,* Newsletter of the National Association of School Psychologists, 17(4), 13.

Slosson, R.L. (1991). *Slosson Oral Reading Test-Revised.* East Aurora, NY: Slosson Educational Publications.

Spache, G.D. (1981). *Diagnostic Reading Scales-Revised*. Monterey, CA: CTB/McGraw-Hill.

Wechsler, D. (1949). *Wechsler Intelligence Scale for Children*. New York: Psychological Corporation.

Wechsler, D. (1974). *Wechsler Intelligence Scale for Children-Revised*. New York: Psychological Corporation.

Wechsler, D. (1991). *Wechsler Intelligence Scale for Children-Third Edition*. San Antonio: Psychological Corporation.

Wechsler, D. (1992). *Wechsler Individual Achievement Test*. San Antonio: Psychological Corporation.

Wiederholt, J.L. & Bryant, B.R. (1986). *Gray Oral Reading Test-Revised*. Austin, TX: Pro-ed.

Wiederholt, J.L. & Bryant, B.R. (1992). *Gray Oral Reading Test-3rd ed*. Austin, TX: Pro-ed.

Willis, J.O. (1977). Overall achievement test—cumulative evaluation reflecting educational ability level. *NH Personnel and Guidance Journal*, 6(1), 9.

Willis, J.O. (1990). *Guide to identification of learning disabilities*. Concord, NH: New Hampshire Department of Education.

Willis, U. (1971). Personal communication.

Woodcock, R.W. (1987). *Woodcock Reading Mastery Tests-Revised*. Circle Pines, MN: American Guidance Service.

Woodcock, R.W., & Johnson, M.B. (1977). *Woodcock-Johnson Psychoeducational Battery*. Allen, TX: DLM Teaching Resources.

Woodcock, R.W. & Johnson, M.B. (1989). *Woodcock-Johnson Psychoeducational Battery-Revised*. Allen, TX: DLM Teaching Resources.

Chapter 12. Program Planning: Forging a Link Between Assessment and Instruction

Sara Brody, EdD
Rivier College

Generally, students are referred for reading assessment or for individualized instruction when someone perceives that their reading ability is lower than anticipated in comparison to the performance of their peers. Usually, assessment is recommended as a means of establishing the area(s) in which reading development is lagging as well as to determine the extent that developmentally earlier foundation skills are present to support further growth (Chall & Curtis, 1990).

In order for the assessment process to be useful, examiners and teachers need to translate assessment findings into instructional objectives that appropriately match the student's reading strengths and needs (Holzman, 1990). This chapter explores the process of forging a link between assessed reading needs and effective instruction. The discussion reviews circumstances in which assessment data indicate that additional testing is needed and also illustrates the relationship between various reading abilities and specific instructional objectives. Table 12.1 (following page) presents a global summary of reading needs, assessments, and related instructional strategies in order to provide an overview of issues under discussion.

Table 12.1. Reading: Linking Needs, Assessment, and Instruction. This brief sketch suggests the sequential scope, but not the depth, of reading development, assessment, and relevant instruction.

Area in Need of Development	Type of Assessment	Reading Stage (Chall, 1983)	Focus of Teaching Strategies
receptive/expressive language; inner language to direct own actions	Oral Language Hearing/Vision	0	See Chapter 2; read to child; talk with child; listen and respond to child's talk
segment spoken words into syllables/sounds; blend spoken syllables into words; blend spoken phonemes into words; remember and retell familiar stories; enjoy listening to stories/making up stories	Phonemic Awareness (Auditory Perception)	Transition 0 - 1	See Chapter 3; read aloud often; chant nursery rhymes/repeating songs/poems; identify words/pictures/objects that begin/end with /x/ sound; orally segment/blend words, syllables, phonemes; discuss activities/experiences when they occur and as memories
correspond letters to sounds; blend sounds to read words; recognize 3- and 4-letter words in rhyme families; recognize "glue" words such as "which, is, that"; read stories written mostly in one-syllable words; enjoy listening to and understanding stories with a variety of common story structures	Word Decoding; Hearing/Vision	1	See Chapters 4, 6; match letters/sounds: display pictures of words with initial letter; teach a few consonants and 1 vowel; form 3-letter word families; dictate words and sentences incorporating the 3-letter words; make book of letters, 3-letter word families, sentences; read aloud often; encourage student to sound initial consonants; encourage student to read selected "glue" words
read familiar, connected text with accuracy; read with appropriate pace/intonation/pausing; read polysyllabic words in connected text; read without drawing attentional resources away from comprehension	Reading Fluency; In addition, measure level of Stage 1 mastery.	2	See Chapters 5, 6; repeated reading of familiar text (oral/silent, choral/independent); teacher tape short text; student reread with tape often; read familiar stories often; offer books and time for free reading
expand knowledge of words and their meanings; select among multiple meanings of a word; recognize specialized meanings of words; recognize words in varied contexts; use many words in varied contexts; in context, learn words for abstract concepts	Reading/Oral Vocabulary; In addition, measure level of Stage 1 & 2 mastery.	3 - 5	See Chapter 9; directly state/explain/demonstrate meanings, applications; create opportunities for students to tell/explain/demonstrate; retrieve/use target word to discuss relevant issues and contexts; read/write target word embedded in sentences/paragraphs; read widely and regularly
locate/state details when reading unfamiliar text; identify central vs extraneous points in text; synthesize details into main ideas; attend to questions or problems that focus learning; identify organizational schema of a passage; summarize, extend, express learnings	Passage Comprehension; In addition, measure Stage 1 & 2 mastery and word meanings.	3 - 5	See Chapters 7, 8, 10; answer teacher/text questions; generate/answer own questions; locate/classify details; sequence events; develop crucial background concepts before/during reading; outline/diagram/summarize/discuss reading material; apply and extend specialized or abstract concepts

HYPOTHESIS TESTING

As discussed in Chapter 11, reading assessment should typically begin with higher-level skills that are noticed to be lacking and then proceed downward until a foundation of more basic skills is established. Testing in this top-down fashion requires that the examiner make many judgments concerning whether reading difficulties revealed by particular assessments are, in fact, actual areas in need of instruction. Alternatively, are the assessments unveiling symptoms of difficulties at a more basic level of reading development?

An accurate answer to this question requires methodical and creative detective work (Budoff, 1972; Kaufman, 1979). The thought and effort put into this process can spare students and teachers from squandering hours of energy and resources on fruitless, inappropriate instruction. Well-targeted instruction depends on an accurate assessment. As noted in Chapter 11, an accurate assessment need not test every conceivable subskill of reading. However, it must be planned and guided by someone with a solid understanding of reading development in order to assure that specific subskills are tested adequately but not unduly. Selection of assessment instruments must also be guided by competency in recognizing the actual information yielded by various testing instruments in contrast to reliance on the name of the test, which may inaccurately suggest what it measures (Willis, 1990).

With practice, attentive examiners increase their ability to stalk a reading problem through the steps of an assessment/instructional cycle:

a) awareness of a difficulty;
b) initial assessment;
c) formation of tentative diagnostic hunches;
d) further assessment if needed;
e) initial instructional recommendations;
f) confirmation, rejection, or adjustment of hypotheses and recommendations to reflect student's on-going progress;
g) additional assessment if needed;
h) formation of better informed hypotheses if needed; and,
i) continuation of the cycle.

Competent examiners and teachers recognize that lack of anticipated progress in a carefully planned program does not indicate a student's failure but instead the need for analysis and adjustment of the program to fit the student's needs and abilities adequately (Brody, 1987a).

CHAPTER ORGANIZATION AND SOME CAUTIONS

This chapter explores the sleuthing process of reading assessment and instruction by examining some common profiles of reading difficulty. These profiles are analyzed by considering strengths and needs presented during referral; types of assessments that document the nature of the specific profile; and related diagnostic findings. In addition, referral and assessment evidence are drawn on to develop recommendations for appropriate instruction.

The profiles selected for discussion are representative of reading difficulties commonly observed in schools. However, the profiles described here are by no means the only common reading difficulties found in schools, nor representative of all types of reading difficulties. It remains the responsibility and challenge of the skilled examiner/teacher to pursue whatever reading behaviors present themselves through a careful step-wise process in order to define the *actual* reading profile of a specific student.

Examiners and teachers are cautioned to avoid assiduously efforts to fit real, individual needs and strengths to prototypic patterns without regard for the nuances of each unique reader. And finally, when making recommendations and carrying out instruction, teachers are urged to help readers develop their strengths even while attending to remediation of weaknesses (Willis, 1990).

With these cautions in mind, the following discussion examines differences among readers in their performance on specific types of reading tests along with the instructional implications of these differences. The discussion begins by considering variation in reading performance on passage comprehension tests and its reflection in several interesting reading profiles. Next, variation in performance on vocabulary meaning tests is considered. This is followed by a review of issues suggested by differing scoring patterns on decoding fluency, decoding word reading, and phonemic awareness tests.

In each assessment area, several profiles are presented in order to illustrate that different instructional needs may underlie similar presenting symptoms. The variety of profiles may provide a sense of the diversity in reading development that appears in schools and the community. Table 12.2 (following page) delineates each reading profile under review by noting assessments used, performance level demonstrated, and instructional strategies recommended.

Table 12.2. Profiles of Common Reading Difficulties: A Very Brief Summary. (Read chapter 12 for necessary detail.)

Pro-file	Passage Comprehension — locate, classify sequence details & concepts; study strategies; application	Vocabulary — word meanings background concepts knowledge breadth knowledge depth	Fluency — oral reading speed accuracy intonation pace	Word Decoding — letter-sound correspondence word analysis strategies	Phonemic Awareness — segment blend phonemes syllables	Diagnostic Hypotheses and Potential Recommendations
A	Low	OK	OK	OK	—	Passage comprehension is low but all other areas seem adequate. Instruction in comprehension and organizational skills is recommended.
B	Mixed	Mixed	OK	OK	—	Passage and vocabulary scores seem to vary in relation to topic familiarity suggesting that basic comprehension strategies are in place. Decoding is adequate. Development of broad background and vocabulary knowledge is recommended.
C	OK	Low Read High Oral	Low	Low	—	Oral vocabulary is high and decoding weak suggesting that comprehension is supported by great background. Nevertheless, decoding instruction is needed to realize potential.
D	Low	Low	OK	OK	—	Passage comprehension and vocabulary are low yet referral indicates basic organization and street-smart understanding is solid. Teach broad background concepts and word meanings.
E	Very Low	Very Low	OK	OK	—	Very low comprehension and vocabulary despite adequate decoding skills suggest limited language development. Intensive, concrete, direct teaching and practice with meanings, background concepts, and text study strategies are needed.
F	Low	Low Read High Oral	Low	Accurate & Slow	—	High oral vocabulary and adequate, slow decoding, along with limited fluency, suggest an instructional need for practice through repeated readings, timed readings, and pleasure reading.
G	Low	Low Read High Oral	Low	Low	—	Oral vocabulary is high despite deficits in passage comprehension, fluency, and decoding. Provide instruction in decoding patterns and strategies along with plenty of practice of these strategies during reading of connected text.
H	Low	Low Read Low Oral	Low	OK	—	Reader needs to develop fluency through repeated readings, reading of connected text, and many opportunities to develop language, vocabulary, and broad experiential knowledge related to a variety of text formats and genres.
J	Low	Low Read High Oral	OK on Basic Low Advanced	OK Basics Low Infrequent	—	Oral vocabulary is high; reading is fluent on basic and intermediate passages; decoding is adequate for most words, but low for infrequent irregular words. Instruction needs to focus on advanced word analysis strategies to decrease dysfluency and increase passage comprehension.
K	Low	Low Reading Low Oral	Low	Low	OK	Comprehension, oral vocabulary, fluency, and decoding are weak. Phonemic awareness is intact from indirect environmental exposure. Needs direct teaching of unknown letter-sound links, word family rhymes, and affix patterns.
L	Low	Low Reading Low Oral	Low	Low	OK	Profile similar to K but with solid phonemic awareness attributable to systematic home instruction. Offer intensive, prolonged teaching and practice of letter-sound correspondences, rhyming word groups, affixes, syllabic patterns.
M	Low	Low	Low	Low	Low	This young student exhibits weaknesses in all areas of reading. Systematic, intensive phonemic awareness instruction is needed with follow-up assessment to determine whether cause is lack of exposure, learning disability, or other issues in order to appropriately pace later plans.
						Note: Emotional disability can inhibit reading progress. Instruction should focus on assessed reading needs; appropriate personnel should be involved to alleviate the emotional stress.

Reading Profiles and Related Recommendations

PASSAGE COMPREHENSION

This discussion of passage comprehension assessment and instruction will consider three profiles. Profile A, Arnold, scored low on passage comprehension by answering many items correctly early in the test, then missing a string of items beyond a clearly observable limit. Profile B, Bethany, also scored low on passage comprehension, but with performance that fluctuated depending on the content of the passage. And Craig scored appropriately for grade placement by comprehending passages written at and below grade level; yet Craig may need some intensive reading instruction. These readers' specific profiles are discussed below in detail.

Profile A. The referral for Arnold indicates that he has difficulty answering questions or developing summaries related to assigned passages in science, social studies, and reading/language arts texts and trade books. It is noted that his vision and hearing were recently tested as normal.[1] In addition, the referral indicates that Arnold seems to possess a good meaning vocabulary relative to peers. Further, he seems to have had many home and school exposures to enriching experiences along with satisfying interactions and relationships with peers, teachers, and family.

Since reading assessment typically begins at the level at which difficulty is perceived, Arnold's assessment begins with tests of passage comprehension—the Kaufman Test of Educational Achievement-Comprehensive Form (K-TEA) (Kaufman & Kaufman, 1985) and the Gates-MacGinitie Reading Tests, 3rd edition (G-MRT) (MacGinitie & MacGinitie, 1989). If, as in Arnold's case, these tests suggest that passage comprehension is weak, additional testing is needed to determine the reading and language processes, as well as any other factors, that may be contributing to weak comprehension. Since Arnold's referral information suggests that vision, hearing, and emotional/social issues are unlikely to be contributing factors, his assessment will focus on reading and language processes that contribute to passage comprehension.

---

[1]It is necessary to check near point, far point, and binocular function to assure vision is not interfering with reading ability. The student who reads a wall chart at some 10 or 20 feet distance may need corrective lenses in order to read print at near point. In addition, complete hearing assessment requires impedance testing.

Measurement of knowledge of word meanings is a logical next step in assessment. Such information can indicate whether lack of word meanings and background concepts is making comprehension of passages difficult (Chall, 1987; Chall & Curtis, 1990). In Arnold's case, this assessment is a useful follow-up on referral information that suggests background is strong. A measure of Arnold's vocabulary, taken with the vocabulary subtest of the Gates-MacGinitie Reading Tests (G-MRT), indicates that word knowledge is similar to that of age and grade peers. Since this is a multiple-choice test, and consequently may not indicate any problems with retrieval of word meanings, word meanings are also assessed with the vocabulary subtest of the Woodcock Reading Mastery Tests-R (WRMT-R) (Woodcock, 1987).

The WRMT-R vocabulary subtest is used with caution since students often score low on it due to their difficulty with synonym, antonym, and analogy constructs, rather than with word meanings. However, Arnold performs well on this vocabulary measure. Together, the solid scores on the G-MRT and WRMT-R provide some assurance that Arnold's passage comprehension difficulty is not an indication of lack of word meaning knowledge. The vocabulary scores also suggest that Arnold's low comprehension is probably not an indication of poor decoding skills since the words on the vocabulary test had to be deciphered in relative isolation.

When passage comprehension difficulties are noted, it is generally a good idea to test reading subskills at least to the level of decoding fluency on connected text. This is done to determine whether a lack of automaticity with the subskill of decoding is drawing attentional resources away from the process of arranging and comprehending thoughts and concepts (Perfetti, 1985; Samuels, Schermer, & Reinking, 1992).

To check his reading fluency, Arnold is given the Gray Oral Reading Test-3 (GORT-3) (Wiederholt & Bryant, 1992). Arnold reads passages written at grade level without reversals, substitutions, inversions, or deletions, as well as with good pace, intonation, and pausing. In addition, he accurately answers questions concerning passages written several grades below current placement, but continues the pattern of weak comprehension of grade-level passages.

Since Arnold's reading fluency seems robust, and polysyllabic words within unfamiliar oral reading passages are read with ease and accuracy, further testing of isolated decoding or phonemic awareness skills may not be necessary. However, there remains some question concerning Arnold's ability to decode fluently without requiring allocation of attention to decoding rather than comprehension. Therefore,

368

the examiner takes a few minutes for an assessment of word decoding on isolated lists using the WRMT-R. Such a test provides targeted evidence that Arnold does not need to rely on context to decode longer words.

With vision, hearing, emotional/social issues, word meaning knowledge, and decoding fluency eliminated as likely underlying factors, the referral and assessment evidence suggest that Arnold's reading comprehension difficulty probably lies in lack of skills such as locating, classifying, or sequencing information and ideas. To confirm this hypothesis, the examiner should study Arnold's errors and successes on the reading comprehension test items. If time permits, it would be instructive to help Arnold work through a few pages of his science textbook. If this is Arnold's difficulty, his comprehension will not be helped by further instruction in decoding or word meanings. Instead, he needs to engage in comprehension development through extensive opportunities to read and apply strategies related to questioning, discussing, and writing about text (Santa, Havens & Harrison, 1989; Stotsky, 1986).

Specifically, the examiner indicates that Arnold seems to need guidance concerning how to: pull information from the text, evaluate relevant and irrelevant details, and apply what is read to what else is under study concerning the topic. In addition, the examiner recommends that teachers supplement reading assignments with study guides that ask specific questions related to important concepts, details, and conclusions. These questions should be sequentially arranged to fill in a clear framework or outline that replicates the text's structure. (See Chapters 7, 8, 10 for detailed descriptions of strategies appropriate for students whose reading difficulties lie in these areas.)

Profile B. Bethany also has difficulty understanding the science text, but she seems to do better with social studies readings. As with Arnold, the referral indicates that Bethany has good vision and hearing and adequate social/emotional adjustment. Similar to Arnold, she performs below peers on the G-MRT and K-TEA passage comprehension subtests. However, unlike Arnold, Bethany's correct and erroneous responses are somewhat scattered.

Bethany answers several items correctly, then misses several, and next performs accurately on a few items that are more difficult. At several points in the testing, Bethany nearly meets the test's ceiling, then answers several advanced items correctly. Noticing this pattern, the examiner asks Bethany to describe the kinds of reading materials that seem easier to read and the kinds that seem more challenging. Bethany indicates that books on music, a hobby, are fun to read, but textbooks are challenging.

Again, with passage comprehension scores below expected levels, the examiner checks Bethany's vocabulary knowledge. Bethany's score on the G-MRT vocabulary subtest is somewhat low, but again with scatter showing greater vocabulary knowledge in some areas than others. To explore whether there is an easily defined pattern to the scatter, the examiner administers the WRMT-R vocabulary subtest. The examiner's record booklet includes a grid to record the vocabulary items by subject area. Bethany's responses do not reflect a clear pattern of error related to science, social studies, or the humanities. Although such a pattern could give useful guidance, Bethany's lack of pattern directly related to an academic subject area in no way rules out the presence of splinter vocabulary knowledge.

To determine whether the vocabulary scatter might reflect splinter deficits in decoding skills rather than a lack of word meaning knowledge, the examiner administers the oral vocabulary subtest from the Diagnostic Assessment of Reading with Trial Teaching Strategies (DARTTS) (Roswell & Chall, 1992). When it is given to Bethany, the scatter again appears, suggesting that her splinter performance is not likely produced by limited decoding skills (since it does not require reading).

The examiner could have skipped the oral vocabulary test and stepped directly to a test of decoding fluency, which would also provide evidence concerning whether decoding deficits impede Bethany's comprehension. Either choice makes sense in Bethany's case since her ability to read and identify some difficult vocabulary words suggests that decoding is not interfering with her knowledge of word meanings. The scatter in her comprehension and vocabulary scores, with some correct responses in the upper range, also leads the examiner to suspect that scattered word meaning and general background knowledge are making passage comprehension difficult when the content area is unfamiliar, and that Bethany is not hampered by a lack of study skills or a weakness in decoding fluency.

Whether the oral vocabulary test is administered or not, decoding fluency should be checked. Such assessment provides evidence concerning potential gaps in decoding mastery and its influence on types of words that can be read and understood. Such assessment suggests whether a lack of decoding fluency is contributing to limited passage comprehension. In Bethany's case, the examiner finds that decoding is fluent since the student does not stumble when orally reading difficult passages. Further, the scatter that appeared in earlier passage comprehension tests surfaces again with passage comprehension items on the GORT-3.

After reviewing the referral and assessment information for Bethany, the examiner hypothesizes that mixed passage comprehension difficulties arise from gaps in knowledge of word meanings and background concepts. Further assessment could include a more comprehensive test of oral vocabulary, such as the Woodcock-Johnson Psychoeducational Battery-Revised (WJPB-R) (Woodcock & Johnson, 1989), and the WJPB-R oral tests of science, social studies, and humanities knowledge. Recommendations for instruction encourage exposure and practice with concepts, vocabulary, and applications in a broad array of areas since the gaps did not appear in selected content areas as measured by the WRMT-R. In addition, the examiner recommends that teachers introduce reading assignments by previewing vocabulary words and their meanings, and by preteaching any crucial background concepts that are prerequisite to understanding an assigned text (Brody, 1993). (See Chapters 8 and 9 for detailed discussion of instructional issues and strategies related to Bethany's profile.)

Profile C. Craig is referred for reading assessment by a teacher who feels that this student is not performing to potential. The referral notes that the science text is written well above grade level and that Craig discusses the concepts competently but avoids reading in class and almost never completes written assignments. Vision and hearing are normal; Craig appears to have several friends; he seems unusually quick to brush aside any mention of academic difficulty.

When given the passage comprehension subtests of the K-TEA and G-MRT, Craig scores similarly to average peers. In fact, he answers most items correctly on passages written at grade level and below; comprehension difficulty is apparent only on passages written above grade level.

When asked to reflect on his reading experiences, Craig indicates contentment with his current reading ability and expresses no desire for assessment or assistance. The examiner is tempted to attribute the referral to the difficulty of the school's science text since Craig scores firmly at grade level on passage comprehension, the goal of reading instruction. However, the entire class has not been referred for testing, and thus the examiner suspects a broader picture may be revealed through more detailed assessment.

In order to develop another perspective, the examiner administers the G-MRT vocabulary test of word meanings and finds low reading vocabulary scores that are incongruent with Craig's grade-level passage comprehension. The examiner recalls the articulate manner in which the youngster discussed the process of assessment. The examiner also considers the critical difference between reading words in isolation on a vocabulary test and reading words in context during passage comprehension testing (Chall & Curtis, 1990; Curtis, 1987). Since Craig's vocabulary scores are much lower than his passage comprehension scores, the examiner begins to suspect that decoding deficits may be contributing to the low vocabulary scores.

It seems that Craig may be guessing from context to compensate for weak decoding when reading relatively simple passages. To test this hypothesis, the examiner gives the DARTTS oral vocabulary subtest, (which does not require the student to read vocabulary items), and discovers that Craig scores extremely well. This suggests that Craig possesses a very broad and deep knowledge of word meanings and concepts that could, indeed, support passage comprehension through the use of context clues until concepts become highly specialized.

Since Craig's oral vocabulary score is high, it is likely that he would be reading passages above grade level if decoding issues were not interfering with comprehension—the referral concern begins to make sense. To clarify the existence and nature of Craig's decoding difficulties, the examiner administers the GORT-3 to test decoding fluency. In addition, the word decoding subtests of the WRMT-R are given to identify specific phonetic difficulties. Craig reads the GORT-3 passages with age-appropriate speed and intonation, but with many substitution errors, particularly on longer content words. Some of the substitutions tended to preserve meaning and Craig's GORT-3 passage comprehension performance is similar to that on the K-TEA and G-MRT. Performance on the WRMT-R suggests that the student can read many one- and two-syllable words in isolation with accuracy, but that word analysis strategies are lacking for the decoding of less-familiar polysyllabic words (Brody, 1987b).

The referral and assessment evidence suggest that Craig has been quite successful in compensating for his limited decoding strategies by using context clues and by memorizing words as logographic wholes. The referring teacher was correct to suspect that Craig could improve reading ability; the assessment evidence suggests that this is likely to occur if Craig learns strategies for decoding longer words. Craig's profile suggests that he can read relatively simple passages with understanding. However, as his ability leads to interests in more specialized areas, it will be very difficult for Craig to keep up with reading that involves technical terms. Accurate reading of such material is difficult when relying only on context clues and the memorization of individual words as logographic wholes (Liberman, 1987).

Effective instruction needs to help Craig take time to learn decoding strategies as well as to provide him with practice in applying word analysis strategies to the decoding of longer words. In addition, teachers can help Craig practice decoding of longer words by presenting polysyllabic content words whole and in syllables to introduce vocabulary before assigning independent reading of text. (See Chapter 5 for a detailed description of advanced decoding strategies.)

Summary of passage comprehension assessment findings. As seen in the profiles of Arnold, Bethany, and Craig, it would be misleading to assume that passage comprehension scores indicate simply the level of reading comprehension at which students should be taught. Instead, results of passage comprehension tests may represent a variety of underlying reading difficulties. Low passage comprehension scores may indicate difficulty with higher-level comprehension skills such as classifying, sequencing, and synthesizing, (Armbruster, 1991), or low scores may represent a lack of broad vocabulary and background knowledge (Chall & Snow, 1988). Further, low scores could suggest a lack of decoding fluency (Brody, 1989; Perfetti, 1984).

In addition, passage comprehension scores commensurate with grade-level peers cannot be assumed to represent proficient reading. Bright students who possess broad and deep vocabulary and background knowledge at times mask an underlying decoding difficulty by managing to compensate with context clues and logographic memorization of individual words.

The masking through compensation can help very bright students hide their reading difficulties until they are in middle school or occasionally even beginning high school. At this point, the need to teach underlying decoding skills often is not understood. This may lead some students to seek help outside the school setting and others to abandon hope of developing reading proficiency commensurate with their intellectual ability.

READING/ORAL VOCABULARY

The following analysis considers the profiles of Daisy and Elroy, readers whose referrals indicate that vision and hearing are fine, passage comprehension scores are consistently low, and decoding fluency and word sounding skills are competent. The discussion considers subtle differences in the assessment performances of Daisy and Elroy that suggest variation in the types of instruction needed to advance their acquisition of enhanced reading proficiency.

Profile D. Daisy has difficulty comprehending texts and trade books written at grade level. Performance on the vocabulary subtest of the G-MRT places her at the bottom of the 2nd quartile—performing near the top of the bottom third of the class. Assessment with the fluency and word recognition subtests of the DARTTS suggests that decoding fluency and word recognition are solid. Daisy converses easily with the examiner concerning daily, familiar topics, but becomes an active listener when encouraged to discuss reactions to an international political event.

Referral information indicates that Daisy is well organized, tries hard, seeks clarification on assignments and directions, and reliably responds in a streetwise, competent manner to unexpected events in the classroom. Although Daisy's assignments are well organized and neat, their content often misses the mark. Referral information also indicates that Daisy bears much responsibility in the care of two younger siblings.

Daisy's referral and assessment data suggest that she seems to possess limited reading comprehension and vocabulary knowledge, although she demonstrates strong organization, sequencing, and synthesizing skills within familiar, non-academic contexts. Daisy also demonstrates competent reading fluency and word decoding. Since Daisy's organizational and decoding skills seem strong, reading comprehension as well as vocabulary knowledge seem to lag due to lack of experiences and exposures (Stanovich, 1994). The WJPB-R vocabulary and knowledge subtests would allow further exploration of this question.

Together, these factors suggest that Daisy's instructional plan should stress many opportunities to develop reading vocabulary meanings and background knowledge through exposure and application. In many ways, Daisy represents an ideal candidate for Chapter I services since her low comprehension skills appear attributable to a lack of opportunity and exposure to broad and deep background experiences and language rather than to learning disabilities.

Profile E. Elroy's assessment procedures and test results are similar to Daisy's except that both vocabulary and passage scores are lower—deep in the 1st quartile. Nevertheless, his decoding and fluency skills are solid. However, referral information suggests that Elroy lacks the organizational skills and streetwise knowledge demonstrated by Daisy.

Elroy's profile seems to reflect limited language development that is more pervasive than Daisy's limited vocabulary and background knowledge. Such a profile may appear whether the underlying difficulty is from lack of exposure, slower intellectual maturation, or a learning disability that affects language processing and ready assimilation of word meanings, syntax patterns, and textual organization. Elroy's apparent language limitations suggest that it would be wise to refer him for a psychoeducational and/or language evaluation.

Students such as Elroy need intensive, concrete, direct, repeated instruction in the areas of vocabulary word meanings and background concepts. These students need intensive, scaffolded opportunities to practice with several text study strategies. They need many opportunities to engage in reading and being read to from challenging text while guided through an explanatory discussion (Brody, 1993; Graves, Cooke, & Laberge, 1983). (Please see chapters 7, 8, 9, 10 for detailed suggestions related to such instruction.)

Summary of vocabulary assessment findings. Students who lack word meaning and background concepts often score low on tests that measure vocabulary orally. Clear, systematic vocabulary meaning instruction is crucial to students who do not extend their word meaning knowledge sufficiently through independent reading and the exposure of weekly class vocabulary tests. Intensive vocabulary instruction is particularly needed by students with learning disabilities, by students with limited cognitive abilities, and by students whose organizational skills and/or background knowledge have been limited by lack of experiential exposure to the academic language of school learning.

Not all students with limited language development have Elroy's and Daisy's advantage of early, systematic, and ample decoding instruction with sufficient practice to produce fluency. However, such instruction is particularly important for students with limited language development. Once decoding is mastered, reading can be used to provide visual (print) exposure to language, vocabulary, and word meanings. Print exposure can reinforce and augment auditory (talk) exposure that is not present in the community environment or that is not processed particularly well by students with learning disabilities (Stanovich, 1986; 1994).

READING FLUENCY

This section presents four profiles related to difficulties with decoding fluency. The number of profiles in this section reflects the importance and complexity of this reading component as the gateway from beginning reading to advanced reading comprehension success (Adams, 1994; Perfetti, 1985). Since many adult illiterates were overcome by failure at this stage of reading development (Chall, 1983), examiners need to be particularly sensitive to assessment of reading fluency.

Published assessment instruments that measure fluency, such as the GORT-3, DARTTS, or Diagnostic Reading Scales-81 (DRS-81) (Spache, 1981), are very useful but somewhat cumbersome to administer. They require use of detailed coding of insertions, omissions, reversals, inversions, and repetitions, and some need timing of passage reading, and noting of intonation and attention to punctuation cues (Salvia

& Ysseldyke, 1991). Nevertheless, proficient and regular use of such tests is crucial since they give an examiner a wealth of diagnostic information concerning a critical juncture in reading development.

Profile F. Fiona illustrates the importance of decoding fluency tests in understanding reading disability. Fiona performs poorly on passage comprehension and reading vocabulary tests, but scores well on the DARTTS oral vocabulary subtest. This suggests to the examiner that Fiona's underlying reading difficulty rests with decoding. Rather than taking the recommended step-wise progression and next testing reading fluency, the examiner hopes to lighten the testing load by skipping the cumbersome fluency tests and going directly to measures of word decoding.

Consequently, the next test administered is the WRMT-R word decoding test. To the examiner's surprise, Fiona performs quite well, reading even unfamiliar polysyllabic words to grade level. The examiner notices that Fiona requires a great deal of **time** to read each word and that some items would have been failed if the test were timed. The Wide Range Achievement Test-Revised (WRAT-R) (Jastak & Wilkinson, 1984) and the Slosson Oral Reading Test-Revised (SORT-R) (Slosson, 1991) are timed for this purpose, and one could have been given for confirmation.

Since Fiona's difficulties remain a mystery, the examiner administers the GORT-3. The results are well below grade level in speed, but accuracy remained good. This suggests that most of her attention is needed to decode accurately, leaving little available for comprehension. Considered along with the WRMT-R word decoding performance, the dysfluency scores suggest that Fiona's decoding draws on attention that could be allocated to comprehension if decoding were practiced to develop fluency. To test this hypothesis, the examiner administers the DARTTS subtests that measure reading fluency with and without accompanying comprehension questions. Fiona performs accurately on both assessments, but with much greater speed when comprehension is not assessed. These findings suggest to the examiner that Fiona may attempt to sacrifice comprehension for speed (when not in a testing situation) in an effort to get through the reading of connected text—a habit that ultimately defeats its own purpose.

Since the referral information indicates no hearing, vision, or emotional issues, and also suggests that Fiona follows discussions of abstract concepts well in class, the examiner recommends intensive practice to develop reading fluency. Recommendations include repeated readings and repeated timed readings (Samuels, Schermer, & Reinking, 1992), supplemented by multiple opportunities and rewards for pleasure reading in materials that were written at Fiona's mastery level. This will be facilitated by a thorough interview to identify current and potential reading interests. (See Chapter 5 for detailed strategies to improve fluency.)

Profile G. Referral information indicates that Gerald demonstrates articulate and focused verbal class participation. However, he seems unable or unwilling to read since he engages in distracting activities when directed to begin reading assignments, and routinely asks to leave the room when assigned a turn at oral reading. Notes from Gerald's cumulative folder indicate that he stumbled often during oral reading in earlier years. Vision and hearing are normal, and Gerald seems otherwise well adjusted.

The referral suggests to the examiner that Gerald's difficulties may lie in the basic decoding processes and that passage comprehension may be thwarted by Gerald's limited decoding abilities. The examiner administers the WRMT-R passage comprehension subtest to record a base-line score against which to measure future instructional effects. Oral vocabulary, rather than reading vocabulary, is tested with the DARTTS and is strong, as anticipated by the referral.

Next, the examiner administers the GORT-3 and finds that Gerald reads very slowly and with many errors. Little time is taken up by the assessment since Gerald quickly reaches the ceiling on the passage comprehension and decoding fluency tests. Now, the examiner focuses on measuring Gerald's skill in decoding of words in isolation. When administering both the real-word and phonetically regular non-word lists on the WRMT-R, the examiner pencils in each nonstandard response (Willis, 1990). Unlike Fiona, Gerald makes many decoding errors.

Based on the referral information and the assessment findings, the examiner stresses the need to teach decoding patterns and principles on controlled word lists. The recommendation suggests that multiple opportunities to practice reading those word patterns for fluency in controlled, connected text will provide reinforcement and speed transfer to connected text (Brody, 1987b).

Further, teachers are reminded that Gerald's strong oral vocabulary is an advantage that can foster continued development of background and concept knowledge at grade level. Teachers can facilitate such growth through lessons that teach content and measure understanding through means other than reading and writing. These supports can be faded gradually when Gerald's decoding and fluency catch up with the potential demonstrated by grade-level oral vocabulary knowledge. If these supports are not provided, Gerald may give up and no longer maintain the intellectual competence that currently far exceeds his reading ability.

Profile H.   In contrast to Fiona and Gerald, Heidi exhibits weak oral vocabulary knowledge in addition to limited reading fluency. The referral for Heidi indicates adequate vision, hearing, and emotional well-being.   Similar to Daisy, whose vocabulary was also limited, Heidi demonstrates good organizational skills and calm application of practical knowledge to a variety of situations arising in the classroom provided that reading is not required.

K-TEA and G-MRT tests of passage comprehension, and DARTTS tests of oral vocabulary and reading fluency, bear out the difficulties predicted by the referral.   However, a test of Heidi's decoding indicates adequate word recognition and knowledge of word analysis strategies.

The referral and assessment results suggest that Heidi needs extensive practice in reading connected text along with equally necessary opportunities for exposure to literary language and conventions. In addition to the practice for fluency needed by Fiona, Heidi needs many opportunities to develop the language, vocabulary, and broad experiential knowledge that foster understanding of a variety of text formats and genres. Such exposure will provide familiarity with a wide range of concepts and, in turn, such familiarity can confirm accurate decoding during independent pleasure reading and fluency practice (Chomsky, 1978).

Unlike Fiona, Heidi does not already recognize a variety of story and text plots, nor have a broad and deep vocabulary and concept background knowledge with which to process living and reading experiences. Until these are developed, Heidi needs direct teacher feedback to assure that fluency practice is done with accuracy since unfamiliar story content cannot predictably confirm whether material was decoded with accuracy.   Teachers can prepare Heidi for independent reading by previewing the vocabulary meanings of words in the assigned material as well as by previewing the gist of the material to be read (Graves, 1987; Graves et al., 1983). (See Chapter 5 for detailed fluency strategies and chapters 8 and 9 for background and vocabulary development strategies.)

Profile J. Jeb was referred for testing due to somewhat lower than average performance on written responses to class reading assignments.   This difficulty contrasts sharply with Jeb's apparent understanding during class discussion and his willing and fluent reading of simple notes and stories. Vision and hearing are reported normal as is his emotional well-being.

Jeb demonstrates a common pattern on the passage comprehension tests with nearly 100 percent accuracy on K-TEA and G-MRT lower-level passages, mixed accuracy on intermediate passages, and failure on advanced passages. The overall pattern and scores suggest a low-average reader—no cause for concern except that oral class performance is reported as at or above average.

The reading vocabulary subtest of the G-MRT reveals scores slightly below grade level, with most of the early and middle items answered correctly and only the more difficult items missed. These scores are commensurate with passage comprehension and, again, unremarkable until the examiner decides to follow a hunch and check oral vocabulary knowledge with the DARTTS. On this test, Jeb scores well at all levels, suggesting that some kind of decoding deficit may be lowering reading comprehension and reading vocabulary performance.

When administered the GORT-3, Jeb reads the beginning passages without error and the middle passages with very few errors—completing the beginning passages with good speed and the middle passages more slowly. When advanced passages are attempted, Jeb's reading speed decreases considerably, and errors on longer words creep into the profile along with substitutions, reversals, and omissions of short "glue" words. The WRMT-R decoding subtests are administered next; they suggest that Jeb has a good grasp of basic decoding strategies but lacks knowledge for decoding longer polysyllabic words that follow infrequent patterns.

Synthesizing the referral and assessment evidence, the examiner hypothesizes that decoding fluency is not an entrenched problem since Jeb performs well on simple text. Instead, fluency seems to break down when attempted with unfamiliar, technical words for which Jeb lacks effective word analysis strategies. The examiner recommends that Jeb's reading comprehension be encouraged through instruction in word analysis strategies for advanced and atypical word patterns.

The report notes that many adult readers are hampered in their otherwise competent reading by lack of these advanced decoding strategies (Chall, 1983). The examiner suggests that teachers assist Jeb in reading with greater speed and understanding by introducing the pronunciation of unfamiliar technical words when assigning a passage for independent reading. (See Chapter 5 for advanced decoding strategies.)

Summary of fluency assessment. Lack of decoding fluency can compromise passage comprehension even when readers possess extensive background and vocabulary knowledge. An adequate reading assessment must determine whether students have developed sufficient fluency to engage fully in reading comprehension. Underdeveloped fluency may arise from an absence of decoding instruction and/or practice in earlier grades. Sometimes this is attributable to a curriculum that is deficient in decoding instruction. Other times, it reflects that a student's learning difficulty requires **intensive** decoding exposure and practice. At times, such instruction must extend beyond the duration typically provided to teach letter-sound correspondences, word families, and advanced word analysis strategies to primary-grade students.

WORD DECODING

We have already considered several profiles in which word decoding is the underlying factor contributing to reading difficulty. Craig, Gerald, and Jeb are representative of the difficulties experienced by readers who have difficulty with decoding despite **strong oral vocabularies and rich experiential backgrounds**. The two profiles considered below illustrate the nature of decoding difficulties and instruction among students who, unlike Craig, Gerald, and Jeb, exhibit **limited oral vocabulary and experiential background**.

Profile K. Kelly's referral indicates that she exhibits halting and inaccurate oral reading, confusions concerning several letter-sound correspondences, and a lack of familiarity with many of the terms that the teacher uses during instruction. Kelly's vision and hearing are adequate. Based on performance in class discussions, activities, and field trips, the teacher suspects that Kelly comes to school with limited exposure to literary language and thought structures.

The examiner quickly takes a baseline passage comprehension measure using the K-TEA Comprehensive. Since it is suspected that problems lie in the more basic processes, the examiner selects the K-TEA, which exposes the student only to those items needed to establish a baseline, record performance, and reach a ceiling. This approach may decrease testing stress for Kelly by avoiding the many items that must be perused to complete the G-MRT.

Since the referral indicates that Kelly has difficulty with decoding, the examiner measures vocabulary word meanings only with the DARTTS oral vocabulary test. As expected, the results are low. Next, the GORT-3 is administered to establish an oral reading fluency baseline; the results are low as expected, but the testing is useful since the examiner records the errors verbatim for later use in instructional planning.

The examiner tests word decoding using only the real-word subtest of the WRMT-R. Again errors are recorded verbatim rather than only correct/incorrect in order to provide useful instructional planning data. Finally, the examiner administers several phonemic awareness measures from the Goldman-Fristoe-Woodcock Auditory Skills Test Battery (GFW) (Goldman, Fristoe, & Woodcock, 1974). Testing suggests that Kelly is able to segment and blend initial and final sounds and syllables.

Since rudimentary phonemic awareness seems to be intact, the referral and assessment evidence suggests that Kelly's weak decoding skills are the result of insufficient instruction in decoding strategies. Although Kelly has limited experience and vocabulary in the realm of academic and literary language, a foundation of phonemic awareness is present to facilitate successful mastery of decoding strategies through direct instruction (Rath, 1990).

The examiner recommends that Kelly receive instruction in letter-sound correspondences that are not yet mastered, in word-family rhyme patterns that are not yet known, and in word analysis strategies such as recognition of common affixes and syllabic patterns (Blachman, 1991). In addition, the recommendation also stresses the need to accompany instruction with exposure to literary language through peer reading, reading books accompanied by tapes, and being read to by the teacher, an aide, or a school volunteer (Chall, 1967; Chomsky, 1978; Reutzel & Cooter, 1992).

Profile L. The reading behaviors of Len are very similar to those of Kelly. Again, class performance suggests that Len has little background exposure to literary language and broad experiences. However, the examiner's contact with the parent contradicts this perception by indicating that the child is read to often and participates in a variety of family outings and experiences. Further, it is learned that the parents interact extensively with the child in language activities. These activities include the repetition of rhymes and the playing of word-sounding games such as forming an onset sound and guessing a word that follows.

The examiner conducts Len's assessment using the same routine followed with Kelly. The evidence gathered from Len's assessment is the same as that for Kelly. However, the examiner suggests a small but crucial difference in recommendations for instruction. Similar to Kelly, Len needs instruction in unfamiliar letter-sound correspondences, unknown word family rhymes, and word analysis strategies such as recognizing common affixes and syllabic patterns.

In contrast, Len needs much more intensive and repeated instruction in decoding strategies since Len's difficulties seem to stem from a learning disability rather than from lack of instruction. While Kelly does not appear to have a learning disability since phonemic awareness skills were developed through incidental home and school exposure, Len's progress likely would be much further behind if he had not received intensive, systematic phonemic awareness training in the home setting.

Summary of word decoding profiles. Readers may exhibit a lack of decoding skill as a result of insufficient instruction or inadequate opportunities for practice. Decoding instruction is typically provided during the primary school years. When decoding instruction is required beyond that time, the need reflects that sufficient instruction was not provided at an earlier, more developmentally appropriate time, or that a learning disability is prolonging the period of time needed to master decoding skills. (See Chapters 3 through 6 for detailed descriptions of decoding instruction techniques.)

A jeopardy to learning decoding skills faces students who come from backgrounds that lack rich literary language, activities, and experiences. This risk is greatly reduced when schools offer ample, clear instruction in letter-sound correspondences, word-family rhymes, and word-analysis elements such as common affixes and syllabic patterns (Blachman, 1991; Rath, 1990).

Timely, clear instruction in decoding skills is particularly important for students whose backgrounds provide only limited literacy exposure. For these readers, mastery of the code opens the world of books as a means of gathering rich literacy experiences. Instruction in the code is equally important for students with learning disabilities. For these students, mastery of decoding can lead to better understanding of language, since reading offers exposure and reinforcement of language through print. This is particularly important for students with learning disabilities, when learning through listening is inefficient (Stanovich, 1986; 1994). Effective decoding instruction includes direct explanation and demonstration of letter cluster patterns *and* opportunities to apply the target patterns to connected text. Such instruction enhances fluency, transfer, and motivation.

Teachers are sometimes tempted to abandon reading instruction and revert to a purely oral language approach when students need intensive decoding instruction. Although oral instruction may offer temporary assistance in fostering learning in math, science, and social studies classes, learning through reading is particularly important for the very students who may need additional instruction to master decoding. As students master decoding fluency and word identification skills, reading can be used to augment language learning.

PHONEMIC AWARENESS

Phonemic awareness typically develops during the preschool and kindergarten years. When environmental exposure and support are insufficient, when a learning disability exists, or when there is a history of intermittent hearing loss, phonemic awareness may not develop in a timely manner (Boucher, 1986). Students who lack adequate phonemic awareness, whether from lack of exposure or from learning disability, exhibit difficulty in learning letter-sound correspondences and in learning to sound and blend letters into words (Liberman, 1987; Rath, 1990).

Profile M. Mattie has been participating in choral reading, student authoring with invented spelling, and peer reading experiences in first grade over the past several months. Each time that the teacher takes an opportunity to hear Mattie read, letter-sound correspondence misunderstandings that arise in the reading are explored within the context of the word, sentence, and story. In early spring, the teacher refers Mattie for assessment since she does not seem to remember the three-letter words introduced through repetitive use in shared stories, consistently misreads "glue" words, and persists in misassociations between the letters she writes and the sounds of the words they are meant to represent. Referral information indicates that vision and hearing are normal.

The examiner follows the procedure used with Kelly and Len and establishes that Mattie's passage comprehension, vocabulary knowledge, and reading fluency are low. Performance on the WRMT-R decoding and letter recognition subtests and supplemental letter checklist indicates that Mattie cannot read many common three-letter words nor basic "glue" words such as "is, the, their." In addition, Mattie does not consistently recognize all the letters of the alphabet nor their sounds. Further, results of the GFW suggest that Mattie lacks phonemic awareness—the ability to segment and blend the sounds of letters and syllables in words.

The examiner recommends systematic, daily instruction in phonemic awareness tasks, both aural and with letters used to represent the sound patterns under study. The examiner also suggests that Mattie's progress be reviewed within a few months to determine her rate of progress with intensive instruction. If Mattie's progress is rapid, it would appear that the initial difficulties arise from a lack of sufficient exposure to phonemic awareness and decoding tasks as well as inconsistent instruction through the school's first-grade curriculum. Rapid progress would also suggest that the newly recommended instruction is providing sufficient intensity and practice.

In contrast, if Mattie's progress is slow, it would appear that she may have a learning or language disability in addition to limited exposure and instruction. The recommended review of progress will provide an opportunity to adjust the pace and frequency of her specialized instruction. In addition, the examiner can use the review as another opportunity to stress the value of practice in phonemic awareness and decoding as well as the importance of supplementing such instruction with exposure to interesting stories through being read to by the teacher, aides, school volunteers, and parents. Also, the review will offer a mechanism to check whether further testing is needed. Whatever the finding, the check-up will help to ensure that further instruction is paced appropriately for Mattie's rate of learning.

Summary of phonemic awareness. Some students who exhibit weak phonemic awareness make good progress and catch up with their peers when given early, timely, and intensive instruction in phonemic awareness and decoding strategies. Others seem to have a specific processing difficulty that interferes with language development at the phoneme level; these students need much prolonged instruction. These students often exhibit poor language skills in general, and it is wise to bring them to the attention of the speech and language pathologist as well. When weaknesses are at the phonemic awareness level and do not turn around in good time with direct instruction, it is important to turn to the language pathologist for further recommendations concerning language deficits and their influence on reading ability and school learning in general. (See Chapters 2 and 3 for detail concerning language development and strategies for teaching phonemic awareness.)

EMOTIONAL ISSUES

During earlier days of remedial reading development, it was believed that emotional issues lay at the base of most reading difficulties (Bettelheim & Zelin, 1981; Dahlberg, Roswell, & Chall, 1952). Although this belief is no longer held, it is recognized that emotional issues can, at times, inhibit reading development. Emotional issues that interfere with expected reading progress may lead to performance that mirrors closely any one of the profiles, A - M, described above. Such reading difficulties may be induced or prolonged by an underlying fear of reading success or an underlying emotional distraction that draws attentional resources away from the project of learning to read. Careful information gathering, through interviews and observation during the referral stage, may highlight the existence of these issues.

Whether reading difficulties arise from emotional issues or not, reading instruction must focus on teaching the reading skills that exhibit a deficit (Dahlberg et al., 1952). However, when an underlying emotional issue exists, instruction must also include a component that focuses on alleviating the emotional stress. Within the instructional setting, teachers can use reading materials in which characters overcome difficulties similar to those that the student is encountering. Or, teachers can use materials that sow and cultivate a spark of interest in an unfamiliar area that promises hope for satisfying engagement and productivity. In addition, appropriate sources should be consulted to assure that adequate psychological treatment and support are provided by qualified personnel.

Conclusion

Linking reading assessment with program planning is a detective activity that attempts to clarify areas of weakness and strength while proposing instructional approaches appropriate to hypothesized needs. Well-designed and implemented assessments can suggest what subskills, if any, contribute to a reading weakness (or strength) and whether an advanced skill may be developed more effectively through instruction that targets that skill or instruction that targets subskills.

Examiners and teachers must remember that the accuracy and effectiveness of their diagnostic hypotheses can be substantiated only by students' progress under recommended instruction. When students do not make expected progress, diagnostic hypotheses must be reconsidered and revised in light of this further evidence.

The assessment and instruction of reading are very challenging, involving, and rewarding. Answers to the puzzles that present themselves, along with effective and appropriate instructional programs, can transform readers' lives. Knowledgeable, committed teachers remain the essence that links effective assessment and instruction. The expertise and dedication of good teachers enable learners to enter a world of knowledge, concepts, and experiences that would be unavailable without the joy and skill of well-developed reading ability.

References

Adams, M.J. (1994). *Beginning to read: Thinking and learning about print.* Cambridge, MA: MIT Press.

Armbruster, B.B. (1991). Framing: A technique for improving learning from science texts. In C.M. Santa & D.E. Alverman (Eds.), *Science learning: Process and applications.* Newark, DE: IRA.

Bettelheim, B. & Zelin, K. (1981). *On Learning to read: The child's fascination with meaning.* New York: Knopf.

Blachman, B.A. (1991). Getting ready to read: Learning how print maps to speech. In J.F. Kavanagh (Ed.), *The language continuum: From infancy to literacy.* Parkton, MD: York Press.

Boucher, J.P. (1986). An investigation of the relationship between middle ear dysfunction and school difficulty in young children. *Dissertation Abstracts International, 47,* 6, 2115-A.

Brody, S. (1987a). *Study skills: Teaching and learning strategies for mainstream and specialized classrooms.* Milford, NH: LARC Publishing.

Brody, S. (1987b). *The Brody reading manual: An implementation guide for teachers.* Milford, NH: LARC Publishing.

Brody, S. (1989). Elements of effective instruction. Unpublished Qualifying Paper, Harvard Graduate School of Education, Cambridge: MA.

Brody, S. (1993). Developing background knowledge: A context enrichment strategy that may provide more consistent results than activation of prior knowledge. In D. Wray (Ed.), *Proceedings: 1992 United Kingdom Reading Association Annual Conference,* Exeter, England: UKRA.

Budoff, M. (1972). Measuring learning potential: An alternative to the traditional intelligence test. In G.R. Gredler (Ed.), *Ethical and legal factors in the practice of school psychology.* Proceedings of the First Annual Conference in School Psychology. Philadelphia: Temple University.

Chall, J.S. (1967). *Learning to read: The great debate.* New York: McGraw-Hill.

Chall, J.S. (1983). *Stages of reading development.* New York: McGraw-Hill.

Chall, J.S. (1987). Two vocabularies for reading: Recognition and meaning. In M.G. McKeown & M.E. Curtis (Eds.), *The nature of vocabulary acquisition.* Hillsdale, NJ: Lawrence Erlbaum Assoc.

Chall, J.S. & Curtis, M.E. (1990). Diagnostic achievement testing in reading. In C.R. Reynolds & R. Kamphaus (Eds.), *Handbook of Psychological and Educational Assessment of Children's Intelligence and Achievement.* NY: Guilford Press.

Chall, J.S. & Snow, C.E. (1988). School influences on the reading development of low-income children, *The Harvard Education Letter,* 4(1), 1-4.

Chomsky, C. (1978). When you still can't read in third grade: After decoding what? In S.J. Samuels (Ed.), *What research has to say about reading instruction.* Newark, DE: International Reading Association.

Curtis, M.E. (1987). Vocabulary testing and vocabulary instruction. In M.G. McKeown & M.E. Curtis (Eds.), *The nature of vocabulary acquisition.* Hillsdale, NJ: Erlbaum.

Dahlberg, M.D., Roswell, F., & Chall, J.S. (1952). Psychotherapeutic principles as applied to remedial reading. *The Elementary School Journal,* December.

386

Goldman, R., Fristoe, M. & Woodcock, R.W. (1974). *Goldman-Fristoe-Woodcock Auditory Skills Test Battery*. Circle Pines, MN: American Guidance Service.

Graves, M.F. (1987). The roles of instruction in fostering vocabulary development. In M.G. McKeown & M.E. Curtis, (Eds.), *The nature of vocabulary acquisition*. Hillsdale, NJ: Lawrence Erlbaum Assoc.

Graves, M.F., Cooke, C.L., & Laberge, M.J. (1983). Effects of previewing difficult short stories on low ability junior high school students' comprehension, recall, and attitudes. *Reading Research Quarterly*. 18(3), 262-276.

Holzman, S. I. (1990). The use of medical-educational test reports in schools. Unpublished doctoral dissertation. Harvard Graduate School of Education, Cambridge, MA.

Jastak, S. & Wilkinson, G.S. (1984). *Wide Range Achievement Test-Revised*. Wilmington, DE: Jastak Associates.

Kaufman, A.S. (1979). *Intelligence testing with the WISC-R*. NY: John Wiley & Sons.

Kaufman, A.S. & Kaufman, N.L. (1985). *Kaufman Test of Educational Achievement, Brief Form* and *Comprehensive Form*. Circle Pines, MN: American Guidance Service.

Liberman, I. (1987). Language and literacy: The obligation of the schools of education. In *Intimacy with language: A forgotten basic in teacher education. Conference proceedings*. Baltimore, MD: The Orton Dyslexia Society.

MacGinitie, W.H. & MacGinitie, R.K. (1989). *Gates-MacGinitie Reading Tests (3rd ed.)*. Chicago: Riverside Publishing Company.

Perfetti, C.A. (1984). Reading acquisition and beyond: Decoding includes cognition. *American Journal of Education*. November, 40 - 60.

Perfetti, C.A. (1985). *Reading ability*. New York: Oxford Press.

Rath, L.K. (1990). Phonemic awareness: Its role in reading development. Unpublished Qualifying Paper, Harvard Graduate School of Education, Cambridge, MA.

Roswell, F.G. & Chall, J.S. (1992). *Diagnostic Assessments of Reading with Trial Teaching Strategies*. Chicago: Riverside Publishing Company.

Reutzel, D.R., & Cooter, R.B. (1992). *Teaching children to read: From basals to books*. NY: Merrill.

Salvia, J. & Ysseldyke, J.E. (1991). *Assessment*. Boston: Houghton Mifflin.

Samuels, S.J., Schermer, N., & Reinking, D. (1992). Reading fluency: Techniques for making decoding automatic. In S.J. Samuels & A.E. Farstrup (Eds.), *What research has to say about reading instruction (2nd ed.)*. Newark, DE: International Reading Association.

Santa, C., Havens, L., & Harrison, S. (1989). Teaching secondary science through reading, writing, studying, and problem solving. In D. Lapp, J. Flood, N. Farnam, (Eds.), *Content area reading and learning: Instructional strategies*. Englewood Cliffs, NJ: Prentice Hall.

Slosson, R.L. (1991). *Slosson Oral Reading Test-Revised*. East Aurora, NY: Slosson Educational Publications.

Spache, G.D. (1981). *Diagnostic Reading Scales-Revised*. Monterey, CA: CTB/McGraw-Hill.

Stanovich, K.E. (1986). Matthew effects in reading: Some consequences of individual differences in the acquisition of literacy. *Reading Research Quarterly*, 21(4), 360-406.

Stanovich, K.E. (1994). Romance and reality. *Reading Teacher.* 47(4), 280-291.

Stotsky, S. (1986). Asking questions about ideas: A critical component in critical thinking. *The Leaflet*, Fall, 39-47.

Wiederholt, J.L. & Bryant, B.R. (1992). *Gray Oral Reading Test-3rd ed.* Austin, TX: Pro-ed.

Willis, J.O. (1990). *Guide to identification of learning disabilities.* Concord, NH: New Hampshire Department of Education.

Woodcock, R.W. (1987). *Woodcock Reading Mastery Tests-Revised.* Circle Pines, MN: American Guidance Service.

Woodcock, R.W., & Johnson, M.B. (1989). *Woodcock-Johnson Psychoeducational Battery-Revised.* Allen, TX: DLM Teaching Resources.

Glossary

ABILITY In educational testing, "ability" usually refers to performance, attainments, or scores on tests, or other measures, that are used to assess intelligence or basic processes.

ACADEMIC In educational jargon, the term has come to mean "relating to skills formally taught in school," so that "academic testing" is likely to mean testing of reading, writing, and arithmetic skills in contrast to scholarly or impractical testing.

ACHIEVEMENT In educational testing, "achievement" usually refers to performance, attainments, or test scores in school subjects.

AGE EQUIVALENT The average age of students who earned the same number of Raw Score points on a test as did the student being tested. Usually written with a hyphen: 10-3 would be ten years and three months. Potentially a very misleading score. See MENTAL AGE and GRADE EQUIVALENT

AUTOMATICITY Successfully performing a task without conscious attention.

BACKGROUND KNOWLEDGE Information related to a topic under study. May be known or unknown by the reader. See also PRIOR KNOWLEDGE.

BACK VOWEL OR CONSONANT Set of sounds made in the back of the mouth such as /h/.

BOTTOM A sufficient number of easy items on a test to allow accurate measurement of the achievement or abilities of students who are weakest in the skills being tested. See TOP.

CHRONOLOGICAL AGE For children who were born prematurely, it is often best to calculate a "due date age" based on the due date instead of the birth date. Writers must be very clear concerning which is used.

CLOZE A technique of testing reading comprehension by asking the student to supply missing words.

CODE Any system of symbols used to transmit information.

COGNITION Thinking.

COGNITIVE PROCESS Any mental process.

CONNECTED TEXT Material written in phrases and sentences to convey meaning, rather than single words or lists of single words.

CONTEXT CLUES A strategy for reading unfamiliar words by inference from the rest of the passage.

CONTINUANT A speech sound such as /m/ that may be prolonged without distortion.

CRITERION-REFERENCED Generally, criterion referenced testing is evaluation in which the student's performance is compared to a set criterion rather than to the scores of other students. Test criteria include, for example, a certain percentage correct or passing an item designed to test a certain skill.

DECODE To transform a printed letter, or group of letters, to its corresponding sound. The process of recognizing words; print-to-sound mapping. Decoding involves pronouncing written words correctly, but not necessarily knowing their meanings.

DIRECT INSTRUCTION Teaching through explicit teacher explanation, demonstration, description direction, etc.

DYSLEXIA A disorder affecting ability to read and/or spell despite good instruction, adequate intelligence, sufficient physical and emotional health, and supportive environmental background.

DYSPEDAGOGIA A failure of teaching. A didagenic disorder.

ENCODING Spelling; matching sounds with their corresponding letters; sound-to-print mapping.

FRONT VOWEL OR CONSONANT Sounds made in the front of the mouth with the blade of the tongue, such as /t/.

GLUE WORDS Common words that are often taught as logographic wholes, such as *and, then, is.*

GRADE EQUIVALENT The average grade placement of students who earned the same number of Raw Score points on a test as did the students being tested. Usually written with a decimal point (3.2 would be the second tenth of third grade or 36 to 53 school days into third grade.)

GRAPHEME The smallest unit in the writing system of a language; letter symbols.

GRAPHIC CODES Neurological codes that process printed symbols for speech.

IQ Intelligence quotient. Originally the ratio of Mental Age (MA) to chronological age (CA), multiplied by 100. The ratio IQ is a very poor score because of the problems with Mental Ages and because the same IQ means different things at different ages. Most IQs today are deviation IQs, simply a form of Standard Score, usually with a Mean of 100 and a Standard Deviation of 15 or 16 points.

INTONATION Variation in pitch from one part of an utterance to another.

LANGUAGE-BASED Based in language, as in a language-based learning disability that reflects deficits in skills requiring the use of language.

LATENCY In testing or research jargon, the time elapsed between display of a test item and initiation of response.

LEXICAL ACCESS Connecting to the lexicon during cognitive activities that make use of language.

LEXICAL CODES Neurological codes that process meaning.

LEXICON Mental dictionary.

LINGUISTICALLY-BASED Information or processes involving language, conveying language, or conveyed by language.

LOGOGRAPH symbol (picture, icon) used to represent a word in a system of writing, such as Chinese, in which words are written in symbols that represent their meaning rather than by symbols that represent their sounds.

MENTAL AGE The average age of students who earned the same number of Raw Score points on a test as did the student being tested. Potentially a very misleading score.

METACOGNITION Attentiveness to one's own thinking during the process of thinking.

METALINGUISTIC AWARENESS Attentiveness to one's own language processing during the process of using language.

MODEL or MODELING In education jargon, to teach by demonstrating the skill, process, or activity under study.

NEURAL CODES In reading jargon, linguistically-based messages carried by nerve cells.

NORMED or NORM-REFERENCED A test is normed if it is administered to a selected sample of people whose scores are then used as a yardstick for assessing the performance of persons who subsequently take the test. To do this, the test must first be standardized.

ORTHOGRAPHY Spelling system.

PHONEME A representation of the smallest sound unit in a language. For example, the phoneme /f/ represents the sound of *f* or the sound of *ph*.

PHONEMIC AWARENESS Ability to segment and blend the sounds of language.

PHONICS A method of teaching reading that is based on decoding words using letter-sound relationships; direct instruction in the spelling and decoding of printed letters.

PHONOLOGICAL CODES Neural codes that process sound stimuli.

POLYSEMOUS Multiple meanings.

PRIOR KNOWLEDGE A reader's knowledge related to a text under study. See also BACKGROUND KNOWLEDGE.

RAW SCORE The simple number of points or items correct on a test.

RELIABILITY In statistics, reliability refers only to the consistency of a test. A test that consistently gives the same, wrong, score to the same person would be considered very reliable. Head size used to be considered a reliable and valid measure of intelligence during the era when most psychologists were men, who tend to have larger skulls than women.

SCAFFOLD A support provided to help a student perform a challenging task that could not be done independently.

SCALED SCORE A form of Standard Score, variously defined by different authors. Wechsler (1939, 1974, 1991) uses Standard Scores with a Mean of 100 and a Standard Deviation of 15 for his broad scales and "Scaled Scores" with a Mean of 10 and a Standard Deviation of 3 for his individual tests. Hammill (1985; Hammill & Larsen, 1988) reverse this usage, much to the confusion of report writers and readers.

SCHEMA, SCHEMATA *(plural)* In reading comprehension jargon, the term refers to a reader's understanding of a text. The reader constructs a schema, or understanding, of a text. Readers construct schemata in their minds as they read texts. Schemata are also constructed during the use of oral language. In this case, a schema is the speaker's, or listener's, understanding of what was said.

SEVERE Extreme or very serious in the opinion of the person using the term; more extreme than whatever that person was last considering.

SEQUENCING Perceiving, understanding, or remembering things in a particular order.

SIGHT WORDS *See* GLUE WORDS

STANDARDIZED A test is standardized if the content and the rules for administering and scoring it are set down in a prescribed manner that is followed by each examiner. A standardized test is not necessarily normed, but a normed test must be standardized.

STANDARD DEVIATION (s, s.d., or S.D.) In a normal distribution, a yardstick that can be used to mark off units. The distance from one Standard Deviation below the Mean to one Standard Deviation above the Mean includes about the middle two-thirds of all the scores in the Normal Distribution. The distance from two Standard Deviations below the Mean to two Standard Deviations above the Mean includes approximately the middle 95% of all the scores in the Normal Distribution. Wechsler IQs use a Standard Deviation with 15 points and a Mean of 100; consequently, approximately two-thirds of the possible scores fall between 85 and 115. Binet IQs use a Standard Deviation of 16 points, with the middle two-thirds of scores falling between 84 and 116.

STANDARD ERROR OF MEASUREMENT SE_M The Standard Deviation of all the scores that a hypothetical student might receive in retaking a test an infinite number of times.

STANDARD SCORE A score defined by the number of Standard Deviation units that it lies away from the Mean of the distribution of scores.

STANINE STAndard NINEs, a nine-point, ascending scale for reporting test scores. Stanines have a Mean of 5 and a Standard Deviation of 1.96. Except for stanines one and nine, which theoretically stretch out infinitely, each Stanine is one-half Standard Deviation in width. Stanine 5 is centered on the Mean.

STREPHOSYMBOLIA A term used by Samuel Orton to describe learning disabilities—literally, twisted symbols.

STRUCTURAL ANALYSIS Decoding words by breaking them into syllables or affixes and base words for easier and more effective phonetic word attack.

TOP A sufficient number of difficult items on a test to allow accurate measurement of the achievement or abilities of students who have strong abilities in the areas the test assesses.

VALIDITY In statistics, validity is the accuracy with which a test measures that which it is supposed to be measuring. The test must, of course, be reliable, but determination of validity requires additional information concerning how accurately it predicts the information it purports to measure.

Z-SCORE A score defined by the number of Standard Deviation units it lies away from the Mean. A Z-Score of -1.00 is exactly one Standard Deviation below the Mean.

Index

To Order: Call **(603) 880-7691**, or write: *LARC Publishing*
P.O. Box 801
Milford, NH 03055

Teaching Reading:
Language, Letters & Thought

Edited by Sara Brody

Teaching Reading: Language, Letters & Thought is the "soup to nuts" of reading instruction. Teachers, teachers-to-be, specialists, and school psychologists will explore a rich background of reading theory and practice in every chapter. Practical strategies range from language-acquisition and phonemic-awareness activities to practices that motivate and guide students in constructing higher-level understanding. Chapters include:

Reading Theory and Practice	Understanding Texts and Literature
Encouraging Emergence of Language	Expanding Background Knowledge
The Phonemic Awareness Bridge	Vocabulary Depth and Breadth
Letter-sound Correspondence Strategies	Writing to Increase Comprehension
Enhancing Automaticity and Fluency	Testing Reading and Its Subskills
Reading and Spelling Connections	Connecting Diagnoses to Lesson Plans

Sara Brody, EdD is Director of the Graduate Program in Educational Disabilities and Reading at Rivier College. Her teaching draws on eighteen years of experience as a public-school teacher, program developer, and educational researcher. Brody's other writings include text-workbooks for teaching reading, writing, and study skills, as well as implementation guides for program improvement efforts.

LARC Publishing   **Milford, NH 03055**   **ISBN 1-886042-12-8**